Annual Editions:
Human Development
43/e

Edited by Karen L. Freiberg

http://create.mcgraw-hill.com

ISBN-10: 125917543X   ISBN-13: 9781259175435

Contents

Preface

In publishing ANNUAL EDITIONS, we recognize the enormous role played by the magazines, newspapers, and journals of the public press in providing current, first-rate educational information in a broad spectrum of interest areas. Many of these articles are appropriate for students, researchers, and professionals seeking accurate, current material to help bridge the gap between principles and theories and the real world. These articles, however, become more useful for study when those of lasting value are carefully collected, organized, indexed, and reproduced in a low-cost format, which provides easy and permanent access when the material is needed. That is the role played by ANNUAL EDITIONS.

In these times of economic uncertainty, students may want to obtain a degree as quickly and as easily as possible. They may prefer rote memorization to deep processing of information. Creativity, however, requires a mastery of concepts such that new insights can occur. In order to become proficient thinkers, students must be exposed to multiple concepts.

The articles chosen for this compendium will help students use the full power of their reasoning abilities. "Student learning outcomes" will focus on the knowledge to be acquired in each selection, and the consequences of possessing this information. Critical thinking questions for each article will help students evaluate their own understanding of the materials which have been read.

As humans develop through the circle of life, it is customary to track changes from infancy through old age. The arrangement of articles in this collection follows this chronology. A Topic Guide is included in this publication to help readers find current, appropriate educational information in the many areas of development that transcend age boundaries.

At conception, a new human being is created, but each unique individual carries genetic materials from biological relatives, alive and dead, and may pass them on to future generations. The first articles in this anthology make the science of genetics, and the possibility of tracing one's ancestry, easier to understand.

Development through infancy proceeds from sensory and motor responses to verbal communication, thinking, conceptualizing, and learning from others.

Childhood brings rapid physical growth, improved cognition, and many types of social learning.

In adolescence, the individual's values and identity are questioned. Separation from parents occurs. Under the influence of sex hormones, the brain undergoes multiple changes. Emotions may fluctuate rapidly.

Early adulthood usually establishes the individual as an independent person. Employment, further education, and the beginning of one's own family are all aspects of setting up a distinct life, with both its own characteristics and the characteristics and customs of previous generations.

During middle adulthood, persons have new situations to face, new transitions with which to cope. Children grow up and leave home. Signs of aging become apparent. Relationships change, roles shift. New abilities may be found and opportunities created.

Finally, during late adulthood, people assess what they've accomplished. Some are pleased. Some feel they could have done more or lived differently. In the best of instances, individuals accept who they are and are comfortable with themselves.

As you explore this collection, you will discover that many articles ask questions that have no answers. As a student, I felt frustrated by such writing. I wanted answers, right answers, right away. However, over time, I learned that maturity includes accepting relativity and acknowledging extenuatory circumstances. Life frequently has no right or wrong answers, but rather various alternatives with multiple consequences. Instead of right versus wrong, a more helpful consideration is "What will bring about the greater good for the greater number?" Controversies, whether about stem cells or global warming, can promote healthy discussions. Different viewpoints should be weighed against societal standards. Different philosophies should be celebrated for what they offer in creating intellectual abilities in human beings to allow them to adapt to changing circumstances.

The Greek sophists were philosophers who specialized in argumentation, rhetoric (using language persuasively), and dialectics (finding synthesis or common ground between contradictory ideas). This was sophistication. However, from their skilled thinking came the derogatory term "sophism," suggesting that some argumentation was deceptive rather than wise. The term sophomore, which now means second-year student, comes from this variation of sophism, combining "sophos" (wise) with "moros" (dull or foolish). "Sophomoric" translates to exhibiting immaturity and lack of judgment, while "sophisticated" translates to having acquired knowledge. Educators strive to have their students move from knowing all the answers (sophomoric) to asking intelligent questions (sophisticated).

This collection is dedicated to seekers of knowledge and searchers for what is true, right, or lasting. To this end, articles have been selected that provide you with information that will stimulate discussion and give your thoughts direction, but that do not tell you what to think. May each suggestive answer you discover open your mind to more erudite (instructive) learning, questioning, and sophistication.

Karen Freiberg, PhD
Editor

Academic Advisory Board

Members of the Academic Advisory Board are instrumental in the final selection of articles for *Annual Editions* books and ExpressBooks. Their review of the articles for content, level, and appropriateness provides critical direction to the editor(s) and staff. We think that you will find their careful consideration reflected here.

Bruce Munson
St. Louis Community College, Forest Park

Pansy Murdock
Keiser University, Fort Lauderdale

Love Nneji
Hampton University

Sylvester Odigie-Osazuwa
Benedict College

Dona Packer
University of Texas, Tyler

Jessie Panko
Saint Xavier University

Anjana Patel
Rowan University

Lynn Patterson
Murray State University

Peter Phipps
Dutchess Community College

Frank Prerost
Midwestern University

Anne Marie Rakip
South Carolina State University

Jean Raniseski
Alvin Community College

Mary Eva Repass
University of Virginia

Grant J. Rich
University of Alaska Southeast

Carol E. Risaliti
Stark State College of Technology

Jane Roda
Pennsylvania State University, Hazelton

Claire N. Rubman
Suffolk County Community College

Terry Salem
Lake Land College

Leo R. Sandy
Plymouth State University

Thomas R. Scheira
Buffalo State College

Hilary Seitz
University of Alaska, Anchorage

Barbara Smith
Johns Hopkins University

Lila Snow
Los Angeles Pierce College

Elizabeth Stern
Milwaukee Area Tech College, North Campus

Fred Stickle
Western Kentucky University

Jacqueline Thompson
Nova Southeastern University

Valerie Wallace
California Lutheran University

Jessie Williams
Mineral Area College

Lois J. Willoughby
Miami-Dade College

Karen M. Zabrucky
Georgia State University

Norma Zunker
Texas A&M University, Corpus Christi

Correlation Guide

The *Annual Editions* series provides students with convenient, inexpensive access to current, carefully selected articles from the public press. **Annual Editions: Human Development, 43/e** is an easy-to-use reader that presents articles on important topics such as *building strong foundations, families and communities, diverse learners, development,* and many more. For more information on *Annual Editions* and other McGraw-Hill Create™ titles, visit www.mcgrawhillcreate.com.

This convenient guide matches the articles in **Annual Editions: Human Development, 43/e** with **Essentials of Life-Span Development, 3/e** by Santrock.

Essentials of Life-Span Development, 3/e by Santrock	Annual Editions: Human Development, 43/e
Chapter 1: Introduction	
Chapter 2: Biological Beginnings	How Long Can You Wait to Have a Baby?
	The Incredible Expanding Adventures of the X Chromosome
	Journey to the Genetic Interior
	Recipe for Immortality
	Unnatural Selection
	The Unspeakable Gift
Chapter 3: Physical and Cognitive Development	Anguish of the Abandoned Child
	Vaccination Nation
Chapter 4: Socioemotional Development in Infancy	Anguish of the Abandoned Child
	Keys to Quality Infant Care
	Use the Science of What Works to Change the Odds for Children at Risk
Chapter 5: Physical and Cognitive Development in Early Childhood	How to Raise a Global Kid
	Ten Tips for Involving Families through Internet-Based Communication
	The Touch-Screen Generation
Chapter 6: Socioemotional Development in Early Childhood	How to Help Your Toddler Begin Developing Empathy
	How to Raise a Global Kid
	Ten Tips for Involving Families through Internet-Based Communication
	Trauma and Children: What We Can Do
Chapter 7: Physical and Cognitive Development in Middle and Late Childhood	Addressing Achievement Gaps with Psychological Interventions
	Creating a Country of Readers
	An Educator's Journey toward Multiple Intelligences
	In Defense of Distraction
	Reformed Schools
	Support Parents to Improve Student Learning
	Visiting Room 501
	What I've Learned
Chapter 8: Socioemotional Development in Middle and Late Childhood	The Angry Smile
	Child Welfare and Children's Mental Health Services
	Do-It-(All)-Yourself Parents
	How to Stop the Bullies
	Support Parents to Improve Student Learning
	Trauma and Children: What We Can Do
	Use the Science of What Works to Change the Odds for Children at Risk
Chapter 9: Physical and Cognitive Development in Adolescence	Build a Curriculum That Includes Everyone
	Digitalk: A New Literacy for a New Generation
	The Incredible Shrinking Childhood: How Early Is Too Early for Puberty?
	In Defense of Distraction
	Portrait of a Hunger Artist
	Reformed Schools
Chapter 10: Socioemotional Development in Adolescence	Build a Curriculum That Includes Everyone
	Foresight Conquers Fear of the Future
	Portrait of a Hunger Artist
	Trauma and Children: What We Can Do
Chapter 11: Physical and Cognitive Development in Early Adulthood	How Long Can You Wait to Have a Baby?
	The Retro Wife
	Unnatural Selection
	The Unspeakable Gift
Chapter 12: Socioemotional Development in Early Adulthood	All Joy and No Fun: Why Parents Hate Parenting
	Heartbreak and Home Runs: The Power of First Experiences
	Peek Hours: What Makes a Neighbor Nosy
	The Retro Wife
	Will Your Marriage Last?

Chapter 13: Physical and Cognitive Development in Middle Adulthood	The Boss Stops Here
	Good Morning, Heartache
	How to Fix the Obesity Crisis
	The New Survivors
	The Switched-On Brain
Chapter 14: Socioemotional Development in Middle Adulthood	The Boss Stops Here
	Good Morning, Heartache
	The New Survivors
	When Privacy Jumped the Shark
	Will Your Marriage Last?
Chapter 15: Physical and Cognitive Development in Late Adulthood	Age-Proof Your Brain:10 Easy Ways to Stay Sharp Forever
	Brutal Truths about the Aging Brain
	Elder Abuse Identification: A Public Health Issue
	How to Fix the Obesity Crisis
	More Good Years
Chapter 16: Socioemotional Development in Late Adulthood	More Good Years
	The New Survivors
	The Old World
	The Real Social Network
Chapter 17: Death, Dying, and Grieving	Elder Abuse Identification: A Public Health Issue
	Recipe for Immortality

Topic Guide

All the articles that relate to each topic are listed below the boldface term.

Adolescence
Build a Curriculum That Includes Everyone
Digitalk: A New Literacy for a Digital Generation
Do-It-(All)-Yourself Parents
Foresight Conquers Fear of the Future
How to Stop the Bullies
The Incredible Shrinking Childhood: How Early Is Too Early for Puberty?
In Defense of Distraction
Portrait of a Hunger Artist
Reformed School
Trauma and Children: What We Can Do

Adulthood
All Joy and No Fun: Why Parents Hate Parenting
The Boss Stops Here
Foresight Conquers Fear of the Future
Heartbreak and Home Runs: The Power of First Experiences
How to Fix the Obesity Crisis
The New Survivors
The Old World
Peek Hours: What Makes a Neighbor Nosy?
The Real Social Network
The Retro Wife
The Switched-On Brain
Will Your Marriage Last?

Aggression
The Angry Smile
Elder Abuse Identification: A Public Health Issue
Foresight Conquers Fear of the Future
How to Stop the Bullies
Trauma and Children: What We Can Do

Aging
Age-Proof Your Brain: 10 Easy Ways to Stay Sharp Forever
Brutal Truths about the Aging Brain
Elder Abuse Identification: A Public Health Issue
How Long Can You Wait to Have a Baby?
The Old World
The Real Social Network
Recipe for Immortality

Brain development
An Educator's Journey toward Multiple Intelligences
Anguish of the Abandoned Child
Brutal Truths about the Aging Brain
Good Morning, Heartache
How to Fix the Obesity Crisis
The Incredible Expanding Adventures of the X Chromosome
The Incredible Shrinking Childhood: How Early Is Too Early for Puberty?
In Defense of Distraction
Keys to Quality Infant Care: Nurturing Every Baby's Life Journey
The Switched-On Brain
The Touch-Screen Generation

Bullying
Build a Curriculum That Includes Everyone
Do-It-(All)-Yourself Parents
How to Stop the Bullies
Trauma and Children: What We Can Do

Career
The Boss Stops Here
Foresight Conquers Fear of the Future
The Old World
The Retro Wife
Will Your Marriage Last?

Children
All Joy and No Fun: Why Parents Hate Parenting
An Educator's Journey toward Multiple Intelligences
The Angry Smile
Anguish of the Abandoned Child
Child Welfare and Children's Mental Health Services: A Decade of Transformation
Do-It-(All)-Yourself Parents
How Long Can You Wait to Have a Baby?
The Incredible Shrinking Childhood: How Early Is Too Early for Puberty?
Reformed School
Trauma and Children: What We Can Do
Use the Science of What Works to Change the Odds for Children at Risk
Visiting Room 501
What I've Learned
Will Your Marriage Last?

Cognition
Addressing Achievement Gaps with Psychological Interventions
An Educator's Journey toward Multiple Intelligences
Anguish of the Abandoned Child
Brutal Truths about the Aging Brain
Creating a Country of Readers
Good Morning, Heartache
The Incredible Expanding Adventures of the X Chromosome
The Incredible Shrinking Childhood: How Early Is Too Early for Puberty?
In Defense of Distraction
The Touch-Screen Generation
Use the Science of What Works to Change the Odds for Children at Risk

Creativity
The Boss Stops Here
Digitalk: A New Literacy for a Digital Generation
Foresight Conquers Fear of the Future
Good Morning, Heartache
The Switched-On Brain
The Touch-Screen Generation

Culture
Addressing Achievement Gaps with Psychological Interventions
The Angry Smile
Creating a Country of Readers
How to Stop the Bullies
In Defense of Distraction
More Good Years
Reformed School
Use the Science of What Works to Change the Odds for Children at Risk
Visiting Room 501
What I've Learned

Death
Good Morning, Heartache
Recipe for Immortality

Drug abuse
Child Welfare and Children's Mental Health Services: A Decade of Transformation
Foresight Conquers Fear of the Future
Good Morning, Heartache
The Switched-On Brain
Trauma and Children: What We Can Do

Early childhood
An Educator's Journey toward Multiple Intelligences
How to Help Your Toddler Begin Developing Empathy

Unit 1

UNIT

Prepared by: Karen L. Freiberg, *University of Maryland*

Genetic and Prenatal Influences on Development

Globalization makes it imperative that all humans learn to think broadly, communicate clearly, and look at the world with a critical eye. How life begins plays a vital role in the kind of humans each of us will become in our futures. Genetic scientists have made quantum leaps recently, finding ways to prevent or treat abnormal human conditions by manipulating cells, genes, and the immune system. The total human genome was mapped in 2003. This knowledge of the human complement of 23 pairs of chromosomes with their associated genes in the nucleus of every cell has the potential for allowing cures for previously incurable diseases. The use of stem cells (undifferentiated embryonic cells) in animal research has documented the possibility of morphing stem cells into any kind of human cells. Stem cells will turn into desired tissue cells when the gene sequences of cytosine, adenine, thymine, and guanine (CATG) of the desired tissues are expressed. Scientists are using their knowledge of the human genome and embryonic stem cells to alter behaviors as well as to cure diseases. Cloning (complete reproduction) of a human already exists when one egg fertilized by one sperm separates into identical twins. Monozygotic twin research suggests that one's genetic CATG sequencing does not determine human behaviors, diseases, and traits without environmental input. Nature versus nurture is better phrased nature plus nurture. Genes appear to have mechanisms by which environmental factors can turn them on or leave them dormant.

Genetic precursors of human development and the use of stem cells, morphing, and cloning will be hot topics of the next several years as more genetic manipulation becomes feasible.

As DNA sequences associated with particular human traits (genetic markers) are uncovered, pressure will appear to alter these traits. Will the focus be on altering the CATG sequencing, or altering the environmental factors that will "operate" on the genes?

If human cells can be repaired or replaced with stem cells, morphing, and cloning, how long will humans be able to live? The world population is growing by about 75 million people per year. Will we eventually need to limit the numbers of new children born?

Human embryology (the study of the first through seventh weeks after conception) and human fetology (the study of the eighth week of pregnancy through birth) have given verification to the idea that behavior precedes birth. The genetic hardwiring of CATG directs much of this behavior. However, the developing embryo/fetus reacts to the internal and external environments provided by the mother as well. Substances diffuse through the placental barrier from the mother's body. The embryo reacts to toxins (viruses, antigens) that pass through the umbilical cord. The fetus reacts to an enormous number of other stimuli, such as the sounds from the mother's body (digestive rumblings, heartbeat) and the mother's movements, moods, and medicines. How the embryo/fetus reacts (weakly to strongly, positively to negatively) depends, in large part, on his or her genetic preprogramming. Genes and environment are so inextricably intertwined that the effect of each cannot be studied separately. Prenatal development always has strong environmental influences and vice versa. A new science of fetal origins is demonstrating this.

Article   Prepared by: Karen L. Freiberg, *University of Maryland*

Journey to the Genetic Interior

What was once known as "junk DNA" turns out to hold hidden treasures, says computational biologist Ewan Birney.

STEPHEN S. HALL

Learning Outcomes

After reading this article, you will be able to:

- Explain why the term "junk DNA" should be expunged from our lexicon.

- Discuss why finding out how much we do not understand about human DNA is good.

I n the 1970s, when biologists first glimpsed the landscape of human genes, they saw that the small pieces of DNA that coded for proteins (known as exons) seemed to float like bits of wood in a sea of genetic gibberish. What on earth were those billions of other letters of DNA there for? No less a molecular luminary than Francis Crick, co-discoverer of DNA's double-helical structure, suspected it was "little better than junk."

The phrase "junk DNA" has haunted human genetics ever since. In 2000, when scientists of the Human Genome Project presented the first rough draft of the sequence of bases, or code letters, in human DNA, the initial results appeared to confirm that the vast majority of the sequence—perhaps 97 percent of its 3.2 billion bases—had no apparent function. The "Book of Life," in other words, looked like a heavily padded text.

But beginning roughly at that same time, a consortium of dozens of international laboratories embarked on a massive, unglamorous and largely unnoticed project to annotate what one biologist has called the "humble, unpretentious non-gene" parts of the human genome. Known as the Encyclopedia of DNA Elements (ENCODE for short), the project required scientists, in essence, to crawl along the length of the double helix as they attempted to identify anything with a biological purpose. In 2007 the group published a preliminary report hinting that, like the stuff all of us park in the attic, there were indeed treasures aplenty amid the so-called junk.

Now, in a series of papers published in September in *Nature* (*Scientific American* is part of Nature Publishing Group) and elsewhere, the ENCODE group has produced a stunning inventory of previously hidden switches, signals and signposts embedded like runes throughout the entire length of human DNA. In the process, the ENCODE project is reinventing the vocabulary with which biologists study, discuss and understand human inheritance and disease.

Ewan Birney, 39, of the European Bio-informatics Institute in Cambridge, England, led the analysis by the more than 400 ENCODE scientists who annotated the genome. He recently spoke with *Scientific American* about the major findings. Excerpts follow.

SCIENTIFIC AMERICAN: The ENCODE project has revealed a landscape that is absolutely teeming with important genetic elements—a landscape that used to be dismissed as "junk DNA." Were our old views of how the genome is organized too simplistic?
BIRNEY: People always knew there was more there than protein-coding genes. It was always clear that there was regulation. What we didn't know was just quite how extensive this was.

Just to give you a sense here, about 1.2 percent of the bases are in protein-coding exons. And people speculated that "maybe there's the same amount again involved in regulation or maybe a little bit more." But even if we take quite a conservative view from our ENCODE data, we end up with something like 8 to 9 percent of the bases of the genome involved in doing something like regulation.

Thus, much more of the genome is devoted to regulating genes than to the protein-coding genes themselves?
And that 9 percent can't be the whole story. The most aggressive view of the amount we've sampled is 50 percent. So certainly it's going to go above 9 percent, and one could easily argue for something like 20 percent. That's not an unfeasible number.

Should we be retiring the phrase "junk DNA" now?
Yes, I really think this phrase does need to be totally expunged from the lexicon. It was a slightly throwaway phrase to describe very interesting phenomena that were discovered in the 1970s. I am now convinced that it's just not a very useful way of describing what's going on.

What is one surprise you have had from the "junk"?
There has been a lot of debate, inside of ENCODE and outside of the project, about whether or not the results from our experiments describe something that is really going on in nature. And then there was a rather more philosophical question, which is whether it matters. In other words, these things may biochemically occur, but evolution, as it were, or our body doesn't actually care.

That debate has been running since 2003. And then work by ourselves, but also work outside of the consortium, has made it much clearer that the evolutionary rules for regulatory elements are different from those for protein-coding elements. Basically the regulatory elements turn over a lot faster. So whereas if you find a particular protein-coding gene in a human, you're going to find nearly the same gene in a mouse most of the time, and that rule just doesn't work for regulatory elements.

In other words, there is more complex regulation of genes, and more rapid evolution of these regulatory elements, in humans?
Absolutely.

That's a rather different way of thinking about genes—and evolution.
I get this strong feeling that previously I was ignorant of my own ignorance, and now I understand my ignorance. It's slightly depressing as you realize how ignorant you are. But this is progress. The first step in understanding these things is having a list of things that one has to understand, and that's what we've got here.

Earlier studies suggested that only, say, 3 to 13 percent of the genome had functional significance—that is, actually did something, whether coding for proteins, regulating how the genes worked or doing something else. Am I right that the ENCODE data imply, instead, that as much as 80 percent of the genome may be functional?
One can use the ENCODE data and come up with a number between 9 and 80 percent, which is obviously a very big range. What's going on there? Just to step back, the DNA inside of our cells is wrapped around various proteins, most of them histones, which generally work to keep everything kind of safe and happy. But there are other types of proteins called transcription factors, and they have specific interactions with DNA. A transcription factor will bind only at 1,000 places, or maybe the biggest bind is at 50,000 specific places across the genome. And so, when we talk about this 9 percent, we're really talking about these very specific transcription-factor-to-DNA contacts.

On the other hand, the copying of DNA into RNA seems to happen all the time—about 80 percent of the genome is actually transcribed. And there is still a raging debate about whether this large amount of transcription is a background process that's not terribly important or whether the RNA that is being made actually does something that we don't yet know about.

Personally, I think everything that is being transcribed is worth further exploration, and that's one of the tasks that we will have to tackle in the future.

There is a widespread perception that the attempts to identify common genetic variants related to human disease through so-called genome-wide association studies, or GWAS, have not revealed that much. Indeed, the ENCODE results now show that about 75 percent of the DNA regions that the GWAS have previously linked to disease lie nowhere near protein-coding genes. In terms of disease, have we been wrong to focus on mutations in protein-coding DNA?
Genome-wide association studies are very interesting, but they are not some magic bullet for medicine. The GWAS situation had everyone sort of scratching their heads. But when we put these genetic associations alongside the ENCODE data, we saw that although the loci are not close to a protein-coding gene, they really are close to one of these new elements that we're discovering. That's been a lovely thing. In fact, when I first saw it, it was a slightly too-good-to-be-true moment. And we spent a long time double-checking everything.

How does that discovery help us understand disease?
It's like opening a door. Think about all the different ways you can study a particular disease, such as Crohn's: Should we look at immune system cells in the gut? Or should we look at the neurons that fire to the gut? Or should we be looking at the stomach and how it does something else?

All those are options. Now suddenly ENCODE is letting you examine those options and say, "Well, I really think you should start by looking at this part of the immune system—the helper T cells—first." And we can do that for a very, very big set of diseases. That's really exciting.

Now that we are retiring the phrase "junk DNA," is there another, better metaphor that might explain the emerging view of the genetic landscape?
What it feels like is genuinely a jungle—a completely dense jungle of stuff that you have to work your way through. You're trying to hack your way to a certain position. And you're really not sure where you are, you know? It's quite easy to feel lost in there.

Over the past 20 years the public has been repeatedly told that these big genomic projects—starting with the Human Genome Project and going on through various other projects—were going to explain everything we needed to know about the "book of life." Is ENCODE simply the latest in this sequence?
I think that each time we always said, "These are foundations. You build on them." Nobody said, "Look, the human genome bases, that's it. It's all done and dusted—we've just got a bit of code breaking to do here." Everybody said, "We're going to be studying this for 50 years, 100 years. But this is the foundation that we start on." I do get the feeling that the ENCODE project is the next layer in that foundational resource for other people to stand on top of and look further. The biggest change here is in our list of known unknowns. And I think people should understand that although finding out how much you don't know can feel regressive and frustrating, identifying the gaps is really good.

Ten years ago we didn't know what we didn't know. There is no doubt that ENCODE poses many, many, many more questions than it directly answers. At the same time, for Crohn's disease, say, and lots of other things, there are some effectively quick wins and low-hanging fruit—at least for researchers—where you start to say to people, "Oh my gosh, have you looked there?"

It's just one more step. It's an important step, but nowhere near the end, I'm afraid.

You sometimes refer to yourself as ENCODE's "cat herder in chief." How many people were involved in the consortium, and what was it like coordinating such a massive effort?

This is very much a different way of doing science. I am only one of 400 investigators, and I am the person who is charged to make sure that the analysis was delivered and that it all worked out. But I had to draw on the talents of many, many people.

So I'm more like the cat herder, the conductor, necessarily, than someone whose brain can absorb all of this. It comes back to that sense that it's a bit of a jungle out there.

Well, you deserve a lot of credit. It's more than just cats. They're pretty opinionated cats.

Yeah, they are. What scientists are not are dogs. Dogs naturally run in packs. Cats? No. And I think that sums up the normal scientific phenotype. And so you have to cajole these people sometimes into sort of taking the same direction.

Do you see a point where all this complex information will resolve into a simpler message about human inheritance and human disease? Or do we have to accept the fact that complexity is, as it were, in our DNA?

We are complex creatures. We should expect that it's complex out there. But I think we should be happy about that and maybe even proud about it.

Critical Thinking

1. What is the goal of the ENCODE project?
2. How do protein-coding elements differ from regulatory elements in humans?

Create Central

www.mhhe.com/createcentral

Internet References

Basic Neural Processes
   www.psych.hanover.edu/Krantz/neurotut.html
Scientific American Online
   www.ScientificAmerican.com/oct2012/genes
The ENCODE Project: Encyclopedia of DNA Elements
   www.genome.gov/10005107

STEPHEN S. HALL has written about science for *The Atlantic*, *The New York Times Magazine*, *New Yorker* and many other magazines.

Article Prepared by: Karen L. Freiberg, *University of Maryland*

Recipe for Immortality

An expert in synthetic biology explains how people could soon live for centuries.

GEORGE CHURCH AND ED REGIS

Learning Outcomes

After reading this article, you will be able to:

- Explain why aging is becoming the most common cause of disease, disability, and death.

- Evaluate the pros and cons of using pluripotent stem cells of humans for replacement or repair of damaged cells.

The yearning for immortality dates back at least to ancient times. As human brain size increased rapidly over the past million years, our ancestors began to think increasingly about the inevitability of death and the redemptive possibility of everlasting life. Ancient pharaohs, queens, and kings used every means to ensure their vestigial persistence through future ages. They had themselves enshrined in legends, songs, and poems; they had their remains preserved in vast pyramids.

Part of the reason for that yearning may lie in the fact that people already live so long and with such self-awareness. Our species is distinctive in its ability to remember and to predict future events based upon past experience. Before the invention of writing, and even afterward, reliable predictions required the presence of memories in a living person. People well past their reproductive years could add value to their tribe by remembering early warning signs of rare phenomena, such as drought, locusts, and disease.

In modern times our learning extends even further. It includes postdoctoral studies and on-the-job training that may continue well into our 60s. Like our ancient predecessors, we enshrine the most important bits of our collective knowledge, only in more sophisticated embodiments: scientific publications, books, music, video, websites. Nevertheless, when people die, their wisdom—the memories and mental processes that produced that knowledge—dies too.

Throughout history, death was associated with assaults, sickness, and privation. Now an increasingly common cause of death is aging. As the wealth of nations increases and exposure to toxins and infectious agents drops, aging will become the cause of most disease, debility, and death. At the same time,

many more people will remain active beyond the age of 100. So, beyond the fear of death, there are practical reasons to explore extending our healthy years.

Scientists have much to learn from the longest-lived humans, many of whom will have their DNA sequenced in the next two years. The effort to extend life—and, even more, to extend life's youthful, vigorous phase—is a clear opportunity for synthetic biology, the technique of extensively engineering the genome. [George Church is a leading researcher in this emerging field.] The cure for aging will probably require a thorough redo of our genome.

We can scour the best of the biosphere for ideas. Species run the gamut when it comes to longevity. Some adult mayflies live, dance, and mate for all of three hours. At the other extreme, some specimens of bowhead whale appear to be more than 120 years old, judging from the age of harpoons lodged in their flesh. The oldest known fish, a koi, was a scarlet female named Hanako, who reportedly died at the age of 226 years on the memorable date 7/7/77. The hard-shell clam *Arctica islandica* can live more than 400 years (judging from annual shell rings) in nearly freezing water, where rates of metabolism are very low.

But it might be possible to evade aging entirely. In one widely cited publication from 1998 ("Mortality Patterns Suggest Lack of Senescence in Hydra," published in *Experimental Gerontology*), Daniel Martinez claimed that hydras—small aquatic animals that look a bit like cacti—may not undergo senescence at all and may be biologically immortal. More astonishing yet is an organism that appears to do something otherwise unheard-of in the animal kingdom: It gets younger. This ability is possessed by *Turritopsis nutricula,* a jellyfish that can return from its sexually mature (medusa) state back to a younger (polyp) state. An entire population of such organisms can do this repeatedly and swiftly, escaping biological death through aging, although members of the species can still be killed through predation, accident, and disease.

This bizarre menagerie of extremely long-lived, possibly immortal, and fountain-of-youth organisms leads us to consider humans. Like these organisms, we are built of cells, and some of those cells can be immortal too.

The possibility of cellular immortality is also suggested by the case of Henrietta Lacks, an African American woman who suffered from cervical cancer and died on October 4, 1951, at Johns Hopkins Hospital at the age of 31. For research purposes, cell samples had been taken from her cervix. They were code-named HeLa cells, using the first two letters of her first and last names.

Prior to Lacks's death, Hopkins researcher George Gey found that HeLa cells could easily be grown in lab glassware and kept alive indefinitely. As other researchers asked for samples, the cells replicated, grew, and proliferated so wildly that they often took over and wiped out cell lines of any kind with which they happened to come in contact. Descendants of the original HeLa cells are still alive today, more than 60 years after they were removed from Henrietta Lacks. HeLa cells are so biologically aberrant in their chromosome makeup that they could never be used to model immortal human life, but they nevertheless point the way.

The healthy cells most capable of making at least some aspects of individuals immortal are germ cells. The germ line, produced by egg and sperm, is the only part of us that naturally survives us in our offspring. Germ-line cells are the all-time champions of cellular survival. We can trace their DNA back through billions, possibly trillions, of binary divisions, back to the dawn of life itself.

Cloning germ cells, then, looks like one possible path to human immortality. Germ cells from a mature animal can be reset to embryonic form; these are the famous "embryonic stem cells." The embryonic cells can develop into replacement organs in the lab or be injected into an egg, where they develop as a viable embryo and are literally born. We can also freeze such cells to keep them healthy and youthful; when the aging donor needs repairs to a damaged genome, the cells could be tapped. Scientists have already cloned more than 20 species, including carp, mice, sheep, monkeys, cattle, cats, dogs, and horses. Cloning is sometimes viewed as dangerous or unethical, but many new technologies are initially perceived that way, then accepted and finally widely embraced—airplanes, for example, or in vitro fertilization.

At present, the main argument against human cloning is that occasional difficulties observed in cloning other animals suggest that human clones would sometimes be born with medical abnormalities. This is a serious concern, but it doesn't mean human cloning can never happen. In one plausible path to that end, veterinary scientists continue to get better at cloning agricultural mammals until the success rate is extremely high. When the chance of error in animal cloning becomes lower than the error rates of natural reproduction, human cloning trials could become socially and ethically acceptable or even recommended.

But even without cloning, life extension could be achieved. For instance, medical researchers might succeed in creating complex tissues and organs derived from patients' own stem cells. These so-called pluripotent stem cells can be derived from a variety of adult cells and be guided into almost any other tissue type. Synthetic biocircuits made of DNA and encoded proteins could be inserted to detect and repair (or kill) cells with mutations known to cause cancer or aging.

In a related approach, new translational codes in the genome—which define how a cell uses DNA to construct proteins—could make organisms resistant to all viruses. Viruses do their damage by entering cells and using the cellular machinery to replicate themselves. They are able to do this because both the viruses and the host cells make use of the same genetic code. But if we changed the code of the host cells, it would thwart the virus's ability to replicate, and so make the host immune.

That may sound like science fiction, but the Church lab at Harvard has already changed portions of the genetic code of *E. coli* bacteria to repel viral attacks. Beyond this, we could take the DNA repair abilities from *Polypedilum vanderplanki,* a fly whose larvae can survive complete desiccation and extremes of heat and cold, and transplant them into human cells.

Ultimately, synthetic biology could free us from obsolete limits set by evolution. We could repair damaged tissue and direct the growth of new tissues to create built-in body and brain parts that could interface with electronic devices. For example, some cells could be engineered to light up and signal if a person is experiencing inflammation, unusual neuronal activity, etc., functioning as noninvasive diagnostic devices.

Globally, life expectancy and the onset of old-age symptoms have been steadily improving at a rate of three months per year. A nearly perfect straight line for the past 170 years! Impressive, but some biotechnologies are improving at up to a tenfold rate per year, meaning that a dramatic change in the slope of that line could happen soon.

The route to long-lived humans will arrive via milestones that we can only guess at. Genome engineering in clinical trials today may become routine by 2014. By 2016 we may have ways to rejuvenate neurons, such as by injecting them with fresh nuclei from engineered stem cells, to make them young again. Or we may have developed miniature electronic circuits capable of monitoring and stimulating neurons, which might be used to augment memory or maintain neural functions during the replacement of neuronal nuclei. Within a decade, we should be able to use these technologies to read and alter the state of neurons for an enormous fraction of the cells in human brains. (We can already do this for dozens of neurons in humans with epilepsy.) This could lead to much longer life spans—semi-immortality, extending progressively toward an unknown limit—both for our cells and for our minds.

With such breakthroughs potentially less than a decade away, now is the time to consider what a world of semi-immortals would look like. One of the most commonly expressed objections to the prospect of human immortality is the unintended consequences of overpopulation, including the fear that long-lived individuals would take away jobs from younger people. Yet our resources have kept expanding.

Thomas Malthus died in 1834, worried about the survival of the world population, which then numbered 1 billion people and was growing by 5 million per year. Today the population stands at 7 billion and is growing by 75 million people per year. But instead of the global starvation and misery that Malthus envisioned, we have seen widespread rises in wealth, standards of living, health, and life expectancy. As economist Julian Simon once explained, "Resources come out of people's minds more than out of the ground or air. Minds matter economically as much as or more than hands or mouths. Human beings create more than they use, on average. It had to be so, or we would be an extinct species." Fertility rates tend to decrease with increasing life span even if the number of fertile years per person increases, which counters the trend toward population increase associated with increased life span.

The vision of a nearly immortal populace squelching the job prospects of youth is reminiscent of 19th-century Luddite concerns about machines' taking over jobs from humans. The likelier scenario is a population implosion marked by increasing numbers of older, healthier citizens, and more women in positions of power, a situation that could be beneficial for child rearing, philanthropy, diplomacy, and other aspects of our civilized life. Look for our values to change: With children a rarer resource, educators may become among the highest-paid workers in the world. Instead of teachers, grammar school kids might be coached by personal tutors on the model of the British university system.

One thing that makes for a robust and long-lived species is diversity among the population. That is as true for *Homo sapiens* as for any other. Personalized tutorial education might yield the advantages of greater human diversity, allowing us to embrace larger spectra of personality types, perceptual and cognitive idiosyncrasies, and high-functioning autistics, bipolars, ADHDs, and hyper-thymesiacs (who can recall autobiographical events in extraordinary detail). People with such traits occasionally succeed today, but in the future could do so more often.

Our new semi-immortals, people of indefinite and unknown longevity, would be a diverse population resistant to all viruses, known and unknown, all other pathogens, and all forms of cancer, autoimmune diseases, environmental toxins, and even radiation—that last attribute particularly handy for space travel. We can acquire such abilities by importing into the human genome the genetic sequences from other organisms that already possess such attributes. Think of it as genetic data mining. We could get radiation-resistance genes, for example, from the *Bdelloid rotifer,* a class of small invertebrates that live in freshwater pools and survive megadoses of ionizing radiation. We will acquire other life-span-enhancing attributes by

combining the best of all genomes of people who are comparatively youthful even though they are older than 100. The Church lab is currently analyzing the genomes of centenarians.

Semi-immortals could combine the best aspects of youthful dynamism with the wisdom of long experience. Such people in abundance would be of great benefit to society. If most of us expect to live possibly indefinitely in good health, there is a strong motivation to help protect humanity from long-term risks like extinction from a new pandemic, the exhaustion of key nonrenewable resources, global nuclear warfare—or a meteor strike. After all, the survival of Earth itself is a prerequisite for the survival of individuals, whether mortal or potentially immortal. One does not want to go to all the trouble of reaching for immortality only to be wiped out by a flying rock.

Critical Thinking

1. Who was Henrietta Lacks and what are HeLa cells?
2. How does the jellyfish *Turritopsis nutricula* get younger?
3. Discuss how changing the genetic codes of human cells could make them immune to viral agents.

Create Central

www.mhhe.com/createcentral

Internet References

Center for Evolutionary Psychology
www.psych.ucsb.edu/research/cep

Pluripotent: definition from Biology-Online.org
www.biology-online.org/dictionary/Pluripotent

The Secret Life of Cells
www.libertymutual.com/Responsibility

What Is Synthetic Biology?
www.synberc.org/what-is-syn-bio

GEORGE CHURCH is a professor of genetics at Harvard Medical School and director of the Center for Computational Genetics. **ED REGIS** is a science writer and author of seven popular science books. Adapted from *Regenesis* by George M. Church and Ed Regis.

Article   Prepared by: Karen L. Freiberg, *University of Maryland*

The Unspeakable Gift

To understand a lifelong genetic condition, I took part in an NIH study. At times I felt isolated and objectified, but I also met others like me and got answers to mysteries that had haunted me for years, of which the biggest was this: Could I accept and love myself as I was?

KATE STEEDLY

Learning Outcomes

After reading this article, you will be able to:

- Summarize the symptoms of Turner syndrome and identify the primary organs affected by this genetic condition.

- Explain how having a genetic condition can affect the person and his or her family.

The minister's sermon was about love. I hadn't yet packed my bag for the hospital, and I was scared and a bit hung over from the mojitos I'd consumed the night before. Church has always been a hopeful and welcoming place for me, and that morning I needed to be held in grace. I looked at the bulletin, and the sermon title made me grit my teeth—"The Unspeakable Gift." In a few hours I'd be checking into the National Institutes of Health in Bethesda to participate in a weeklong medical study. My mind was too preoccupied to worry about love.

The sermon started with a poem by Raymond Carver, "Late Fragment":

> And did you get what
> you wanted from this life, even so?
> I did.
> And what did you want?
> To call myself beloved, to feel myself
> beloved on the earth.

The minister, Mark, continued with a reading from St. Paul's letter to the Corinthians: "Thanks be to God for his unspeakable gift."

The message focused on our ability to give and receive love. Mark explained that our capacity to love is one of our most precious. He related the story of a friend who would end a conversation by saying, "I love you. Do you know how much I love you?" (*Who says those words?* I thought.) Mark spoke about the

fact that the words made him feel weird and that it wasn't until his friend's death that he really grappled with their meaning.

Not feeling particularly lovable or loving that morning, I tried to allow the message to wash over me, seep into my sadness, and change my heart a bit. I sat there numb and weepy. The service ended, and I headed home to pack.

I had known about the study for years and ignored the quiet voice that said the road forward leads through NIH. Then a few years ago, I was in a class at the Writer's Center in Bethesda and did a short assignment about being 15. In the process of researching it, I learned about the study. I turned the story in and thought that was that.

I lived five miles from where some of the most renowned scientists in the world were studying people like me, but I chose denial and fear—until something clicked and I knew I had to live differently.

The journey had started when I was 15. My first menstrual cycle had been excruciating, and that had set in motion a series of doctors' appointments. Finding answers meant that my parents and I became private investigators in a search to make me well. My blood was sent to lab after lab. At 15, I learned the languages of endocrinology, genetics, and high-risk gynecology.

Sleuthing and vials of blood led to a diagnosis of Turner syndrome, a genetic condition in which a female is missing all or part of her X chromosomes. (Females generally have two X chromosomes, males an X and a Y.) The syndrome occurs in one of every 2,500 live female births. Ninety-eight percent of fetuses with Turner syndrome are miscarried. The syndrome usually manifests itself in extremely short stature and infertility. It can also mean heart and kidney problems, cognitive difficulty, spatial-reasoning issues, hearing loss, dry eyes, diabetes, and osteoporosis. My case was a bit more complicated in that I was missing only part of an X chromosome, which meant I had a "mosaic" form of the disorder.

I'm not sure if my endocrinologist had ever made a Turner-syndrome diagnosis before. His reaction was one of both concern and curiosity. I remember him saying, "By the time this is an issue for you, who knows what technology will be able to do?"

After we left his office, my mother and father took me to a Mexican restaurant. Maybe they were as scared as I was, but we didn't discuss what the doctor had said. I ordered a burrito and soldiered on.

A mosaic form of a genetic disorder allows doctors to hedge their bets. They're never really sure how the condition will express itself until they poke around inside. My endocrinologist wanted to find out exactly what Turner syndrome looked like in me, so he sent me to a gynecologist who was known to handle unusual cases.

A laparoscopic procedure, which required general anesthesia and a small incision below my belly button, confirmed that I had "streak ovaries" (scar tissue that doesn't produce eggs). A bone-density scan revealed that at age 15 I was already on the road to osteoporosis. I wanted to be thinking about guys and driver's ed, not bone degeneration and ovulation.

The years that followed were filled with treatment typically prescribed to postmenopausal women—hormone-replacement therapy, bone-density scans, bone-strengthening drugs. As my doctor tried different hormones, I endured the same emotional shifts, night sweats, and weight gain familiar to many grown women. I never looked any deeper into Turner syndrome than the initial investigation. I even kept the same gynecologist until I was 33, scheduling appointments months in advance and making special trips home to Louisville from Washington so I wouldn't have to explain my situation to anyone.

I grew weary of educating doctors about Turner syndrome when I was being treated for everything from strep throat to pinched nerves. The question about medications always required that I disclose hormone-replacement therapy, which meant I had to explain why someone of my age was taking hormones.

Disclosure became more complicated once I became an adult and health insurance entered the picture. When asking about preexisting conditions, an insurance investigator once said, "When did the condition start?" and I replied, "Mitosis."

A pause, then the follow-up: "When do you expect treatment to end?"

"When I die."

Again and again, I cringed at the thought of coming out as a person with Turner syndrome. I tried to retreat into a kind of normality that deflected reality as much as possible.

The decision to participate in an NIH study was an attempt to confront the silence. I was 35 years old. It was time.

I arrived at the NIH Clinical Center alone, early, and unprepared. The nurse responsible for checking me in wasn't even on duty yet. I had packed my suitcase as if for a four-day business conference, not a hospital stay—slacks, blouses, and pumps rather than T-shirts, sweats, and tennis shoes. That was probably a function of my denial as well as my "don't leave home without lipstick" impulse. I'd never spent a night in a hospital, never had an MRI or CT scan.

People generally don't go to NIH when they have a garden-variety illness. NIH takes the sickest of the sick and offers hope. Old and young gather there. The common denominator is illness—the kind so serious that it generates platitudes and whispers. To be a patient at NIH feels like being a contestant on a reality show in which all the cameras are turned on you—or being a lottery winner when the prize is assuming a large debt at a huge interest rate.

My mom arrived from Louisville that evening to hold my hand. She had gathered some hospital-friendly clothes from my apartment in response to my SOS call and set up my closet while I tried to make sense of my hospital schedule.

A nurse came by and pointed out the container into which I'd need to pee. She told me they'd be taking my heart rate and blood pressure every few hours. She noted the times I'd need to fast and the times they'd be drawing blood. She said the study director would arrive in the morning to make sure my paperwork was complete. She revealed very little, other than time and location, about the alphabet soup of tests on my schedule: "The specifics will be explained by the doctors."

All my meals would be in my room. I shared the first one with my mom. The food looked like it was supposed to taste good. I had been assigned the least restrictive diet and could eat as much as I wanted when I wasn't fasting. I ordered enough for two, and my mother and I sat there talking about her trip and what the nurse had described. After dinner, she headed to my apartment.

While we were eating, my roommate, Annie, arrived. Roughly my age, she was the first person with Turner syndrome I'd ever met.

Annie was from Texas, where I'd gone to grad school, so we talked about barbecue and line dancing. At five feet, she was a shade taller than I was, with wavy red hair hanging down her back. Her disarming drawl and openness stood in opposition to the short sentences and hard edges that would characterize my time at NIH. Before I met her, my image of Turner syndrome was based on pictures in 1950s textbooks of people who looked like a cross between *Dawn of the Dead* zombies and Frankenstein. She was beautiful.

I had someone to talk to during the nights that would prove difficult. Annie was in love, and we spent hours talking about the wonderful man with whom she planned to spend her life and who was supporting her through the Turner-syndrome journey. I wasn't in a relationship, so her story was a hopeful example of love and connection. The study occurred in September and I was planning a trip to New Zealand in November, so she listened to me talk about my plans as I thumbed through my *Let's Go* and *Lonely Planet* guides.

Annie had participated in the study three years before and was now doing the follow-up longitudinal component. Doctors had found problems with her heart during her earlier stay, so a great deal was at stake. She knew the ropes and could sometimes assuage, sometimes confirm, my fears.

Most of all, we shared a bond that widened my circle of what it meant to be normal. She knew what it was like to have the "So . . . let me explain about my having children" discussion with a boyfriend. She knew about hormone-replacement therapy and what it was like to hear a doctor say, "Well, your aorta could be malformed and your kidneys could cease functioning." She had osteoporosis, and clothes didn't really fit her, either.

I met the principal investigator (PI) of the study on Monday. Her salt-and-pepper hair and wire-rimmed glasses projected deep knowledge. Very scientific, she discussed the history of the study and explained how it fit with other Turner-syndrome work around the world. She had a perpetual-motion air that didn't seem to allow her to sit down and hear my story.

I quickly learned that my experience wasn't the point of the study. Doctors were primarily interested in the clinical and genetic factors related to Turner syndrome. The PI talked about an additional study on blood glucose in which I'd be asked to participate. Our eyes never really met. My mom took notes. The PI was politely interested and left after ten minutes. Her assistant provided copies of articles published by the NIH research team.

The first major procedure during my first full day at NIH was the insertion of a PICC (peripherally inserted central catheter) line—a thin tube that runs under the skin from the arm to the heart. I chose to have the PICC line so as not to be stuck with a needle every time someone needed to draw blood or administer a substance during a test. (Quite a choice.) PICC lines are generally used for the long-term administration of chemotherapy or antibiotics.

I went to the PICC area and signed more papers while someone talked very quickly about what the papers said. Then I was escorted to the sterile room where the line would be inserted. The *Today* show was on a TV in the corner. I watched a segment about Paris Hilton as they administered a local anesthetic and began to search for a vein.

The nurse, an athletic thirtysomething guy, said, "I'm glad you're nice. This is the first time I'm doing this, so you might have to be a little patient." He laughed, and my heart sank, unsure if he was joking.

Inserting the line involved inching a small tube toward my heart. It slithered through the muscles of my upper arm, pointing toward my chest, where blood flowed freely. Centimeter by centimeter, the technician charmed the snake toward its destination. (I felt nothing.) He checked the placement, made sure I was "responding correctly," explained cleaning procedures, and sent me on my way. The line would remain in for the duration of my stay.

I wandered through corridors and elevators—around silk ferns and muted sofas positioned for comfort and community— trying to find my room. I thought of the direct line to my heart that now existed. If only it were that easy to make way for emotions to move and dance, for the substance of grief and pain to flow in and out, for memories to live and transition to some higher place.

In elevators and waiting rooms, I witnessed the frailty of the human body—bald children with defeated eyes, families speaking in somber codes. I saw a man gently holding his wife's hand as she rested her head on his shoulder. A child of no more than eight walked up to the reception desk and relayed information with the swagger of a surgeon. He shouldn't have had to be that smart. I saw old people present file folders the size of encyclopedias to nurses. I saw infants staring at mortality. We were all on the same road, traveling at different speeds.

On my third day, I had a 3-D cardiac MRI. Like the entrance to a dragon ride at a carnival, the rolling, bed-like platform takes you into the mouth of the beast. I walked into the room, and the nurse—who looked as if she could run a marathon in two hours—asked about buckles or other metal on my clothes. She handed me a headset-like contraption to mitigate the loud noise. I'd be inside the machine for an hour while the doctor administered the test, which would produce a three-dimensional movie of my heart's activity. The doctor arrived and the procedure began. The sound of the machine was deafening, and I seemed to lie there forever.

The movie my heart produced—part video game, part Discovery Channel—was brief. I saw my heart beating on a small screen. Muscles moved with the fluidity of a ballet dancer. Blood flowed like a river. Valves opened and closed as elegantly as a bird's wings. The components of my heart worked together in such a way that I left convinced of a God. The experience of seeing a 3-D film of my heart was intimate and distant, natural and artificial.

The cardiac MRI was one of many tests focused on my heart. The heart is one of the primary organs affected by Turner syndrome, so it received a thorough evaluation. The knowledge that this organ would get a tremendous amount of attention was one of the primary reasons I'd been scared to participate in the study, but I knew I needed to do it. Every inch of the grand muscle was checked for shape, strength, and function.

I had lived my entire life not knowing my heart. Finishing a marathon seven years earlier hadn't convinced me it was healthy. My family history of cardiac disease surrounded my heart in a shroud. I can't describe the relief on the face of the technician who broke the rules (only doctors are supposed to reveal test results) and told me my aorta had fully functioning valves or the affirming nod by another one who read my EKG. I can only say a weight in me was lifted with each revelation. Textbook pictures of malformed hearts no longer matched mine. The premature deaths of family members were countered with each piece of positive evidence.

On my third afternoon, I reported to radiology for a pelvic ultrasound. Pregnant friends had described this test and shared black-and-white images of life as it grew inside them, so I went in knowing a little about what to expect. The technician, a stern woman, instructed me to take off my shirt and pants and put on the gown. I sat on a bed and watched her prepare the jelly that had been warming in a toaster-oven-like appliance. I was truly excited. She asked me to lie down and moved my gown to the side.

The technician rubbed the warm substance across my belly and moved a small implement firmly over me from left to right. I watched her slow, steady hands and thought about the fact that I now shared something with friends who were mothers. For a moment, I felt as if I were joining the sorority of women who could have babies.

She gently pushed the instrument, and I prayed that things could be different. On the screen, I saw a large, empty space that I think was my uterus. The technician said, "The doctors will provide analysis of the images later."

Happiness turned to grief as I contemplated the truth this test would likely confirm: the scar-tissue ovaries that had been revealed years earlier. The test ended, and the technician left. I wiped off my stomach and dried my eyes. I lay on the table for a few minutes, thinking about how different this experience was for most others.

How do I negotiate being fully female but somehow not? I felt as though a fundamental choice—the decision whether to have children—had been taken from me. I never got to weigh the pros and cons, dream about baby names, or anticipate pointy elbows and knees protruding from beneath exhausted ribs.

My diagnosis had forced me to approach the question of children not as an easy assumption but as a challenge I'd confront later—when technology would make pregnancy possible or adoption would bring children into my life.

As I sat in that room, the issue no longer swirled in my head as an abstract concept to contemplate in the future. A visceral grief settled in my bones. I lay there breathing and crying, hearing the deafening silence. I was cold and lonely. Emotionally bare, I prayed to understand how I could love myself if I was never a mother. I prayed to be whole, to feel the grief that I had buried for so long.

Somehow I gathered myself enough to put my clothes on and move on to the next test. To say I found resolution would be a lie. I still struggle with the feelings that surfaced in that room every time I consider motherhood.

Seeing a 3-D film of my heart was both intimate and distant.

The study required that photographs be taken of me. I don't like having my picture taken in the best of circumstances, and I was angry at being subjected to a camera's eye.

The experience reminded me of the pictures of women and girls with Turner syndrome I had seen over the years. I couldn't help but think about the grotesque pictures of females with the condition that appeared in textbooks, depicting abnormal bodies, webbed necks, malformed hearts, horseshoe-shaped kidneys. The subjects were never smiling; they were simply ugly. I was now being forced into an experience similar to what I imagined they had endured.

I couldn't look at the photographer when I entered the small room. He seemed nice enough, but my mood was such that I resented the very oxygen he demanded. He asked me to remove my shirt but let me leave on my bra, camisole, and jeans. (I was relieved beyond belief.) The fluorescent lights made my skin appear corpse-like.

I was to stand in front of a screen and let my arms hang, not allowing my shoulders to tense up and curl forward. The photographer said he was particularly interested in the way my elbows extended. He didn't give me instructions for my face, so I'm not sure it was included in the picture. He asked me to turn to the left and remain relaxed. (It's really hard to relax when someone requests it.) I turned to the right. He came closer for what I assume were close-ups of my face and neck from various angles. I wish I'd been clever enough to think of an expression that passive-aggressively said "F--- you" or that subliminally said "Really see me" to everyone who would look at these pictures in the future.

The photo session put me in touch with an anger I hadn't been able to articulate. I was angry that I just had to stand and have pictures taken of me. I was angry that I was hungry and hadn't been able to eat because I'd had a blood test that afternoon. I was angry because a nurse had tried to stick me with a needle at 5:30 in the morning. I was angry that I had Turner syndrome. I was angry that I was different. I was angry that there was no cure.

One of the final tests on my last day was a comprehensive hearing exam. The audiologist looked as if he'd stepped out of a J. Crew catalog, and he had an empathetic demeanor. We had a long discussion about the connection between Turner syndrome and hearing loss. He asked me a battery of questions, then handed me a buzzer and stood in front of what looked like a rock-music soundboard.

The test was easy at first. I was told to press the buzzer when I heard a sound. I detected a variety of sounds at a variety of pitches and volumes. As the test progressed, there were centuries of silence. I got a sick feeling and began randomly pressing the button—like choosing C on a multiple-choice test when you have no idea of the answer. Every once in a while, I actually heard a sound. I couldn't tell what pitches or volumes were more audible. I knew in my gut I was failing.

After the test, the audiologist printed the results and told me I had significant hearing loss within the pitch range of the human voice and explained this was common for Turner patients. He suggested I consider hearing aids.

A wave of fear washed over me, and tears welled. I had been through so much, and now this information pushed me over an edge I didn't even know I was near. Somehow I heard the news as more evidence that I was less than whole. I thought about all the ways in which I was imperfect or broken, about every time I'd asked for clarification when someone spoke or nodded in agreement when I hadn't heard something, about my need over the last few years to see people's mouths when they talked—all the subconscious coping mechanisms I'd developed. Being flawed had now been scientifically verified. I knew hearing aids wouldn't make that feel any better.

The study culminated in a conference in which the research team would come to my hospital room and share my results with me. I had my PICC line removed that morning and would be released after the meeting.

My mother and I were waiting, a mixture of fatigue and fear churning in my stomach, when a chaplain came to the door. She had been ordained in the same denomination in which I'd grown up, the United Church of Christ, so our theological waters converged immediately. The chaplain asked about my story and shared her own—she had a social-justice background that had taken her around the world, and she was new to NIH. She asked if my mother and I wanted her to pray with us. We said yes. (We were both exhausted from the week—my mom had spent every day with me, leaving only to sleep at my apartment—and scared about the final conference.) After about 15 minutes, the chaplain held our hands and asked that the God of health and safety watch over us. She affirmed the fullness of God's grace and asked that it be present in our comings and goings.

Her visit brought a measure of peace and warmth to the clinical experience I'd lived at NIH. She was a reminder of my faith. She was God made real in that moment.

After the chaplain left, the research team began to assemble. One by one, a sea of spectacled anonymity filled my room and a buzz akin to that of an AM radio in the desert descended. The group of about a dozen circled as I sat on my bed and listened. My mother took notes. The principal investigator led the discussion, with analysis by one of the chief scientists. Their students listened as they explained the results of my 20 or so tests. They talked about my heart, hormones, bones, kidneys, blood glucose, blood pressure, eyes, skin, and liver. They concluded that I was pre-diabetic, had a fatty liver, needed to lose 20 to 25 pounds, had osteoporosis, and had significant hearing loss.

They wrote no prescriptions. They made no referrals to specialists. They didn't seem alarmed by the findings. The atmosphere seemed strangely relaxed given what my body had endured—they seemed to have told this story a million times.

I tried to not interpret their lack of interest as cavalier indifference. I was both relieved and angry. Somehow this meeting didn't provide the closure that I craved. I'm not sure what would have—short of someone saying, "We'd like to enroll you in a genetic-therapy experiment in which we'll correct your chromosomes. You'll grow six inches, and your ovaries, ears, and bones will be fixed."

I know that wouldn't have satisfied me, either. I think I yearned for acknowledgement of who I was and for the knowledge that emerges when the body is examined to the degree that physical truths are revealed and our understanding of ourselves is changed. The NIH doctors weren't concerned with what I'd learned or experienced. That wasn't their job.

I left bruised and a bit lighter. Years of silence had been shattered: I'd met my heart and confronted the grief I felt about my fertility issues. Somehow normal grew to include me.

How do I negotiate between being fully female but somehow not?

I'd never again wonder if my aorta allowed blood to flow in the right direction (it does) or if my bones were as thin as lace (not quite, but I have to take calcium and vitamin D supplements). I learned that my eyes produced enough tears. I received answers to long-held questions about my physical state. I learned I was strong enough to ask questions. I learned that being whole is a complicated journey that starts with breaking our silences and learning to love the parts of ourselves we fear. I wanted to start more conversations, continuing and expanding the spiritual and psychic excavation that began within those stark halls.

I'd have a conversation with my minister in the courtyard of my church, on the stone benches where I'd passed hours. I wanted to ask him about the relationship between loving oneself and being loving in the world.

He might say, "Being loving in the world starts with loving oneself." Or he might talk about Martin Luther King Jr. and invoke the idea that real love takes courage—the kind of which peace, compassion, and reconciliation are born—and that loving oneself is a profound act of courage. He might invoke poet Mary Oliver and remind me to "let the soft animal of [my] body love what it loves." I would then ask him why St. Paul called love the "unspeakable gift."

I'm not sure how he would answer. I think he would talk about how hard it is to love sometimes, and that the ability to love, even when it's hard, is a gift.

I would have a conversation with myself at age 15. I hear this conversation as clearly as the sea knows the tide and the sky knows the sunrise. We would meet by the tallest tree in the back yard of the house where I grew up. My 15-year-old self would be wearing her Rocky's Sub Pub uniform and pounds of blue eye shadow. I would tell her everything was going to be okay. I would show her the NIH results and explain how they describe her but don't define her. I would tell her it's all right to be mad as hell. I would stroke her hair and tell her she's beautiful and whole. I would hold her and explain that she could be a world traveler, fearless warrior, and loving spirit.

Then I'd have a conversation with myself at 80. We would sit on the porch of her mountainside home. She would offer me something to drink and I'd ask for sweet tea. Her long, wavy gray hair would be gathered in a bun. I would ask why it took me 20 years to find out about Turner syndrome's effects on my body. I'd say, "Why was I so scared?"

"We come to things when we are ready," she'd say.

I'd ask, "How would I live my life differently if I really knew I was whole?"

She would respond with questions: "Don't you love completely? Aren't you guided by your passions even when that path is difficult? Do you frame each day in gratitude? Don't you act generously with loved ones and strangers?"

Then she would say, "Being whole looks like that."

She might even hold my hands in hers and add, "I love you. Do you know how much I love you?"

Critical Thinking

1. How can medical professionals help patients feel less isolated and objectified when study procedures are performed?

2. Support the need for health insurance to pay for conditions present from conception to death.

3. Why does confronting one's situation help ease the angers and fears associated with it?

Create Central

www.mhhe.com/createcentral

Internet References

Genetics Education Center
www.kumc.edu/gec

International Hap Map Project
www.hapmap.org

National Institute of Child Health and Human Development
http://turners.nichd.nih.gov/clinfrintro.html

Turner Syndrome: What Is It, Symptoms, Causes
www.turnersyndrome.org

KATIE STEEDLY lived in Washington for seven years. She currently lives and writes in Cincinnati.

Article   Prepared by: Karen L. Freiberg, *University of Maryland*

The Incredible Expanding Adventures of the X Chromosome

Genes housed on the powerhouse X chromosome shed new light on the human mind, including why identical female twins differ more than their male counterparts, why there are more male geniuses and male autists, and why you may have mom to thank for your brains.

CHRISTOPHER BADCOCK

Learning Outcomes

After reading this article, you will be able to:

- Distinguish between the genetic potential of the X compared to the Y chromosome.

- Explain why you may have your mother to thank for your intelligence.

In the early 1980s I met and began an unofficial training with Anna Freud—Sigmund Freud's youngest daughter, and his only child to follow him into psychoanalysis. I was a young social scientist who had been carrying out a self-analysis for some years.

Anna Freud's couch was a daybed on which I lay, with her seated in a chair at its head. On one or two occasions I couldn't help but think that the voice I heard coming from her chair was in fact that of her father, speaking to me from beyond the grave.

I can even recall her exact words in one case. I had been free-associating about my attempt to analyze myself when Anna Freud remarked, "In your self-analysis you sank a deep but narrow shaft into your unconscious. Here we clear the whole area, layer by layer." This produced a spine-tingling reaction in me, and I surprised Miss Freud (as I called her) by stating that her remark reminded me of her father, because he was particularly fond of archaeological metaphors in his published writings. Most people would simply attribute her statement to the influence of her father's writing on her own choice of words. Thirty years ago, I would probably have said the same. But today, having spent decades researching the links between genetics and psychology, I can offer a different hypothesis, one that goes to the core of all we now know about the inheritance and expression of genes in the brain.

The Royal X

Everyone inherits 23 chromosomes from each parent, 46 in all, making 23 matched pairs—with one exception. One pair comprises the chromosomes that determine sex. Female mammals get an X chromosome from each parent, but males receive an X from their mother and a Y sex chromosome from their father.

The X chromosome a woman inherits from her mother is, like any other chromosome, a random mix of genes from both of her mother's Xs, and so does not correspond as a whole with either of her mother's X chromosomes. By contrast, the X a woman inherits from her father is his one and only X chromosome, complete and undiluted. This means that a father is twice as closely related to his daughter via his X chromosome genes as is her mother. To put it another way: Any X gene in a mother has a 50/50 chance of being inherited by her daughter, but every X gene in a father is certain to be passed on to a daughter.

These laws of genetic transmission have major implications for family lineages. When it comes to grandparents, women are always most closely X-related to their paternal grandmother and less related to their paternal grandfather. Consider how this plays out in the current British royal family. The late Diana, Princess of Wales, will be more closely related to any daughter born to William and Kate than will Kate's parents, thanks to William's passing on his single X from her. Kate's mother's X genes passed on to a granddaughter, by contrast, will be diluted by those of Kate's father in the X this girl would receive from Kate, meaning that the X-relatedness of the Middletons to any granddaughter would be half that of Princess Diana. Prince Charles, however, would be the least related of all four grandparents to Prince William's daughters because he confers no sex chromosome genes on them.

Prince Charles would be the least related grandparent to any daughters of prince William and Kate because he confers no sex chromosome to girls.

Of course, if William and Kate produce a son, the situation is reversed, and now Prince Charles is most closely related to his grandson, via his Y chromosome. Princess Diana will have no sex-chromosome relatedness to William and Kate's sons because the X she bequeathed William will not be passed on to the grandsons.

Calculations of X-relatedness may seem abstract, but they have probably played a huge role in European history, thanks to the fact that Queen Victoria passed on hemophilia, an X-chromosome disorder that was in the past fatal to males. Victoria and her female descendants were protected by a second, unaffected X, but princes in several European royal houses—not least the Romanovs—were affected, with disastrous consequences for successions based on male primogeniture.

The X in Sex

Not only are X chromosomes bequeathed and inherited differently, depending on whether you are male or female, they also have different patterns of expression in the body. For example, in 1875, Darwin described a disorder that appeared in each generation of one family's male members, affecting some but sparing others: ". . . small and weak incisor teeth . . . very little hair on the body . . . excessive dryness of the skin. . . . Though the daughters in the . . . family were never affected, they transmit the tendency to their sons; and no case has occurred of a son transmitting it to his sons."

Today we know this to be anhidrotic ectodermal dysplasia (AED), a disorder involving sweat glands, among other things, that affects males and females differently. Because AED is carried on an X chromosome, affected males have no sweat glands whatsoever. They express their one and only X in all their cells. Affected females with the AED gene on only one X have different patterns of expression because areas of their body randomly express one or the other of their two X chromosomes. It is perfectly possible for an affected woman to have one armpit that sweats and one that doesn't.

X chromosome expression can explain not only differences between males and females but also differences between identical female twins. Such twins may routinely differ more than their male counterparts, because in each woman, one of their two X chromosomes is normally silenced. Identical twins result when the cells of the fertilized egg have divided only a few times and the egg then splits into two individuals. The pattern of differential X expression in cells is set at this stage. In females, an X chromosome gene called Xist effectively tosses a coin and decides which of the two X chromosomes will be expressed and which silenced in any particular cell.

Differential X chromosome gene expression explains why one of a pair of living Americans is a successful athlete yet her identical twin sister suffers from Duchenne muscular dystrophy (DMD), an X-linked genetic disease that predominantly affects males and leaves sufferers unable to walk. In this case only one twin was unfortunate enough to inherit the cell lineages that expressed the DMD gene from one parental X chromosome, while the other twin inherited those expressed from the other parent's unaffected X.

A predisposition to sex-linked disorders is just one of the ways female identical twins differ more than males. A recent study found that compared with male twins, female identical twins vary more on measures of social behavior and verbal ability. This is also due to differential expression of genes on their two X chromosomes in contrast to male twins' single, truly identical X. In the past, such differences between identical twins would have been attributed to nongenetic or environmental factors, but now we know that these dissimilarities are in fact the result of gene expression. Where X chromosome genes are concerned, what once seemed to be nurture now turns out to be nature.

The X Factor in IQ

Another important factor in sex chromosome expression is the huge dissimilarity between the information carried on the X and Y chromosomes. The Y has a mere 100 or so genes, and there is no evidence that any of them are linked to cognition. This contrasts sharply with the 1,200-odd genes on the X chromosome. There is mounting evidence that at least 150 of these genes are linked to intelligence, and there is definite evidence that verbal IQ is X-linked. It suggests that a mother's contribution to intelligence may be more significant than a father's—especially if the child is male, because a male's one and only X chromosome always comes from his mother. And in females, the X chromosome derived from the father is in fact bequeathed directly from the father's mother, simply setting the maternal X-effect back one generation, so to speak.

The fact that males have only a single X, uniquely derived from the mother, has further implications for variations in intelligence. Look at it this way: If you are the son of a highly intelligent mother and if there is indeed a major X chromosome contribution to IQ, you will express your one and only maternal X chromosome without dilution by the second X chromosome that a female would inherit. The effects cut both ways: If you are a male with a damaged IQ-linked gene on your X, you are going to suffer its effects much more obviously than a female, who can express the equivalent, undamaged gene from her second X chromosome. This in itself likely explains why there are more males than females with very high and very low IQs: males' single X chromosome increases variance in IQ, simply because there is not a second, compensatory X chromosome.

If you are the son of a highly intelligent mother and there is indeed a major X chromosome contribution to IQ, you're in luck.

The Case against "Genius" Sperm Banks

IF INTELLIGENCE IS X-linked to the degree that some researchers speculate, there are important implications for our views of the heritability of talent—and even genius. The Repository for Germinal Choice was a California sperm bank that operated in the 1980s and 1990s and claimed that its donors reflected a range of Nobel laureates. (In fact the only confirmed Nobel Prize-winning donor was William Shockley, and most donors are now known not to have been laureates at all.) But beyond the actual composition of the sperm bank, there is a fundamental problem with an enterprise founded on the belief that Nobel Prize-winning talent might be heritable from the father, given the likely role of the X chromosome in intelligencê.

In the case of a "genius" sperm bank, only half the sperm donated would on average be carrying the Nobel laureate's X chromosome, and any child resulting from such a fertilization would be female, and so would have a second X from the mother to dilute its effect. In the beginning, mothers receiving Nobel laureates' sperm from the Repository for Germinal Choice had to be members of Mensa, and so would have had high IQs to pass on to their offspring of either sex via their X chromosomes. Indeed, this in itself might explain any apparent heritability of Nobel laureate "genius" via the Repository.

The other half of the preserved sperm would have a Y chromosome instead of an X. These sperm assuredly would produce sons, but there is no evidence that the Y is implicated in intelligence. On the contrary, the sole X of sons conceived this way would increase their vulnerability to intellectual impairment in the way that it does for all males, and would also mean that any "genius" seen in them most likely came from their single, undiluted maternal X.

Finally, there is the environmental factor in IQ. Clearly this too would be wholly attributable to the mothers in the case of a sperm bank, because the father provides only his genes.

Ironically then, mothers with children of "genius" sperm-bank fathers were probably laboring under something of a delusion. Any intellectual talent in their children was most likely predominantly attributable to them, both via their X chromosome genes and the home environment they provided. However, the single mothers who nowadays constitute the major clientele for sperm banks may not be too displeased to realize that, where heritability of intelligence is concerned, Mother Nature is something of a feminist.

The inheritance of intelligence is not limited to the influence of sex-linked genes. Non-sex-chromosome genes can also vary in their pattern of expression depending on which parent they come from (so-called genomic imprinting). One such gene on chromosome 6 (IGF2R) has been found to correlate with high IQ in some studies. The mouse version of this gene is expressed only from the maternal chromosome, and to that extent such genes resemble X chromosome ones in their maternal bias. Although it remains highly controversial to what extent the same is true of the human version of this gene, several syndromes that feature mental retardation are associated with imprinted genes on others of the 22 non-sex chromosomes.

X Expression in Autism

Autism spectrum disorder is yet another phenomenon that can be clarified through the prism of X chromosome inheritance and expression. Researchers have recently begun to suspect that autism is X-linked, in part because more males than females are affected by ASD, particularly at the high-functioning end of the spectrum—Asperger's syndrome—where males outnumber females by at least 10 to 1. Asperger's syndrome impairs pro-social behavior, peer relations, and verbal ability (among other deficits)—the very same traits that vary between identical female as opposed to identical male twins, and all of which are thought to have some linkage to the X chromosome. Because males have only a single X, they could be much more vulnerable to such X-linked deficits than are females, who normally have a second X chromosome to compensate and dilute the effect.

Indeed, women afflicted with autism spectrum disorders may be among the minority of females who disproportionately express one parent's X. Women on the autism spectrum are probably among the 35 percent of women who have a greater than 70:30 skew in their pattern of X expression in favor of one rather than the other parent's X. Indeed, 7 percent of women have more than a 90:10 skew. Such a hugely one-sided expression of one X would closely resemble the single X chromosome found in males. And if X expression peculiarities affect critical genes implicated in autism in the case of these women, Asperger's would result, just as it does in males. Furthermore, the fact that only a small minority of females have such highly skewed X expression could explain why so many more males than females are affected. Most females have more equitable patterns of X expression and are therefore protected by their second X.

The peculiarities of X chromosome gene expression might even explain the often-remarked variability of the symptoms in Asperger's. Classically heritable single-gene disorder like anhidrotic ectodermal dysplasia or Duchenne muscular dystrophy usually have strikingly consistent symptoms because only one gene is affected, often in the same way. But if variable expression of several X-linked genes is the norm in Asperger's syndrome, the outcome in each case might be surprisingly different, and the combined effects highly variable—just as researchers find.

Female identical twins differ more than their male counterparts, because in each woman one of their two X chromosomes is normally silenced.

X Marks the Spot in the Brain

What light might this shed on Anna Freud's eerie use of metaphors favored by her father? In her case, the woman who became a psychoanalyst just like her father might have been among the minority of women who disproportionately express one parent's set of X-linked genes in the brain. We saw earlier that anhidrotic ectodermal dysplasia affects only some areas of a woman's skin, depending on where the affected X is expressed. Both the skin and the brain develop from the same layer in the ball of cells (or blastocyst) from which the embryo first forms. We also saw that in females this can result in some cells expressing one parent's X and some expressing the other's, and if this can happen to the skin, then it could also occur in the brain: Some parts might express the father's X and some parts the mother's. Indeed, there is persuasive evidence that this occurs in mice, and circumstantial evidence that it also does in humans.

Given the possibility of an extreme skew in the pattern of X expression, such as likely occurs in women with Asperger's syndrome, we can envisage a situation in which critical parts of a woman's brain are built entirely by one parent's genes. And if that parent is the father, then the same genes that constructed his brain would be expressed in his daughter's brain. Theoretically, a woman could be an X chromosome clone of her father in that each and every X gene he has would be inherited and expressed by her, perhaps in exactly the same regions of the brain. This could result in a daughter's mind being very like her father's—and surprisingly dissimilar to her mother's.

Freud emphasized the importance of the relationship between mothers and sons, but in my experience it pales in comparison to that between many fathers and daughters, who often seem to have a close emotional bond that intensifies with time.

Sigmund Freud's own relationship with his daughter Anna certainly seems a case in point, as I was able to observe firsthand—at least in the daughter at the end of her life. At the time, I felt I was hearing the voice of Freud speaking from beyond the grave. But of course only a person's DNA can survive his or her death, and even then it has to be packaged in a living descendant. So today I am more inclined to think that the words I heard may indeed have been those of Sigmund Freud, but expressed from his daughter's paternal X chromosome.

Critical Thinking

1. Identify the approximate number of genes found on each X chromosome and the approximate number on each Y chromosome.

2. Explain why genius and autism are related to the X chromosome, and why they both are more common in males.

3. How can identical female twins differ on traits related to genes on their X chromosomes?

Create Central

www.mhhe.com/createcentral

Internet References

Biological Basis of Heredity: Sex Linked Genes
    http://anthro.palomar.edu/biobasis/bio_4.htm
Genetic Science Learning Center
    www.learn.genetics.utah.edu
Identical Twins Facts
    www.ask.com/Identical+Twins+Facts

CHRISTOPHER BADCOCK, PhD, is the author of *The Imprinted Brain*. He retired this year as a Reader in Sociology at the London School of Economic and Political Science.

Article   Prepared by: Karen L. Freiberg, *University of Maryland*

How Long Can You Wait to Have a Baby?

Jean M. Twenge

Learning Outcomes

After reading this article, you will be able to:

- Analyze the accurate chances of a woman's ability to procreate in her mid- to late-30's.

- Identify the more common reasons for in vitro fertilization (IVF), rather than the mother's age.

- Identify new technologies for allowing babies to be born to older mothers.

In the tentative, post-9/11 spring of 2002, I was, at 30, in the midst of extricating myself from my first marriage. My husband and I had met in graduate school but couldn't find two academic jobs in the same place, so we spent the three years of our marriage living in different states. After I accepted a tenure-track position in California and he turned down a postdoctoral research position nearby—the job wasn't good enough, he said—it seemed clear that our living situation was not going to change.

I put off telling my parents about the split for weeks, hesitant to disappoint them. When I finally broke the news, they were, to my relief, supportive and understanding. Then my mother said, "Have you read *Time* magazine this week? I know you want to have kids."

Time's cover that week had a baby on it. "Listen to a successful woman discuss her failure to bear a child, and the grief comes in layers of bitterness and regret," the story inside began. A generation of women who had waited to start a family was beginning to grapple with that decision, and one media outlet after another was wringing its hands about the steep decline in women's fertility with age: "When It's Too Late to Have a Baby," lamented the U.K.'s *Observer;* "Baby Panic," *New York MAGAZINE* announced on its cover.

The panic stemmed from the April 2002 publication of Sylvia Ann Hewlett's headline-grabbing book, *Creating a Life,* which counseled that women should have their children while they're young or risk having none at all. Within corporate America, 42 percent of the professional women interviewed by Hewlett had no children at age 40, and most said they deeply regretted it. Just as you plan for a corner office, Hewlett advised her readers, you should plan for grandchildren.

The previous fall, an ad campaign sponsored by the American Society for Reproductive Medicine (ASRM) had warned, "Advancing age decreases your ability to have children." One ad was illustrated with a baby bottle shaped like an hourglass that was—just to make the point glaringly obvious—running out of milk. Female fertility, the group announced, begins to decline at 27. "Should you have your baby now?" asked *Newsweek* in response.

For me, that was no longer a viable option.

I had always wanted children. Even when I was busy with my postdoctoral research, I volunteered to babysit a friend's preschooler. I frequently passed the time in airports by chatting up frazzled mothers and babbling toddlers—a 2-year-old, quite to my surprise, once crawled into my lap. At a wedding I attended in my late 20s, I played with the groom's preschool-age nephews, often on the floor, during the entire rehearsal and most of the reception. ("Do you fart?" one of them asked me in an overly loud voice during the rehearsal. "Everyone does," I replied solemnly, as his grandfather laughed quietly in the next pew.)

But, suddenly single at 30, I seemed destined to remain childless until at least my mid-30s, and perhaps always. Flying to a friend's wedding in May 2002, I finally forced myself to read the *Time* article. It upset me so much that I began doubting my divorce for the first time. "And God, what if I want to have two?" I wrote in my journal as the cold plane sped over the Rockies. "First at 35, and if you wait until the kid is 2 to try, more than likely you have the second at 38 or 39. If at all." To reassure myself about the divorce, I wrote, "Nothing I did would have changed the situation." I underlined that.

I was lucky: within a few years, I married again, and this time the match was much better. But my new husband and I seemed to face frightening odds against having children. Most books and Web sites I read said that one in three women ages 35 to 39 would not get pregnant within a year of starting to try. The first page of the ASRM's 2003 guide for patients noted that women in their late 30s had a 30 percent chance of remaining childless altogether. The guide also included statistics that

I'd seen repeated in many other places: a woman's chance of pregnancy was 20 percent each month at age 30, dwindling to 5 percent by age 40.

Every time I read these statistics, my stomach dropped like a stone, heavy and foreboding. Had I already missed my chance to be a mother?

As a psychology researcher who'd published articles in scientific journals, some covered in the popular press, I knew that many scientific findings differ significantly from what the public hears about them. Soon after my second wedding, I decided to go to the source: I scoured medical-research databases, and quickly learned that the statistics on women's age and fertility—used by many to make decisions about relationships, careers, and when to have children—were one of the more spectacular examples of the mainstream media's failure to correctly report on and interpret scientific research.

The widely cited statistic that one in three women ages 35 to 39 will not be pregnant after a year of trying, for instance, is based on an article published in 2004 in the journal *Human Reproduction.* Rarely mentioned is the source of the data: French birth records from 1670 to 1830. The chance of remaining childless—30 percent—was also calculated based on historical populations.

In other words, millions of women are being told when to get pregnant based on statistics from a time before electricity, antibiotics, or fertility treatment. Most people assume these numbers are based on large, well-conducted studies of modern women, but they are not. When I mention this to friends and associates, by far the most common reaction is: "No . . . No way. *Really?*"

Surprisingly few well-designed studies of female age and natural fertility include women born in the 20th century—but those that do tend to paint a more optimistic picture. One study, published in *Obstetrics & Gynecology* in 2004 and headed by David Dunson (now of Duke University), examined the chances of pregnancy among 770 European women. It found that with sex at least twice a week, 82 percent of 35-to-39-year-old women conceive within a year, compared with 86 percent of 27-to-34-year-olds. (The fertility of women in their late 20s and early 30s was almost identical—news in and of itself.) Another study, released this March in *Fertility and Sterility* and led by Kenneth Rothman of Boston University, followed 2,820 Danish women as they tried to get pregnant. Among women having sex during their fertile times, 78 percent of 35-to-40-year-olds got pregnant within a year, compared with 84 percent of 20-to-34-year-olds. A study headed by Anne Steiner, an associate professor at the University of North Carolina School of Medicine, the results of which were presented in June, found that among 38- and 39-year-olds who had been pregnant before, 80 percent of white women of normal weight got pregnant naturally within six months (although that percentage was lower among other races and among the overweight). "In our data, we're not seeing huge drops until age 40," she told me.

Even some studies based on historical birth records are more optimistic than what the press normally reports: One found

that, in the days before birth control, 89 percent of 38-year-old women were still fertile. Another concluded that the typical woman was able to get pregnant until somewhere between ages 40 and 45. Yet these more encouraging numbers are rarely mentioned—none of these figures appear in the American Society for Reproductive Medicine's 2008 committee opinion on female age and fertility, which instead relies on the most-ominous historical data.

In short, the "baby panic"—which has by no means abated since it hit me personally—is based largely on questionable data. We've rearranged our lives, worried endlessly, and forgone countless career opportunities based on a few statistics about women who resided in thatched-roof huts and never saw a lightbulb. In Dunson's study of modern women, the difference in pregnancy rates at age 28 versus 37 is only about 4 percentage points. Fertility does decrease with age, but the decline is not steep enough to keep the vast majority of women in their late 30s from having a child. And that, after all, is the whole point.

I am now the mother of three children, all born after I turned 35. My oldest started kindergarten on my 40th birthday; my youngest was born five months later. All were conceived naturally within a few months. The toddler in my lap at the airport is now mine.

Instead of worrying about my fertility, I now worry about paying for child care and getting three children to bed on time. These are good problems to have.

Yet the memory of my abject terror about age-related infertility still lingers. Every time I tried to get pregnant, I was consumed by anxiety that my age meant doom. I was not alone. Women on Internet message boards write of scaling back their careers or having fewer children than they'd like to, because they can't bear the thought of trying to get pregnant after 35. Those who have already passed the dreaded birthday ask for tips on how to stay calm when trying to get pregnant, constantly worrying—just as I did—that they will never have a child. "I'm scared because I am 35 and everyone keeps reminding me that my 'clock is ticking.' My grandmother even reminded me of this at my wedding reception," one newly married woman wrote to me after reading my 2012 advice book, *The Impatient Woman's Guide to Getting Pregnant,* based in part on my own experience. It's not just grandmothers sounding this note. "What science tells us about the aging parental body should alarm us more than it does," wrote the journalist Judith Shulevitz in a *New Republic* cover story late last year that focused, laser-like, on the downsides of delayed parenthood.

How did the baby panic happen in the first place? And why hasn't there been more public pushback from fertility experts?

One possibility is the "availability heuristic": when making judgments, people rely on what's right in front of them. Fertility doctors see the effects of age on the success rate of fertility treatment every day. That's particularly true for in vitro fertilization, which relies on the extraction of a large number of eggs from the ovaries, because some eggs are lost at every stage of the difficult process. Younger women's ovaries respond better to the drugs used to extract the eggs, and younger women's eggs are more likely to be chromosomally normal. As a result, younger women's IVF success rates are indeed much higher—about 42 percent of those younger than 35 will give birth to a live baby after one IVF cycle, versus 27 percent for those ages 35 to 40, and just 12 percent for those ages 41 to 42. Many studies have examined how IVF success declines with age, and these statistics are cited in many research articles and online forums.

Yet only about 1 percent of babies born each year in the U.S. are a result of IVF, and most of their mothers used the technique not because of their age, but to overcome blocked fallopian tubes, male infertility, or other issues: about 80 percent of IVF patients are 40 or younger. And the IVF statistics tell us very little about natural conception, which requires just one egg rather than a dozen or more, among other differences.

Studies of natural conception are surprisingly difficult to conduct—that's one reason both IVF statistics and historical records play an outsize role in fertility reporting. Modern birth records are uninformative, because most women have their children in their 20s and then use birth control or sterilization surgery to prevent pregnancy during their 30s and 40s. Studies asking couples how long it took them to conceive or how long they have been trying to get pregnant are as unreliable as human memory. And finding and studying women who are trying to get pregnant is challenging, as there's such a narrow window between when they start trying and when some will succeed.

Another problem looms even larger: women who are actively trying to get pregnant at age 35 or later might be less fertile than the average over-35 woman. Some highly fertile women will get pregnant accidentally when they are younger, and others will get pregnant quickly whenever they try, completing their families at a younger age. Those who are left are, disproportionately, the less fertile. Thus, "the observed lower fertility rates among older women presumably overestimate the effect of biological aging," says Dr. Allen Wilcox, who leads the Reproductive Epidemiology Group at the National Institute of Environmental Health Sciences. "If we're overestimating the biological decline of fertility with age, this will only be good news to women who have been most fastidious in their birth-control use, and may be more fertile at older ages, on average, than our data would lead them to expect."

These modern-day research problems help explain why historical data from an age before birth control are so tempting. However, the downsides of a historical approach are numerous. Advanced medical care, antibiotics, and even a reliable food supply were unavailable hundreds of years ago. And the decline in fertility in the historical data may also stem from older couples' having sex less often than younger ones. Less-frequent sex might have been especially likely if couples had been married for a long time, or had many children, or both. (Having more children of course makes it more difficult to fit in sex, and some couples surely realized—*eureka!*—that they could avoid having another mouth to feed by scaling back their nocturnal activities.) Some historical studies try to control for these problems in various ways—such as looking only at just-married couples—but many of the same issues remain.

The best way to assess fertility might be to measure "cycle viability," or the chance of getting pregnant if a couple has sex on the most fertile day of the woman's cycle. Studies based on cycle viability use a prospective rather than retrospective design—monitoring couples as they attempt to get pregnant instead of asking couples to recall how long it took them to get pregnant or how long they tried. Cycle-viability studies also eliminate the need to account for older couples' less active sex lives. David Dunson's analysis revealed that intercourse two days before ovulation resulted in pregnancy 29 percent of the time for 35-to-39-year-old women, compared with about 42 percent for 27-to-29-year-olds. So, by this measure, fertility falls by about a third from a woman's late 20s to her late 30s. However, a 35-to-39-year-old's fertility two days before ovulation was the same as a 19-to-26-year-old's fertility three days before ovulation: according to Dunson's data, older couples who time sex just one day better than younger ones will effectively eliminate the age difference.

Don't these numbers contradict the statistics you sometimes see in the popular press that only 20 percent of 30-year-old women and 5 percent of 40-year-old women get pregnant per cycle? They do, but no journal article I could locate contained these numbers, and none of the experts I contacted could tell me what data set they were based on. The American Society for Reproductive Medicine's guide provides no citation for these statistics; when I contacted the association's press office asking where they came from, a representative said they were simplified for a popular audience, and did not provide a specific citation.

Dunson, a biostatistics professor, thought the lower numbers might be averages across many cycles rather than the chances of getting pregnant during the first cycle of trying. More women will get pregnant during the first cycle than in each subsequent one because the most fertile will conceive quickly, and those left will have lower fertility on average.

Most fertility problems are not the result of female age. Blocked tubes and endometriosis (a condition in which the cells lining the uterus also grow outside it) strike both younger and older women. Almost half of infertility problems trace back to the man, and these seem to be more common among older men, although research suggests that men's fertility declines only gradually with age.

Fertility problems unrelated to female age may also explain why, in many studies, fertility at older ages is considerably higher among women who have been pregnant before. Among couples who haven't had an accidental pregnancy—who, as Dr. Steiner put it, "have never had an 'oops'"—sperm issues and blocked tubes may be more likely. Thus, the data from women who already have a child may give a more accurate picture of the fertility decline due to "ovarian aging." In Kenneth Rothman's study of the Danish women, among those who'd given birth at least once previously, the chance of getting pregnant at age 40 was similar to that at age 20.

Older women's fears, of course, extend beyond the ability to get pregnant. The rates of miscarriages and birth defects rise with age, and worries over both have been well ventilated in the popular press. But how much do these risks actually rise? Many miscarriage statistics come from—you guessed it—women who undergo IVF or other fertility treatment, who may have a higher miscarriage risk regardless of age. Nonetheless, the *National Vital Statistics Reports,* which draw data from the general population, find that 15 percent of women ages 20 to 34, 27 percent of women 35 to 39, and 26 percent of women 40 to 44 report having had a miscarriage. These increases are hardly insignificant, and the true rate of miscarriages is higher, since many miscarriages occur extremely early in a pregnancy—before a missed period or pregnancy test. Yet it should be noted that even for older women, the likelihood of a pregnancy's continuing is nearly three times that of having a known miscarriage.

What about birth defects? The risk of chromosomal abnormalities such as Down syndrome does rise with a woman's age—such abnormalities are the source of many of those very early, undetected miscarriages. However, the probability of having a child with a chromosomal abnormality remains extremely low. Even at early fetal testing (known as chorionic villus sampling), 99 percent of fetuses are chromosomally normal among 35-year-old pregnant women, and 97 percent among 40-year-olds. At 45, when most women can no longer get pregnant, 87 percent of fetuses are still normal. (Many of those that are not will later be miscarried.) In the near future, fetal genetic testing will be done with a simple blood test, making it even easier than it is today for women to get early information about possible genetic issues.

W hat does all this mean for a woman trying to decide when to have children? More specifically, how long can she safely wait?

This question can't be answered with absolutely certainty, for two big reasons. First, while the data on natural fertility among modern women are proliferating, they are still sparse. Collectively, the three modern studies by Dunson, Rothman, and Steiner included only about 400 women 35 or older, and they might not be representative of all such women trying to conceive.

Second, statistics, of course, can tell us only about probabilities and averages—they offer no guarantees to any particular person. "Even if we had good estimates for the average biological decline in fertility with age, that is still of relatively limited use to individuals, given the large range of fertility found in healthy women," says Allen Wilcox of the NIH.

So what is a woman—and her partner—to do?

The data, imperfect as they are, suggest two conclusions. No. 1: fertility declines with age. No. 2, and much more relevant: the vast majority of women in their late 30s will be able to get pregnant on their own. The bottom line for women, in my view, is: plan to have your last child by the time you turn 40. Beyond that, you're rolling the dice, though they may still come up in your favor. "Fertility is relatively stable until the late 30s, with the inflection point somewhere around 38 or 39," Steiner told me. "Women in their early 30s can think about years, but in their late 30s, they need to be thinking about months."

That's also why many experts advise that women older than 35 should see a fertility specialist if they haven't conceived after six months—particularly if it's been six months of sex during fertile times.

There is no single best time to have a child. Some women and couples will find that starting—and finishing—their families in their 20s is what's best for them, all things considered. They just shouldn't let alarmist rhetoric push them to become parents before they're ready. Having children at a young age slightly lowers the risks of infertility and chromosomal abnormalities, and moderately lowers the risk of miscarriage. But it also carries costs for relationships and careers. Literally: an analysis by one economist found that, on average, every year a woman postpones having children leads to a 10 percent increase in career earnings.

For women who aren't ready for children in their early 30s but are still worried about waiting, new technologies—albeit imperfect ones—offer a third option. Some women choose to freeze their eggs, having a fertility doctor extract eggs when they are still young (say, early 30s) and cryogenically preserve them. Then, if they haven't had children by their self-imposed deadline, they can thaw the eggs, fertilize them, and implant the embryos using IVF. Because the eggs will be younger, success rates are theoretically higher. The downsides are the expense—perhaps $10,000 for the egg freezing and an average of more than $12,000 per cycle for IVF—and having to use IVF to get pregnant. Women who already have a partner can, alternatively, freeze embryos, a more common procedure that also uses IVF technology.

At home, couples should recognize that having sex at the most fertile time of the cycle matters enormously, potentially making the difference between an easy conception in the bedroom and expensive fertility treatment in a clinic. Rothman's study found that timing sex around ovulation narrowed the fertility gap between younger and older women. Women older than 35 who want to get pregnant should consider recapturing the glory of their 20-something sex lives, or learning to predict ovulation by charting their cycles or using a fertility monitor.

I wish i had known all this back in the spring of 2002, when the media coverage of age and infertility was deafening. I did, though, find some relief from the smart women of *Saturday Night Live.*

"According to author Sylvia Hewlett, career women shouldn't wait to have babies, because our fertility takes a steep drop-off after age 27," Tina Fey said during a "Weekend Update" sketch. "And Sylvia's right; I *definitely* should have had a baby when I was 27, living in Chicago over a biker bar, pulling down a cool $12,000 a year. That would have worked out great." Rachel Dratch said, "Yeah. Sylvia, um, thanks for reminding me that I have to hurry up and have a baby. Uh, me and my four cats will get *right* on that."

"My neighbor has this adorable, cute little Chinese baby that speaks Italian," noted Amy Poehler. "So, you know, I'll just buy one of those." Maya Rudolph rounded out the rant: "Yeah, Sylvia, maybe your next book should tell men our age to stop playing Grand Theft Auto III and holding out for the chick from *Alias*." ("You're *not* gonna get the chick from *Alias,*" Fey advised.)

Eleven years later, these four women have eight children among them, all but one born when they were older than 35. It's good to be right.

Critical Thinking

1. Using information from this article, what would you tell a 30-something woman about her chances of conceiving and bearing her own child?

2. Why are the data on fertility in 30-something women considered "questionable"?

Create Central

www.mhhe.com/createcentral

Internet References

Conception
www.thefertilitydiet.com

Fast Stats: Infertility: Centers for Disease Control and Prevention
www.cdc.gov/nchs/faststats/fertile.htm

Infertility Fact Sheet: Womenshealth.gov
www.womenshealth.gov/publications/factsheet/infertility.html

JEAN M. TWENGE is a professor of psychology at San Diego State University, and the author of *The Impatient Woman's Guide to Getting Pregnant*.

Article   Prepared by: Karen L. Freiberg, *University of Maryland*

Unnatural Selection

The gaping gender gap in Asia—the result of sex-selective abortion—has a burgeoning (and to some, equally alarming) counterpart here in the U.S.

MARA HVISTENDAHL

Learning Outcomes

After reading this article, you will be able to:

- Identify developmental disabilities more common in children born prematurely.

- Evaluate a future with one-third more males than females.

New Delhi, India

For Dr. Puneet Bedi, the intensive care unit in Apollo Hospital's maternity ward is a source of both pride and shame. The unit's technology is among the best in Delhi—among the best, for that matter, in all of India. But as a specialist in high-risk births, he works hard so that babies can be born. The fact that the unit's technology also contributes to India's skewed sex ratio at birth gnaws at him. Seven out of 10 babies born in the maternity ward, Bedi says, are male. He delivers those boys knowing that many of them are replacements for aborted girls.

A tall, broad-shouldered man with a disarmingly gentle voice, Bedi stands in the unit's control room, gazing into a sealed, temperature-controlled room lined with rows of cribs. He performs abortions himself. For sex-selective abortions, however, he reserves a contempt bordering on fury. To have his work negated by something as trifling as sex preference feels like a targeted insult. "You can choose whether to be a parent," he says. "But once you choose to be a parent, you cannot choose whether it's a boy or girl, black or white, tall or short."

A broad interpretation of parental choice, indeed, is spreading throughout India—along with China, Taiwan, Vietnam, Georgia, Azerbaijan, and Albania. Preliminary results from India's 2011 census show a sex ratio of only 914 girls for every 1,000 boys ages 6 and under, a decline from 2001. In some Chinese counties the sex ratio at birth has reached more than 150 boys for every 100 girls. "We are dealing with genocide," Bedi says. Sex-selective abortion, he adds, is "probably the single most important issue in the next 50 years that India and China are going to face. If you're going to wipe out 20 percent of your population, nature is not going to sit by and watch."

If you're going to wipe out 20 percent of your population, nature will not sit by and watch.

Bedi speaks with an immaculate British accent that hints at years spent studying at King's College London. The accent helps in this part of Delhi, where breeding can trump all else. His patients are the sort who live in spacious homes tended by gardeners, belong to bucolic country clubs, and send their children to study in the United States. India's wealthy are among the most frequent practitioners of sex selection, and in their quest to have a son Bedi is often an obstacle. His refusal to identify sex during ultrasound examinations disappoints many women, he says: "They think it's just a waste of time and money if you don't even know whether it's a boy or a girl."

India outlawed fetal sex identification and sex-selective abortion in 1994, but so many physicians and technicians break the law that women have little trouble finding one willing to scan fetal sex. Bedi says sex-selective abortion has caught on in Delhi because it bears the imprint of a scientific advance. "It's sanitized," he says. The fact that sex selection is a medical act, he adds, neatly divides the moral burden between two parties: Parents tell themselves their doctor knows best, while doctors point to overwhelming patient demand for the procedure.

Hospital administrators, for their part, have little incentive to do anything about the problem because maternity wards bring in substantial business. (At Apollo, a deluxe delivery suite outfitted with a bathtub, track lighting, a flat screen television, and a large window looking out onto landscaped grounds runs to $200 a night.) "When you confront the medical profession, there is a cowardly refusal to accept blame," Bedi says. "They say, 'We are doctors; it's a noble profession.' This is bullshit. When it comes to issues like ethics and morality, you can have an opinion, but there is a line which you do not cross. Everybody who [aborts for reasons of sex selection] knows it's unethical. It's a mass medical crime."

For as long as they have counted births, demographers have found an average of 105 boys born for every 100 girls. This is our natural sex ratio at birth. (The small gap neatly makes up for the fact that males are more likely to die early in life.) If Asia had maintained that ratio over the past few decades, the continent would today have an additional 163 million women and girls.

For Westerners, such a gender gap may be difficult to fathom: 163 million is more than the entire female population of the United States. Walk around Delhi's posh neighborhoods, or visit an elementary school in eastern China, and you can see the disparity: Boys far outnumber girls.

At first glance, the imbalance might seem to be the result of entrenched gender discrimination and local practices. Scholars and journalists typically look to the Indian convention of dowry, which makes daughters expensive, and to China's one-child policy, which makes sons precious, to explain sex selection in Asia. (Sons have long been favored in China, as in many other parts of the world.) But this logic doesn't account for why South Koreans also aborted female fetuses in large numbers until recently, or why a sex ratio imbalance has lately spread to the Caucasus countries—Azerbaijan, Georgia, and Armenia— and the Balkans, or why sex-selective abortion occurs among some immigrant communities in the United States.

What impact will hundreds of million of "surplus" men have on everything from health care to crime?

The world's missing females are an apparent paradox: Sex selection is occurring at a time when women are better off than ever before. "More and more girls are going to school and getting educated," says T.V. Sekher, a demographer at the International Institute for Population Studies in Mumbai. And in India, educated women are more likely to have a son than those with no degree. The women who select for sex include lawyers and doctors and businesspeople. Economic development has accompanied a drop in fertility rates, which decreases the chances of a couple getting the son they want without resorting to technology.

We might have seen this coming. Decades ago, Western hysteria over what many saw as an impending "population explosion" led American scholars and policymakers to scour the world for solutions to reducing the global birth rate. Studies from India and East Asia showed the major barrier to acceptance of contraception was that couples wanted at least one son. The advocates of population control saw that the barrier might be turned into an opportunity, however: If parents could be guaranteed a son the first time around, they might happily limit themselves to one or two children.

Beginning in the late 1960s, influential U.S. experts sounded their approval for sex selection everywhere from the pages of major scientific journals to the podiums at government sponsored seminars. "[I]f a simple method could be found to guarantee that first-born children were males," Paul Ehrlich wrote in *The Population Bomb* in 1968, "then population control problems in many areas would be somewhat eased."

Meanwhile, another group of scientists was figuring out how to determine fetal sex. These scientists' efforts focused on amniocentesis, which entails inserting a needle through a pregnant women's abdomen into the amniotic sac surrounding the fetus and removing a small amount of protective amniotic fluid, a substance rich with fetal cells that reveal its sex. They saw sex determination as a way to help women carrying sex-linked diseases like hemophilia have healthy children. But when amniocentesis, and later ultrasound, found their way to Asia decades later, it was their use as a population-control tool that stuck.

Sex selection's proponents argued that discrimination against women and girls wouldn't endure. As women became scarce, several prominent Western theorists proposed, they would also become more valuable, prompting couples to have daughters again. But in fact the opposite has happened. In their scarcity, women are being turned into commodities to be sold to and exploited by what demographers call "surplus men": the ones left over in an imagined world in which everyone who can marry does so. Scholars have begun to calculate the impact hundreds of millions of such men will have on everything from health care to crime.

Suining County, China

In a village in eastern China's agricultural belt, I meet Zhang Mei, a 37-year-old woman clad in men's pants and a black-and-white polka-dot shirt that billows around her thin frame. Zhang is from distant Yunnan province, a poor mountain region near the border with Tibet. Her neighbors say she arrived 20 years ago, after a long journey in which a trafficker took her east to deliver her into marriage. She had no idea where she was headed beyond the vague promise that she would find work there, and yet she had some faith in the trafficker, for she hadn't been kidnapped. Her parents had sold her.

The man who became her husband was gentle, but 15 years her senior, undeniably ugly, and one of the poorest residents of the village. Zhang learned that she had to work hard to make ends meet, and that she could not leave, even for a short trip home. Soon after she married, she found herself under pressure to have a son. One came on the third try, after two girls. But as the children grew, her husband complained it cost too much to educate their daughters, and since it is sons that matter in Suining, he sent one of the girls back to Yunnan to be raised by Zhang's parents: a return, one generation later, of a lost girl.

Today Zhang copes with lifelong detention by gambling at raucous *majiang* games, burying herself in soap operas, and praying. (She is Christian.) "I carry some burdens," she tells me, as we sit on the couch in her one-room home. "If I didn't pray, I would keep them all in my heart."

Zhang's story is perhaps the most obvious way in which the gender imbalance is altering societies in Asia. The U.S. Department of State lists the dearth of women in Asia as one of the principal causes of sex trafficking in the region. Some of those women, like Zhang, are sold into marriage. Others become prostitutes. But what happens to the men who can't find partners is significant as well.

Nothing can fully predict the effect of gathering tens of millions of young bachelors in one place for years on end. But preliminary conclusions can be drawn from places where the first generation touched by sex selection has reached adulthood. One line of speculation centers on testosterone, which occurs in high levels among young unmarried men. While testosterone does not directly cause violence in a young man, it can elevate existing aggressive tendencies, serving as a "facilitative effect" that predicts whether he will resort to violence. Gauging whether millions of high-testosterone men together spark more violence is complicated, particularly in China and India, which have experienced great social change in the past few decades. But some answers can be found through breaking down crime rates by region and time period.

In a 2007 study, Columbia University economist Lena Edlund and colleagues at Chinese University of Hong Kong used the fact that China's sex ratio at birth spiked in some provinces earlier than others to explore a link between crime rates and a surplus of men. The researchers found a clear link, concluding a mere 1 percent increase in sex ratio at birth resulted in a 5- to 6-point increase in an area's crime rate.

Other scholars speculate the gender imbalance is yielding depression and hopelessness among young men—which may explain why China has lately been hit with the sort of senseless violence that was once America's domain. In 2004 and 2010 the country saw separate waves of attacks on elementary schools and child care centers in which murderers went on rampages and bludgeoned and stabbed children to death.

Eight out of the 10 killers (all male) lived in eastern Chinese provinces with high sex ratios at birth; several were unemployed. One man told neighbors, before he was arrested and summarily executed, that he was frustrated with his life and wanted revenge on the rich and powerful. Another apparently told police he was upset because his girlfriend had left him.

Los Angeles, U.S.

"Be certain your next child will be the gender you're hoping for," promises the Web site of L.A.'s Fertility Institutes. Dr. Jeffrey Steinberg founded the clinic in 1986, just as in-vitro fertilization was taking off.

Today 70 percent of his patients come to select the sex of their baby. Steinberg's favored method is preimplantation genetic diagnosis, PGD, an add-on to in-vitro fertilization that allows parents to screen embryos before implanting them in the mother. Like amniocentesis and ultrasound before it, PGD was developed to test for defects or a propensity toward certain diseases.

But lab technicians working with eight-celled embryos can also separate XY embryos from XX ones, thus screening for sex—the first nonmedical condition to be turned into a choice. PGD thus attracts Americans who are perfectly capable of having babies the old-fashioned way but are hell-bent on having a child of a certain sex. So determined are they that they're willing to submit to the diet of hormones necessary to stimulate ovulation, pay a price ranging from $12,000 to $18,000, and live with IVF's low success rate. Decades after America's elite introduced sex selection to the developing world, they have taken it up themselves.

High-tech sex selection has its critics. They point to a litany of ethical issues: that the technology is available only to the rich, that it gives parents a degree of control over their offspring they shouldn't have, that it marks the advent of designer babies. But in surveys of prospective American parents over the past 10 years, 25 to 35 percent say they would use sex selection techniques if they were readily available; presumably that means more affordable and less invasive.

A squat, balding man who exudes a jovial confidence, Dr. Steinberg talks as if he has all the time in the world, peppering his stories with Hollywood gossip. (To wit: The producers of the show *CSI* once stopped by the clinic to evaluate a sperm cryopreservation tank's potential as a weapon.) The patient response to his clinic offering sex selection, Steinberg tells me after ushering me into a spacious corner office, has been "crazy."

The fertility doctors who perform preimplantation sex selection take care to distinguish it from sex-selective abortion. In America, they point out, patriarchy is dead, at least when it comes to choosing the sex of our children. As late as the 1970s, psychologists and sociologists found that Americans were far more likely to prefer sons to daughters. Not anymore.

National figures are not available, but two of America's leading clinics—HRC Fertility in Los Angeles and Genetics and IVF Institute in Fairfax, Virginia—independently report that between 75 and 80 percent of their patients want girls. The demand for daughters may explain why at Steinberg's clinic everything from the entrance wall to the scrubs worn by the laboratory workers are pink.

For the most part, however, Americans don't talk about gender preference. We say "family balancing," a term that implies couples have an inherent right to an equal number of boys and girls. (Many patients seeking sex selection via PGD already have a child of the opposite sex.) We talk about "gender disappointment," a deep grief arising from not getting what we want. The author of the reproductive technology guide *Guarantee the Sex of Your Baby* explains: "The pain that these mothers feel when they fail to bear a child of the 'right' sex is more than just emotional angst. The longing that they hold in their hearts can translate into real physical pain."

Rhetorical differences aside, "family balancing" is not in fact all that different from what is happening in China and India. In Asia, too, most parents who select for sex do so for the second or third birth. And examining why American parents are set on girls suggests another similarity: Americans who want girls, like Asians who opt for boys, have preconceived notions of how a child of a certain gender will turn out.

Bioethicist Dena S. Davis writes that people who take pains to get a child of a certain sex "don't want just the right chromosomes and the attendant anatomical characteristics, they want a set of characteristics that go with 'girlness' or 'boyness.' If parents want a girl badly enough to go to all the trouble of sperm sorting and artificial insemination, they are likely to make it more difficult for the actual child to resist their expectations and follow her own bent."

When Dr. Sunita Puri surveyed Bay Area couples undergoing PGD for sex selection, most of them white, older, and affluent, 10 out of 12 wanted girls for reasons like "barrettes and pink dresses."

Some mention that girls do better in school, and on this point the research backs them up: Girls are more likely to perform and less likely to misbehave, while boys have lately become the source of a good deal of cultural anxiety. Others mention more noble goals. They talk about raising strong daughters; women mention having the close relationship they had—or didn't have—with their own mother.

But regardless of the reason, bioethicists point out, sex selection prioritizes the needs of one generation over another, making having children more about bringing parents satisfaction than about responsibly creating an independent human being.

At stake with preimplantation sex selection is much more than the global balance of males and females, as if that weren't enough. If you believe in the slippery slope, then sex-selective embryo implantation definitely pushes us a little further down it.

In 2009 Jeffrey Steinberg announced that the clinic would soon offer selection for eye color, hair color, and skin color. The science behind trait selection is still developing, and some later doubted whether he in fact was capable of executing it. Still, Steinberg might have eventually gone through with the service had his advertisement not set off an uproar. The press descended, the Vatican issued a statement criticizing the "obsessive search for the perfect child," and couples who had used PGD for medical reasons balked, fearing frivolous use of reproductive technology would turn public sentiment against cases like theirs. For the moment, at least, Americans had problems with selecting for physical traits, and Steinberg retreated.

Having children has become more about bringing parents satisfaction than creating independent human beings.

"The timing was off is all," he tells me. "It was just premature. We were ahead of our time. So we said, 'OK, fine. We'll put it on the back burner.'" In the meantime, he says, couples obsessed with blue or green eyes continue to call the office. He keeps their names on a mailing list.

Critical Thinking

1. Differentiate between sex-selective abortion and preimplantation sex selection.

2. What are some negative consequences in a society where males far outnumber females?

3. Why would selection for offspring traits (e.g., skin color, eye color, hair color) create ethical issues in a society?

4. If you could afford it, would you choose to preselect traits for your own offspring using preimplantation genetic diagnosis (PGD)?

Create Central

www.mhhe.com/createcentral

Internet References

American Academy of Pediatrics
  www.aap.org
Medicine Plus Health Information/Prenatal Care
  www.nim.nih.gov/medicineplus/prenatalcare.html
National Children's Study
  www.nationalchildrensstudy.gov

MARA HVISTENDAHL is a China-based correspondent with *Science* magazine. She's also written for *Harper's, Scientific American,* and *Popular Science.* This piece is adapted from her new book, *Unnatural Selection: Choosing Boys Over Girls, and the Consequences of a World Full of Men* (PublicAffairs, 2011).

Unit 2

UNIT

Prepared by: Karen L. Freiberg, *University of Maryland*

Development during Infancy and Early Childhood

Development during infancy and early childhood is more rapid than in any other life stage, excluding the prenatal period. Newborns are quite well developed in some areas, and incredibly deficient in others. Babies' higher cerebral hemispheres already have their full complement of neurons (worker cells). The neuroglia (supportive cells) are almost completely developed and will reach their final numbers by age one. In contrast, babies' legs and feet are tiny, weak, and barely functional. Look at newborns from another perspective, however, and their brains seem somewhat less superior. The neurons and neuroglia present at birth must be protected. By contrast, the cells of the baby's legs and feet (skin, fat, muscles, bones, blood vessels) are able to replace themselves by mitosis indefinitely. Their numbers will continue to grow through early adulthood, and then their quantity and quality can be regenerated through advanced old age.

The developing brain in infancy is a truly fascinating organ. At birth, it is poorly organized. The lower (primitive) brain parts (brain stem, pons, medulla, cerebellum) are developed enough to allow the infant to live. The lower brain directs vital organ systems (heart, lungs, kidneys, etc.). The higher (advanced) brain parts (cerebral hemispheres) have allocated neurons, but the nerve cells and cell processes (axons, dendrites) are small, underdeveloped, and unorganized. During infancy, these higher (cerebral) nerve cells (that allow the baby to think, reason, and remember) grow at astronomical rates. They migrate to permanent locations in the hemispheres, develop myelin sheathing (insulation), and conduct messages. Many 20th-century researchers, including Jean Piaget, the father of cognitive psychology, believed that all brain activities in the newborn were reflexive, based on instincts for survival. They underestimated babies. New research has documented that fetuses can learn, and newborns can think as well as learn.

The role played by the electrical and chemical activity of neurons in actively shaping the physical structure of the brain is particularly awe-inspiring. The neurons are produced prenatally. After birth, the flood of sensory inputs from the environment (sights, sounds, smells, tastes, touch, balance, and kinesthetic sensations) drives the neurons to form circuits and become wired to each other. Trillions of connections are established in a baby's brain. During childhood, the connections that are seldom or never used are eliminated or pruned. The first three years are critical for establishing these connections. Environments that provide both good nutrition and lots of sensory stimulation actually produce richer, more connected brains.

Article   Prepared by: Karen L. Freiberg, *University of Maryland*

Keys to Quality Infant Care
Nurturing Every Baby's Life Journey

Alice Sterling Honig

Learning Outcomes

After reading this article, you will be able to:

- Distinguish between three infant temperament types and explain why each baby's unique personality should be explored.

- Defend the author's assertion that love and intimate connections are paramount requirements for quality infant care.

Teachers of infants need a large bunch of key ideas and activities of all kinds to unlock in each child the treasures of loving kindness, thoughtful and eloquent use of language, intense active curiosity to learn, willingness to cooperate, and the deep desire to work hard to master new tasks. Here are some ideas that teachers can use during interactions with infants to optimize each child's development.

Get to Know Each Baby's Unique Personality

At 4 months, Luci holds her hands in front of her face and turns them back and forth so she can see the curious visual difference between the palms and backs. Jackson, an 8-month-old, bounces happily in accurate rhythm as his teacher bangs on a drum and chants, "Mary had a little lamb whose fleece was white as snow!" Outdoors, 1-year-old Jamie sits in an infant swing peering down at his feet sticking out of the leg holes. How interesting! Those are the same feet he has watched waving in the air while being diapered and has triumphantly brought to his mouth to chew on.

Teachers can tune in to each child's special personality—especially the child's temperament. There are three primary, mostly inborn, styles of temperament (Honig 1997). Some babies are more low-key; they tend to be slow to warm up to new caregivers, new foods, and new surroundings. They need reassuring hand-holding and more physical supports to try a new activity. Others are more feisty and sometimes irritable. They tend to be impetuous, intense in their emotional reactions, whether of anger or of joy. Easygoing babies are typically friendly, happy, accept new foods and caregivers without much fuss, and adapt fairly quickly and more flexibly after

experiencing distress or sudden change. Try to find out whether each baby in your care tends to be shy and slow to warm up *or* mostly feisty and intense *or* easygoing. A caring adult's perceptive responses in tune with individual temperament will ease a child's ability to adapt and flourish in the group setting.

Physical Loving

Your body is a safe haven for an infant. Indeed, some babies will stay happy as a clam when draped over a shoulder, across your belly as you rock in a rocking chair, or, especially for a very young baby, snuggled in a sling or carrier for hours. As Montagu (1971) taught decades ago, babies need *body loving:* "To be tender, loving, and caring, human beings must be tenderly loved and cared for in their earliest years. . . . caressed, cuddled, and comforted" (p. 138).

As you carry them, some babies might pinch your neck, lick your salty arm, pull at your hair, tug at eyeglasses, or show you in other ways how powerfully important your body is as a sacred and special playground. Teach gentleness by calmly telling a baby you need your glasses on to read a story. Use the word *gently* over and over and over. Dance cheek-to-cheek with a young child in arms to slow waltz music—good for dreary days! Also carry the baby while you do a routine task such as walking to another room to get something.

Provide lap and touch times generously to nourish a child's sense of well-being. Slowly caress a baby's hair. Rub a tense shoulder soothingly. Kiss one finger and watch as a baby offers every other finger to kiss. Rock a child with your arms wrapped around him for secure comfort. Babies learn to become independent as we confirm and meet their dependency needs in infancy. A sense of well-being and somatic certainty flows from cherishing adults who generously hold, caress, and drape babies on shoulders and tummies.

Create Intimate Emotional Connections

Scan the environment so you can be close to every baby. Notice the quiet baby sitting alone, mouthing a toy piece and rocking back and forth with vacant eyes. Notice shy bids for attention, such as a brief smile with lowered lids. The child with an easy or cautious temperament needs your loving attention as much as the one who impulsively climbs all over you for attention.

> **A caring adult's perceptive responses in tune with individual temperament will ease a child's ability to adapt and flourish in the group setting.**

Shine admiring eyes at the children, whether a baby is cooing as she lies in her crib, creeping purposefully toward a toy she desires, or feeding herself happily with messy fingers. Speak each child's name lovingly and frequently. Even if they are fussing, most babies will quiet when you chant and croon their names.

Although babies do not understand the meanings of the words, they do understand *tonal* nuances and love when your voice sounds admiring, enchanted with them, and happy to be talking with them. While diapering, tell the baby he is so delicious and you love his plump tummy and the few wispy hairs on that little head. Watch him thrust out his legs in delight on the diapering table. Your tone of voice entrances him into a deep sense of pleasure with his own body (Honig 2002).

Harmonizing Tempos

Tempo is important in human activities and is reflected in how abruptly or smoothly adults carry out daily routines. Because adults have so many tasks to do, sometimes we use impatient, too-quick motions, for example, while dressing a baby to play outdoors. When dressing or feeding, more leisurely actions are calming. They signal to children that we have time for them. Rub backs slowly and croon babies into soothing sleep.

A baby busily crawling across the rug sees a toy, grasps it, then plops himself into a sitting position to examine and try to pull it apart. He slowly looks back and forth at the toy as he leisurely passes it from hand to hand. He has no awareness that a teacher is about to interrupt because she is in a hurry to get him dressed because his daddy is coming to pick him up. Young children need time and cheerful supports to finish up an activity in which they are absorbed. If they are hurried, they may get frustrated and even have a tantrum.

Enhance Courage and Cooperation

Your presence can reassure a worried baby. Stay near and talk gently to help a child overcome his fear of the small infant slide. Pascal sits at the top, looking uncertain. Then he checks your face for a go-ahead signal, for reassurance that he can bravely try to slide down this slide that looks so long to him. Kneeling at the bottom of the slide, smile and tell him that you will be there to catch him when he is ready to slide down.

Be available as a "refueling station"—Margaret Mahler's felicitous term (Kaplan 1978). Sometimes a baby's independent learning adventure comes crashing down—literally. Your body and your lap provide the emotional support from which a baby regains courage to tackle the learning adventure again.

Create loving rituals during daily routines of dressing, bath times, nap times, feeding times. Babies like to know what will happen and when and where and how. Babies have been known to refuse lunch when their familiar, comfortable routines were changed. At cleanup times, older babies can be more flexible and helpful if you change some chores into games. Through the use of sing-song chants, putting toys away becomes an adventure in finding the big fat blocks that need to be placed together on a shelf and then the skinny blocks that go together in a different place.

> **Young children need time and cheerful supports to finish up an activity in which they are absorbed. If they are hurried, they may get frustrated and even have a tantrum.**

Address Stress

Attachment research shows that babies who develop secure emotional relationships with a teacher have had their distress signals noticed, interpreted correctly, and responded to promptly and appropriately (Honig 2002). At morning arrival times, watch for separation anxiety. Sometimes holding and wordlessly commiserating with a baby's sad feelings can help more than a frenzied attempt to distract her (Klein, Kraft, & Shohet 2010). As you become more expert at interpreting a baby's body signals of distress and discomfort, you will become more sensitively attuned in your responses (Honig 2010).

Learn Developmental Milestones

Learning developmental norms helps teachers figure out when to wonder, when to worry, and when to relish and feel overjoyed about a child's milestone accomplishments. Day and night toilet learning can be completed anywhere from 18 months to 5 years. This is a *wide* time window for development. In contrast, learning to pick up a piece of cereal from a high chair tray with just thumb and forefinger in a fine pincer grasp is usually completed during a *narrow* time window well before 13 months. By 11 months, most babies become expert at using just the first two fingers.

Hone Your Detective Skills

If a baby is screaming and jerking knees up to his belly, you might suspect a painful gas bubble. Pick up the baby and jiggle and thump his back until you get that burp up. What a relief, for you as well as baby. Maybe an irritable, yowling baby just needs to be tucked in quietly and smoothly for a nap after an expert diaper change. Suppose baby is crying and thrashing about, and yet he has been burped and diapered. Use all your detective skills to determine the cause. Is it a hot day? He might be thirsty. A drink of water can help him calm down.

Notice Stress Signs

Scan a child's body for stress signs. Dull eyes can signal the need for more intimate loving interactions. Tense shoulders and a grave look often mean that a child is afraid or worried (Honig 2010). Compulsive rocking can mean a baby feels forlorn. Watch for lonesomeness and wilting.

Some babies melt down toward day's end. They need to be held and snuggled. Murmur sweet reassurances and provide a small snack of strained applesauce to soothe baby's taste buds and worries. Check his body from top to bottom for signs of stresses or tensions, such as eyes avoiding contact, teeth grinding, fingernail chewing, frequently clenched fists, so that you can develop an effective plan for soothing. Be alert, and tend to children's worrisome bodily signs; these will tell you what you need to know long before children have enough language to share what was stressful (Honig 2009).

Play Learning Games

Parents and teachers are a baby's preferred playmates. While playing learning games with infants, pay attention to their actions. Ask yourself if the game has become so familiar and easy that it is time to "dance up the developmental ladder" (Honig 1982) and increase the game's challenge. Or perhaps the game is still too baffling and you need to "dance down" and simplify the activity so that the child can succeed.

Provide safe mirrors at floor level and behind the diapering table so children can watch and learn about their own bodies. Hold babies in arms up to a mirror to reach out and pat the face in the mirror. Lying on the floor in front of a securely attached safety mirror, a young child twists and squirms to get an idea of where his body begins and ends.

Your body can serve as a comforting support for some early learning activities. Sit an infant on your lap and watch as he coordinates vision and grasp to reach and hold a toy you are dangling. Babies love "Peek-a-boo! I see you!" These games nurture the development of object permanence—the understanding that objects still exist even when they are out of sight. Peek-a-boo games also symbolically teach that even when a special adult is not seen, that dear person will reappear.

Provide Physical Play Experiences

Play pat-a-cake with babies starting even before 6 months. As you gently hold a baby's hands and bring them out and then back together, chant slowly and joyously, "Pat-a-cake, pat-a-cake, baker's man; bake me a cake just as fast as you can. Pat it, and roll it, and mark it with a *B,* and put it in the oven for [baby's name] and me." Smile with joy as you guide the baby's hands rhythmically and slowly through the game, and use a high-pitched voice as you emphasize her name in the sing-song chant. Over the next months, as soon as you begin chanting the words, the baby will begin to bring hands to the midline and do the hand motions that belong with this game. Babies who are 9 to 11 months old will even start copying the hand-rolling motions that belong with this game.

To encourage learning, try to arrange games with more physical actions. Sit on the floor with your toes touching the baby's toes, then model how to roll a ball back and forth.

Introduce Sensory Experiences

Safe sensory and tactile experiences are ideal for this age group. As he shifts a toy from hand to hand, turns it over, pokes, tastes, bangs, and even chews on it, a baby uses his senses to learn about the toy's physical properties. Teachers can blow bubbles so babies can reach for and crawl after them. Provide play-dough made with plenty of salt to discourage children from putting it in their mouths. Older babies enjoy exploring finger paints or nontoxic tempera paint and fat brushes.

Play Sociable Games

Give something appealing to a seated baby. Put out your hand, smile, and say "Give it to me, please." The baby may chew on the "gift," such as a safe wooden block or chunky plastic cylinder peg. After the baby passes it to you, say thank you, then give the object back with a smile. Give-and-take games with you are a sociable pleasure for babies and teach them turn-taking skills that are crucial for friendly social interchanges years later.

Seated on a chair, play a bouncing game, with the baby's back resting snuggly against your tummy. After you stop bouncing and chanting "Giddyup, horsie," a baby often bounces on his or her tush as if to remind you to start this game over and over. An older baby vigorously demands "More horsie!" to get you to restart this game. Babies enjoy kinesthetic stimulation too, such as when you swing them gently in a baby swing. A baby will grin with glee as you pull or push him in a wagon around the room or playground.

Observe Babies' Ways of Exploring and Learning

Observe a baby to learn what and how she is learning, then adapt the activity to offer greater challenge. Observation provides information that lets teachers determine when and how to arrange for the next step in a child's learning experience. Watch quietly as a baby tries with determination to put the round wood top piece for a ring stack set on the pole. His eyes widen in startled amazement as he gradually realizes that when the hole does not go through the middle, then that piece will not go down over the pole—a frustrating but important lesson. Calmly, a teacher can demonstrate how to place the piece on top of the pole while using simple words to describe how this piece is different. She can also gently guide the baby's hands so he feels successful at placing the piece on top.

Enhance Language and Literacy in Everyday Routines

Talk back and forth with babies; respond to their coos and babbles with positive talk. When the baby vocalizes, tell her, "What a terrific talker you are. Tell me some more."

The diapering table is a fine site for language games. With young babies, practice "parentese"—a high-pitched voice, drawn-out vowels, and slow and simple talk. This kind of talk fires up the brain neurons that carry messages to help a baby learn (Doidge 2007). Cascades of chemicals and electrical signals course down the baby's neural pathways. A baby responds when you are an attentive and delighted talking partner. Pause so the baby gets a turn to talk too, and bring the game to a graceful close when baby fatigue sets in.

Talk about body parts on dolls, stuffed animals, yourself, and the babies in the room. Talk about what the baby sees as you lift her onto your lap and then onto your shoulders. Talk at mealtimes. Use every daily routine as an opportunity to enhance oral language (Honig 2007).

Daily reading is an intimate one-on-one activity that young babies deeply enjoy in varied spaces and at varied times of the day (Honig 2004). Hook your babies on books as early as possible. Frequent shared picture-book experiences are priceless gifts. Early pleasurable reading experiences empower success in learning to read years later in grade school (Jalongo 2007).

Cuddle with one or several children as you read and share books together every day. Use dramatic tones along with loving and polite words. You are the master of the story as you read aloud. Feel free to add to or to shorten picture-book text according to a particular child's needs. Group reading times can be pleasurable when infants lean against you as you sit on the rug and share a picture book. Teachers often prefer the intimacy of individual reading times with babies (Honig & Shin 2001). Individual reading can help a tense or fussy baby relax in your lap as he becomes deeply absorbed in sharing the picture-book experience.

Encourage Mastery Experiences

Children master many linguistic, physical, and social skills in the first years of life. Watch the joy of mastery and self-appreciation as a baby succeeds at a task, such as successfully placing Montessori cylinders into their respective sockets. Babies enjoy clapping for their own efforts. Mastery experiences arranged in thoughtful doses bring much pleasure, such an eagerness to keep on exploring, trying, and learning. Watch the baby's joy as he proudly takes a long link chain out of a coffee can and then stuffs it slowly back in the can. He straightens his shoulders with such pride as he succeeds at this game of finding a way to put a long skinny chain into a round container with a small diameter opening.

Mastery experiences arranged in thoughtful doses bring much pleasure, such an eagerness to keep on exploring, trying, and learning.

Vygotsky taught that the *zone of proximal development* is crucial for adult-child coordination in learning activities. You the teacher are so important in helping a child to succeed when a task may be slightly too difficult for the child to solve alone. Hold the baby's elbow steady when she feels frustrated while trying to stack one block on top of another. For a difficult puppy puzzle, a teacher taped down a few of the pieces so a baby could succeed in getting the puppy's tail and head pieces

in the right spaces. If a baby has been struggling with a slippery nesting cup for a while, just steady the stack of cups so he can successfully insert a smaller cup into the next largest one.

Promote Socioemotional Skills

Babies learn empathy and friendliness from those who nurture them. Empathy involves recognizing and feeling the distress of another and trying to help in some way. A young baby who sees another baby crying may look worried and suck his thumb to comfort himself. Fifteen-month-old Michael tussles over a toy with Paul, who starts to cry. Michael looks worried and lets go of the toy so Paul has it. As Paul keeps crying, Michael gives him his own teddy bear. But Paul continues crying. Michael pauses, then runs to the next room and gets Paul's security blanket for him. And Paul stops crying (Blum 1987).

When teachers showed deeply respectful caregiving, then they observed that babies did develop early empathy and internalize the friendly interactions they had experienced.

Friendliness includes making accommodations so children can play together. For example, move a child over to make room for a peer, or make overtures to invite other babies to engage in peer play. Perhaps they could take turns toddling in and out of a cardboard house. Babies act friendly when they sit near each other and companionably play with toys, happy to be close together. McMullen and colleagues (2009) observed that positive social-emotional interactions were rare in some infant rooms. But when teachers showed deeply respectful caregiving, then they observed that babies did develop early empathy and internalize the friendly interactions they had experienced. One teacher is described below:

> Her wonderful gentle manner, the way she speaks to the babies, how they are all her friends . . . only someone who utterly respects and values babies could put that kind of effort into this the way she does, almost like she is setting a beautiful table for honored guests each and every morning. (McMullen et al. 2009, p. 27)

Conclusion

Later in life, a baby will not remember your specific innumerable kindly caring actions in the earliest years. However, a child's *feelings* of being lovable and cherished will remain a body-memory for life. These feelings of having been loved will permeate positive emotional and social relationships decades later.

Keep your own joy pipes open. How brief are the years of babyhood. All too soon young children grow into the mysterious world of teenagers who prefer hanging out with peers to snuggling on an adult lap. Reflect with deep personal satisfaction on your confidence and delight in caring for tiny ones—hearing the first words, seeing the joy at a new accomplishment, watching the entranced look of an upturned face as you tell a story, feeling the trust as a baby sleepily settles onto your lap for refreshment of spirit, for a breath of the loving comfort that emanates from your body.

Life has grown more complicated in our technological, economically difficult, and more and more urbanized world. But you, the teacher, remain each baby's priceless tour guide into the world of "growing up!" You gently take each little person by the hand—literally and figuratively—and lure each and every baby into feeling the wonder and the somatic certainty of being loved, lovable, and cherished so that each baby can fully participate in the adventure of growing, loving, and learning.

Your nurturing strengthens a baby's determination to keep on learning, keep on cooperating, keep on being friendly, and keep on growing into a loving person—first in the world of the nursery and later in the wider world. You can give no greater gift to a child than to be the best guide possible as each child begins his or her unique life journey.

References

Blum, L. 1987. Particularity and responsiveness. In *The emergence of morality in young children,* eds. J. Kagan & S. Lamb, 306–37. Chicago: University of Chicago Press.

Doidge, N. 2007. *The brain that changes itself.* New York: Penguin.

Honig, A.S. 1982. *Playtime learning games for young children.* Syracuse, NY: Syracuse University Press.

Honig, A.S. 1997. Infant temperament and personality: What do we need to know? *Montessori Life* 9 (3): 18–21.

Honig, A.S. 2002. *Secure environments: Nurturing infant/toddler attachment in child care settings.* Washington, DC: NAEYC.

Honig, A.S. 2004. Twenty ways to boost your baby's brain power. *Scholastic Parent and Child* 11 (4): 55–56.

Honig, A.S. 2007. Oral language development. *Early Child Development and Care* 177 (6): 581–613.

Honig, A.S. 2009. Stress and young children. In *Informing our practice: Useful research on young children's development,* eds. E. Essa & M.M. Burnham, 71–88. Washington, DC: NAEYC.

Honig, A.S. 2010. *Little kids, big worries: Stress-busting tips for early childhood classrooms.* Baltimore: Brookes.

Honig, A.S., & M. Shin. 2001. Reading aloud to infants and toddlers in childcare settings: An observational study. *Early Childhood Education Journal* 28 (3): 193–97.

Jalongo, M.R. 2007. *Early childhood language arts.* 4th ed. New York: Pearson.

Kaplan, L. 1978. *Oneness and separateness: From infant to individual.* New York: Simon & Schuster.

Klein, P.S., R.R. Kraft, & C. Shohet. 2010. Behavior patterns in daily mother-child separations: Possible opportunites for stress reduction. *Early Child Development and Care* 180: 387–96.

McMullen, M.B., J.M. Addleman, A.M. Fulford, S. Moore, S.J. Mooney, S.S. Sisk, & J. Zachariah. 2009. Learning to be *me* while coming to understand *we.* Encouraging prosocial babies in group settings. *Young Children* 64 (4): 20–28. www.naeyc.org/files/yc/file/200907/McMullenWeb709.pdf

Montagu, A. 1971. *Touching: The human significance of the skin.* New York: Harper & Row.

Critical Thinking

1. Identify the three primary, inborn styles of temperament.
2. Why is physical contact an important aspect of quality infant care?
3. What are ways to enhance language development in infants?

Create Central

www.mhhe.com/createcentral

Internet References

Baby Center
www.babycenter.com

Early Childhood Care and Development
www.ecdgroup.com

Project Viva
www.dacp.org/viva

The National Association for the Education of Young Children (NAEYC)
www.naeyc.org

Zero to Three: National Center for Infants, Toddlers, and Families
www.zerotothree.org

ALICE STERLING HONIG, PhD, is professor emerita of child development in the College of Human Ecology at Syracuse University, where she has taught the QIC (Quality Infant/Toddler Caregiving) Workshop for 34 years. She is the author or editor of more than two dozen books and more than 500 articles and chapters on early childhood. As a licensed New York State clinician, she works with children and families coping with a variety of troubles, such as divorce or learning difficulties. ahonig@syr.edu.

Article   Prepared by: Karen L. Freiberg, *University of Maryland*

Vaccination Nation

The decadelong controversy surrounding the safety of vaccines is over—or is it? A fierce debate continues wover what really puts our children at risk.

CHRIS MOONEY

Learning Outcomes

After reading this article, you will be able to:

- Defend the pro-vaccine group's position of "Every Child by Two."

- Explain the apparent increase in autistic spectrum disorders today.

Vaccines do not cause autism. That was the ruling in each of three critical test cases handed down on February 12 by the U.S. Court of Federal Claims in Washington, D.C. After a decade of speculation, argument, and analysis—often filled with vitriol on both sides—the court specifically denied any link between the combination of the MMR vaccine and vaccines with thimerosal (a mercury-based preservative) and the spectrum of disorders associated with autism. But these rulings, though seemingly definitive, have done little to quell the angry debate, which has severe implications for American public health.

The idea that there is something wrong with our vaccines—that they have poisoned a generation of kids, driving an "epidemic" of autism—continues to be everywhere: on cable news, in celebrity magazines, on blogs, and in health news stories. It has had a particularly strong life on the Internet, including the heavily trafficked *The Huffington Post,* and in pop culture, where it is supported by actors including Charlie Sheen and Jim Carrey, former *Playboy* playmate Jenny McCarthy, and numerous others. Despite repeated rejection by the scientific community, it has spawned a movement, led to thousands of legal claims, and even triggered occasional harassment and threats against scientists whose research appears to discredit it.

You can see where the emotion and sentiment come from. Autism can be a terrible condition, devastating to families. It can leave parents not only aggrieved but desperate to find any cure, any salvation. Medical services and behavioral therapy for severely autistic children can cost more than $100,000 a year, and these children often exhibit extremely difficult behavior.

Moreover, the incidence of autism is apparently rising rapidly. Today one in every 150 children has been diagnosed on the autism spectrum; 20 years ago that statistic was one in 10,000. "Put yourself in the shoes of these parents," says journalist David Kirby, whose best-selling 2005 book, *Evidence of Harm,* dramatized the vaccine-autism movement. "They have perfectly normal kids who are walking and happy and everything—and then they regress." The irony is that vaccine skepticism—not the vaccines themselves—is now looking like the true public-health threat.

The decadelong vaccine-autism saga began in 1998, when British gastroenterologist Andrew Wakefield and his colleagues published evidence in *The Lancet* suggesting they had tracked down a shocking cause of autism. Examining the digestive tracts of 12 children with behavioral disorders, nine of them autistic, the researchers found intestinal inflammation, which they pinned on the MMR (measles, mumps, and rubella) vaccine. Wakefield had a specific theory of how the MMR shot could trigger autism: The upset intestines, he conjectured, let toxins loose in the bloodstream, which then traveled to the brain. The vaccine was, in this view, effectively a poison. In a dramatic press conference, Wakefield announced the findings and sparked an instant media frenzy. For the British public, a retreat from the use of the MMR vaccine—and a rise in the incidence of measles—began.

In the United States, meanwhile, fears would soon arise concerning another means by which vaccines might induce autism. Many vaccines at the time contained thimerosal, a preservative introduced in the 1930s to make vaccines safer by preventing bacterial contamination. But thimerosal is 50 percent mercury by weight, and mercury is known to be a potent neurotoxin, at least in large doses. In 1999 new federal safety guidelines for mercury in fish stirred concerns about vaccines as well.

The U.S. government responded by ordering that thimerosal be removed from all vaccines administered to children under age 6, or reduced to trace amounts. (Some inactivated influenza vaccines were exempted.) The step was described as a "precautionary" measure. There was no proof of harm, government researchers said, just reason to worry that there might be. Meanwhile, scientists launched numerous studies to determine whether thimerosal had actually caused an autism epidemic, while some parents and their lawyers started pointing fingers and developing legal cases.

Within weeks of this year's federal court decisions—which examined and vindicated both the MMR vaccine and thimerosal environmental lawyer Robert F. Kennedy Jr. wrote a column in *The Huffington Post* in which he continued to press his case that the government has peddled unsafe vaccines to an unsuspecting public. It is a cause he has championed since 2005, when he published "Deadly Immunity" in *Rolling Stone* and *Salon* magazines. The article was a no-holds-barred denunciation of the U.S. public-health establishment, purporting to tell the story of how "government health agencies colluded with Big Pharma to hide the risks of thimerosal from the public . . . a chilling case study of institutional arrogance, power, and greed." Half a decade after the original thimerosal concerns were first raised, Kennedy claimed to have found the smoking gun: the transcript of a "secret" 2000 meeting of government, pharmaceutical, and independent researchers with expertise in vaccines. Kennedy's conclusion: The generational catastrophe was real; our kids had been poisoned. If true, it would be perhaps the greatest biomedical catastrophe in modern history.

But for Kennedy to be right, a growing consensus in the medical establishment had to be wrong. Indeed, Kennedy blasted a leading organ of science that had just vindicated both the MMR vaccine and thimerosal, the Institute of Medicine (IOM). "The CDC [Centers for Disease Control and Prevention] paid the Institute of Medicine to conduct a new study to whitewash the risks of thimerosal," Kennedy wrote, "ordering researchers to 'rule out' the chemical's link to autism." In reality, the IOM—a branch of the National Academy of Sciences (NAS), the government's top independent scientific adviser—carefully creates firewalls between the funding it receives to conduct scientific assessments and the results it ultimately produces. "Funders don't control the composition of the committee, and they don't meet with the committee," says Harvard public-health researcher Marie McCormick, who chaired the IOM vaccine-safety committee in question. "And on no NAS or IOM committee are the members paid; they all work pro bono. There's no reason for them not to look at the data."

The same year Kennedy's article came out, journalist David Kirby published *Evidence of Harm—Mercury in Vaccines and the Autism Epidemic: A Medical Controversy.* He followed a group of parents from the Coalition for SafeMinds, an autism activist organization. They had grown convinced that vaccines and other environmental factors had caused their children's conditions. Kirby's chronicle of the parents' efforts to publicize the dangers of vaccines became a best seller and greatly advanced SafeMinds' cause.

"It's not hard to scare people," says pediatrician and leading vaccine advocate Paul Offit. "But it's extremely difficult to unscare them."

Yet even as vaccine hysteria reached a fever pitch in the wake of Kennedy's and Kirby's writings, the scientific evidence was leaning strongly in the other direction. In discounting the dangers of both the MMR vaccine and thimerosal, the IOM had multiple large epidemiological studies to rely on. For MMR, the IOM examined 16 studies. All but two, which were dismissed because of "serious methodological flaws," showed no evidence of a link. For thimerosal, the IOM looked at five studies, examining populations in Sweden, Denmark, the United Kingdom, and the United States (studies that vaccine critics contend were flawed). Since then, further research has strengthened and vindicated the committee's original conclusion. It is a conclusion that has been "independently reached by scientific and professional committees around the world," as a recent science journal commentary noted. Either the scientific community has found a clear, reassuring answer to the questions raised about thimerosal in vaccines, or there is a global scientific conspiracy to bury the truth.

Whether the public is hearing the scientific community's answer is another matter. "It's not hard to scare people," says pediatrician and leading vaccine advocate Paul Offit, who himself coinvented a vaccine. "But it's extremely difficult to unscare them."

A backlash against vaccine skeptics is beginning to mount. Standing up to fellow celebrities, actress Amanda Peet, who recently vaccinated her baby daughter, has become a spokeswoman for the provaccine group Every Child by Two. Offit's book *Autism's False Prophets* has further galvanized vaccine defenders—not only by debunking the science of those who claim vaccines are dangerous but also by contending that the parents of autistic children and the children themselves are indeed victims, not of vaccines but of medical misinformation.

The provaccine case starts with some undeniable facts: Vaccines are, as the IOM puts it, "one of the greatest achievements of public health." The CDC estimates that thanks to vaccines, we have reduced morbidity by 99 percent or more for smallpox, diphtheria, measles, polio, and rubella. Averaged over the course of the 20th century, these five diseases killed nearly 650,000 people annually. They now kill fewer than 100. That is not to say vaccines are perfectly safe; in rare cases they can cause serious, well-known adverse side effects. But what researchers consider unequivocally unsafe is to avoid them. As scientists at the Johns Hopkins Bloomberg School of Public Health recently found while investigating whooping cough outbreaks in and around Michigan, "geographic pockets of vaccine exemptors pose a risk to the whole community."

When it comes to autism, vaccine defenders make two central claims. First, the condition is likely to be mostly genetic rather than environmentally caused; and second, there are reasons to doubt whether there is really a rising autism epidemic at all.

It is misleading to think of autism as a single disorder. Rather, it is a spectrum of disorders showing great variability in symptoms and expression but fundamentally characterized by failed social development, inability to communicate, and obsessive repetitive behavior. Autism generally appears in children at early ages, sometimes suddenly, and its genetic component has long been recognized. Studies have shown that if one identical twin has autism, there is at least a 60 percent chance that the other also does. "From my point of view, it's a condition associated with genetic defects and developmental biology problems," says Peter Hotez, a George Washington University microbiologist and father of an autistic child. Hotez, who is also president of the Sabin Vaccine Institute, says, "I don't think it's possible to explain on the basis of any vaccine toxin that is acquired after the baby is born." Still, scientists cannot fully rule out environmental triggers—including various types of toxicity—that might interact with a given individual's preexisting genetic inclination. Autism is a complex disorder with multiple forms of expression and potentially multiple types of causation that are incompletely understood.

As for whether autism is rising, a number of experts say it is hard to know. Is the increase real, or is it largely the result of more attention to the condition, an expansion of the autism spectrum to embrace many different heterogeneous disorders, a new focus on children classified as autistic in federal special education programs during the 1990s, and other factors? It could be some combination of all these things.

But if environmental triggers of autism cannot be ruled out, the idea that those triggers can be found in the MMR vaccine or in thimerosal has crumbled under the weight of scientific refutation. Epidemiological studies have cast grave doubt on Andrew Wakefield's MMR hypothesis—and so have subsequent scandals. Nearly all of Wakefield's coauthors have since retracted the autism implications of their work; *The Lancet* has also backed away from the study. A series of investigative stories published in *The Times* of London unearthed Wakefield's undisclosed ties to vaccine litigation in the U.K. and, more recently, suggested he fabricated his data (which Wakefield denies).

As for thimerosal, government precautions notwithstanding, it was never clear how threatening it might be. The federal mercury standards that first heightened concern were developed for methylmercury, not ethylmercury, the form contained in thimerosal. Ethylmercury has less risk of accumulating to a toxic dose because it does not last as long in the body. And, according to the IOM's 2004 report, there had never been any evidence of a major incident of mercury poisoning leading to autism.

The strongest argument against the idea that thimerosal poisoned a generation of children does not emerge from the body of published studies alone. There is the added detail that although thimerosal is no longer present in any recommended childhood vaccines save the inactivated influenza vaccine—and hasn't been, beyond trace amounts, since 2001—no one is hailing the end of autism. "If you thought thimerosal was related to autism, then the incidence of autism should have gone down," Harvard's McCormick explains. "And it hasn't."

Children who would have been classified as mentally retarded or learning disabled were now being classified on the autism spectrum.

In 2005 David Kirby stated that if autism rates didn't begin to decline by 2007, "that would deal a severe blow to the autism-thimerosal hypothesis." But as McCormick notes, despite the absence of thimerosal in vaccines, reports of autism cases have not fallen. In a 2008 study published in *Archives of General Psychiatry,* two researchers studying a California Department of Developmental Services database found that the prevalence of autism had actually continued increasing among the young. Kirby concedes that these findings about the California database represent a "pretty serious blow to the thimerosal-causes-autism hypothesis," though he does not think they thoroughly bury it. In an interview, he outlined many problems with relying on the California database, suggesting potential confounding factors such as the state's high level of immigration. "Look, I understand the desire to try to end this and not scare parents away from vaccination," Kirby says. "But I also feel that sometimes that desire to prove or disprove blinds people on both sides."

Kirby says—and even some vaccine defenders agree—that some small subgroup of children might have a particular vulnerability to vaccines and yet be missed by epidemiological studies. But the two sides disagree as to the possible size of that group. "If one or two or three children every year are getting autism from vaccines, you would never pick that up," Offit says. Kirby, in contrast, feels that while the idea of thimerosal as the "one and only cause of autism has gone out the window," he still believes there is an "epidemic" with many environmental triggers and with thimerosal as a possible contributing factor.

Meanwhile, in the face of powerful evidence against two of its strongest initial hypotheses—concerning MMR and thimerosal—the vaccine skeptic movement is morphing before our eyes. Advocates have begun moving the goalposts, now claiming, for instance, that the childhood vaccination schedule hits kids with too many vaccines at once, overwhelming their immune systems. Jenny McCarthy wants to "green our vaccines," pointing to many other alleged toxins that they contain. "I think it's definitely a response to the science, which has consistently shown no correlation," says David Gorski, a cancer surgeon funded by the National Institutes of Health who in his spare time blogs at Respectful Insolence, a top medical blog known for its provaccine stance. A hardening of antivaccine attitudes, mixed with the despair experienced by families living under the strain of autism, has heightened the debate—sometimes leading to blowback against scientific researchers.

Paul Shattuck did not set out to enrage vaccine skeptics and the parents of autistic children. Currently an assistant professor at the George Warren Brown School of Social Work at Washington University in St. Louis, he has dedicated the last decade of his professional life to helping people with autism in their families. "Some of my dearest friends have kids with autism," he says.

But in 2006 Shattuck came under fire after he published an article in the journal *Pediatrics* questioning the existence of an autism epidemic. No one doubts that since the early 1990s the number of children diagnosed with autism has dramatically increased, a trend reflected in U.S. special education programs, where children enrolled as autistic grew from 22,445 in 1994–1995 to 140,254 in 2003–2004. Yet Shattuck's study found reasons to doubt that these numbers were proof of an epidemic. Instead, he suggested that "diagnostic substitution"—in which children who previously would have been classified as mentally retarded or learning disabled were now being classified on the autism spectrum—played a significant role in the apparent increase.

Shattuck did not reject the idea that rising autism levels might be in part due to environmental causes; he merely showed the increase was largely an artifact of changing diagnostic practices, which themselves had been enabled by rising levels of attention to autism and its listing as a diagnostic category in special education. Yet simply by questioning autism epidemic claims in a prominent journal, he became a target. "People were obviously Googling me and tracking me down," he recalls. Shattuck emphasizes that most e-mails and calls merely delivered "heartfelt pleas from people with very sick kids who've been led to believe a particular theory of etiology." The bulk weren't menacing, but a few certainly were.

Others attacked Shattuck's research on the Web and insinuated that he had fabricated his data or committed scientific misconduct. "It was dismaying to feel like people were calling me a traitor to autistic kids and families," he says.

"If there has been a more harmful urban legend circulating in our society than the vaccine-autism link," University of Pennsylvania bioethicist Arthur Caplan wrote in *The Philadelphia Inquirer*, "it's hard to know what it might be." One type of harm, as Shattuck's story shows, is to individual scientists and the scientific process. There is a real risk that necessary research is being held back as scientists fear working in such a contested field. Shattuck's experience is not unique. Offit cannot go on a book tour to promote *Autism's False Prophets* because of the risk involved in making public appearances. He has received too many threats.

Yet another cost comes in the rush toward unproven, and potentially dangerous, alternative therapies to treat autism. It is easy to sympathize with parents of autistic children who desperately want to find a cure, but this has led to various pseudoremedies whose efficacy and safety have been challenged by science. These include facilitated communication, secretin infusion, chelation therapy (which involves pumping chemicals into the blood to bind with heavy metals such as mercury), and hormonal suppression. It is estimated that more than half of all children with autism are now using "complementary and alternative" treatments.

D isease, however, is the greatest danger associated with holding back vaccines amid the ongoing investigation of dubious claims. Both the vaccinated and the unvaccinated populations are placed at greater risk. Given enough vaccine exemptions and localized outbreaks, it is possible that largely vanquished diseases could become endemic again. (That is precisely what happened with measles in 2008 in the U.K., following the retreat from the MMR vaccine in the wake of the 1998 scare.) The public-health costs of such a

development would be enormous—and they would not impact everyone equally. "If vaccine rates start to drop, who's going to get affected?" Peter Hotez asks. "It's going to be people who live in poor, crowded conditions. So it's going to affect the poorest people in our country."

Paradoxically, the great success of vaccines is a crucial reason why antivaccination sentiment has thrived, some scientists say. Most of the diseases that vaccines protect against have largely been licked. As a consequence, few people personally remember the devastation they can cause. So with less apparently on the line, it is easier to indulge in the seeming luxury of vaccine skepticism and avoidance. Even before the recent spike in attention to thimerosal, members of the public were alarmingly skeptical of vaccines. In a 1999 survey, 25 percent felt their children's immune systems could be harmed by too many vaccinations, and 23 percent shared the sentiment that children receive more vaccinations than are healthy. There is every reason to think that those numbers—gathered before the vaccine-autism controversy reached anything like its current intensity—have risen since.

In the United States, population pockets with low vaccination rates (such as in Boulder, Colorado, and Ashland, Oregon) have existed for some time, and the great fear among many governmental medical authorities is that high-profile claims about vaccine dangers will widen the phenomenon, with potentially disastrous consequences. Already, medical and religious vaccination exemptions are climbing: In New York State they totaled 4,037 in 2006, nearly twice as many as in 1999. In New Jersey they came to 1,923 in 2006 versus only 727 in 1990. It is not just exemptors: The far larger concern, according to McCormick and others, is those parents referred to as "vaccine hesitaters." They have heard all the noise about vaccines and will probably get their children shots because they feel they have to, but their skepticism is growing.

Offit points to still another threat: litigation. The wave of autism-related claims filed with the U.S. government's Vaccine Injury Compensation Program is unprecedented. Since 2001 autism claims have outnumbered nonautism cases almost four to one. Following the science, the court has now dismissed many of them, but there is the possibility that civil litigation will follow. "I still think it's going to be another 10 years before this really washes out in litigation," Offit says. If the legal atmosphere becomes too difficult for vaccine manufacturers, they could stop producing them or be forced out of business.

U ltimately, that is why the vaccine-autism saga is so troubling—and why it is so important to explore how science and so many citizens fell out of touch.

"It wouldn't have been possible without the Internet," says journalist Arthur Allen, who has covered the vaccine-autism story since 2002, when he wrote a high-profile *The New York Times Magazine* article that took the thimerosal risk seriously. Over time Allen changed his mind, coming to reject the idea that vaccines are to blame. Still, he recognizes why it persists. "If people believe something happened to them, there are so many people on the Web you can find who believe the same thing." The Internet has become a haven for a number of autism support groups that continually reinforce the vaccine-autism argument. This has led to the radicalization of some elements who have denounced scientists as "vaccine barbarians," "pharmaceutical and medical killers," and so on. And after all we have heard about environmental and chemical risks—some accurate, some not—people are now easily persuaded about all manner of toxin dangers.

But if the Internet has made it easier for pockets of antiscience feeling to grow and flourish, scientific authorities also deserve some of the blame. "I don't think they woke up that this was a serious problem until maybe 2008," David Gorski says about the growing antivaccine sentiment. George Washington University's Hotez notes that "the office of the surgeon general, the secretary of Health and Human Services, and the head of the CDC have not been very vocal on this issue." True, the CDC, the Food and Drug Administration, and other governmental organizations feature accurate and up-to-date information about vaccine risks on their websites. But that is very different from launching a concerted communications campaign to ensure that the public retains faith in vaccination.

Some outspoken scientists may have actually increased the polarization on this issue. For example, calling those against vaccines "scientifically illiterate"—or, as CDC vaccine expert Stephen Cochi reportedly put it to one journalist, "junk scientists and charlatans"—may just lead to a further circling of the wagons.

The most promising approach to the vaccine-autism issue comes from the government itself. Consider the work of Roger Bernier, a CDC scientist who turned to emphasizing the public-engagement aspects of the vaccine problem after hearing one parent declare any new government research on the topic "dead on arrival." The central problem Bernier has confronted: how to deal with a situation in which so many parents are unswervingly convinced that their children have been harmed, in which they could be harming their children even more by using untested therapies, and in which dangerous misinformation abounds.

"There's no end to the kind of noise people can make about vaccines," he observes. "And so if you're in the vaccine community, what's the best approach to this? I don't think it is ignoring people." Instead, Bernier has headed up a series of award-winning projects that bring together average citizens with scientists and policymakers to reach joint recommendations on vaccines, holding public dialogues across the country to break down boundaries between the experts and everybody else, literally putting multiple perspectives around a table. His example suggests that while science's first and greatest triumph in this area was to develop vaccinations to control or eradicate many diseases, the challenge now—not yet achieved, and in some ways even more difficult—is to preserve public support for vaccine programs long after these scourges have largely vanished from our everyday lives.

"The problem is not only research," Bernier says. "The problem is trust."

Critical Thinking

1. Explain why some people still believe that vaccinations cause autism.

2. Identify known factors which are correlated with autistic spectrum disorders.

3. Provide reasons why every child should have vaccinations.

Create Central

www.mhhe.com/createcentral

Internet References

Autism
www.autism-society.org

Autism Information
www.hhs.gov/autism

Autism Signs May Show Up as Early as First Month
www.keyt.com/news/health/study-autism

CHRIS MOONEY will continue to report on the vaccine-autism controversy on his blog. The Intersection, at blogs.discovermagazine.com/intersection.

Article   Prepared by: Karen L. Freiberg, *University of Maryland*

Anguish of the Abandoned Child

The plight of orphaned Romanian children reveals the psychic and physical scars from first years spent without a loving, responsive caregiver.

CHARLES A. NELSON III, NATHAN A. FOX AND CHARLES H. ZEANAH, JR.

Learning Outcomes

After reading this article, you will be able to:

- Explain the policy of the Romanian president, Ceauşescu, between 1965 and 1989.

- Evaluate the "orphan problem" of Romania and estimate the psychological impact of early life in a state institution.

In a misguided effort to enhance economic productivity, Nicolae Ceauşescu decreed in 1966 that Romania would develop its "human capital" via a government-enforced mandate to increase the country's population. Ceauşescu, Romania's leader from 1965 to 1989, banned contraception and abortions and imposed a "celibacy tax" on families that had fewer than five children. State doctors—the menstrual police—conducted gynecologic examinations in the workplace of women of child-bearing age to see whether they were producing sufficient offspring. The birth rate initially skyrocketed. Yet because families were too poor to keep their children, they abandoned many of them to large state-run institutions. By 1989 this social experiment led to more than 170,000 children living in these facilities.

The Romanian revolution of 1989 deposed Ceauşescu, and over the next 10 years his successors made a series of halting attempts to undo the damage. The "orphan problem" Ceauşescu left behind was enormous and did not disappear for many years. The country remained impoverished, and the rate of child abandonment did not change appreciably at least through 2005. A decade after Ceauşescu had been removed from power, some government officials could still be heard saying that the state did a better job than families in bringing up abandoned children and that those confined in institutions were, by definition, "defective"—a view grounded in the Soviet-inspired system of educating the disabled, dubbed "defectology."

Even after the 1989 revolution, families still felt free to abandon an unwanted infant to a state-run institution. Social scientists had long suspected that early life in an orphanage could have adverse consequences. A number of mostly small, descriptive studies that lacked control groups were conducted from the 1940s to the 1960s in the West that compared children in orphanages with those in foster care and showed that life in an institution did not come close to matching the care of a parent—even if that parent was not the natural mother or father. One issue with these studies was the possibility of "selection bias": children removed from institutions and placed into adoptive or foster homes might be less impaired, whereas the ones who remained in the institution were more disabled. The only way to counter any bias would require the unprecedented step of randomly placing a group of abandoned children into either an institution or a foster home.

Understanding the effects of life in an institution on children's early development is important because of the immensity of the orphan problem worldwide (an orphan is defined here as an abandoned child or one whose parents have died). War, disease, poverty and sometimes government policies have stranded at least eight million children worldwide in state-run facilities. Often these children live in highly structured but hopelessly bleak environments, where typically one adult oversees 12 to 15 children. Research is still lacking to gain a full understanding of what happens to children who spend their first years in such deprived circumstances.

In 1999, when we approached Cristian Tabacaru, then secretary of state for Romania's National Authority for Child Protection, he encouraged us to conduct a study on institutionalized children because he wanted data to address the question of whether to develop alternative forms of care for the 100,000 Romanian children then living in state institutions. Yet Tabacaru faced stiff resistance from some government officials, who believed for decades that children received a better upbringing in institutions than in foster care. The problem was exacerbated because some government agencies' budgets were funded, in part, by their role in making institutional care arrangements. Faced with these challenges, Tabacaru thought that scientific evidence about putative advantages of foster care for young children over state institutions would make a convincing case for reform, and so he invited us to go ahead with a study.

Infancy in an Institution

With the assistance of some officials within the Romanian government and especially with help from others who worked for SERA Romania (a nongovernmental organization), we implemented a study to ascertain the effects on a child's brain and behavior of living in a state institution and whether foster care could ameliorate the effects of being reared in conditions that run counter to what we know about the needs of young children. The Bucharest Early Intervention Project was launched in 2000, in cooperation with the Romanian government, in part to provide answers that might rectify the aftereffects of previous policies. The unfortunate legacy of Ceauşescu's tenure provided a chance to examine, with greater scientific rigor than any previous study, the effects of institutionalized care on the neurological and emotional development of infants and young children. The study was the first-ever randomized controlled study that compared a group of infants placed in foster care with another raised in institutions, providing a level of experimental precision that had been hitherto unavailable.

We recruited, from all six institutions for infants and young children in Bucharest, a group of 136 whom we considered to be free of neurological, genetic and other birth defects based on pediatric exams conducted by a member of the study team. All had been abandoned to institutions in the first weeks or months of life. When the study began, they were, on average, 22 months old—the range of ages was from six to 31 months.

Immediately after a series of baseline physical and psychological assessments, half the children were randomly assigned to a foster care intervention our team developed, maintained and financed. The other half remained in an institution—what we called the "care as usual" group. We also recruited a third group of typically developing children who lived with their families in Bucharest and had never been institutionalized. These three groups of children have been studied for more than 10 years. Because the children were randomly assigned to foster care or to remain in an institution, unlike previous studies, it was possible to show that any differences in development or behavior between the two groups could be attributed to where they were reared.

Because there was virtually no foster care available for abandoned children in Bucharest when we started, we were in the unique position of having to build our own network. After extensive advertising and background checks, we eventually recruited 53 families to foster 68 children (we kept siblings together).

Of course, many ethical issues were involved in conducting a controlled scientific study of young children, a trial in which only half the participants were initially removed from institutions. The design compared the standard intervention for abandoned children—institutional rearing—with foster care, an intervention that had never been available to these children. Ethical protections put in place included oversight by multiple Romanian and U.S.-based institutions, implementation of "minimal risk" measures (all used routinely with young children), and noninterference with government decisions about changes in placement when children were adopted, returned to biological parents or later placed in government-sponsored foster care that at the outset did not exist.

No child was moved back from foster care to an institution at the end of the study. As soon as the early results became available, we communicated our findings to the Romanian government at a news conference.

To ensure high-quality foster care, we designed the program to incorporate regular involvement of a social work team and provided modest subsidies to families for child-related expenses. All foster parents had to be licensed, and they were paid a salary as well as a subsidy. They received training and were encouraged to make a full psychological commitment to their foster children.

Sensitive Periods

The study set about to explore the premise that early experience often exerts a particularly strong influence in shaping the immature brain. For some behaviors, neural connections form in early years in response to environmental influences during windows of time, called sensitive periods. A child who listens to spoken language or simply looks around receives aural and visual inputs that shape neural connections during specific periods of development. The results of the study supported this initial premise of a sensitive period: the difference between an early life spent in an institution compared with foster care was dramatic. At 30, 40 and 52 months, the average IQ of the institutionalized group was in the low to middle 70s, whereas it was about 10 points higher for children in foster care. Not surprisingly, IQ was about 100, the standard average, for the group that had never been institutionalized. We also discovered a sensitive period when a child was able to achieve a maximum gain in IQ: a boy or girl placed in a home before roughly two years of age had a significantly higher IQ than one put there after that age.

The findings clearly demonstrate the devastating impact on mind and brain of spending the first two years of life within the impersonal confines of an institution. The Romanian children living in institutions provide the best evidence to date that the initial two years of life constitute a sensitive period in which a child must receive intimate emotional and physical contact or else find personal development stymied.

Infants learn from experience to seek comfort, support and protection from their significant caregivers, whether those individuals are natural or foster parents—and so we decided to measure attachment. Only extreme conditions that limit opportunities for a child to form attachments can interfere with a process that is a foundation for normal social development. When we measured this variable in the institutionalized children, we found that the overwhelming majority displayed incompletely formed and aberrant relationships with their caregivers.

When the children were 42 months of age, we made another assessment and found that the children placed in foster care displayed dramatic improvements in making emotional attachments. Almost half had established secure relationships with another person, whereas only 18 percent of the institutionalized children had done so. In the community children, those never institutionalized, 65 percent were securely attached. Children placed into foster care before the end of the 24-month sensitive period were more likely to form secure attachments compared with children placed there after that threshold.

These numbers are more than just statistical disparities that separate the institutionalized and foster groups. They translate into very real experiences of both anguish and hope. Sebastian (none of the children's names in this article are real), now 12, has spent virtually his entire life in an orphanage and has seen his IQ drop 20 points to a subpar 64 since he was tested during his fifth year. A youth who may have never formed an attachment with anyone, Sebastian drinks alcohol and displays other risk-prone behaviors. During an interview with us, he became irritable and erupted with flashes of anger.

Bogdan, also 12, illustrates the difference that receiving individualized attention from an adult makes. He was abandoned at birth and lived in a maternity ward until two months of age, after which he lived in an institution for nine months. He was then recruited into the project and randomized to the foster care group, where he was placed in the family of a single mother and her adolescent daughter. Bogdan started to catch up quickly and managed to overcome mild developmental delays within months. Although he had some behavioral problems, project staff members worked with the family, and by his fifth birthday the foster mother had decided to adopt him. At age 12, Bogdan's IQ continues to score at an above-average level. He attends one of the best public schools in Bucharest and has the highest grades in his class.

Because children raised in institutions did not appear to receive much personal attention, we were interested in whether a paucity of language exposure would have any effect on them. We observed delays in language development, and if children arrived in foster care before they reached approximately 15 or 16 months, their language was normal, but the later children were placed, the further behind they fell.

We also compared the prevalence of mental health problems among any children who had ever been institutionalized with those who had not. We found that 53 percent of the children who had ever lived in an institution had received a psychiatric diagnosis by the age of four and a half, compared with 20 percent of the group who had never been institutionalized. In fact, 62 percent of the institutionalized children approaching the age of five had diagnoses, ranging from anxiety disorders—44 percent—to attention-deficit hyperactivity disorder (ADHD)—23 percent.

Foster care had a major influence on the level of anxiety and depression—reducing their incidence by half—but did not affect behavioral diagnoses (ADHD and conduct disorder). We could not detect any sensitive period for mental health. Yet relationships were important for assuring good mental health. When we explored the mechanism to explain reduced emotional disorders such as depression, we found that the more secure the attachment between a child and foster parent, the greater probability that the child's symptoms would diminish.

We also wanted to know whether first years in a foster home affected brain development differently than living in an institution. An assessment of brain activity using electroencephalography (EEG)—which records electrical signals—showed that infants living in institutions had significant reductions in one component of EEG activity and a heightened level in another (lower alpha and higher theta waves), a pattern that may reflect delayed brain maturation. When we assessed the children at the eight-year mark, we again recorded EEG scans. We could then see that the pattern of electrical activity in children placed in foster care before two years of age could not be distinguished from that of those who had never passed time in an institution. Children taken out of an orphanage after two years and those who never left showed a less mature pattern of brain activity.

The noticeable decrease in EEG activity among the institutionalized children was perplexing. To interpret this observation, we turned to data from magnetic resonance imaging, which can visualize brain structures. Here we observed that the institutionalized children showed a large reduction in the volume of both gray matter (neurons and other brain cells) and white matter (the insulating substance covering neurons' wirelike extensions).

On the whole, all the children who were institutionalized had smaller brain volumes. Placing children in foster care at any age had no effect on increasing the amount of gray matter—the foster care group showed levels of gray matter comparable to those of the institutionalized children. Yet the foster care children showed more white matter volume than the institutionalized group, which may account for the changes in EEG activity.

To further examine the biological toll of early institutionalization, we focused attention on a crucial area of the genome. Telomeres, regions at the ends of chromosomes that provide protection from the stresses of cell division, are shorter in adults who undergo extreme psychological stresses than those who escape this duress. Shorter telomeres may even be a mark of accelerated cellular aging. When we examined telomere length in the children in our study, we observed that, on the whole, those who had spent any time in an institution had shorter telomeres than those who had not.

Lessons for All

The Bucharest early intervention project has demonstrated the profound effects early experience has on brain development. Foster care did not completely remedy the profound developmental abnormalities linked to institutional rearing, but it did mostly shift a child's development toward a healthier trajectory.

The identification of sensitive periods—in which recovery from deprivation occurs the earlier the child begins to experience a more favorable living environment—may be one of the most significant findings from our project. This observation has implications beyond the millions of children living in institutions, extending to additional millions of maltreated children whose care is being overseen by child-protection authorities. We caution readers, however, not to make unwarranted assumptions that two years can be rigidly defined as a sensitive period for development. Yet the evidence suggests that the earlier children are cared for by stable, emotionally invested parents, the better their chances for a more normal development trajectory.

We are continuing to follow these children into adolescence to see if there are "sleeper effects"—that is, significant behavioral or neurological differences that appear only later in youth or even adulthood. Further, we will determine whether the effects of a sensitive period we observed at younger ages will still be observed as children enter adolescence. If they are, they will reinforce a growing body of literature that speaks to the role of early life experiences in shaping development across one's life span. This insight, in turn, may exert pressure on governments throughout the world to pay more attention to the toll that early adversity and institutionalization take on the capacity of a maturing child to traverse the emotional hazards of adolescence and acquire the needed resiliency to cope with the travails of adult life.

Critical Thinking

1. Why is foster care for orphans better than care in an institutional setting?

2. How did the research scientists select infants for the foster care and the care-as-usual groups?

3. What ethical issues were involved in leaving some infants in the care of state institutions?

Create Central

www.mhhe.com/createcentral

Internet References

Importance of Early-Life Caregiving
www.ScientificAmerican.com/apr2013/orphans

Proven Benefits of Early Childhood Interventions
www.rand.org/pubs/research_briefs/RB9145

Why Is Early Intervention of Great Importance?
www.articlesbase.com/health-articles

Article   Prepared by: Karen L. Freiberg, *University of Maryland*

How to Help Your Toddler Begin Developing Empathy

REBECCA PARIAKIAN AND CLAIRE LERNER

Learning Outcomes

After reading this article, you will be able to:

- Contrast popular versus rejected children in terms of their empathy abilities.

- Describe ways for adults to model empathy to young children.

Empathy is the ability to imagine how someone else is feeling in a particular situation and respond with care. This is a very complex skill to develop. Being able to empathize with another person means that a child:

- Understands that he is a separate individual, his own person;
- Understands that others can have different thoughts and feelings than he has;
- Recognizes the common feelings that most people experience—happiness, surprise, anger, disappointment, sadness, etc.;
- Is able to look at a particular situation (such as watching a peer saying good-bye to a parent at child care) and imagine how he—and therefore his friend—might feel in this moment; and
- Can imagine what response might be appropriate or comforting in that particular situation—such as offering his friend a favorite toy or teddy bear to comfort her.

Understanding and showing empathy is the result of many social-emotional skills that are developing in the first years of life. Some especially important milestones include:

- Establishing a secure, strong, loving relationship with you. Feeling accepted and understood by you helps your child learn how to accept and understand others as he grows.
- Beginning to use social referencing, at about 6 months old. This is when a baby will look to a parent or other loved one to gauge his or her reaction to a person or situation. For example, a 7-month-old looks carefully at her father as he greets a visitor to their home to see if this new person is good and safe. The parent's response to the visitor influences how the baby responds. (This is why parents are encouraged to be upbeat and reassuring—not anxiously hover—when saying good-bye to children at child care. It sends the message that "this is a good place" and "you will be okay.") Social referencing, or being sensitive to a parent's reaction in new situations, helps the babies understand the world and the people around them.

- Developing a theory of mind. This is when a toddler (between 18 and 24 months old) first realizes that, just as he has his own thoughts, feelings and goals, others have their own thoughts and ideas, which may be different from his.

- Recognizing one's self in a mirror. This occurs between 18 and 24 months and signals that a child has a firm understanding of himself as a separate person.

What Can You Do: Nurturing Empathy in Your Toddler

Empathize with your child. *Are you feeling scared of that dog? He is a nice dog but he is barking really loud. That can be scary. I will hold you until he walks by.*

Talk about others' feelings. *Kayla is feeling sad because you took her toy car. Please give Kayla back her car and then you choose another one to play with.*

Suggest how children can show empathy. *Let's get Jason some ice for his boo-boo.*

Read stories about feelings. Some suggestions include:

- *I Am Happy: A Touch and Feel Book of Feelings* by Steve Light
- *My Many Colored Days* by Dr. Seuss

- *How Are You Feeling* by Saxton Freymann and Joost Elffers
- *Feelings* by Aliki
- *The Feelings Book* by Todd Parr
- *Baby Happy Baby Sad* by Leslie Patricelli
- *Baby Faces* by DK Publishing
- *When I Am/Cuando Estoy* by Gladys Rosa-Mendoza

Be a role model. When you have strong, respectful relationships and interact with others in a kind and caring way, your child learns from your example.

Use "I" messages. This type of communication models the importance of self-awareness: I don't like it when you hit me. It hurts.

Validate your child's difficult emotions. Sometimes when our child is sad, angry, or disappointed, we rush to try and fix it right away, to make the feelings go away because we want to protect him from any pain. However, these feelings are part of life and ones that children need to learn to cope with. In fact, labeling and validating difficult feelings actually helps children learn to handle them: *You are really mad that I turned off the TV. I understand. You love watching your animal show. It's okay to feel mad. When you are done being mad you can choose to help me make a yummy lunch or play in the kitchen while mommy makes our sandwiches.* This type of approach also helps children learn to empathize with others who are experiencing difficult feelings.

Use pretend play. Talk with older toddlers about feelings and empathy as you play. For example, you might have your child's stuffed hippo say that he does not want to take turns with his friend, the stuffed pony. Then ask your child: *How do you think pony feels? What should we tell this silly hippo?*

Think through the use of "I'm sorry." We often insist that our toddlers say "I'm sorry" as a way for them to take responsibility for their actions. But many toddlers don't fully understand what these words mean. While it may feel "right" for them to say "I'm sorry", it doesn't necessarily help toddlers learn empathy. A more meaningful approach can be to help children focus on the other person's feelings: *Chandra, look at Sierra—she's very sad. She's crying. She's rubbing her arm where you pushed her. Let's see if she is okay.* This helps children make the connection between the action (shoving) and the reaction (a friend who is sad and crying).

Be patient. Developing empathy takes time. Your child probably won't be a perfectly empathetic being by age three. (There are some teenagers and even adults who haven't mastered this skill completely either!) In fact, a big and very normal part of being a toddler is focusing on *me, mine,* and *I.* Remember, empathy is a complex skill and will continue to develop across your child's life.

Critical Thinking

1. Describe some of the attributes of empathy.
2. Name some of the social-emotional milestones that foster the development of empathy.
3. Explain why some teenagers and adults do not know how to empathize with others.

Create Central

www.mhhe.com/createcentral

Internet References

Early Childhood Care and Development
www.ecdgroup.com

The National Association for the Education of Young Children
www.naeyc.org

Zero to Three: National Center for Infants, Toddlers, and Families
www.zerotothree.org

Article   Prepared by: Karen L. Freiberg, *University of Maryland*

How to Raise a Global Kid

Taking Tiger Mom tactics to radical new heights, these parents are packing up the family for a total Far East Immersion.

LISA MILLER

Learning Outcomes

After reading this article, you will be able to:

- Explain why some parents want to raise bilingual children and immerse them in a different culture for at least a portion of their childhoods.

- Identify some of the benefits of global experiences.

Happy Rogers, age 8, stands among her classmates in the schoolyard at dismissal time, immune, it seems, to the cacophonous din. Her parents and baby sister are waiting outside, but still she lingers, engrossed in conversation. A poised and precocious blonde, Hilton Augusta Parker Rogers, nicknamed Happy, would be at home in the schoolyard of any affluent American suburb or big-city private school. But here, at the elite, bilingual Nanyang Primary School in Singapore, Happy is in the minority, her Dakota Fanning hair shimmering in a sea of darker heads. This is what her parents have traveled halfway around the world for. While her American peers are feasting on the idiocies fed to them by junk TV and summer movies, Happy is navigating her friendships and doing her homework entirely in Mandarin.

Fluency in Chinese, she says—in English—through mouthfuls of spaghetti bolognese at a Singapore restaurant, "is going to make me better and smarter."

American parents have barely recovered from the anxiety attacks they suffered at the hands of the Tiger Mom—oh, no, my child is already 7 and she can't play a note of Chopin—and now here comes Happy's father, the multimillionaire American investor and author Jim Rogers, to give them something new to fret about. It is no longer enough to raise children who are brave, curious, hardworking, and compassionate. Nor is it sufficient to steer them toward the right sports, the right tutors, the right internships, and thus engineer their admittance to the right (or at least a good enough) college. According to Rogers, who in 2007 left New York's Upper West Side to settle in Singapore with his wife, Paige Parker, and Happy (Beeland Anderson

Parker Rogers, called Baby Bee, was born the next year), parents who really care about their children must also ponder this: are we doing enough to raise "global" kids?

"I'm doing what parents have done for many years," Jim Rogers says. "I'm trying to prepare my children for the future, for the 21st century. I'm trying to prepare them as best I can for the world as I see it." Rogers believes the future is Asia—he was recently on cable television flogging Chinese commodities. "The money is in the East, and the debtors are in the West. I'd rather be with the creditors than the debtors," he adds.

It has become a convention of public discourse to regard rapid globalization—of economies and business; of politics and conflict; of fashion, technology, and music—as the great future threat to American prosperity. The burden of meeting that challenge rests explicitly on our kids. If they don't learn—now—to achieve a comfort level with foreign people, foreign languages, and foreign lands, this argument goes, America's competitive position in the world will continue to erode, and their future livelihood and that of subsequent generations will be in jeopardy. Rogers is hardly the only person who sees things this way. "In this global economy, the line between domestic and international issues is increasingly blurred, with the world's economies, societies, and people interconnected as never before," said U.S. Education Secretary Arne Duncan in remarks in the spring of 2010 at the Asia Society in New York. "I am worried that in this interconnected world, our country risks being disconnected from the contributions of other countries and cultures."

Despite Duncan's articulate urgency (and the public example of Rogers and a few others like him), America is so far utterly failing to produce a generation of global citizens. Only 37 percent of Americans hold a passport. Fewer than 2 percent of America's 18 million college students go abroad during their undergraduate years—and when they do go, it's mostly for short stints in England, Spain, or Italy that are more like vacations. Only a quarter of public primary schools offer any language instruction at all, and fewer high schools offer French, German, Latin, Japanese, or Russian than they did in 1997. The number of schools teaching Chinese and Arabic is so tiny as to be nearly invisible.

Meanwhile, 200 million Chinese schoolchildren are studying English. South Korean parents recently threw a collective hissy fit, demanding that their children begin English instruction in first grade, rather than in second. Nearly 700,000 students from all over the world attended U.S. universities during the 2009–10 school year, with the greatest increases in kids from China and Saudi Arabia. "Not training our kids to be able to work and live in an international environment is like leaving them illiterate," says David Boren, the former U.S. senator and current president of the University of Oklahoma. The gap between our ambition and reality yawns wide.

There is no consensus on remedies. According to a white paper issued in 2009 by the Institute on International Education, most colleges and universities say they want to increase participation in study-abroad programs, but only 40 percent are actually making concerted efforts to do so. Long immersion programs are expensive, and in an environment of tough statewide budget cuts, students and professors are too crunched for time to make international experience a priority. Educators disagree on which kinds of experiences are most advantageous for kids—or even what advantageous means. Is it enough for a teenager who has never traveled farther than her grandma's house to get a passport and order a pint in a London pub? Or does she have to spend a year in Beijing, immersed in Mandarin and economic policy? Is the goal of foreign experience to learn a language or gain some special expertise—in auto engineering or peace mediation? Or is it to be of service to others by giving mosquito nets to poor children in an African village?

Jim Rogers sees an America in decline, and his solution has been to immerse himself in the countries and cultures that are ascendant. "We think we're the world leader, but we're not," he says. "I don't like saying that. I'm an American. I vote. I pay taxes. But the level of knowledge is not very high, and that's going to hurt us, I'm afraid." In the Rogers family's five-bedroom bungalow, there is no TV. Instead, there are more than a dozen globes to look at and maps to ponder, a nanny and a maid who speak only Mandarin to the kids, bicycles to ride, and a new karaoke machine so the girls can learn Chinese songs.

A generation ago and as far back as Thomas Jefferson, a certain kind of child from a certain kind of family went abroad because it was done; a sojourn in Europe was as crucial to becoming a cultivated person as knowing the works of Mozart or Rembrandt. The point was to see the Great Museums, of course, but also to breathe the air—to learn to converse in another tongue, to adapt to the rhythms of another place. Hemingway did this, of course, but so did Benjamin Franklin and Johnny Depp. This is what Pamela Wolf, who just returned to New York City with her husband and children from a year in Barcelona, did. She enrolled her teenagers in an international school, where they made friends with kids from around the world and learned to speak fluent Spanish. Her children have a global perspective not only because of their language skills but also because arriving in a new place, knowing no one, forced them to be resilient. "It's pushing yourself out of your comfort zone," Wolf says. "It builds a very compassionate child. While,

yes, grades and academics are as important to me as anyone, you need resilience to understand and have sympathy for other people."

Such lengthy sojourns, though, are available to only a few: the very adventurous or the very rich. Wolf and her husband are both self-employed. "Financially," she says, "we have the great privilege of earning money while we're away."

Without resources and connections, a foreign experience can be a misery. Two years ago, Maribeth Henderson moved from San Antonio with her husband, her college-age son, and her adopted 5-year-old daughter, Wei Wei, to a remote part of China, in Guangdong province. Wei Wei didn't learn much Mandarin—her school taught mainly Cantonese—and Henderson felt lonely and alienated. "It was so Chinese that I couldn't assimilate and feel comfortable," she says. "I couldn't speak the language; it was hard for us to even order food in a restaurant. If you ordered a chicken, they would literally hand you a chicken. You were lucky if it wasn't alive." Henderson abandoned ship, returning to Texas with Wei Wei ahead of schedule and leaving her husband and son in Guangzhou. Now, though, she's planning to try again. This summer she and Wei Wei will move to Beijing, and Henderson hopes the big city will ameliorate her former isolation. About her goal—helping Wei Wei learn Chinese—Henderson has no doubts. "For children to be competitive and successful in a global economy," she says, "it's important for them to be bilingual."

For parents who want to give their children global experience while keeping them safely on the straight and narrow American path of PSATs, SATs, and stellar extracurriculars, there's an ever-growing field of options. Immersion schools have exploded over the past 40 years, growing from none in 1970 to 440 today, according to the Center for Applied Linguistics, and Mandarin, especially, is seen among type-A parents as a twofer: a child who learns Mandarin starting at 5 increases her brain capacity and is exposed to the culture of the future through language. (One mom in San Francisco laughs when she recalls that her daughter learned about Rosa Parks and the Montgomery bus boycott in Chinese.) The education entrepreneur Chris Whittle and colleagues recently announced plans for the new Avenues school, to open in New York City in September 2012 and designed to compete with the city's most exclusive (and expensive) private schools. Its curriculum will be fully bilingual—parents choose a Mandarin or Spanish track when their kids are 3—providing the Happy Rogers experience but with all the conveniences of home. "We think that any child that graduates from high school a monoglot is automatically behind," Whittle says. Fourteen months before the school's doors open, Avenues had already received 1,200 applications.

Study abroad is now a prerequisite on some college campuses, and a few professional schools, especially in business and engineering, have begun to require international study as part of their curricula. Nursing students at a community college in Utah must all spend a month at a hospital in Vietnam as part of their training. But Margaret Heisel, director of the Center for Capacity Building in Study Abroad, believes that a real global education comes from a long stay in a strange place; it gives kids skills that no amount of study can teach.

My own experience proves this point. During my sophomore year in high school, my father, a university professor, moved our entire family to Amsterdam for his sabbatical year and enrolled my brothers and me in local public schools. During that glorious year, I rode my bike through city streets, learned to roll a cigarette one-handed, and eventually spoke Dutch like a 15-year-old native. (I can still say "That's so stupid" and "This is so boring.") We saw Stonehenge and the Rijksmuseum and drove to Burgundy for the grape harvest, but the real impact of that adventure was that I learned a degree of self-reliance—a 15-year-old girl needs to make friends and will cross any cultural boundary to do so—that I didn't know I had.

"I think it's liberating to some extent," Heisel says. "It touches people in places that being in a familiar place doesn't. It requires versatility, flexibility. It's a different culture and it's pressing on kids in different ways." Baby Bee is equally at home on visits to the U.S. and in Singapore, where her father rides her to school each day on his personal pedicab. There she sings the Singapore national anthem and pledges the Singapore flag. "She's no different from the Chinese kids," says her teacher, Fu Su Qin. "And her Chinese is just as good."

Critical Thinking

1. Who would you describe as a "global kid"?
2. What languages should schoolchildren in the United States learn now to best prepare for a future global economy?
3. Identify several advantages of living in a foreign country during childhood.
4. When would be the best ages for childhood immersion in a different culture? Why did you choose this age range?

Create Central

www.mhhe.com/createcentral

Internet References

Benefits of Study Abroad
www.sit.edu/studyabroad/1050.htm

Six Benefits of Studying Abroad/AFS USA High School Student
www.afsusa.org/study-abroad/parents

Top Five Advantages of Studying Abroad/HCCMIS
www.hccmis.com

With reporting by **LENNOX SAMUELS** in Singapore.

Article   Prepared by: Karen L. Freiberg, *University of Maryland*

The Touch-Screen Generation

HANNA ROSIN

Learning Outcomes

After reading this article, you will be able to:

- Evaluate what tablets, iPads, and smartphones are doing to young children's brains.

- Distinguish between digital natives and digital immigrants and give characteristics of each.

On a chilly day last spring, a few dozen developers of children's apps for phones and tablets gathered at an old beach resort in Monterey, California, to show off their games. One developer, a self-described "visionary for puzzles" who looked like a skateboarder-recently-turned-dad, displayed a jacked-up, interactive game called Puzzingo, intended for toddlers and inspired by his own son's desire to build and smash. Two 30-something women were eagerly seeking feedback for an app called Knock Knock Family, aimed at 1-to-4-year-olds. "We want to make sure it's easy enough for babies to understand," one explained.

The gathering was organized by Warren Buckleitner, a longtime reviewer of interactive children's media who likes to bring together developers, researchers, and interest groups—and often plenty of kids, some still in diapers. It went by the Harry Potter-ish name Dust or Magic, and was held in a drafty old stone-and-wood hall barely a mile from the sea, the kind of place where Bathilda Bagshot might retire after packing up her wand. Buckleitner spent the breaks testing whether his own remote-control helicopter could reach the hall's second story, while various children who had come with their parents looked up in awe and delight. But mostly they looked down, at the iPads and other tablets displayed around the hall like so many open boxes of candy. I walked around and talked with developers, and several paraphrased a famous saying of Maria Montessori's, a quote imported to ennoble a touch-screen age when very young kids, who once could be counted on only to chew on a square of aluminum, are now engaging with it in increasingly sophisticated ways: "The hands are the instruments of man's intelligence."

What, really, would Maria Montessori have made of this scene? The 30 or so children here were not down at the shore poking their fingers in the sand or running them along mossy stones or digging for hermit crabs. Instead they were all inside, alone or in groups of two or three, their faces a few inches from a screen, their hands doing things Montessori surely did not imagine. A couple of 3-year-old girls were leaning against a pair of French doors, reading an interactive story called *Ten Giggly Gorillas* and fighting over which ape to tickle next. A boy in a nearby corner had turned his fingertip into a red marker to draw an ugly picture of his older brother. On an old oak table at the front of the room, a giant stuffed Angry Bird beckoned the children to come and test out tablets loaded with dozens of new apps. Some of the chairs had pillows strapped to them, since an 18-month-old might not otherwise be able to reach the table, though she'd know how to swipe once she did.

Not that long ago, there was only the television, which theoretically could be kept in the parents' bedroom or locked behind a cabinet. Now there are smartphones and iPads, which wash up in the domestic clutter alongside keys and gum and stray hair ties. "Mom, everyone has technology but me!" my 4-year-old son sometimes wails. And why shouldn't he feel entitled? In the same span of time it took him to learn how to say that sentence, thousands of kids' apps have been developed—the majority aimed at preschoolers like him. To us (his parents, I mean), American childhood has undergone a somewhat alarming transformation in a very short time. But to him, it has always been possible to do so many things with the swipe of a finger, to have hundreds of games packed into a gadget the same size as *Goodnight Moon*.

In 2011, the American Academy of Pediatrics updated its policy on very young children and media. In 1999, the group had discouraged television viewing for children younger than 2, citing research on brain development that showed this age group's critical need for "direct interactions with parents and other significant care givers." The updated report began by acknowledging that things had changed significantly since then. In 2006, 90 percent of parents said that their children younger than 2 consumed some form of electronic media. Nonetheless, the group took largely the same approach it did in 1999, uniformly discouraging passive media use, on any type of screen, for these kids. (For older children, the academy noted, "high-quality programs" could have "educational benefits.") The 2011 report mentioned "smart cell phone" and "new screen" technologies, but did not address interactive apps. Nor did it broach the possibility that has likely occurred to those 90 percent of American parents, queasy though they might be: that some good might come from those little swiping fingers.

I had come to the developers' conference partly because I hoped that this particular set of parents, enthusiastic as they were about interactive media, might help me out of this conundrum, that they might offer some guiding principle for American parents who are clearly never going to meet the academy's ideals, and at some level do not want to. Perhaps this group would be able to articulate some benefits of the new technology that the more cautious pediatricians weren't ready to address. I nurtured this hope until about lunchtime, when the developers gathering in the dining hall ceased being visionaries and reverted to being ordinary parents, trying to settle their toddlers in high chairs and get them to eat something besides bread.

I fell into conversation with a woman who had helped develop Montessori Letter Sounds, an app that teaches preschoolers the Montessori methods of spelling.

She was a former Montessori teacher and a mother of four. I myself have three children who are all fans of the touch screen. What games did her kids like to play?, I asked, hoping for suggestions I could take home.

"They don't play all that much."

Really? Why not?

"Because I don't allow it. We have a rule of no screen time during the week," unless it's clearly educational.

No screen time? None at all? That seems at the outer edge of restrictive, even by the standards of my overcontrolling parenting set.

"On the weekends, they can play. I give them a limit of half an hour and then stop. Enough. It can be too addictive, too stimulating for the brain."

Her answer so surprised me that I decided to ask some of the other developers who were also parents what their domestic ground rules for screen time were. One said only on airplanes and long car rides. Another said Wednesdays and weekends, for half an hour. The most permissive said half an hour a day, which was about my rule at home. At one point I sat with one of the biggest developers of e-book apps for kids, and his family. The toddler was starting to fuss in her high chair, so the mom did what many of us have done at that moment—stuck an iPad in front of her and played a short movie so everyone else could enjoy their lunch. When she saw me watching, she gave me the universal tense look of mothers who feel they are being judged. "At home," she assured me, "I only let her watch movies in Spanish."

By their pinched reactions, these parents illuminated for me the neurosis of our age: as technology becomes ubiquitous in our lives, American parents are becoming more, not less, wary of what it might be doing to their children. Technological competence and sophistication have not, for parents, translated into comfort and ease. They have merely created yet another sphere that parents feel they have to navigate in exactly the right way. On the one hand, parents want their children to swim expertly in the digital stream that they will have to navigate all their lives; on the other hand, they fear that too much digital media, too early, will sink them. Parents end up treating tablets like precision surgical instruments, gadgets that might perform miracles for their child's IQ and help him win some nifty robotics competition—but only if they are used just so. Otherwise, their child could end up one of those sad, pale creatures who can't make eye contact and has an avatar for a girlfriend.

Norman Rockwell never painted *Boy Swiping Finger on Screen,* and our own vision of a perfect childhood has never adjusted to accommodate that now-common tableau. Add to that our modern fear that every parenting decision may have lasting consequences—that every minute of enrichment lost or mindless entertainment indulged will add up to some permanent handicap in the future—and you have deep guilt and confusion. To date, no body of research has definitively proved that the iPad will make your preschooler smarter or teach her to speak Chinese, or alternatively that it will rust her neural circuitry—the device has been out for only three years, not much more than the time it takes some academics to find funding and gather research subjects. So what's a parent to do?

In 2001, the education and technology writer Marc Prensky popularized the term *digital natives* to describe the first generations of children growing up fluent in the language of computers, video games, and other technologies. (The rest of us are *digital immigrants,* struggling to understand.) This term took on a whole new significance in April 2010, when the iPad was released. iPhones had already been tempting young children, but the screens were a little small for pudgy toddler hands to navigate with ease and accuracy. Plus, parents tended to be more possessive of their phones, hiding them in pockets or purses. The iPad was big and bright, and a case could be made that it belonged to the family. Researchers who study children's media immediately recognized it as a game changer.

Previously, young children had to be shown by their parents how to use a mouse or a remote, and the connection between what they were doing with their hand and what was happening on the screen took some time to grasp. But with the iPad, the connection is obvious, even to toddlers. Touch technology follows the same logic as shaking a rattle or knocking down a pile of blocks: the child swipes, and something immediately happens. A "rattle on steroids," is what Buckleitner calls it. "All of a sudden a finger could move a bus or smush an insect or turn into a big wet gloopy paintbrush." To a toddler, this is less magic than intuition. At a very young age, children become capable of what the psychologist Jerome Bruner called "enactive representation"; they classify objects in the world not by using words or symbols but by making gestures—say, holding an imaginary cup to their lips to signify that they want a drink. Their hands are a natural extension of their thoughts.

I have two older children who fit the early idea of a digital native—they learned how to use a mouse or a keyboard with some help from their parents and were well into school before they felt comfortable with a device in their lap. (Now, of course, at ages 9 and 12, they can create a Web site in the time it takes me to slice an onion.) My youngest child is a whole different story. He was not yet 2 when the iPad was released. As soon as he got his hands on it, he located the Talking Baby Hippo app that one of my older children had downloaded. The little purple hippo repeats whatever you say in his own squeaky voice, and responds to other cues. My son said his name ("Giddy!"); Baby Hippo repeated it back. Gideon poked Baby Hippo; Baby Hippo laughed. Over and over, it was funny every time. Pretty soon he discovered other apps. Old MacDonald, by Duck Duck Moose, was a favorite. At first he would get frustrated trying to zoom between screens, or not knowing what to do when a message popped up. But after about two weeks, he figured all that out. I must admit, it was eerie to see a child still in diapers so competent and intent, as if he were forecasting his own adulthood. Technically I was the owner of the iPad, but in some ontological way it felt much more his than mine.

Without seeming to think much about it or resolve how they felt, parents began giving their devices over to their children to mollify, pacify, or otherwise entertain them. By 2010, two-thirds of children ages 4 to 7 had used an iPhone, according to the Joan Ganz Cooney Center, which studies children's media. The vast majority of those phones had been lent by a family member; the center's researchers labeled this the "pass-back effect," a name that captures well the reluctant zone between denying and giving.

The market immediately picked up on the pass-back effect, and the opportunities it presented. In 2008, when Apple opened up its App Store, the games started arriving at the rate of dozens a day, thousands a year. For the first 23 years of his career, Buckleitner had tried to be comprehensive and cover every children's game in his publication, *Children's Technology Review*. Now, by Buckleitner's loose count, more than 40,000 kids' games are available on iTunes, plus thousands more on Google Play. In the iTunes "Education" category, the majority of the top-selling apps target preschool or elementary-age children. By age 3, Gideon would go to preschool and tune in to what was cool in toddler world, then come home, locate the iPad, drop it in my lap, and ask for certain games by their approximate description: "Tea? Spill?" (That's Toca Tea Party.)

As these delights and diversions for young children have proliferated, the pass-back has become more uncomfortable, even unsustainable, for many parents:

He'd gone to this state where you'd call his name and he wouldn't respond to it, or you could snap your fingers in front of his face . . .

But, you know, we ended up actually taking the iPad away for—from him largely because, you know, this example, this thing we were talking about, about zoning out. Now, he would do that, and my wife and I would stare at him and think, *Oh my God, his brain is going to turn to mush and come oozing out of his ears.* And it concerned us a bit.

This is Ben Worthen, a *Wall Street Journal* reporter, explaining recently to NPR's Diane Rehm why he took the iPad away from his son, even though it was the only thing that could hold the boy's attention for long periods, and it seemed to be sparking an interest in numbers and letters. Most parents can sympathize with the disturbing sight of a toddler, who five minutes earlier had been jumping off the couch, now subdued and staring at a screen, seemingly hypnotized. In the somewhat

alarmist *Endangered Minds: Why Children Don't Think—and What We Can Do About It,* author Jane Healy even gives the phenomenon a name, the " 'zombie' effect," and raises the possibility that television might "suppress mental activity by putting viewers in a trance."

Ever since viewing screens entered the home, many observers have worried that they put our brains into a stupor. An early strain of research claimed that when we watch television, our brains mostly exhibit slow alpha waves—indicating a low level of arousal, similar to when we are daydreaming. These findings have been largely discarded by the scientific community, but the myth persists that watching television is the mental equivalent of, as one Web site put it, "staring at a blank wall." These common metaphors are misleading, argues Heather Kirkorian, who studies media and attention at the University of Wisconsin at Madison. A more accurate point of comparison for a TV viewer's physiological state would be that of someone deep in a book, says Kirkorian, because during both activities we are still, undistracted, and mentally active.

Because interactive media are so new, most of the existing research looks at children and television. By now, "there is universal agreement that by at least age 2 and a half, children are very cognitively active when they are watching TV," says Dan Anderson, a children's-media expert at the University of Massachusetts at Amherst. In the 1980s, Anderson put the zombie theory to the test, by subjecting roughly 100 children to a form of TV hell. He showed a group of children ages 2 to 5 a scrambled version of *Sesame Street*: he pieced together scenes in random order, and had the characters speak backwards or in Greek. Then he spliced the doctored segments with unedited ones and noted how well the kids paid attention. The children looked away much more frequently during the scrambled parts of the show, and some complained that the TV was broken. Anderson later repeated the experiment with babies ages 6 months to 24 months, using *Teletubbies.* Once again he had the characters speak backwards and chopped the action sequences into a nonsensical order—showing, say, one of the Teletubbies catching a ball and then, after that, another one throwing it. The 6- and 12-month-olds seemed unable to tell the difference, but by 18 months the babies started looking away, and by 24 months they were turned off by programming that did not make sense.

Anderson's series of experiments provided the first clue that even very young children can be discriminating viewers—that they are not in fact brain-dead, but rather work hard to make sense of what they see and turn it into a coherent narrative that reflects what they already know of the world. Now, 30 years later, we understand that children "can make a lot of inferences and process the information," says Anderson. "And they can learn a lot, both positive and negative." Researchers never abandoned the idea that parental interaction is critical for the development of very young children. But they started to see TV watching in shades of gray. If a child never interacts with adults and always watches TV, well, that is a problem. But if a child is watching TV instead of, say, playing with toys, then that is a tougher comparison, because TV, in the right circumstances, has something to offer.

How do small children actually experience electronic media, and what does that experience do to their development? Since the '80s, researchers have spent more and more time consulting with television programmers to study and shape TV content. By tracking children's reactions, they have identified certain rules that promote engagement: stories have to be linear and easy to follow, cuts and time lapses have to be used very sparingly, and language has to be pared down and repeated. A perfect example of a well-engineered show is Nick Jr.'s *Blue's Clues,* which aired from 1996 to 2006. Each episode features Steve (or Joe, in later seasons) and Blue, a cartoon puppy, solving a mystery. Steve talks slowly and simply; he repeats words and then writes them down in his handy-dandy notebook. There are almost no cuts or unexplained gaps in time. The great innovation of *Blue's Clues* is something called the "pause." Steve asks a question and then pauses for about five seconds to let the viewer shout out an answer. Small children feel much more engaged and invested when they think they have a role to play, when they believe they are actually helping Steve and Blue piece together the clues. A longitudinal study of children older than 2 and a half showed that the ones who watched *Blue's Clues* made measurably larger gains in flexible thinking and problem solving over two years of watching the show.

For toddlers, however, the situation seems slightly different. Children younger than 2 and a half exhibit what researchers call a "video deficit." This means that they have a much easier time processing information delivered by a real person than by a person on videotape. In one series of studies, conducted by Georgene Troseth, a developmental psychologist at Vanderbilt University, children watched on a live video monitor as a person in the next room hid a stuffed dog. Others watched the exact same scene unfold directly, through a window between the rooms. The children were then unleashed into the room to find the toy. Almost all the kids who viewed the hiding through the window found the toy, but the ones who watched on the monitor had a much harder time.

A natural assumption is that toddlers are not yet cognitively equipped to handle symbolic representation. (I remember my older son, when he was 3, asking me if he could go into the TV and pet Blue.) But there is another way to interpret this particular phase of development. Toddlers are skilled at seeking out what researchers call "socially relevant information." They tune in to people and situations that help them make a coherent narrative of the world around them. In the real world, fresh grass smells and popcorn tumbles and grown-ups smile at you or say something back when you ask them a question. On TV, nothing like that happens. A TV is static and lacks one of the most important things to toddlers, which is a "two-way exchange of information," argues Troseth.

A few years after the original puppy-hiding experiment, in 2004, Troseth reran it, only she changed a few things. She turned the puppy into a stuffed Piglet (from the Winnie the Pooh stories). More important, she made the video demonstration explicitly interactive. Toddlers and their parents came into a room where they could see a person—the researcher—on a monitor. The researcher was in the room where Piglet would be hidden, and could in turn see the children on a monitor. Before hiding Piglet, the researcher effectively engaged the children in a form of media training. She asked them questions about their siblings, pets, and toys. She played Simon Says with them and invited them to sing popular songs with her. She told them to look for a sticker under a chair in their room. She gave them the distinct impression that she—this person on the screen—could interact with them, and that what she had to say was relevant to the world they lived in. Then the researcher told the children she was going to hide the toy and, after she did so, came back on the screen to instruct them where to find it. That exchange was enough to nearly erase the video deficit. The majority of the toddlers who participated in the live video demonstration found the toy.

Blue's Clues was on the right track. The pause could trick children into thinking that Steve was responsive to them. But the holy grail would be creating a scenario in which the guy on the screen did actually respond—in which the toddler did something and the character reliably jumped or laughed or started to dance or talk back.

Like, for example, when Gideon said "Giddy" and Talking Baby Hippo said "Giddy" back, without fail, every time. That kind of contingent interaction (I do something, you respond) is what captivates a toddler and can be a significant source of learning for even very young children—learning that researchers hope the children can carry into the real world. It's not exactly the ideal social partner the American Academy of Pediatrics craves. It's certainly not a parent or caregiver. But it's as good an approximation as we've ever come up with on a screen, and it's why children's-media researchers are so excited about the iPad's potential.

A couple researchers from the Children's Media Center at Georgetown University show up at my house, carrying an iPad wrapped in a bright-orange case, the better to tempt Gideon with. They are here at the behest of Sandra Calvert, the center's director, to conduct one of several ongoing studies on toddlers and iPads. Gideon is one of their research subjects. This study is designed to test whether a child is more likely to learn when the information he hears comes from a beloved and trusted source. The researchers put the iPad on a kitchen chair; Gideon immediately notices it, turns it on, and looks for his favorite app. They point him to the one they have invented for the experiment, and he dutifully opens it with his finger.

Onto the screen comes a floppy kangaroo-like puppet, introduced as "DoDo." He is a nobody in the child universe, the puppet equivalent of some random guy on late-night public-access TV. Gideon barely acknowledges him. Then the narrator introduces Elmo. "Hi," says Elmo, waving. Gideon says hi and waves back.

An image pops up on the screen, and the narrator asks, "What is this?" (It's a banana.)

"This is a banana," says DoDo.

"This is a grape," says Elmo.

I smile with the inner glow of a mother who knows her child is about to impress a couple strangers. My little darling knows what a banana is. Of course he does! Gideon presses on Elmo. (The narrator says, "No, not Elmo. Try again.") As far as I know, he's never watched *Sesame Street,* never loved an Elmo doll or even coveted one at the toy store. Nonetheless, he is tuned in to the signals of toddler world and, apparently, has somehow figured out that Elmo is a supreme moral authority. His relationship with Elmo is more important to him than what he knows to be the truth. On and on the game goes, and sometimes Gideon picks Elmo even when Elmo says an orange is a pear. Later, when the characters both give made-up names for exotic fruits that few children would know by their real name, Gideon keeps doubling down on Elmo, even though DoDo has been more reliable.

As it happens, Gideon was not in the majority. This summer, Calvert and her team will release the results of their study, which show that most of the time, children around age 32 months go with the character who is telling the truth, whether it's Elmo or DoDo—and quickly come to trust the one who's been more accurate when the children don't already know the answer. But Calvert says this merely suggests that toddlers have become even more savvy users of technology than we had imagined. She had been working off attachment theory, and thought toddlers might value an emotional bond over the correct answer. But her guess is that something about tapping the screen, about getting feedback and being corrected in real time, is itself instructive, and enables the toddlers to absorb information accurately, regardless of its source.

Calvert takes a balanced view of technology: she works in an office surrounded by hardcover books, and she sometimes edits her drafts with pen and paper. But she is very interested in how the iPad can reach children even before they're old enough to access these traditional media.

"People say we are experimenting with our children," she told me. "But from my perspective, it's already happened, and there's no way to turn it back. Children's lives are filled with media at younger and younger ages, and we need to take advantage of what these technologies have to offer. I'm not a Pollyanna. I'm pretty much a realist. I look at what kids are doing and try to figure out how to make the best of it."

Despite the participation of Elmo, Calvert's research is designed to answer a series of very responsible, high-minded questions: Can toddlers learn from iPads? Can they transfer what they learn to the real world? What effect does interactivity have on learning? What role do familiar characters play in children's learning from iPads? All worthy questions, and important, but also all considered entirely from an adult's point of view. The reason many kids' apps are grouped under "Education" in the iTunes store, I suspect, is to assuage parents' guilt (though I also suspect that in the long run, all those "educational" apps merely perpetuate our neurotic relationship with technology, by reinforcing the idea that they must be sorted vigilantly into "good" or "bad"). If small children had more input, many "Education" apps would logically fall under a category called "Kids" or "Kids' Games." And many more of the games would probably look something like the apps designed by a Swedish game studio named Toca Boca.

The founders, Emil Ovemar and Bjorn Jeffery, work for Bonnier, a Swedish media company. Ovemar, an interactive-design expert, describes himself as someone who never grew up. He is still interested in superheroes, Legos, and animated movies, and says he would rather play stuck-on-an-island with his two kids and their cousins than talk to almost any adult. Jeffery is the company's strategist and front man; I first met him at the conference in California, where he was handing out little temporary tattoos of the Toca Boca logo, a mouth open and grinning, showing off rainbow-colored teeth.

In late 2010, Ovemar and Jeffery began working on a new digital project for Bonnier, and they came up with the idea of entering the app market for kids. Ovemar began by looking into the apps available at the time. Most of them were disappointingly "instructive," he found—"drag the butterfly into the net, that sort of thing." They were missing creativity and imagination." Hunting for inspiration, he came upon Frank and Theresa Caplan's 1973 book *The Power of Play,* a quote from which he later e-mailed to me:

> What is it that often puts the B student ahead of the A student in adult life, especially in business and creative professions? Certainly it is more than verbal skill. To create, one must have a sense of adventure and playfulness. One needs toughness to experiment and hazard the risk of failure. One has to be strong enough to start all over again if need be and alert enough to learn from whatever happens. One needs a strong ego to be propelled forward in one's drive toward an untried goal. Above all, one has to possess the ability to play!

Ovemar and Jeffery hunted down toy catalogs from as early as the 1950s, before the age of exploding brand tie-ins. They made a list of the blockbusters over the decades—the first Tonka trucks, the Frisbee, the Hula-Hoop, the Rubik's Cube. Then they made a list of what these toys had in common: None really involved winning or losing against an opponent. None were part of an effort to create a separate child world that adults were excluded from, and probably hostile toward; they were designed more for family fun. Also, they were not really meant to teach you something specific—they existed mostly in the service of having fun.

In 2011 the two developers launched Toca Tea Party. The game is not all that different from a real tea party. The iPad functions almost like a tea table without legs, and the kids have to invent the rest by, for example, seating their own plushies or dolls, one on each side, and then setting the theater in motion. First, choose one of three tablecloths. Then choose plates, cups, and treats. The treats are not what your mom would feed you. They are chocolate cakes, frosted doughnuts, cookies. It's very easy to spill the tea when you pour or take a sip, a feature added based on kids' suggestions during a test play (kids love spills, but spilling is something you can't do all that often at a real tea party, or you'll get yelled at). At the end, a sink filled with soapy suds appears, and you wash the dishes, which is also part of the fun, and then start again. That's it. The game is either very boring or terrifically exciting, depending on what you make of it. Ovemar and Jeffery knew that some parents wouldn't get it, but for kids, the game would be fun every time, because it's dependent entirely on imagination. Maybe today the stuffed bear will be naughty and do the spilling, while naked Barbie will pile her plate high with sweets. The child can take on the voice of a character or a scolding parent, or both. There's no winning, and there's no reward. Like a game of stuck-on-an-island, it can go on for five minutes or forever.

Soon after the release of Toca Tea Party, the pair introduced Toca Hair Salon, which is still to my mind the most fun game out there. The salon is no Fifth Avenue spa. It's a rundown-looking place with cracks in the wall. The aim is not beauty but subversion. Cutting off hair, like spilling, is on the list of things kids are not supposed to do. You choose one of the odd-looking people or creatures and have your way with its hair, trimming it or dyeing it or growing it out. The blow-dryer is genius; it achieves the same effect as Tadao Cern's Blow Job portraits, which depict people's faces getting wildly distorted by high winds. In August 2011, Toca Boca gave away Hair Salon for free for nearly two weeks. It was downloaded more than 1 million times in the first week, and the company took off. Today, many Toca Boca games show up on lists of the most popular education apps.

Are they educational? "That's the perspective of the parents," Jeffery told me at the back of the grand hall in Monterey. "Is running around on the lawn educational? Every part of a child's life can't be held up to that standard." As we talked, two girls were playing Toca Tea Party on the floor nearby. One had her stuffed dragon at a plate, and he was being especially naughty, grabbing all the chocolate cake and spilling everything. Her friend had taken a little Lego construction man and made him the good guy who ate neatly and helped do the dishes. Should they have been outside at the beach? Maybe, but the day would be long, and they could go outside later.

The more I talked with the developers, the more elusive and unhelpful the "Education" category seemed. (Is *Where the Wild Things Are* educational? Would you make your child read a textbook at bedtime? Do you watch only educational television? And why don't children deserve high-quality fun?) Buckleitner calls his conference Dust or Magic to teach app developers a more subtle concept than pedagogy. By *magic,* Buckleitner has in mind an app that makes children's fingers move and their eyes light up. By *dust,* he means something that was obviously (and ploddingly) designed by an adult. Some educational apps, I wouldn't wish on the naughtiest toddler. Take, for example, Counting With the Very Hungry Caterpillar, which turns a perfectly cute book into a tedious app that asks you to "please eat 1 piece of chocolate cake" so you can count to one.

Before the conference, Buckleitner had turned me on to Noodle Words, an app created by the California designer and children's-book writer Mark Schlichting. The app is explicitly educational. It teaches you about active verbs—*spin, sparkle, stretch.* It also happens to be fabulous. You tap a box, and a verb pops up and gets acted out by two insect friends who have the slapstick sensibility of the Three Stooges. If the word is *shake,* they shake until their eyeballs rattle. I tracked down Schlichting at the conference, and he turned out to be a little like Maurice Sendak—like many good children's writers, that is: ruled by id and not quite tamed into adulthood. The app, he told me, was inspired by a dream he'd had in which he saw the word *and* floating in the air and sticking to other words like a magnet. He woke up and thought, *What if words were toys?*

During the course of reporting this story, I downloaded dozens of apps and let my children test them out. They didn't much care whether the apps were marketed as educational or not, as long as they were fun. Without my prompting, Gideon fixated on a game called Letter School, which teaches you how to write letters more effectively and with more imagination than any penmanship textbooks I've ever encountered. He loves the Toca Boca games, the Duck Duck Moose games, and random games like Bugs and Buttons. My older kids love The Numberlys, a dark fantasy creation of illustrators who have worked with Pixar that happens to teach the alphabet. And all my kids, including Gideon, play Cut the Rope a lot, which is not exclusively marketed as a kids' game. I could convince myself that the game is teaching them certain principles of physics—it's not easy to know the exact right place to slice the rope. But do I really need that extra convincing? I like playing the game; why shouldn't they?

Every new medium has, within a short time of its introduction, been condemned as a threat to young people. Pulp novels would destroy their morals, TV would wreck their eyesight, video games would make them violent. Each one has been accused of seducing kids into wasting time that would otherwise be spent learning about the presidents, playing with friends, or digging their toes into the sand. In our generation, the worries focus on kids' brainpower, about unused synapses withering as children stare at the screen. People fret about television and ADHD, although that concern is largely based on a single study that has been roundly criticized and doesn't jibe with anything we know about the disorder.

There are legitimate broader questions about how American children spend their time, but all you can do is keep them in mind as you decide what rules to set down for your own child. The statement from the American Academy of Pediatrics assumes a zero-sum game: an hour spent watching TV is an hour not spent with a parent. But parents know this is not how life works. There are enough hours in a day to go to school, play a game, and spend time with a parent, and generally these are different hours. Some people can get so drawn into screens that they want to do nothing else but play games. Experts say excessive video gaming is a real problem, but they debate whether it can be called an addiction and, if so, whether the term can be used for anything but a small portion of the population. If your child shows signs of having an addictive personality, you will probably know it. One of my kids is like that; I set stricter limits for him than for the others, and he seems to understand why.

In her excellent book *Screen Time,* the journalist Lisa Guernsey lays out a useful framework—what she calls the three

C's— for thinking about media consumption: content, context, and your child. She poses a series of questions—Do you think the content is appropriate? Is screen time a "relatively small part of your child's interaction with you and the real world?"—and suggests tailoring your rules to the answers, child by child. One of the most interesting points Guernsey makes is about the importance of parents' attitudes toward media. If they treat screen time like junk food, or "like a magazine at the hair salon"—good for passing the time in a frivolous way but nothing more—then the child will fully absorb that attitude, and the neurosis will be passed to the next generation.

"The war is over. The natives won." So says Marc Prensky, the education and technology writer, who has the most extreme parenting philosophy of anyone I encountered in my reporting. Prensky's 7-year-old son has access to books, TV, Legos, Wii—and Prensky treats them all the same. He does not limit access to any of them. Sometimes his son plays with a new app for hours, but then, Prensky told me, he gets tired of it. He lets his son watch TV even when he personally thinks it's a "stupid waste." *SpongeBob SquarePants,* for example, seems like an annoying, pointless show, but Prensky says he used the relationship between SpongeBob and Patrick, his starfish sidekick, to teach his son a lesson about friendship. "We live in a screen age, and to say to a kid, 'I'd love for you to look at a book but I hate it when you look at the screen' is just bizarre. It reflects our own prejudices and comfort zone. It's nothing but fear of change, of being left out."

Prensky's worldview really stuck with me. Are books always, in every situation, inherently better than screens? My daughter, after all, often uses books as a way to avoid social interaction, while my son uses the Wii to bond with friends. I have to admit, I had the exact same experience with *Sponge-Bob.* For a long time I couldn't stand the show, until one day I got past the fact that the show was so loud and frenetic and paid more attention to the story line, and realized I too could use it to talk with my son about friendship. After I first interviewed Prensky, I decided to conduct an experiment. For six months, I would let my toddler live by the Prensky rules. I would put the iPad in the toy basket, along with the remote-control car and the Legos. Whenever he wanted to play with it, I would let him.

Gideon tested me the very first day. He saw the iPad in his space and asked if he could play. It was 8 A.M. and we had to get ready for school. I said yes. For 45 minutes he sat on a chair and played as I got him dressed, got his backpack ready, and failed to feed him breakfast. This was extremely annoying and obviously untenable. The week went on like this—Gideon grabbing the iPad for two-hour stretches, in the morning, after school, at bedtime. Then, after about 10 days, the iPad fell out of his rotation, just like every other toy does. He dropped it under the bed and never looked for it. It was completely forgotten for about six weeks.

Now he picks it up every once in a while, but not all that often. He has just started learning letters in school, so he's back to playing LetterSchool. A few weeks ago his older brother played with him, helping him get all the way through the uppercase and then lowercase letters. It did not seem beyond the range of possibility that if Norman Rockwell were alive, he would paint the two curly-haired boys bent over the screen, one small finger guiding a smaller one across, down, and across again to make, in their triumphant finale, the small *z.*

Critical Thinking

1. Why did the American Academy of Pediatrics (2011) discourage any passive media use for children younger than age 2?
2. What are the advantages of learning to navigate digital technology in early childhood?

Create Central

www.mhhe.com/createcentral

Internet References

Internet Safety Rules: The Constant Pursuit of Keeping Your Child Safe Online
   www.articlesbase.com/parenting-articles/internet-safety-rules
Study: 40 Percent of Kids Use iPads Before They Can Speak
   http://nymag.com/thecut/2013
Tech and Young Children
   www.techandyoungchildren.org

HANNA ROSIN is a national correspondent for *The Atlantic.*

Article   Prepared by: Karen L. Freiberg, *University of Maryland*

Ten Tips for Involving Families through Internet-Based Communication

SASCHA MITCHELL, TERESA S. FOULGER, AND KEITH WETZEL

Learning Outcomes

After reading this article, you will be able to:

- Defend the idea that parents need to be involved in their child's early education.

- Describe the possible contents of emails between teachers and parents.

The research is clear that a family's involvement in their child's early education improves outcomes in areas such as the child's language, self-help, social, and motor skills (Connell & Prinz 2002; Henderson & Mapp 2002; Sheldon 2003; Epstein 2004; Weiss, Caspe, & Lopez 2006). The more frequent the contact between home and school, the more the child benefits (McWayne et al. 2004).

While traditional forms of home-school partnerships (for example, parents participating in class activities and teachers sending home children's work) are associated with positive results, they are limited in their ability to effectively reach all families. Some children divide their time between two households as a result of divorce, and some parents cannot volunteer in the classroom due to daytime work hours. In such cases, teachers need to use different methods of home-program communication.

A variety of Internet-based communication methods exist to help increase the frequency and outreach of communication between families and early childhood programs. We recommend these strategies after observing and interviewing teachers who have successfully used them in their own classrooms.

Using Technology to Improve Home-school Communication

All of the following methods emphasize two-way communication. Unlike one-way communication approaches, in which families are merely informed of their child's progress, two-way communication approaches invite parents to participate in their child's learning process, thus creating an ongoing dialogue

between home and program (Abdal-Haqq 2002; Vazquez-Nuttall, Li, & Kaplan 2006).

1. **Create a classroom Web site.** Many schools and programs have Web sites that teachers can add to. For teachers without this option, tools to create Web pages, such as Google Sites and Facebook, are free and accessible from any computer. In addition to using print sources to give families information about your classroom activities, post items on the Web site. Embed a calendar, your family handbook, newsletters, homework assignments (for primary grades), announcements, wish lists, permission slips, and volunteer opportunities. It is best if your Web site is password-protected and accessible only to the families of children in the class. Be sure to keep the information on the Web site current. If you have a large number of families whose home language is not English, post all key messages in families' home languages.

2. **Send individual e-mails to share positive information about a particular child's activities and accomplishments.** Teachers need to reach out to families when a child is facing challenges at school; e-mail can be too impersonal and too easily misinterpreted for these types of communications. On the other hand, teachers *can* send e-mails to share short anecdotes about children's developing interests, their newly acquired skills, or their ability to be a good friend that day. These types of positive, spontaneous communications can create two-way conversations when parents reply with similar anecdotes or questions.

3. **Post photo stories on the class Web site.** To help families focus on the process through which their child learns rather than just an end product, create photo essays—a series of photos with captions that capture children engaged in a project (for example, building with blocks, painting a picture, planting seeds). Post the photo essays for families to view; many software programs and Web sites provide easy ways to upload photos. (As photos can be copied on the Internet

by anyone with access to the originating page, take special care to select photos for your Web site that do not show children's faces or names.) Sequenced photos give families a more accurate picture of their child's developmental progress. Also post photos of children's work. Change the photos often, and make sure to display each child's work at least once a month.

4. **Provide at-home educational activities.** Your Web site can help families use home computers as avenues for extended learning. Prepare a short list of activities that use readily accessible materials and include links to age-appropriate sites related to classroom topics. For example, if the children are learning about birds, add a link to the National Audobon Society Web site, which familes can explore with their children. Encourage families to document their children's learning at home by keeping a portfolio of their work, taking photos, and jotting down their child's questions. Also ask them to share links to good sites they have found while investigating topics of interest to their children.

Teachers *can* send e-mails to share short anecdotes about children's developing interests, their newly acquired skills, or their ability to be a good friend that day.

---

5. **Create a family response link or form on the Web page to elicit comments, questions, and feedback.** This is a good strategy for inviting families to monitor and comment on their child's progress. Parents can complete a short online form to provide comments and questions and e-mail them directly to the teacher.

6. **Establish and moderate a family support discussion forum.** The purpose of discussion forums is to offer a place where families can share their thoughts and questions. As the discussion forum moderator, you can instigate forums, but work toward families becoming the major contributors. Check the forum regularly to highlight important points, pose follow-up questions, and delete contributions that are inappropriate. As new topics emerge, archive old forums for future reference. Examples of topics might include how to address challenging behavior or develop nutritious meal or snack ideas for children. Also share listings of upcoming family events in the community.

7. **Communicate logistical information through group e-mails.** In addition to using informal communication (conversations at drop-off and pickup) and formal communication (parent-teacher conferences, print), send group e-mails to remind all families of upcoming events, such as field trips and parent-teacher conferences.

Techniques for Addressing Challenges

While the above methods are opportunities to increase communication between programs and families of young children, they also raise concerns of equity. The following techniques offer ideas on how to increase access to computer technology for all teachers and families.

8. **Ensure families' access to technology.** To ensure that families who do not have computers at home are included, continue to communicate through traditional means and by printing and sending home hard copies of your Web site announcements and general e-mails.

Remember, some families may need these items in their home languages. You might choose to apply for funding from various public and private sources to secure laptop computers that families can check out for home use. For example, the following

---

Resources for Creating a Web Site

Google sites
http://sites.google.com

Provides Web-based templates for creating Web pages and announcements, plus file cabinet (<10mb document upload), dashboard, and lists. Web pages can be modified easily by anyone who has editing privileges, and can include videos, Google docs, spreadsheets, presentations, photo slide shows, and calendars. The site manager designates members as owners, viewers, or collaborators. No advertisements.

webs (formerly freewebs)
www.webs.com

Template-driven Web site construction lets you create blogs, discussion forums, and calendars, and allow for comments. Share ideas, information, photos, and videos. Can accommodate group publishing, and can be set up for either public or member-only viewing. Web-based construction allows editing from any computer with Internet connectivity. Fee-based version does not contain advertisements.

Wikispaces
www.wikispaces.com

Classroom version features
www.wikispaces.com/site/for/teachers

Features include page editing, file and image uploads (including video), and links to Web pages. Allows unlimited members and discussion posts. RSS feeds can notify members of changes to the site. Free version for educators contains no advertisements.

Ten Tips for Involving Families through Internet-Based Communication by Sascha Mitchell, Teresa S. Foulger, and Keith Wetzel

67

organizations award computer grants to schools serving pre-K through grade 12 students: (1) Computers for Learning, http:// computersforlearning.gov; (2) Sun Microsystems Open Gateways Grant program, www.sun.com/aboutsun/comm_invest/ giving/education.html; and (3) the HP Technology for Teaching Grant, www.hp.com/hpinfo/grants/us/programs/tech_teaching/ k12_main.html. In addition, the Teachers Network posts technology grant opportunities at www.teachersnetwork.org/Grants/ grants_technology.htm. Computers acquired through grants can be placed in the family area of your center or school.

9. **Provide opportunities for families to increase their technology skills.** In certain circumstances, technology-based solutions can produce an unintended communications gap. To ensure that families receive your communications, offer a brief orientation to your classroom Web site during Open House or parent-teacher conferences. Demonstrate how to access and navigate the site. Focus on teaching families how to use the interactive features (discussion board, e-mail response). Distribute information about computer availability at public libraries and any other local organizations that provide computer access.

Staff members could take turns becoming "experts" and train others in how to use the technology.

10. **Set aside time for technology-based communication.** Teachers need time for training, maintaining a Web site, keeping information current, and preparing regular communications. Seek professional development opportunities to learn how to use new technology, or consider contacting experts (or an older student) who can assist with the initial setup. Alternatively, access free online tutorials. Staff members could take turns becoming "experts" and train others in how to use the technology. Visit the Web site of the NAEYC Technology and Young Children Interest Forum, www .techandyoungchildren.org, for more information.

References

Abdal-Haqq, I. 2002. *Connecting schools and communities through technology.* Alexandria, VA: National School Boards Association.

Connell, C.M., & R.J. Prinz. 2002. The impact of childcare and parent-child interactions on school readiness and social skills development for low-income African American children. *Journal of School Psychology* 40 (2): 177–93.

Epstein, J.L. 2004. Foreword. In *Children's literacy development: Making it happen through school, family, and community involvement,* by P.A. Edwards, ix–xiv. Boston: Pearson Education.

Henderson, A.T., & K.L. Mapp. 2002. *A new wave of evidence: The impact of school, family, and community connections on student achievement.* Austin, TX: Southwest Educational Development Laboratory, National Center for Family & Community Connections with Schools.

McWayne, C., V. Hampton, J. Fantuzzo, H.L. Cohen, & Y. Sekino. 2004. A multivariate examination of parent involvement and the social and academic competencies of urban kindergarten children. *Psychology in the Schools* 41 (3): 363–77.

Sheldon, S.B. 2003. Linking school-family-community partnerships in urban elementary schools to student achievement on state tests. *Urban Review* 35 (2): 149–65.

Vazquez-Nuttall, E., C. Li, & J.P. Kaplan. 2006. Home-school partnerships with culturally diverse families: Challenges and solutions for school personnel. Special issue, *Journal of Applied School Psychology* 22 (2): 81–102.

Weiss, H., M. Caspe, & M.E. Lopez. 2006. Family involvement in early childhood education. *Family Involvement Makes a Difference* 1 (Spring). Cambridge, MA: Harvard Family Research Project, www.hfrp.org/publications-resources/browse-our -publications/family-involvement-in-early-childhood -education.

Critical Thinking

1. What are some examples of home-school partnerships?
2. How can preschool teachers create home-school websites?
3. Why are home-school discussion forums useful?

Create Central

www.mhhe.com/createcentral

Internet References

Google Sites
   http://sites.google.com
The National Association for the Education of Young Children (NAEYC)
   www.naeyc.org
Webs (formerly Freewebs)
   www.webs.com
Wikispaces: Classroom version features
   www.wikispaces.com/site/for/teachers
Zero to Three: National Center for Infants, Toddlers, and Families
   www.zerotothree.org

Article Prepared by: Karen L. Freiberg, *University of Maryland*

Trauma and Children: What We Can Do

Linda Goldman

Learning Outcomes

After reading this article, you will be able to:

- Defend the premise that adults should encourage children to talk about bad things (e.g., bullying).

- Estimate what would be age-appropriate language, facts, and responses to children's experiences with trauma during early childhood.

The events of September 11, 2001, caused significant trauma to all of us. Children witnessed a terrorist assault on our nation over and over again on television, in newspapers and magazines and on the Internet. We have recently memorialized the 10th anniversary of the tragedy, and, with that have all witnessed the photos and films once again. This unprecedented horror was and may continue to be a traumatic overlay, potentially triggering all of the pre-existing, grief-related issues that our children were carrying before that awful day. Since then, our young people have also been traumatized by natural disasters (Hurricane Katrina, Haiti's earthquake, tornadoes, floods and the tsunami in Asia), man-made disasters such as oil spills, rampage shootings, political assassinations, plane crashes and many other scenes that have played repeatedly through media sounds and images.

Each day, our kids are impacted directly or vicariously by death-related tragedies involving suicide, homicide, and sudden death- and non-death-related traumas such as bullying and victimization, divorce and separation, foster care and abandonment, violence and abuse, drugs and alcohol and sexuality and gender issues. These experiences can result in overwhelmed feelings and distracted thoughts that may create traumatic grief for girls and boys.

Children processing their grief and trauma may not necessarily progress in a linear way through typical grief phases. The four phases of grief are shock and disbelief, searching and yearning, disorganization and despair, and rebuilding and healing (Life and Loss, 2nd Ed, 2000). These phases may surface and resurface in varying order, intensity and duration. Grief and trauma work can be messy, with waves of feelings and thoughts flowing through children when they least expect them. Kids can be unsuspectingly hit with "grief and trauma bullets" just about anywhere, with everyday sights and sounds triggering sudden intense feelings without any warning.

Talking to Children about "the Bad Stuff"

One question weighing heavily on the minds of parents, educators and mental health professionals is, "How do we talk to our children about war, terrorism, violence, natural disasters and destruction?" Sometimes, it may help to ask children if they have been "thinking about world events" and, if they have, then opening a dialogue. Some children don't want to talk about it. Some live in fear they will be killed or hurt, while others say there is nothing to worry about. Some may want to know the facts; therefore, we need to choose words that will help them understand what is happening around them. We need to be able to discuss each piece of traumatic experiences a little at a time.

Creating Dialogues

When creating dialogues with children, use accurate, real and age-appropriate language, avoiding clichés or denial of their experience. Concentrate on giving the facts and keep responses to questions simple. This helps adults follow the lead of children as to how much information they choose to take in. Especially with young children, minimize the scope of external tragedies, without contemplating with them what did or may happen. Keeping explanations developmentally appropriate allows children to process this information at their own level. Ask them what they think happened to clarify their understandings.

- Young elementary school children need simple information balanced with reassurance that trustworthy adults are bringing stability to their day-to-day life.
- Middle school children may seek out more facts and want to know more about what is being done to keep them safe and healthy at home, school and in the community.
- High school students may outspokenly voice opinions about what has happened and why, and may need to develop tactics for combating terrorism, rationalizing war and preventing world annihilation. (Adapted from National Association of School Psychologists, NASP, www.nasponline.org.)

Prepare Children for Dialogue

Reassure children that what they are feeling is very common. Emphasize to them that adults are feeling the same things that they are when learning about tragic events. Remind them that everyone has different ways of showing their feelings, and that is OK. Restore confidence by reassuring them that problems are being handled, and you are there to help them with their personal traumas. Mature modeling guides children to create responsible ways to be helpful during the crisis. This can mean collecting money to help victims or removing some of the sources of their distress. One example is helping them establish a new email account that they can keep private and avoid cyber-bullying.

Accept Children's Reactions

While there are several commonly seen reactions to trauma in children, these reactions range widely. Some children will listen to your explanation then go out to play. Others will want to stay near you and talk about it for a length of time, or maybe ask you to drive them to school instead of taking the bus. Still others may be angry that adults can't immediately fix the problem. Encourage children to use a variety of activities to safely tell their story, including drawing, writing and acting out with puppets or other expressive means of describing their traumas.

Activities to Help Children Participate in Dealing with Grief over World Events

Since 9/11, adults have been more supportive of children and helping them express their grief. Young people can create rituals that allow commemoration and avenues to voice feelings. Lighting candles, planting flowers, writing letters, raising money for victims or saying prayers for victims allow children to be recognized mourners.

Communities can involve children in participating in fundraisers for the survivors of disasters. Making patriotic pins and selling them to raise money to help victims and survivors, creating websites for world peace or having a poster contest at school on "What We Can Do to Feel Safe" are ways to give children back a sense of control and participation in their own lives. One group of children in Washington, DC, initiated a backpack project to collect backpacks for the children of Hurricane Katrina.

What Kids Can Do

Talk about their feelings. Allow children ways to tell their story as much as they need to. Draw pictures, create poems, write letters or offer suggestions about ways to help. Make a fear box. Cut out pictures from newspapers and magazines about what frightens them and paste these around the box. Write down their fears and put them inside. Create a worry list. Make a list of worries from 1 to 5; number 1 is the biggest. Suggest that children talk about this list with someone they trust, like their mom or dad, their sister or brother, their guidance counselor or a good friend. Put together a "peaceful box." Ask kids to find toys, stuffed animals and pictures that make them feel safe and peaceful and keep these items in the box. Monitor TV viewing and create a "teachable moment" for dialoguing as a family.

Help others. Help boys and girls give food or clothing to people who need it. Suggest that the family donate money to a good cause like the Red Cross, the fund for victims and survivors of disasters or the children in war-torn countries. Display an American flag and create an original global flag. Children can place these flags together outside their house to remind everyone of their support for their country and their hope for world peace. As a family, say a nightly prayer and light a candle for world peace.

Helping Our Children Grieve

Our world contains millions of grieving, traumatized children who have seen and experienced too much. They have been abused; witnessed adults and teens gunned down; lost a parent to death, divorce, deportation or deployment; watched their family dissolve due to economic problems; looked at pictures of starving children; been placed in foster care; and experienced bullying from peers and older kids or adults. If we can help our kids to see the relationship between terrorist attacks, bullying behaviors and issues of power and control, we can begin rooting out the behaviors that create oppression, prejudice, misguided rage and destruction of people and property. Responsible adults need to help children cope with trauma, loss and grief over issues within their homes, schools, community and nation.

Providing information, understanding and skills on these essential issues may well aid them in becoming more compassionate, caring human beings and thereby increase their chances of living in a future world of inner and outer peace. We need extensive training in schools and universities to prepare to work with kids in the context of a new paradigm of trauma and grief. Educators, parents, health professionals and all caring adults must become advocates in creating understanding and procedures to work with our children facing a present and future so different from their past.

Our task is to help our children stay connected to their feelings during the continuing traumas of terrorism, war, and man-made and natural disasters. The 9/11 terrorist attack has transformed us all into a global community joining together to re-instill protection and a sense of safety for America and for the world. Helping our children grieve can only help the grieving child in each one of us.

Critical Thinking

1. When should children be encouraged to talk about trauma?
2. How can parents, adult counselors, etc. help children talk about their intense feelings related to "bad stuff"?
3. Can helping a child grieve also help an adult? Why?

Create Central

www.mhhe.com/createcentral

Internet References

National Association of School Psychologists (NASP)
www.nasponline.org

The Penn Resiliency Project
www.ppc.sas.upenn.edu

Turnaround for Children
www.turnaroundusa.org

Read more in Linda Goldman's books: *Breaking the Silence: A Guide to Help Children with Complicated Grief/Suicide, Homicide, AIDS, Violence, and Abuse* (Taylor and Francis, 2002) and *Raising Our Children to Be Resilient: A Guide to Help Children with Trauma in Today's World* (Taylor and Francis, 2005) and *Great Answer to Children's Questions About Death: What Children Need to Know* (Jessica Kingsley, 2010).

LINDA GOLDMAN has a Fellow in Thanantology: Death, Dying, and Bereavement (FT) with an MS degree in counseling and Master's Equivalency in early childhood education. She is a Licensed Clinical Professional Counselor (LCPC) and a National Certified Counselor (NBCC) and has worked as a teacher and counselor for almost twenty years. Currently, she has a private grief therapy practice in Chevy Chase, MD, where she works with children, teenagers, families with prenatal loss, and grieving adults and presents workshops, courses and trainings on children and grief and trauma and teaches at the Graduate Program of Counseling at Johns Hopkins University. Linda is the author of *Life and Loss: A Guide to Help Grieving Children* (First edition, 1994/Second edition 2000) Taylor and Francis Publishers; *Breaking the Silence: a Guide to Help Children with Complicated Grief* (First edition, 1996/ Second edition 2002); *Bart Speaks Out: An Interactive Storybook for Young Children On Suicide* (1998) WPS publishers, a Phi Delta Kappan International fastback; *Raising Our Children to Be Resilient: A Guide for Helping Children Cope with Trauma in Today's World* (2005); and *Coming Out, Coming In: Nurturing the Well Being and Inclusion of Gay Youth in Mainstream Society* (2008); *Great Answers to Difficult Questions about Death* (2009); and *Great Answers to Difficult Questions about Sex* (2010).

Unit 3

UNIT

Prepared by: Karen L. Freiberg, *University of Maryland*

Development during Childhood: Cognition and Schooling

The mental process of knowing—cognition—includes aspects such as sensing, understanding, associating, and discriminating. Cognitive research has been hampered by the limitations of trying to understand what is happening inside the minds of living persons without doing harm. It has also been challenged by the problem of defining concepts such as intuition, unconsciousness, unawareness, implicit learning, incomprehension, and all the aspects of knowing present behind our sensations and perceptions (metacognition). Many kinds of achievement that require cognitive processes (awareness, perception, reasoning, judgment) cannot be measured with intelligence tests or with achievement tests.

Intelligence is the capacity to acquire and apply knowledge. It is usually assumed that intelligence can be measured. The ratio of tested mental age to chronological age is expressed as intelligence quotient (IQ). For years, schoolchildren have been classified by IQ scores. The links between IQ scores and school achievement are positive, but no significant correlations exist between IQ scores and life success. Consider, for example, the motor coordination and kinesthetic abilities of Hall of Fame baseball player Cal Ripken, Jr. He had a use of his body that surpassed the capacity of most other athletes and nonathletes. Is knowledge of kinesthetics a form of intelligence? Many people believe it is.

Some psychologists have suggested that uncovering more about how the brain processes various types of intelligences will soon be translated into new educational practices. Today's tests of intelligence only measure abilities in the logical/mathematical, spatial, and linguistic areas of intelligence, which is what schools now teach. Jean Piaget, the Swiss founder of cognitive psychology, was involved in the creation of the world's first intelligence test, the Binet-Simon Scale. He became disillusioned with trying to quantify how much children knew at different chronological ages. He was much more intrigued with what they did not know, what they knew incorrectly, and how they came to know the world as they did. He started the Centre for Genetic Epistemology in Geneva, Switzerland, where he began to study the nature, extent, and validity of children's knowledge. He discovered qualitative, rather than quantitative, differences in cognitive processes over the life span. Infants know the world through their senses and their motor responses. After language develops, toddlers and preschoolers know the world through their language/symbolic perspective. Piaget likened early childhood cognitive processes to bad thought, or thought akin to daydreams. By school age, children know things in concrete terms, which allows them to number, seriate, classify, conserve, think backward and forward, and think about their own thinking (metacognition). However, Piaget believed that children do not acquire the cognitive processes necessary to think abstractly and to use clear, consistent, logical patterns of thought until early adolescence. Their moral sense and personal philosophies of behavior are not completed until adulthood.

Article   Prepared by: Karen L. Freiberg, *University of Maryland*

An Educator's Journey toward Multiple Intelligences

SCOTT SEIDER

Learning Outcomes

After reading this article, you will be able to:

- Support the addition of more project-based creative activities to schools.

- Defend the notion that traditional IQ tests cannot measure the wide range of human intelligences.

During my first year as a high school English teacher, I got into the habit each Friday afternoon of sitting in the bleachers and grading papers while the players on the freshman football team squared off against their counterparts from nearby towns. I had been assigned four classes of rambunctious freshmen, and several of my most squirrelly students were football players. I hoped that demonstrating my interest in their gridiron pursuits might make them a bit easier to manage in the classroom.

My presence at their games unquestionably helped on the management front, but a second, unexpected benefit emerged as well. A couple of those freshmen—kids in my class who struggled mightily with subject-verb agreement and the function of a thesis statement—had clearly committed several dozen complex plays to memory. During one particularly impressive series of plays, I remember thinking, "These guys are really smart! I'm underestimating what they're capable of!" And over the course of my first year in the classroom, that same thought emerged several more times—at the school musical, visiting the graphic design class, and even just watching a couple of students do their math homework during study hall. Without my realizing it, my relationship with multiple-intelligences (MI) theory had begun.

Rethinking IQ

What has become a powerful force in the world of education all started in 1983, when Harvard University professor Howard Gardner began his book *Frames of Mind: The Theory of Multiple Intelligences*[1] with some simple but powerful questions: Are talented chess players, violinists, and athletes "intelligent" in their respective disciplines? Why are these and other abilities not accounted for on traditional IQ tests? Why is the term *intelligence* limited to such a narrow range of human endeavors?

From these questions emerged multiple-intelligences theory. Stated simply, it challenges psychology's definition of intelligence as a general ability that can be measured by a single IQ score. Instead, MI theory describes eight intelligences (see Howard Gardner's Eight Intelligences) that people use to solve problems and create products relevant to the societies in which they live.

MI theory asserts that individuals who have a high level of aptitude in one intelligence do not necessarily have a similar aptitude in another intelligence. For example, a young person who demonstrates an impressive level of musical intelligence may be far less skilled when it comes to bodily-kinesthetic or logical-mathematical intelligence. Perhaps that seems obvious, but it's important to recognize that this notion stands in sharp contrast to the traditional (and still dominant) view of intelligence as a general ability that can be measured along a single scale and summarized by a single number.

Multiple Misconceptions

During my eight years as a high school English teacher and an administrator, MI theory came up periodically. Colleagues shared assignments with me that sought to tap into the multiple intelligences. At parent-teacher conferences, I fielded questions about whether schools today are too focused (or, alternatively, not focused enough) on verbal-linguistic and logical-mathematical intelligences. In professional-development seminars, I was urged to keep multiple intelligences in mind while developing curriculum.

I also assured my students that everyone is gifted in at least one of the intelligences—a sentiment uttered with the best of intentions, but not entirely accurate.

Not only didn't I fully understand the theory, but when I began teaching at an urban public high school in Boston, I believed I had no time to concern myself with it. I was determined to help my students develop the tools they needed to make it into college: reading comprehension, writing skills, critical thinking, SAT vocabulary. I was certain there simply weren't enough hours in the day to foster students' musical intelligence or bodily-kinesthetic intelligence.

And, then, in 2004, my views began to change. I started working on my doctorate at Harvard University and asked Professor Howard Gardner to be my adviser. My interest in working with Gardner had more to do with his work on ethics than on MI theory, but over the next four years, MI theory was like fluoride in the water. There was a constant clamor from educators across the globe to hear from him about MI theory. Working each day about 20 yards away, I couldn't help overhearing the uproar and, amid that din, I started to pick up on my own misconceptions.

What MI Is—and Is Not

MI theory asserts that, barring cases of severe brain damage, everyone possesses all eight of the intelligences with varying levels of aptitude, giving each person a unique profile. And MI theory makes no claims about everyone being gifted in at least one of the intelligences.

I also discovered that neither Gardner nor MI theory has ever argued that educators should spend equal amounts of time teaching to the eight intelligences, or that every lesson should provide students with eight options for demonstrating their learning. In fact, MI theory offers neither a curriculum nor a goal toward which educators are expected to strive. Rather, MI theory is an *idea* about the concept of intelligence. A psychologist by training, Gardner left it to educators to decide how MI theory can be useful in the particular community and context in which they teach.

Nowadays, as a professor of education myself, when students or colleagues learn that I trained with Gardner, I am often asked facetiously, "How many intelligences is he up to now?" In truth, the original formulation of MI theory included seven intelligences, and Gardner has added just one (naturalistic intelligence) over the past 25 years.

Many other scholars and educators have proposed other intelligences—everything from moral intelligence to cooking intelligence to humor intelligence—but none have provided compelling evidence to justify an addition to the list. That said, advances in fields like neuroscience and genetics may well lead in coming years to the identification of new intelligences or the reorganization of existing intelligences. Ultimately, what is important about MI theory is not the number of identified intelligences, but, rather, its core premise that intelligence is better conceived of as multiple rather than general.

Far-Reaching Impact

Since its inception 26 years ago, thousands of schools, teachers, and researchers across the globe have drawn on MI theory to improve teaching and learning. There are Howard Gardner MI schools in Indiana, Pennsylvania, and Washington State and "multiple intelligences" schools in Bangalore, India, and Quezon City, Philippines. A 2002 conference on MI theory in Beijing attracted 2,500 educators from nine provinces and six neighboring countries. In 2005, a theme park opened in Nordborg, Denmark, that allows Danish children and adults to explore their aptitudes across the intelligences.

Some schools, like Indianapolis's *Key Learning Community*[2], aim to build all eight intelligences for each student. Others, like *New City School*[3], in St. Louis, focus on the two personal intelligences. Both schools are exemplary practitioners of MI theory.

It also happens that MI theory is used in ways that are neither educationally sound nor appropriate. Perhaps the most glaring example has been a state ministry in Australia that compiled a list of ethnic groups within the state as well as the particular intelligences that each group supposedly possessed and lacked—a practice Gardner has denounced as a perversion of his theory.

In Gardner's view, MI theory is used most effectively by educators who have a particular goal they are seeking to achieve and who conceive of the theory as a tool for achieving this goal. For instance, at the start of the school year, an elementary school teacher might want to identify students' strengths and weaknesses among the eight intelligences. That teacher might carefully observe the students' activities and interactions on the playground during recess or, alternatively, ask both students and parents to fill out a short survey identifying what they believe to be their (or their child's) strengths among the eight intelligences. Such information can facilitate lesson and unit planning down the road.

Or perhaps a school leader or department head seeks to improve communication among faculty about student achievement. For this objective, MI theory could serve as a framework or common language for discussing the strengths and challenges of individual students. In this instance, the concept of multiple intelligences may not even be raised directly with students, but, rather, may serve as a tool for fostering dialogue and collaboration among their teachers.

The irony of MI theory's tremendous impact on the educational community is that the theory was not developed with educators in mind. Rather, Gardner wrote his 1983 book, *Frames of Mind,* with the goal of inciting debate among psychologists about the nature of intelligence. By and large, such a debate did not occur. The psychology community has demonstrated relatively little interest in Gardner's theory, perhaps because, in sharp contrast to the traditional IQ test, it offers no easy scale for measuring aptitude across the various intelligences.

In what amounted to a sort of grassroots uprising, however, educators at all grade levels in many types of communities have embraced MI theory with a genuine passion. In describing this groundswell of support, Gardner has often speculated that MI theory provided empirical and conceptual support for what educators had known all along: that the notion of a single, general intelligence does not accurately depict the children that educators see in their classrooms each day.

Perhaps it is for this reason that the earliest groups of educators to embrace MI theory were teachers whose daily work entailed supporting students with learning disabilities. Even more so than their general-ed colleagues, special educators see first-hand that youth who struggle with, say, language can simultaneously possess a strong aptitude for numbers or music or graphic design, and vice-versa. These teachers knew intuitively that IQ tests were not measuring what they purported to measure.

Howard Gardner's Eight Intelligences

- Verbal-linguistic intelligence refers to an individual's ability to analyze information and produce work that involves oral and written language, such as speeches, books, and memos.
- Logical-mathematical intelligence describes the ability to develop equations and proofs, make calculations, and solve abstract problems.
- Visual-spatial intelligence allows people to comprehend maps and other types of graphical information.
- Musical intelligence enables individuals to produce and make meaning of different types of sound.
- Naturalistic intelligence refers to the ability to identify and distinguish among different types of plants, animals, and weather formations found in the natural world.
- Bodily-kinesthetic intelligence entails using one's own body to create products or solve problems.
- Interpersonal intelligence reflects an ability to recognize and understand other people's moods, desires, motivations, and intentions.
- Intrapersonal intelligence refers to people's ability to recognize and assess those same characteristics within themselves.

Source: www.edutopia.org/multiple-intelligences-theory-teacher

A Broader View

Perhaps the greatest contribution of MI theory, I would argue, has been its role over the past decade as a counterbalance to an educational climate increasingly focused on high-stakes testing, such as the IQ test, the SAT, and the various state assessments that have emerged from the No Child Left Behind Act.

Even if one believes that these assessments have contributions to offer to the practice of teaching and learning, it seems equally true that these tests have presented new challenges to the educational world as well. The IQ test and the SAT, two assessments unquestionably correlated with an individual's class status and schooling opportunities, have been utilized to declare some children intrinsically "smarter" than others and more deserving of seats in gifted-and-talented programs, magnet schools, and elite universities. Particularly in urban schools, the pressure from testing has narrowed the curriculum to focus on those subjects on which graduation and accreditation rest—at the expense of art, music, theater, physical education, foreign language, and even science and social studies.

In the face of these powerful forces, MI theory has served as a reminder to educators to focus on the strengths and weaknesses of the individual child and has also offered conceptual

support for educators seeking to prevent individual students from being stigmatized by a low score on one of these standardized tests. On a schoolwide scale, administrators contemplating eliminating or reducing funding for the subjects not covered by state assessments are likely to hear protests (from parents, teachers, students, and even internally) about neglecting children's multiple intelligences. I would argue that MI theory has offered an important check on the standards-based reform movement that has dominated American education for the past decade.

Or, put more simply, MI theory has helped facilitate in the heads of thousands of educators the same sort of appreciation I experienced while watching my students march down the football field: "These guys are really smart! I'm underestimating what they're capable of!" MI theory is neither a curriculum nor a goal nor an endpoint, but it remains, 26 years after its birth, a powerful tool for helping educators to teach more effectively and students to learn more deeply and enduringly.

Links

1. www.perseusbooksgroup.com/basic/book_detail.jsp?isbn=0465025102
2. www.616.ips.k12.in.us
3. www.newcityschool.org
4. www.ribasassociates.com/books.htm

Critical Thinking

1. Repeat Howard Gardner's eight intelligences.
2. Share reasons why some intelligences cannot be measured on IQ tests.
3. Recognize why multiple intelligence recognition supports students with learning disabilities.

Create Central

www.mhhe.com/createcentral

Internet References

Concept to Classroom: Tapping into Multiple Intelligences
www.thirteen.org/edonline/concept2class/mi
Gardner's Intelligences
www.edutopia.org/multiple-intelligences-theory-teacher
How to Address Multiple Intelligences in the Classroom
www.edutopia.org/multiple-intelligences-resources
Howard Gardner, Multiple Intelligences, and Education
http://infed.org/mobi/howard-gardner-multiple-intelligences
Multiple Intelligences: PBS
www.pbs.org/wnet/gperf/education/ed_mi_overview.html

SCOTT SEIDER, a former public school teacher, is an assistant professor of curriculum and teaching at Boston University. He is coauthor of *Instructional Practices That Maximize Student Achievement.*

Article   Prepared by: Karen L. Freiberg, *University of Maryland*

Creating a Country of Readers

Sid Trubowitz

Learning Outcomes

After reading this article, you will be able to:

- Identify five ways to get children to read more.

- Explain why book reading and storytelling are considered preferable to talking on a cell phone or watching TV or movies.

When I consider what can be done to create a society in which people read regularly, I recall strolling down a street in Italy and hearing a sanitation worker humming an aria from an opera as he swept debris into his cart. As I sat in a Rome barbershop, I heard strains from a Puccini opera filling the air. In a Milan opera house, I was part of an audience of people from every economic and social stratum.

If the United States is to become a nation of readers, we must do more than just develop programs to increase standardized test scores. If we could create a society where hunger for books is pervasive, there would be less need for concern about scores on standardized tests. If we want reading to permeate our culture and infiltrate every corner of our society in the same way opera is an everyday element in the life of Italy, we must think broadly about how we can accomplish this. Here are a few of my ideas.

Begin each school day with reading as a meditative experience. As students enter a room, they seat themselves, breathe in the surrounding quiet, take out a book, and proceed to read. In this way, a morning of rushing to get to school on time gives way to a time for relaxing and focusing.

Schools, towns, and cities can periodically highlight different writers and encourage residents to read their publications. On a trip to Scotland, I was struck by the fact that the entire country was celebrating the birthday of Robert Burns. Why not a Robert Frost, John Steinbeck, or E.B. White Day in the United States?

Prenatal and postnatal instruction for new mothers ought to include guidance on reading to children. Every new parent on leaving the hospital should be provided with reading kits that include nursery rhymes, books, and lists of appropriate reading material for children at different ages.

Books should be available for sale and casual reading at different locations—at supermarket checkout counters, in hospital emergency rooms, in banks, in post offices.

Extend rather than diminish library hours. Libraries should have children's rooms that are attractive, welcoming areas with games for toddlers, stuffed animals for cuddling, and comfortable corners where youngsters can read, browse, or listen to an adult read.

The President can appoint a Secretary of Cultural Development who is responsible for feeding the soul of the country. This person can promote library funding, invite writers to meet government officials, and arrange reading events such as poetry slams. The President and First Lady can also talk regularly about what they've been reading and why.

Investment in reading in many and varied ways would be required to develop a widespread love of reading in the United States.

Communities can agree to television blackout hours devoted to reading before bedtime. They can sponsor events in which the entire population is encouraged to read a designated book. Iowa City, Iowa, for example, invited local residents to read *The Tortilla Curtain* by T.C. Boyle (Viking 1995) in preparation for his visit to the city. For nearly 10 years, Chicago has been inviting its diverse population to read and discuss a single book in its citywide One Book, One Chicago activity.

Businesses can join this effort to integrate reading into everyday life. One pizza chain distributed a poem along with the pizzas it delivered or had picked up. Marc Kelly Smith, a Midwestern poet supporting this idea, commented, "Poetry is an everyman thing. I wonder if there's a family who's never had pizza." Companies could include brief biographies of such people as Alexander Graham Bell, Samuel Morse, and Thomas Edison along with their monthly bills. Tenants' associations and co-op boards can set aside a room in their buildings as a lending library for residents.

I imagine a country in which people walk down the streets book in hand, rather than a cell phone, a place where book readings prevail over sugarcoated movies, and where storytelling is an integral part of family living.

Critical Thinking

1. When should a child first experience a parent or caregiver reading to him/her? Why?

2. What is the Chicago citywide activity known as "One Book, One Chicago" designed to accomplish?

3. How would you react to a silent reading/meditative experience every school day before your classes begin?

4. Indicate how reading and storytelling are related.

Create Central

www.mhhe.com/createcentral

Internet References

Reach Out and Read
www.reachoutandread.org

10 Reasons Why Reading Is Important (for Kids and Adults)
http://everydayadventure//.blogspot.com

The Importance of Reading
http://esl.fisedu/parents/advice/read.htm

SID TRUBOWITZ is professor emeritus at Queens College of the City University of New York, N.Y.

Article

Prepared by: Karen L. Freiberg, *University of Maryland*

Addressing Achievement Gaps with Psychological Interventions

Carefully devised and delivered psychological interventions catalyze the effects of high-quality educational reforms, but don't replace them.

DAVID YEAGER, GREGORY WALTON, AND GEOFFREY L. COHEN

Learning Outcomes

After reading this article, you will be able to:

- Explain why the "fixed mindset" (intelligence is fixed and cannot change) is detrimental to learning.

- Discuss how a teacher's belief in a student's potential to learn can help a student achieve up to that potential.

- Explain how psychological interventions raise students' achievements.

Besides being researchers, each of us is also a teacher. Like anyone who has taught, we know the feeling of failing to connect with some students. It's disheartening. Before going into research, one of us (Yeager) taught middle school. He wanted to help kids in tough straits get a good education. Yet, looking at his gradebook at the end of his first year teaching 7th-grade English in Tulsa, Okla., he saw large gains for more advantaged students but much smaller gains for less advantaged students, including racial and ethnic minority students. He thought that he'd given these students just as much attention, if not more, and that he'd held them to equally high standards. He'd given them plenty of helpful critical feedback and cared about their success. What had gone wrong? And what could be done differently?

Many teachers have such experiences. Our research investigates why, sometimes, no matter how hard you work to create a good lesson plan or provide high-quality feedback, some students don't stay as motivated or learn as much as teachers would like. We also look at what can be done to improve their outcomes.

Take the Student's Perspective

When confronted with a problem in education—students falling behind in math, for example—we tend to focus on what teachers teach and how they teach it. We tend to prescribe solutions that take the perspective of the teacher, like *How can we teach math differently?*

That is an important perspective. But it can also help to adopt the vantage point of a student. How does the classroom look to a student sitting at a desk in the third row? What is he or she concerned about? How does the student feel about his or her potential? Does the student feel accepted by the teacher and fellow classmates? When you begin with questions like these, a different picture emerges—one that focuses on the psychology of students. This approach suggests that teachers should look beyond how they communicate academic content and try to understand and, where appropriate, change how students experience school. Even when a classroom seems to be the same for all students—for instance, when all students are treated similarly—different students can experience the class very differently. Understanding what school feels like for different students can lead to nonobvious but powerful interventions.

A common problem is that students have beliefs and worries in school that prevent them from taking full advantage of learning opportunities. For example, students who struggle in math may think that they are "dumb" or that teachers or peers could see them as such. Or girls in advanced math or minority students in general may wonder if other people will look at them through the lens of a negative stereotype about their group instead of judging them on their merits.

These beliefs and worries don't reflect low self-esteem, insecurity, or flaws in the student. From the students' viewpoint, they're often reasonable. If students are aware that negative stereotypes exist about their group, it makes sense for them to be alert to the possibility that stereotypes are in play (Steele, Spencer, & Aronson, 2002). Likewise, if a student has learned that many people see math ability as something that you either have or don't, it makes sense for that student to worry about being seen as "dumb" in math. Below we look at some of these beliefs in more detail and describe how they can be addressed.

Growth mindset

Carol Dweck has shown that some students think that people's amount of intelligence is fixed and cannot change (2006). Students who have this belief—called a *fixed mindset*—who then struggle in math may find it hard to stay motivated. They may think, "I'll never get it" and avoid math. But countering this belief can have powerful effects.

Teaching students that intelligence can be developed—that, like a muscle, it grows with hard work and good strategies—can help students view struggles in school not as a threat ("Am I dumb?") but as an opportunity to grow and learn ("This will make my brain stronger!"). In rigorous randomized experiments, even relatively brief messages and exercises designed to reinforce this *growth mindset* improved student achievement over several months, including the achievement of low-income and minority students (Aronson, Fried, & Good, 2002; Blackwell, Trzesniewski & Dweck, 2007).

Buttressing belonging and reducing stress

Worrying about belonging—"Do I belong? Will other students and teachers value me?"—is a chronic stressor. Students from historically marginalized groups, like black and Latino students or women in quantitative fields, may worry more about belonging. When students worry about belonging and something goes wrong—for instance, when a student feels left out, criticized, or disrespected—it can seem like proof that they don't belong. This can increase stress and undermine students' motivation and engagement over time.

Two types of interventions can remedy these worries. First, social-belonging interventions convey the positive message that almost all students worry about belonging at some point ("your concerns are not unique to you") and that these worries fade with time ("things will get better"). Such interventions can require as little as an hour to administer, and, by using persuasive delivery mechanisms that quickly change students' beliefs, they can be successful. One such intervention improved minority college students' grades for three years with no reinforcement from researchers, halving the achievement gap (Walton & Cohen, 2011).

Stealthy approaches don't feel controlling and don't stigmatize students as in need of help, factors that could do more harm than good.

Second, values affirmation interventions give students opportunities to reflect on personal values that bring them a sense of belonging and identity, such as relationships with friends and family, religion, or artistic pursuits. Students reflect on these values through structured in-class writing assignments timed to coincide with stressors throughout the year. These interventions shore up belonging in school and boost the GPAs of students contending with negative stereotypes in both adolescence and college.

High standards and assurance

Many students, but especially students who face negative stereotypes, worry that a teacher could be biased or unfair. They may wonder if critical feedback is a genuine attempt to help them or reflects bias against their group—something understandable given the historical marginalization of their group. Even a little mistrust can harm a student's learning. But when minority students were encouraged to see critical feedback as a sign of their teacher's high standards and his or her belief in their potential to reach those standards, they no longer perceived bias (Cohen, Steele, & Ross, 1999). In rigorous field studies, interventions of this sort boosted urban black youths' GPAs and reduced the black-white achievement gap several months after the intervention (Yeager et al., 2012).

Psychological Interventions aren't "Magic"

Understanding what students worry about in school can help us develop targeted interventions. These interventions can require only one or several class periods and modest resources. Sometimes they can even be delivered over the Internet (see www.perts.net). Yet all of these interventions have been experimentally evaluated and can have powerful effects on students' grades and test scores. But they are not "magic." They are not worksheets or phrases that will universally or automatically raise grades. Psychological interventions will help students only when they are delivered in ways that change how students think and feel in school, and when student performance suffers in part from psychological factors rather than entirely from other problems like poverty or neighborhood trauma. That means interventions depend critically on the school context, as we elaborate below.

How Psychological Interventions Work

Psychological interventions raise student achievement by:

- Changing students' subjective experience in school—what school feels like for them, their *construals* of themselves and the classroom;
- Leveraging powerful but *psychologically wise* tactics that deliver the treatment message effectively without generating problematic side effects like stigmatizing recipients; and
- Tapping into self-reinforcing or *recursive processes* that sustain the effects of early interventions (Garcia & Cohen, 2012; Yeager & Walton, 2011).

Construal

Each psychological intervention began by understanding what school feels like to students. These interventions may seem small to outside observers, and often they are in terms of time and cost relative to other school reforms. But to a student who worries that a poor test score means that she is stupid or could be seen as stupid, learning that the brain can grow and form new connections when challenged, or being told that a teacher believes that she can meet a higher standard, can be powerful. Despite its subtlety—or perhaps *because* of it—the message assuages fears that might stifle learning.

Psychologically wise delivery

Psychological interventions change how students think or feel about school or about themselves in school. If they don't deliver their message in a way that leads to these changes, they won't be effective. Each intervention used a delivery mechanism that drew on research into how to make messages stick. Rather than simply presenting an appeal to a student, each intervention enlisted students to actively generate the intervention itself. For instance, one delivery mechanism involves asking students to write letters to younger students advocating for the intervention message (e.g., "Tell a younger student why the brain can grow"). As research on the "saying-is-believing" effect shows, generating and advocating a persuasive message to a receptive audience is a powerful means of persuasion (Aronson, 1999). Similarly, rather than telling students that they are successfully meeting important values in their lives, values affirmations have students self-generate ways in which this is the case.

Although such delivery mechanisms are psychologically powerful, they are also stealthy, which may increase their effectiveness. None of the interventions expose students to a persuasive appeal (e.g., "You should know that your teachers are not biased") or tell them they are receiving "an intervention" to help them. Stealthy approaches don't feel controlling and don't stigmatize students as in need of help, factors that could do more harm than good (Ross & Nisbett, 1991).

Often psychological interventions are brief—not extensive or repeated. Excessive repetition risks sending the message that students are seen as needing help or may undermine the credibility of a reassuring message (as in "thou doth protest too much"). In this way, delivering psychological interventions differs markedly from teaching academic content. Academic content is complex and taught layer on layer: The more math students are taught, the more math they learn. Changing students' psychology, by contrast, can call for a light touch.

One mistake is to encourage students to give "more effort" when they really need not only to apply more effort but also change strategy.

Recursive processes

What can seem especially mysterious is how a brief or one-shot psychological intervention can generate effects that persist over long periods. For instance, people may assume that an intervention must remain on students' minds to retain its effects. But, like many experiences, a psychological intervention will become less salient as it recedes in time. A key to understanding the long-lasting effects of psychological interventions is to understand how they tap into self-reinforcing processes in schools—like how students make friends and then feel more

confident they belong, how they build relationships with teachers who give them more support and encouragement, and how they simply feel more confident in their ability to learn and succeed.

In education, early success begets more success. As students study, learn, and build academic skills, they're better prepared to learn and perform in the future. As students form better relationships in school, these become sources of support and learning that promote feelings of belonging and academic success. When students achieve success beyond what they thought possible, their beliefs about their own agency often improve, leading them to become more invested in school, further improving performance, and reinforcing their belief in their potential for growth. As students perform well, they're placed in higher-level classes—gateways that raise expectations, expose them to high-achieving peers, and put them on a trajectory of success. A well-timed, well-targeted psychological intervention can improve students' relationships, experiences, and performance at a critical stage and thus improve their trajectory through their school careers (Yeager & Walton, 2011). It is thus essential to intervene early, before a negative recursive process has gained momentum, if we are to improve students' outcomes over long periods (Garcia & Cohen, 2012).

Education occurs in a complex system. If students are to succeed, they need both learning opportunities and openness to these opportunities. As a result, it would be absurd to replace traditional educational reforms, like improving curricula, pedagogy, or teacher quality, with psychological interventions. Indeed, making students optimistic about school without actually giving them opportunities to learn could not only be ineffective but counterproductive. Psychological interventions work only because they catalyze the student's potential and the classroom resources for growth.

Use Psychological Interventions Thoughtfully

Excellent teachers already use versions of the techniques discussed here. But, when trying to improve those techniques by applying psychological interventions, practitioners will want to be thoughtful. Psychology is subtle, and you can make many mistakes when trying to change it (believe us—we've made them).

One mistake is to encourage students to give "more effort" when they really need not only apply more effort but also change strategy. Effort is necessary but it is not the sole ingredient for success. When confronted with continued failures despite heightened effort, students might conclude that they can't succeed, sapping their motivation. Effective growth mindset interventions challenge the myth that raw ability matters most by teaching the fuller formula for success: effort + strategies + help from others.

Psychological interventions complement—and do not replace—traditional education reforms.

Second, any psychological intervention can be implemented poorly. The devil is in the details: An intervention to instill belonging, a growth mindset, or a sense of affirmation hinges on subtle and not-so-subtle procedural craft. Classroom activities that promote a rah-rah ethos or that express platitudes ("everyone belongs here") but don't make students feel personally valued and respected will fail. Bolstering a sense of belonging for poor-performing students requires establishing credible norms that worry about belonging are common and tend to fade with time—not rah-rah boosterism. Similarly, values affirmation exercises might backfire if they're delivered in a cursory way or seen as something that the teacher cares little about.

A third example of well-intended but unwise strategies for changing student psychology involves teacher feedback. Many teachers are tempted to overpraise students for mediocre performance, especially students who face negative stereotypes, so as to appear unbiased and boost student self-esteem (Harber, Gorman, Gengaro, & Butisingh, in press). Sometimes, teachers go out of their way to praise student ability on classroom tasks. But such overpraising risks worsening student psychology by conveying low expectations or by sending the message that ability rather than effort and strategy matter the most.

Good teachers often know the importance of belonging, growth, and positive affirmation. But they may not know the best ways to bring these about. Well-intended practices can sometimes even do more harm than good. At the same time, researchers may not always know the best way to make their interventions speak to students in a given class. And many of the interventions developed here were borne of observations of real-world success stories—educators who boosted the performance and life chances of their at-risk youth. This is why, going forward, we believe it is critical for educators and practitioners to work together to develop ways to change students' psychology in school for the better.

Conclusion

Psychological interventions complement—and do not replace—traditional educational reforms. They don't teach students academic content or skills, restructure schools, or improve teaching. A psychological intervention will never teach a student to spell or do fractions. Instead, it will allow students to seize opportunities to learn. Psychological and structural interventions when combined could go a long way toward solving the nation's educational problems.

References

Aronson, E. (1999). The power of self-persuasion. *American Psychologist, 54,* 875–884.

Aronson, J., Fried, C., & Good, C. (2002). Reducing the effects of stereotype threat on African-American college students by shaping theories of intelligence. *Journal of Experimental Social Psychology, 38,* 113–125.

Blackwell, L.A., Trzesniewski, K.H., & Dweck, C.S. (2007). Theories of intelligence and achievement across the junior high school transition: A longitudinal study and an intervention. *Child Development, 78,* 246–263.

Cohen, G.L., Steele, C.M., & Ross, L.D. (1999). The mentor's dilemma: Providing critical feedback across the racial divide. *Personality and Social Psychology Bulletin, 25,* 1302–1318.

Dweck, C.S. (2006). *Mindset.* New York, NY: Random House.

Garcia, J. & Cohen, G.L. (2012). A social-psychological approach to educational intervention. In E. Shafir (Ed.), *Behavioral foundations of policy,* pp. 329–350. Princeton, NJ: Princeton University Press. https://ed.stanford.edu/sites/default/files/social_psych_perspective_education.pdf.

Harber, K.D., Gorman, J.L., Gengaro, F.P., & Butisingh, S. (in press). Students' race and teachers' social support affect the positive feedback bias in public schools. *Journal of Educational Psychology, 104* (4), 1149–1161.

Ross, L. & Nisbett, R.E. (1991). *The person and the situation: Perspectives of social psychology.* New York, NY: McGraw-Hill.

Steele, C.M., Spencer, S.J., & Aronson, J. (2002). Contending with group image: The psychology of stereotype and social identity threat. In M.P. Zanna (Ed.), *Advances in experimental social psychology* (vol. 34), pp. 379–440. San Diego, CA: Academic Press.

Walton, G.M. & Cohen, G.L. (2011). A brief social-belonging intervention improves academic and health outcomes of minority students. *Science, 331,* 1447–1451.

Yeager, D.S., Purdie-Vaughns, V., Garcia, J., Pebley, P., & Cohen, G.L. (2012). *Lifting a barrier of mistrust: "Wise" feedback to racial minorities.* Unpublished manuscript. Austin, TX: University of Texas.

Yeager, D.S. & Walton, G. (2011). Social-psychological interventions in education: They're not magic. *Review of Educational Research, 81,* 267–301.

Critical Thinking

1. What do you see as the greatest challenge in helping students develop a "growth mindset" over a "fixed mindset"?

2. How can social-belonging interventions reduce the stress of marginalized students?

3. Why is it important to help students change strategies rather than give more time and effort to studying?

Create Central

www.mhhe.com/createcentral

Internet References

Support All Students to Close the Achievement Gap
   www.wholechildeducation.org

The Achievement Gap
   www.achievementfirst.org

The Challenge: Why Are Some Students Unmotivated?
   www.perts.net/home/about.php

DAVID YEAGER (yeager@psy.utexas.edu) is an assistant professor of developmental psychology at University of Texas, Austin, Texas. **GREGORY WALTON** (gwalton@stanford.edu) is an assistant professor of psychology and **GEOFFREY L. COHEN** (glc@stanford.edu) is a professor of education and psychology at Stanford University, Stanford, Calif.

Yeager et al., David . From *Phi Delta Kappan,* February 2013, pp. 62–65. Reprinted with permission of Phi Delta Kappa International. All rights reserved. www.pdkintl.org.

Article   Prepared by: Karen L. Freiberg, *University of Maryland*

In Defense of Distraction

Twitter, Adderall, lifehacking, mindful jogging, power browsing, Obama's BlackBerry, and the benefits of overstimulation.

SAM ANDERSON

Learning Outcomes

After reading this article, you will be able to:

- Synthesize what is known about neuroenhancers and attention.
- Explain why Albert Einstein's and John Lennon's genius are considered similar.

I. The Poverty of Attention

I'm going to pause here, right at the beginning of my riveting article about attention, and ask you to please get all of your precious 21st-century distractions out of your system now. Check the score of the Mets game; text your sister that pun you just thought of about her roommate's new pet lizard ("iguana hold yr hand LOL get it like Beatles"); refresh your work e-mail, your home e-mail, your school e-mail; upload pictures of yourself reading this paragraph to your "me reading magazine articles" Flickr photostream; and alert the fellow citizens of whatever Twittertopia you happen to frequent that you will be suspending your digital presence for the next twenty minutes or so (I know that seems drastic: Tell them you're having an appendectomy or something and are about to lose consciousness). Good. Now: Count your breaths. Close your eyes. Do whatever it takes to get all of your neurons lined up in one direction. Above all, resist the urge to fixate on the picture, right over there, of that weird scrambled guy typing. Do not speculate on his ethnicity (German-Venezuelan?) or his backstory (Witness Protection Program?) or the size of his monitor. Go ahead and cover him with your hand if you need to. There. Doesn't that feel better? Now it's just you and me, tucked like fourteenth-century Zen masters into this sweet little nook of pure mental focus. (Seriously, stop looking at him. I'm over here.)

Over the last several years, the problem of attention has migrated right into the center of our cultural attention. We hunt it in neurology labs, lament its decline on op-ed pages, fetishize it in grassroots quality-of-life movements, diagnose its absence in more and more of our children every year, cultivate it in

yoga class twice a week, harness it as the engine of self-help empires, and pump it up to superhuman levels with drugs originally intended to treat Alzheimer's and narcolepsy. Everyone still pays some form of attention all the time, of course—it's basically impossible for humans not to—but the currency in which we pay it, and the goods we get in exchange, have changed dramatically.

Back in 1971, when the web was still twenty years off and the smallest computers were the size of delivery vans, before the founders of Google had even managed to get themselves born, the polymath economist Herbert A. Simon wrote maybe the most concise possible description of our modern struggle: "What information consumes is rather obvious: It consumes the attention of its recipients. Hence a wealth of information creates a poverty of attention, and a need to allocate that attention efficiently among the overabundance of information sources that might consume it." As beneficiaries of the greatest information boom in the history of the world, we are suffering, by Simon's logic, a correspondingly serious poverty of attention.

If the pundits clogging my RSS reader can be trusted (the ones I check up on occasionally when I don't have any new e-mail), our attention crisis is already chewing its hyperactive way through the very foundations of Western civilization. Google is making us stupid, multitasking is draining our souls, and the "dumbest generation" is leading us into a "dark age" of bookless "power browsing." Adopting the Internet as the hub of our work, play, and commerce has been the intellectual equivalent of adopting corn syrup as the center of our national diet, and we've all become mentally obese. Formerly well-rounded adults are forced to MacGyver worldviews out of telegraphic blog posts, bits of YouTube videos, and the first nine words of *Times* editorials. Schoolkids spread their attention across 30 different programs at once and interact with each other mainly as sweatless avatars. (One recent study found that American teenagers spend an average of 6.5 hours a day focused on the electronic world, which strikes me as a little low; in South Korea, the most wired nation on earth, young adults have actually died from exhaustion after multiday online-gaming marathons.) We are, in short, terminally distracted. And *distracted,* the alarmists will remind you, was once a synonym for *insane*. (Shakespeare: "poverty hath distracted her.")

The most advanced Buddhist monks become world-class multitaskers. Meditation might speed up their mental processes enough to handle information overload.

This doomsaying strikes me as silly for two reasons. First, conservative social critics have been blowing the apocalyptic bugle at every large-scale tech-driven social change since Socrates' famous complaint about the memory-destroying properties of that newfangled technology called "writing." (A complaint we remember, not incidentally, because it was written down.) And, more practically, the virtual horse has already left the digital barn. It's too late to just retreat to a quieter time. Our jobs depend on connectivity. Our pleasure-cycles—no trivial matter—are increasingly tied to it. Information rains down faster and thicker every day, and there are plenty of non-moronic reasons for it to do so. The question, now, is how successfully we can adapt.

Although attention is often described as an organ system, it's not the sort of thing you can pull out and study like a spleen. It's a complex process that shows up all over the brain, mingling inextricably with other quasi-mystical processes like emotion, memory, identity, will, motivation, and mood. Psychologists have always had to track attention second-hand. Before the sixties, they measured it through easy-to-monitor senses like vision and hearing (if you listen to one voice in your right ear and another in your left, how much information can you absorb from either side?), then eventually graduated to PET scans and EEGs and electrodes and monkey brains. Only in the last ten years—thanks to neuroscientists and their functional MRIs—have we been able to watch the attending human brain in action, with its coordinated storms of neural firing, rapid blood surges, and oxygen flows. This has yielded all kinds of fascinating insights—for instance, that when forced to multitask, the overloaded brain shifts its processing from the hippocampus (responsible for memory) to the striatum (responsible for rote tasks), making it hard to learn a task or even recall what you've been doing once you're done.

When I reach David Meyer, one of the world's reigning experts on multitasking, he is feeling alert against all reasonable odds. He has just returned from India, where he was discussing the nature of attention at a conference with the Dalai Lama (Meyer gave a keynote speech arguing that Buddhist monks multitask during meditation), and his trip home was hellish: a canceled flight, an overnight taxi on roads so rough it took thirteen hours to go 200 miles. This is his first full day back in his office at the University of Michigan, where he directs the Brain, Cognition, and Action Laboratory—a basement space in which finger-tapping, card-memorizing, tone-identifying subjects help Meyer pinpoint exactly how much information the human brain can handle at once. He's been up since 3 A.M. and has by now goosed his attention several times with liquid stimulants: a couple of cups of coffee, some tea. "It does wonders," he says.

My interaction with Meyer takes place entirely via the technology of distraction. We scheduled and rescheduled our appointment, several times, by e-mail. His voice is now projecting, tinnily, out of my cell phone's speaker and into the microphone of my digital recorder, from which I will download it, as soon as we're done, onto my laptop, which I currently have open on my desk in front of me, with several windows spread across the screen, each bearing nested tabs, on one of which I've been reading, before Meyer even had a chance to tell me about it, a blog all about his conference with the Dalai Lama, complete with RSS feed and audio commentary and embedded YouTube videos and pictures of His Holiness. As Meyer and I talk, the universe tests us with a small battery of distractions. A maximum-volume fleet of emergency vehicles passes just outside my window; my phone chirps to tell us that my mother is calling on the other line, then beeps again to let us know she's left a message. There is, occasionally, a slight delay in the connection. Meyer ignores it all, speaking deliberately and at length, managing to coordinate tricky subject-verb agreements over the course of multi-clause sentences. I begin, a little sheepishly, with a question that strikes me as sensationalistic, nonscientific, and probably unanswerable by someone who's been professionally trained in the discipline of cautious objectivity: Are we living through a crisis of attention?

Before I even have a chance to apologize, Meyer responds with the air of an Old Testament prophet. "Yes," he says. "And I think it's going to get a lot worse than people expect." He sees our distraction as a full-blown epidemic—a cognitive plague that has the potential to wipe out an entire generation of focused and productive thought. He compares it, in fact, to smoking. "People aren't aware what's happening to their mental processes," he says, "in the same way that people years ago couldn't look into their lungs and see the residual deposits."

I ask him if, as the world's foremost expert on multitasking and distraction, he has found his own life negatively affected by the new world order of multitasking and distraction.

"Yep," he says immediately, then adds, with admirable (although slightly hurtful) bluntness: "I get calls all the time from people like you. Because of the way the Internet works, once you become visible, you're approached from left and right by people wanting to have interactions in ways that are extremely time-consuming. I could spend my whole day, my whole night, just answering e-mails. I just can't deal with it all. None of this happened even ten years ago. It was a lot calmer. There was a lot of opportunity for getting steady work done."

Over the last twenty years, Meyer and a host of other researchers have proved again and again that multitasking, at least as our culture has come to know and love and institutionalize it, is a myth. When you think you're doing two things at once, you're almost always just switching rapidly between them, leaking a little mental efficiency with every switch.

Meyer says that this is because, to put it simply, the brain processes different kinds of information on a variety of separate "channels"—a language channel, a visual channel, an auditory channel, and so on—each of which can process only one stream of information at a time. If you overburden a channel, the brain becomes inefficient and mistake-prone. The classic example is driving while talking on a cell phone, two tasks that conflict across a range of obvious channels: Steering and dialing are both manual tasks, looking out the windshield and reading a phone screen are both visual, etc. Even talking on a hands-free phone can be dangerous, Meyer says. If the person on the other end of the phone is describing a visual scene—say, the layout of a room full of furniture—that conversation can actually occupy your visual channel enough to impair your ability to see what's around you on the road.

The only time multitasking does work efficiently, Meyer says, is when multiple simple tasks operate on entirely separate channels—for example, folding laundry (a visual-manual task) while listening to a stock report (a verbal task). But real-world scenarios that fit those specifications are very rare.

This is troubling news, obviously, for a culture of Black-Berrys and news crawls and Firefox tabs—tools that, critics argue, force us all into a kind of elective ADHD. The tech theorist Linda Stone famously coined the phrase "continuous partial attention" to describe our newly frazzled state of mind. American office workers don't stick with any single task for more than a few minutes at a time; if left uninterrupted, they will most likely interrupt themselves. Since every interruption costs around 25 minutes of productivity, we spend nearly a third of our day recovering from them. We keep an average of eight windows open on our computer screens at one time and skip between them every twenty seconds. When we read online, we hardly even read at all—our eyes run down the page in an *F* pattern, scanning for keywords. When you add up all the leaks from these constant little switches, soon you're hemorrhaging a dangerous amount of mental power. People who frequently check their e-mail have tested as less intelligent than people who are actually high on marijuana. Meyer guesses that the damage will take decades to understand, let alone fix. If Einstein were alive today, he says, he'd probably be forced to multitask so relentlessly in the Swiss patent office that he'd never get a chance to work out the theory of relativity.

II. The War on the Poverty of Attention

For Winifred Gallagher, the author of *Rapt,* a new book about the power of attention, it all comes down to the problem of jackhammers. A few minutes before I called, she tells me, a construction crew started jackhammering outside her apartment window. The noise immediately captured what's called her bottom-up attention—the broad involuntary awareness that roams the world constantly looking for danger and rewards: shiny objects, sudden movements, pungent smells. Instead of letting this distract her, however, she made a conscious choice to go into the next room and summon her top-down

attention—the narrow, voluntary focus that allows us to isolate and enhance some little slice of the world while ruthlessly suppressing everything else.

This attentional self-control, which psychologists call executive function, is at the very center of our struggle with attention. It's what allows us to invest our focus wisely or poorly. Some of us, of course, have an easier time with it than others.

Gallagher admits that she's been blessed with a naturally strong executive function. "It sounds funny," she tells me, "but I've always thought of paying attention as a kind of sexy, visceral activity. Even as a kid, I enjoyed focusing. I could feel it in almost a mentally muscular way. I took a lot of pleasure in concentrating on things. I'm the sort of irritating person who can sit down to work at nine o'clock and look up at two o'clock and say, 'Oh, I thought it was around 10:30.'"

Gallagher became obsessed with the problem of attention five years ago, when she was diagnosed with advanced and aggressive breast cancer. She was devastated, naturally, but then realized, on her way out of the hospital, that even the cancer could be seen largely as a problem of focus—a terrifying, deadly, internal jackhammer. It made her realize, she says, that attention was "not just a latent ability, it was something you could marshal and use as a tool." By the time she reached her subway station, Gallagher had come up with a strategy: She would make all the big pressing cancer-related decisions as quickly as possible, then, in order to maximize whatever time she had left, consciously shift her attention to more positive, productive things.

One of the projects Gallagher worked on during her recovery (she is now cancer free) was *Rapt,* which is both a survey of recent attention research and a testimonial to the power of top-down focus. The ability to positively wield your attention comes off, in the book, as something of a panacea; Gallagher describes it as "the sine qua non of the quality of life and the key to improving virtually every aspect of your experience." It is, in other words, the Holy Grail of self-help: the key to relationships and parenting and mood disorders and weight problems. (You can apparently lose seven pounds in a year through the sheer force of paying attention to your food.)

"You can't be happy all the time," Gallagher tells me, "but you can pretty much focus all the time. That's about as good as it gets."

The most promising solution to our attention problem, in Gallagher's mind, is also the most ancient: meditation. Neuroscientists have become obsessed, in recent years, with Buddhists, whose attentional discipline can apparently confer all kinds of benefits even on non-Buddhists. (Some psychologists predict that, in the same way we go out for a jog now, in the future we'll all do daily 20- to 30-minute "secular attentional workouts.") Meditation can make your attention less "sticky," able to notice images flashing by in such quick succession that regular brains would miss them. It has also been shown to elevate your mood, which can then recursively stoke your attention: Research shows that positive emotions cause your visual field to expand. The brains of Buddhist monks asked to meditate on "unconditional loving-kindness and compassion" show instant and remarkable changes: Their left prefrontal cortices (responsible for positive emotions) go into overdrive, they produce gamma waves 30 times more powerful than novice meditators, and their wave activity is coordinated in a way often seen in patients under anesthesia.

Gallagher stresses that because attention is a limited resource—one psychologist has calculated that we can attend to only 110 bits of information per second, or 173 billion bits in an average lifetime—our moment-by-moment choice of attentional targets determines, in a very real sense, the shape of our lives. *Rapt*'s epigraph comes from the psychologist and philosopher William James: "My experience is what I agree to attend to." For Gallagher, everything comes down to that one big choice: investing your attention wisely or not. The jackhammers are everywhere—iPhones, e-mail, cancer—and Western culture's attentional crisis is mainly a widespread failure to ignore them.

It's possible that we're evolving toward a new techno-cognitive nomadism, in which restlessness will be an advantage.

"Once you understand how attention works and how you can make the most productive use of it," she says, "if you continue to just jump in the air every time your phone rings or pounce on those buttons every time you get an instant message, that's not the machine's fault. That's your fault."

Making the responsible attention choice, however, is not always easy. Here is a partial list, because a complete one would fill the entire magazine, of the things I've been distracted by in the course of writing this article: my texting wife, a very loud seagull, my mother calling from Mexico to leave voice mails in terrible Spanish, a man shouting "Your weed-whacker fell off! Your weed-whacker fell off!" at a truck full of lawn equipment, my *Lost*-watching wife, another man singing some kind of Spanish ballad on the sidewalk under my window, streaming video of the NBA playoffs, dissertation-length blog breakdowns of the NBA playoffs, my toenail spontaneously detaching, my ice-cream-eating wife, the subtly shifting landscapes of my three different e-mail in-boxes, my Facebooking wife, infinite YouTube videos (a puffin attacking someone wearing a rubber boot, Paul McCartney talking about the death of John Lennon, a chimpanzee playing Pac-Man), and even more infinite, if that is possible, Wikipedia entries: puffins, *MacGyver,* Taylorism, the phrase "bleeding edge," the Boston Molasses Disaster. (If I were going to excuse you from reading this article for any single distraction, which I am not, it would be to read about the Boston Molasses Disaster.)

When the jackhammers fire up outside my window, in other words, I rarely ignore them—I throw the window open, watch for a while, bring the crew sandwiches on their lunch break, talk with them about the ins and outs of jackhammering, and then spend an hour or two trying to break up a little of the sidewalk

myself. Some of my distractions were unavoidable. Some were necessary work-related evils that got out of hand. Others were pretty clearly inexcusable. (I consider it a victory for the integrity of pre-web human consciousness that I was able to successfully resist clicking on the first "related video" after the chimp, the evocatively titled "Guy shits himself in a judo exhibition.") In today's attentional landscape, it's hard to draw neat borders.

I'm not ready to blame my restless attention entirely on a faulty willpower. Some of it is pure impersonal behaviorism. The Internet is basically a Skinner box engineered to tap right into our deepest mechanisms of addiction. As B. F. Skinner's army of lever-pressing rats and pigeons taught us, the most irresistible reward schedule is not, counterintuitively, the one in which we're rewarded constantly but something called "variable ratio schedule," in which the rewards arrive at random. And that randomness is practically the Internet's defining feature: It dispenses its never-ending little shots of positivity—a life-changing e-mail here, a funny YouTube video there—in gloriously unpredictable cycles. It seems unrealistic to expect people to spend all day clicking reward bars—searching the web, scanning the relevant blogs, checking e-mail to see if a coworker has updated a project—and then just leave those distractions behind, as soon as they're not strictly required, to engage in "healthy" things like books and ab crunches and undistracted deep conversations with neighbors. It would be like requiring employees to take a few hits of opium throughout the day, then being surprised when it becomes a problem. Last year, an editorial in the *American Journal of Psychiatry* raised the prospect of adding "Internet addiction" to the *DSM,* which would make it a disorder to be taken as seriously as schizophrenia.

A quintessentially Western solution to the attention problem—one that neatly circumvents the issue of willpower—is to simply dope our brains into focus. We've done so, over the centuries, with substances ranging from tea to tobacco to NoDoz to Benzedrine, and these days the tradition seems to be approaching some kind of zenith with the rise of neuroenhancers: drugs designed to treat ADHD (Ritalin, Adderall), Alzheimer's (Aricept), and narcolepsy (Provigil) that can produce, in healthy people, superhuman states of attention. A grad-school friend tells me that Adderall allowed him to squeeze his mind "like a muscle." Joshua Foer, writing in *Slate* after a weeklong experiment with Adderall, said the drug made him feel like he'd "been bitten by a radioactive spider"—he beat his unbeatable brother at Ping-Pong, solved anagrams, devoured dense books. "The part of my brain that makes me curious about whether I have new e-mails in my in-box apparently shut down," he wrote.

Although neuroenhancers are currently illegal to use without a prescription, they're popular among college students (on some campuses, up to 25 percent of students admitted to taking them) and—if endless anecdotes can be believed—among a wide spectrum of other professional focusers: journalists on deadline, doctors performing high-stakes surgeries, competitors in poker tournaments, researchers suffering through the grind of grant-writing. There has been controversy in the chess world recently about drug testing at tournaments.

In December, a group of scientists published a paper in *Nature* that argued for the legalization and mainstream acceptance of neuroenhancers, suggesting that the drugs are really no different from more traditional "cognitive enhancers" such as laptops, exercise, nutrition, private tutoring, reading, and sleep. It's not quite that simple, of course. Adderall users frequently complain that the drug stifles their creativity—that it's best for doing ultrarational, structured tasks. (As Foer put it, "I had a nagging suspicion that I was thinking with blinders on.") One risk the scientists do acknowledge is the fascinating, horrifying prospect of "raising cognitive abilities beyond their species-typical upper bound." Ultimately, one might argue, neuroenhancers spring from the same source as the problem they're designed to correct: our lust for achievement in defiance of natural constraints. It's easy to imagine an endless attentional arms race in which new technologies colonize ever-bigger zones of our attention, new drugs expand the limits of that attention, and so on.

One of the most exciting—and confounding—solutions to the problem of attention lies right at the intersection of our willpower and our willpower-sapping technologies: the grassroots Internet movement known as "lifehacking." It began in 2003 when the British tech writer Danny O'Brien, frustrated by his own lack of focus, polled 70 of his most productive friends to see how they managed to get so much done; he found that they'd invented all kinds of clever little tricks—some high-tech, some very low-tech—to help shepherd their attention from moment to moment: ingenious script codes for to-do lists, software hacks for managing e-mail, rituals to avoid sinister time-wasting traps such as "yak shaving," the tendency to lose yourself in endless trivial tasks tangentially related to the one you really need to do. (O'Brien wrote a program that prompts him every ten minutes, when he's online, to ask if he's procrastinating.) Since then, lifehacking has snowballed into a massive self-help program, written and revised constantly by the online global hive mind, that seeks to help you allocate your attention efficiently. Tips range from time-management habits (the 90-second shower) to note-taking techniques (mind mapping) to software shortcuts (how to turn your Gmail into a to-do list) to delightfully retro tech solutions (turning an index card into a portable dry-erase board by covering it with packing tape).

When I call Merlin Mann, one of lifehacking's early adopters and breakout stars, he is running late, rushing back to his office, and yet he seems somehow to have attention to spare. He is by far the fastest-talking human I've ever interviewed, and it crosses my mind that this too might be a question of productivity—that maybe he's adopted a time-saving verbal lifehack from auctioneers. He talks in the snappy aphorisms of a professional speaker ("Priorities are like arms: If you have more than two of them, they're probably make-believe") and is always breaking ideas down into their atomic parts and reassessing the way they fit together: "What does it come down to?" "Here's the thing." "So why am I telling you this, and what does it have to do with lifehacks?"

Mann says he got into lifehacking at a moment of crisis, when he was "feeling really overwhelmed by the number of inputs in my life and managing it very badly." He founded one of the original lifehacking websites, 43folders.com (the name is a reference to David Allen's Getting Things Done, the legendarily complex productivity program in which Allen describes, among other things, how to build a kind of "three-dimensional calendar" out of 43 folders) and went on to invent such illustrious hacks as "in-box zero" (an e-mail-management technique) and the "hipster PDA" (a stack of three-by-five cards filled with jotted phone numbers and to-do lists, clipped together and tucked into your back pocket). Mann now makes a living speaking to companies as a kind of productivity guru. He Twitters, podcasts, and runs more than half a dozen websites.

Despite his robust web presence, Mann is skeptical about technology's impact on our lives. "Is it clear to you that the last fifteen years represent an enormous improvement in how everything operates?" he asks. "Picasso was somehow able to finish the *Desmoiselles of Avignon* even though he didn't have an application that let him tag his to-dos. If John Lennon had a BlackBerry, do you think he would have done everything he did with the Beatles in less than ten years?"

One of the weaknesses of lifehacking as a weapon in the war against distraction, Mann admits, is that it tends to become extremely distracting. You can spend solid days reading reviews of filing techniques and organizational software. "On the web, there's a certain kind of encouragement to never ask yourself how much information you really need," he says. "But when I get to the point where I'm seeking advice twelve hours a day on how to take a nap, or what kind of notebook to buy, I'm so far off the idea of lifehacks that it's indistinguishable from where we started. There are a lot of people out there that find this a very sticky idea, and there's very little advice right now to tell them that the only thing to do is action, and everything else is horseshit. My wife reminds me sometimes: 'You have all the information you need to do *something* right now.'"

For Mann, many of our attention problems are symptoms of larger existential issues: motivation, happiness, neurochemistry. "I'm not a physician or a psychiatrist, but I'll tell you, I think a lot of it is some form of untreated ADHD or depression," he says. "Your mind is not getting the dopamine or the hugs that it needs to keep you focused on what you're doing. And any time your work gets a little bit too hard or a little bit too boring, you allow it to catch on to something that's more interesting to you." (Mann himself started getting treated for ADD a year ago; he says it's helped his focus quite a lot.)

Mann's advice can shade, occasionally, into Buddhist territory. "There's no shell script, there's no fancy pen, there's no notebook or nap or Firefox extension or hack that's gonna help you figure out why the fuck you're here," he tells me. "That's on you. This makes me sound like one of those people who swindled the Beatles, but if you are having attention problems, the best way to deal with it is by admitting it and then saying, 'From now on, I'm gonna be in the moment and more cognizant.' I said not long ago, I think on Twitter—God, I quote myself a lot, what an asshole—that really all self-help is Buddhism with a service mark."

"Where you allow your attention to go ultimately says more about you as a human being than anything that you put in your mission statement," he continues. "It's an indisputable receipt for your existence. And if you allow that to be squandered by other people who are as bored as you are, it's gonna say a lot about who you are as a person."

III. Embracing the Poverty of Attention

Sometimes I wonder if the time I'm wasting is actually being wasted. Isn't blowing a couple of hours on the Internet, in the end, just another way of following your attention? My life would be immeasurably poorer if I hadn't stumbled a few weeks ago across the Boston Molasses Disaster. (Okay, seriously, forget it: I hereby release you to go look up the Boston Molasses Disaster. A giant wave of molasses destroyed an entire Boston neighborhood 90 years ago, swallowing horses and throwing an elevated train off its track. It took months to scrub all the molasses out of the cobblestones! The harbor was brown until summer! The world is a stranger place than we will ever know.)

The prophets of total attentional melt-down sometimes invoke, as an example of the great culture we're going to lose as we succumb to e-thinking, the canonical French juggernaut Marcel Proust. And indeed, at seven volumes, several thousand pages, and 1.5 million words, *Á la Recherche du Temps Perdu* is in many ways the anti-Twitter. (It would take, by the way, exactly 68,636 tweets to reproduce.) It's important to remember, however, that the most famous moment in all of Proust, the moment that launches the entire monumental project, is a moment of pure distraction: when the narrator, Marcel, eats a spoonful of tea-soaked madeleine and finds himself instantly transported back to the world of his childhood. Proust makes it clear that conscious focus could never have yielded such profound magic: Marcel has to abandon the constraints of what he calls "voluntary memory"— the kind of narrow, purpose-driven attention that Adderall, say, might have allowed him to harness—in order to get to the deeper truths available only by distraction. That famous cookie is a kind of hyperlink: a little blip that launches an associative cascade of a million other subjects. This sort of free-associative wandering is essential to the creative process; one moment of judicious unmindfulness can inspire thousands of hours of mindfulness.

My favorite focusing exercise comes from William James: Draw a dot on a piece of paper, then pay attention to it for as long as you can. (Sitting in my office one afternoon, with my monkey mind swinging busily across the lush rain forest of online distractions, I tried this with the closest dot in the vicinity: the bright-red mouse-nipple at the center of my laptop's keyboard. I managed to stare at it for 30 minutes, with mixed results.) James argued that the human mind can't actually focus on the dot, or any unchanging object, for more than a few seconds at a time: It's too hungry for variety, surprise, the adventure of the unknown. It has to refresh its attention by continually finding new aspects of the dot to focus on: subtleties of its shape, its relationship to the edges of the paper,

metaphorical associations (a fly, an eye, a hole). The exercise becomes a question less of pure unwavering focus than of your ability to organize distractions around a central point. The dot, in other words, becomes only the hub of your total dot-related distraction.

This is what the web-threatened punditry often fails to recognize: Focus is a paradox—it has distraction built into it. The two are symbiotic; they're the systole and diastole of consciousness. Attention comes from the Latin "to stretch out" or "reach toward," distraction from "to pull apart." We need both. In their extreme forms, focus and attention may even circle back around and bleed into one other. Meyer says there's a subset of Buddhists who believe that the most advanced monks become essentially "world-class multitaskers"—that all those years of meditation might actually speed up their mental processes enough to handle the kind of information overload the rest of us find crippling.

The truly wise mind will harness, rather than abandon, the power of distraction. Unwavering focus—the inability to be distracted—can actually be just as problematic as ADHD. Trouble with "attentional shift" is a feature common to a handful of mental illnesses, including schizophrenia and OCD. It's been hypothesized that ADHD might even be an advantage in certain change-rich environments. Researchers have discovered, for instance, that a brain receptor associated with ADHD is unusually common among certain nomads in Kenya, and that members who have the receptor are the best nourished in the group. It's possible that we're all evolving toward a new techno-cognitive nomadism, a rapidly shifting environment in which restlessness will be an advantage again. The deep focusers might even be hampered by having too much attention: Attention Surfeit Hypoactivity Disorder.

I keep returning to the parable of Einstein and Lennon— the great historical geniuses hypothetically ruined by modern distraction. What made both men's achievements so groundbreaking, though, was that they did something modern technology is getting increasingly better at allowing us to do: They very powerfully linked and synthesized things that had previously been unlinked—Newtonian gravity and particle physics, rock and blues and folk and doo-wop and bubblegum pop and psychedelia. If Einstein and Lennon were growing up today, their natural genius might be so pumped up on the possibilities of the new technology they'd be doing even more dazzling things. Surely Lennon would find a way to manipulate his BlackBerry to his own ends, just like he did with all the new technology of the sixties—he'd harvest spam and text messages and web snippets and build them into a new kind of absurd poetry. The Beatles would make the best viral videos of all time, simultaneously addictive and artful, disposable and forever. All of those canonical songs, let's remember, were created entirely within a newfangled mass genre that was widely considered to be an assault on civilization and the sanctity of deep human thought. Standards change. They change because of great creations in formerly suspect media.

Which brings me, finally, to the next generation of attenders, the so-called "net-gen" or "digital natives," kids who've grown up with the Internet and other time-slicing technologies. There's been lots of hand-wringing about all the skills they might lack, mainly the ability to concentrate on a complex task from beginning to end, but surely they can already do things their elders can't—like conduct 34 conversations simultaneously across six different media, or pay attention to switching between attentional targets in a way that's been considered impossible. More than any other organ, the brain is designed to change based on experience, a feature called neuroplasticity. London taxi drivers, for instance, have enlarged hippocampi (the brain region for memory and spatial processing)—a neural reward for paying attention to the tangle of the city's streets. As we become more skilled at the 21st-century task Meyer calls "flitting," the wiring of the brain will inevitably change to deal more efficiently with more information. The neuroscientist Gary Small speculates that the human brain might be changing faster today than it has since the prehistoric discovery of tools. Research suggests we're already picking up new skills: better peripheral vision, the ability to sift information rapidly. We recently elected the first-ever BlackBerry president, able to flit between sixteen national crises while focusing at a world-class level. Kids growing up now might have an associative genius we don't—a sense of the way ten projects all dovetail into something totally new. They might be able to engage in seeming contradictions: mindful web-surfing, mindful Twittering. Maybe, in flights of irresponsible responsibility, they'll even manage to attain the paradoxical, Zenlike state of focused distraction.

Critical Thinking

1. Explain how a wealth of information creates a poverty of attention.

2. Identify simple tasks you can perform together where multitasking is efficient.

3. Defend meditation as a solution to our attention problems.

Create Central

www.mhhe.com/createcentral

Internet References

Information Overload or Attention Deficiency?
www.sambemer.com/documents/KM/infoglut.pdf

Recovering from Information Overload
www.mckinsey.com/insights/organization

The Net, Info Overload, and Our Fragmented Attention Spans
http://techliberation.com/2011/03/16

Article   Prepared by: Karen L. Freiberg, *University of Maryland*

What I've Learned

We can't keep politics out of school reform. Why I'm launching a national movement to transform education.

MICHELLE RHEE

Learning Outcomes

After reading this article, you will be able to:

- Explain why a child's relationship with his/her teacher matters in education.

- Describe the changes Michelle Rhee wants to see in public schools.

After my boss, Washington, D.C., mayor Adrian Fenty, lost his primary in September, I was stunned. I had never imagined he wouldn't win the contest, given the progress that was visible throughout the city—the new recreation centers, the turnaround of once struggling neighborhoods, and, yes, the improvements in the schools. Three and a half years ago, when I first met with Fenty about becoming chancellor of the D.C. public-school system, I had warned him that he wouldn't want to hire me. If we did the job right for the city's children, I told him, it would upset the status quo—I was sure I would be a political problem. But Fenty was adamant. He said he would back me—and my changes—100 percent. He never wavered, and I convinced myself the public would see the progress and want it to continue. But now I have no doubt this cost him the election.

The timing couldn't have been more ironic. The new movie *Waiting for Superman*—which aimed to generate public passion for school reform the way *An Inconvenient Truth* had for climate change—premiered in Washington the night after the election. The film championed the progress Fenty and I had been making in the District, and lamented the roadblocks we'd faced from the teachers' union. In the pro-reform crowd, you could feel the shock that voters had just rejected this mayor and, to some extent, the reforms in their schools.

When I started as chancellor in 2007, I never had any illusions about how tough it would be to turn around a failing system like D.C.'s; the city had gone through seven chancellors in the 10 years before me. While I had to make many structural changes—overhauling the system for evaluating teachers and principals, adopting new reading and math programs, making

sure textbooks got delivered on time—I believed the hardest thing would be changing the culture. We had to raise the expectations that people had about what was possible for our kids.

I quickly announced a plan to close almost two dozen schools, which provoked community outrage. We cut the central office administration in half. And I also proposed a new contract for teachers that would increase their salaries dramatically if they abandoned the tenure system and agreed to be paid based on their effectiveness.

Though all of these actions caused turmoil in the district, they were long overdue and reaped benefits quickly. In my first two years in office, the D.C. schools went from being the worst performing on the National Assessment of Educational Progress examination, the national test, to leading the nation in gains at both the fourth and eighth grade in reading as well as math. By this school year we reversed a trend of declining enrollment and increased the number of families choosing District schools for the first time in 41 years.

Because of results like these, I have no regrets about moving so fast. So much needed to be fixed, and there were times when I know it must have felt overwhelming to the teachers because we were trying to fix everything at once. But from my point of view, waiting meant that another year was going by when kids were not getting the education they deserved.

My comments about ineffective teachers were often perceived as an attack on all teachers.

I know people say I wasn't good enough at building consensus, but I don't think consensus can be the goal. Take, for example, one of our early boiling points: school closures. We held dozens of community meetings about the issue. But would people really have been happier with the results if we had done it more slowly? I talked to someone from another district that spent a year and a half defining the criteria that outlined which schools would close. But when the results were announced, everyone went nuts. They had seen the criteria. What did they think was going to happen? That's when I realized there is no good way to close a school.

Still, I could have done a better job of communicating. I did a particularly bad job letting the many good teachers know that I considered them to be the most important part of the equation. I should have said to the effective teachers, "You don't have anything to worry about. My job is to make your life better, offer you more support, and pay you more." I totally fell down on doing that. As a result, my comments about ineffective teachers were often perceived as an attack on all teachers. I also underestimated how much teachers would be relying on the blogs, random rumors, and innuendo. Over the last 18 to 24 months, I held teacher-listening sessions a couple of times a week. But fear was already locked in. In the end, the changes that we needed to make meant that some teachers and principals would lose their jobs in a punishing economy. I don't know if there was any good way to do that.

Some people believed I had disdain for the public. I read a quote where a woman said it seemed like I was listening, but I didn't do what she told me to do. There's a big difference there. It's not that I wasn't listening; I just didn't agree and went in a different direction. There's no way you can please everyone.

But it's true that I didn't do enough to bring parents along, either. I saw a poll of people who live in a part of the city where the schools experienced a significant turnaround, and everyone agreed that they were overwhelmingly much better now. But when they were asked, did we need to fire the teachers to see this turnaround, they said no. We didn't connect the dots for them.

After the shock of Fenty's loss, it became clear to me that the best way to keep the reform going in the D.C. schools was for me to leave my job as chancellor. That was tough for me to accept. I called the decision heartbreaking, and I meant it, because there is a piece of my heart in every classroom, and always will be. To this day, I get mail from D.C. parents and kids who say, "Why did you leave us? The job wasn't done. Why did you give up on us?" Those kinds of letters are really hard to read and respond to. I loved that job. But I felt that Mayor-elect Vincent Gray should have the same ability that Fenty had to appoint his own chancellor. And I knew I had become a lightning rod and excuse for the anti-reformers to oppose the changes that had to be made.

After stepping down, I had a chance to reflect on the challenges facing our schools today and the possible solutions. The truth is that despite a handful of successful reforms, the state of American education is pitiful, and getting worse. Spending on schools has more than doubled in the last three decades, but the increased resources haven't produced better results. The U.S. is currently 21st, 23rd, and 25th among 30 developed nations in science, reading, and math, respectively. The children in our schools today will be the first generation of Americans who will be less educated than the previous generation.

When you think about how things happen in our country—how laws get passed or policies are made—they happen through the exertion of influence. From the National Rifle Association to the pharmaceutical industry to the tobacco lobby, powerful interests put pressure on our elected officials and government institutions to sway or stop change.

The truth is, the state of American education is pitiful, and it's getting worse.

Education is no different. We have text-book manufacturers, teachers' unions, and even food vendors that work hard to dictate and determine policy. The public-employee unions in D.C., including the teachers' union, spent huge sums of money to defeat Fenty. In fact, the new chapter president has said his No. 1 priority is job security for teachers, but there is no big organized interest group that defends and promotes the interests of children.

You can see the impact of this dynamic playing out every day. Policymakers, school-district administrators, and school boards who are beholden to special interests have created a bureaucracy that is focused on the adults instead of the students. Go to any public-school-board meeting in the country and you'll rarely hear the words "children," "students," or "kids" uttered. Instead, the focus remains on what jobs, contracts, and departments are getting which cuts, additions, or changes. The rationale for the decisions mostly rests on which grown-ups will be affected, instead of what will benefit or harm children.

The teachers' unions get the blame for much of this. Elected officials, parents, and administrators implore them to "embrace change" and "accept reform." But I don't think the unions can or should change. The purpose of the teachers' union is to protect the privileges, priorities, and pay of their members. And they're doing a great job of that.

What that means is that the reform community has to exert influence as well. That's why I've decided to start StudentsFirst, a national movement to transform public education in our country. We need a new voice to change the balance of power in public education. Our mission is to defend and promote the interests of children so that America has the best education system in the world.

From the moment I resigned, I began hearing from citizens from across this country. I got e-mails, calls, and letters from parents, students, and teachers who said, "Don't give up. We need you to keep fighting!" Usually, they'd then share with me a story about how the education system in their community was not giving students what they need or deserve. I got one e-mail from two people who have been trying to open a charter school in Florida and have been stopped every step of the way by the school district. No voices have moved me more than those of teachers. So many great teachers in this country are frustrated with the schools they are working in, the bureaucratic rules that bind them, and the hostility to excellence that pervades our education system.

We're hoping to sign up 1 million StudentsFirst members and raise $1 billion in our first year.

The common thread in all of these communications was that these courageous people felt alone in battling the bureaucracy.

They want help and advocates. There are enough people out there who understand and believe that kids deserve better, but until now, there has been no organization for them. We'll ask people across the country to join StudentsFirst—we're hoping to sign up 1 million members and raise $1 billion in our first year.

StudentsFirst will work so that great teachers can make a tremendous difference for students of every background. We believe every family can choose an excellent school—attending a great school should be a matter of fact, not luck. We'll fight against ineffective instructional programs and bureaucracy so that public dollars go where they make the biggest difference: to effective instructional programs. Parent and family involvement are key to increased student achievement, but the entire community must be engaged in the effort to improve our schools.

Though we'll be nonpartisan, we can't pretend that education reform isn't political. So we'll put pressure on elected officials and press for changes in legislation to make things better for kids. And we'll support and endorse school-board candidates and politicians—in city halls, statehouses, and the U.S. Congress—who want to enact policies around our legislative agenda. We'll support any candidate who's reform-minded, regardless of political party, so reform won't just be a few courageous politicians experimenting in isolated locations; it'll be a powerful, nationwide movement.

Lastly, we can't shy away from conflict. I was at Harvard the other day, and someone asked about a statement that Secretary of Education Arne Duncan and others have made that public-school reform is the civil-rights issue of our generation. Well, during the civil-rights movement they didn't work everything out by sitting down collaboratively and compromising. Conflict was necessary in order to move the agenda forward. There are some fundamental disagreements that exist right now about what kind of progress is possible and what strategies will be most effective. Right now, what we need to do is fight. We can be respectful about it. But this is the time to stand up and say what you believe, not sweep the issues under the rug so that we can feel good about getting along. There's nothing more worthwhile than fighting for children. And I'm not done fighting.

Critical Thinking

1. What role does politics play in public school education?
2. How do you feel about the "last hired, first fired" policy of unionized workers? Why?
3. Why is public school reform needed in the United States?

Create Central

www.mhhe.com/createcentral

Internet References

Is School Reform Making America Less Competitive?
   www.washingtonpost.com/blogs/answer-sheet/wp/2013/02/06
School Reform: False Assumptions That Drive School Reform
   http://teaching.about.com/od/Parentalinvolvement
StudentsFirst
   www.studentsfirst.org

Rhee, Michelle. From *Newsweek*, December 13, 2010, pp. 38–41. Copyright © 2010 by Michelle Rhee. Reprinted by permission of StudentsFirst. www.studentsfirst.org.

Article   Prepared by: Karen L. Freiberg, *University of Maryland*

Reformed School

Ramón González's Middle School 223 in the Bronx is a model for how an empowered principal can transform a troubled school. But can he maintain that success when the forces of reform are now working against him?

Jonathan Mahler

Learning Outcomes

After reading this article, you will be able to:

- Point out how some educational reforms are preventing schools from succeeding.

- Identify some of Ramón González's traits that led him to be an "empowered" principal.

On a recent morning, Ramón González, the principal of M.S. 223, a public middle school in the South Bronx, arrived at work as usual at 7:30, stripped off his coat and suit jacket, deposited his tea and toast from a nearby diner on the cluttered conference table in his office and hustled down the hallway to the school's back door to greet arriving students. González had a busy agenda for the day. Among other things, he needed to get to work on a proposal for the city's Department of Education to expand 223 into a high school.

At 10, González was finally about to sit down at his computer, when he was interrupted. A young teacher came into his office in tears, unable to figure out what was going on with an eighth grader who had just transferred to 223 from a public school in Florida, was way behind in class and had been wandering around the school's hallways between periods, looking lost. González knew almost nothing about the girl. Like many of his students, she turned up at 223 with no more than a utility bill to prove she lived in the neighborhood. He calmed the teacher and started trying to figure out what was happening. (When he finally reached an administrator at the girl's old school days later, he discovered that she had been classified with a severe learning disability.)

Next, González was informed that the three free books that each of his school's students was entitled to—under a nonprofit program to promote literacy in poor communities—had never arrived. He needed to chase them down. (As it turned out, they wound up at the wrong school.) As he was doing so, he learned that a former teacher who had physically threatened him, members of his faculty and even some students, and whom González had spent years trying to remove from the classroom, was challenging his termination.

There was also the matter of the eye tests. For five straight days, González had been trying to get through to someone at an organization that does free vision tests at public schools and fits children with glasses on the spot. "I can guarantee you right now that at least 20 percent of our kids need glasses," he told me, after leaving yet another message on someone's voice mail to "please, please, *please* call me back." González, a light-skinned, baby-faced Latino, was sitting at a table in his office, his untouched tea and toast in front of him. Hanging on the bulletin board above him were the school's last three report cards from the city, straight A's, and an elaborately color-coded chart tracking all of his 486 students' test scores. "They're in their classrooms right now, staring at blackboards with no idea what they're looking at," he said. "You can have the best teachers, the best curriculum and the greatest after-school programs in the world, but if your kids can't see, what does it matter?"

González has been principal of M.S. 223, on 145th Street near Willis Avenue, since the school's creation in September 2003. One of the first schools opened by Joel Klein, the New York City schools chancellor at the time, 223 was intended to help replace a notoriously bad junior high school that the city had decided to shut down. Thirteen percent of its first incoming class of sixth graders were at grade level in math and just 10 percent were at grade level in English. Last year, after seven years under González, 60 percent of its students tested at or above grade level in math and 30 percent in English. Not something to brag about in most school districts, but those numbers make 223 one of the top middle schools in the South Bronx. According to its latest progress report from the Department of Education, which judges a school's growth against a peer group with similar demographics, 223 is the 10th-best middle school in the entire city.

Success stories like this in high-poverty neighborhoods are becoming more common in the era of charter schools, but 223 is no charter. There is no clamoring of parents trying to game a spot for their kids in a lottery, no screening of applicants, no visits from educators hoping to learn the secret of the school's success, no shadow philanthropist supplying Kindles to all of its students. M.S. 223 is just a regular public school. González isn't even allowed to see the files of incoming students before they arrive. "You know what you have to do to come to school here?" González told me. "Walk through that door."

Late last year, as I was first getting to know González and M.S. 223, I spent some time with Klein during his final days on the job, joining him on a couple of his last school visits and talking to him about his tenure as chancellor.

Now that education reform has become an established national movement, backed by countless multimillionaires and endorsed by President Obama himself, it's easy to forget that Klein was once a lonely pioneer, if not the first chancellor to try to overhaul his schools, then surely the first to undertake such an ambitious effort to do so, and in the city with the largest—1.1 million students—and most complicated school system in the country.

During our conversations, Klein, a former lawyer, cloaked his revolutionary ideology in a technocrat's rhetoric, describing how he implemented "disruptive strategies" designed to transform the city's schools "from a provider-driven system to a consumer-driven one." What he meant was that he turned the city's school system upside down, opening hundreds of new schools and shutting down dozens of others. Individual schools were given control over their own budgets, hiring and curriculums. In exchange, they were expected to earn good grades on their report cards from the city—another Klein innovation—or risk closure.

Klein's successor, Cathleen Black, made it clear that she planned to continue the bold policies that he started implementing after his appointment by Mayor Bloomberg in 2002. (Black has since resigned.) While it may still be too early to evaluate Klein's legacy, some statistics certainly suggest meaningful progress. When Klein started, for instance, less than 50 percent of New York's incoming high-school freshmen were graduating in four years. That number is now 63 percent. Since 2006, according to an analysis of state testing data by the city's Department of Education (which used 2010's recalibrated proficiency levels to compare 2006's testing data to 2010's), the city's elementary and middle schools have seen a 22-point increase in the percentage of students at or above grade level in math (to 54 percent) and a 6-point increase in English (to 42 percent).

At the center of Klein's vision was the notion that New York should not aspire to have a great school system but a system of great schools run by talented and empowered educators. To help reach this goal, Klein created an academy to train principals in the new skills the job would require and dispatched its graduates to the city's most difficult neighborhoods with a mandate for change and the authority and autonomy to try to effect it. "I think one of our core accomplishments is that we transformed the principal from an agent of the bureaucracy to the C.E.O. of his or her school," Klein told me.

I thought about this notion a lot over the course of the months I spent with González at 223. It's an incongruous metaphor to apply to someone whose office overlooks one of the largest, most dangerous housing projects in New York. Still, González has shown the kind of entrepreneurial thinking that, were he a C.E.O., would attract attention: he joined the board of the Randall's Island Sports Foundation in part to gain access to its playing fields, hired a part-time grant writer to raise money for the school, brought in a number of nonprofits to support the school's extracurricular activities and even rented out space in his building to underwrite 223's two-week summer-school program.

In certain respects, 223 is a monument to Klein's success: empower the right principals to run their own schools and watch them bloom. Thanks to Klein, González has been able to avoid having teachers foisted on him on the basis of seniority. He has been able to create his own curriculums, micromanage his students' days (within the narrow confines of the teachers' union contract, anyway) and spend his annual budget of $4 million on the personnel, programs and materials he deems most likely to help his kids.

And yet even as school reform made it possible for González to succeed, as the movement rolls inexorably forward, it also seems in many ways set up to make him fail. The grading system imposed by Klein that has bestowed three consecutive A's on González is based in part on how well 223 does on state tests. But the school's relative success on these tests and other measures also disqualifies him from additional state resources earmarked for failing schools. The ever-growing number of charter schools, often privately subsidized and rarely bound by union rules, that Klein unleashed on the city skims off the neighborhood's more ambitious, motivated families. And every year, as failing schools are shut down around González, a steady stream of children with poor intellectual habits and little family support continues to arrive at 223. González wouldn't want it any other way—he takes pride in his school's duty to educate all comers—but the endless flow of underperforming students drags down test scores, demoralizes teachers and makes the already daunting challenge of transforming 223 into a successful school, not just a relatively successful one, that much more difficult.

The school day at 223 begins at 7:50 A.M. This is 10 minutes before the United Federation of Teachers officially permits New York City public schools to start, which means that every year a majority of 223's teachers has to vote to approve the earlier opening bell. The early start is a way to create more time for after-school programs, especially academic tutoring, before it gets dark and the streets surrounding the school become more threatening. "The research says it's better to start your school day later," González says, referring to studies showing that adolescents often need to get more sleep in order to be at their best. "But those researchers don't live in my neighborhood."

M.S. 223 is in the heart of School District 7, which is part of the poorest Congressional district in the nation. More than 90 percent of its students live in one of five housing projects, most prominently the Patterson Houses, a sprawling complex of 15 towers across the street from the school. About 70 percent of its students are Hispanic, predominantly Puerto Rican and Dominican. The remainder are black, either African-American or recent immigrants from West African countries like Senegal. Roughly 11 percent of the school's students are ELLs, or English-language learners. (Another 60 to 70 percent of its students are former ELLs.) About 17 percent have learning disabilities.

Upon arrival at 223, students pass through a gantlet of smiling teachers. González requires that faculty members stand outside their doors at the start of the school day, part of his effort to set the school off from the grim streets surrounding it. "In our location, kids have to want to come to school," he says. "This is a very sick district. Tuberculosis, AIDS, asthma rates, homeless shelters, mental-health needs—you name the physical or social ill, and we're near the top for the city. Which means that when our kids come to school in the morning, when they come through that door, we have to welcome them."

There's another, no less compelling reason for this policy: posting teachers outside their classrooms helps maintain order in the hallways. It's one of a number of things, like moving students' lockers into their homerooms, that González has done to ensure that kids spend as little time as possible in the halls, where so much middle-school trouble invariably begins. (Chaotic hallways also tend to make for chaotic classrooms.)

Watching students pour into the school, some barely five feet tall, others over six feet, it can be hard to believe that all of 223's kids are within just a few years of one another. This is the nature of middle school, which straddles childhood and adolescence, an awkward period for most children and one of the many reasons that educators will tell you that middle-schoolers are unusually challenging, even in the best of circumstances.

It's hard to say definitively how successful González has been at controlling 223's halls. During the weeks I spent at the school, I never saw anything much more serious than one kid yanking another's backpack, but the wave of students crashing noisily toward their homerooms bore little resemblance to the silent, single-file lines you see in many charter schools.

Those schools have a distinct advantage over 223, though. Their families have already chosen to be at a charter and have often jumped through numerous hoops to get there. This makes it easier for charters to create their own cultures. They can define the length of their days, dictate exactly how children dress and enforce strict codes of conduct. Those students—scholars, in charter parlance—who fall out of line don't last.

Much of what González does involves creating a culture for 223 too, one that he essentially tricks children into embracing. Look closely at just about any aspect of 223, and you will invariably discover a hidden agenda. Students at 223 are required to wear white shirts and blue pants or skirts. González would like all of his boys to dress more formally, but rather than insisting that they wear ties, the custom at many charters, he has encouraged the school's athletes to do so in the hope that the trend would spread. Most charters extend the school day until 5 P.M., an easy way to maximize their influence over students. Traditional public schools, however, are permitted to require that children be in school for only about six hours each day, so González has had to find creative ways to keep kids in the building, for example, mandating that students attend math or English tutoring before participating in after-school sports, clubs and music programs.

Career Day was held at 223 on a Monday morning in late January. Participants, a professionally diverse crowd of about 25, mostly minorities, that included a fashion designer, a corporate lawyer and a parole officer, started assembling at around 9 o'clock in an overheated classroom. A few picked at an unappetizing buffet of cold eggs, dinner rolls and limp, greasy bacon. Most scrolled through their BlackBerrys and waited, with growing impatience, to be told where to go and what to do.

If they expected to deliver a perfunctory description of their jobs, answer a few questions and be done, González had other plans. At about 9:15 he strode into the room and got right to the point. "Some of these kids have never left the Bronx or even the area," he said, casting a stern eye around the group. "For a lot of our kids, this is going to be a life-changing experience, and I want to make sure you see it that way. I'll be out in the hallway cheering you on, keeping that fire going, but I have to stress that this is an opportunity for them, and you don't want to lose it." Then he walked out.

González, who is Cuban and Puerto Rican, has a term for encounters between his students and adults with the potential to affect them: touches. As he describes it, it was a touch that changed the course of his own life when he was in middle school. González was raised in East Harlem by his mother, who supported seven children on welfare. A Puerto Rican stockbroker who volunteered at the Boys' Club where González spent most of his free time took an interest in him and encouraged him to take a test to qualify for a high-school scholarship. González aced the test and was accepted to Middlesex, a prep school outside Boston. "I always had this weird feeling of having one foot in one world and one foot in another," he says. "My financial-aid package paid for me to fly up to Boston, then I'd fly home for vacation and kids in the neighborhood would be getting shot." From Middlesex, he went on to Cornell.

González's background is similar to that of many of his students, and he can personally relate to some of the obstacles that stand in the way of their academic achievement: as a boy, he would take a pillow into the bathtub and close the bathroom door, because it was the only quiet place to read in the apartment. But González had at least one thing going for him. While his father, a veteran who returned from the Vietnam War addicted to heroin, was in and out of jail for much of González's life and ultimately died of AIDS during his senior year at Cornell, he was self-educated and politically aware, a member of the Young Lords, the Puerto Rican equivalent of the Black Panthers. He recognized that his son was bright, and even if he wasn't a provider or a role model, he did have aspirations for his son. He wanted him to go to law school and become a neighborhood defense lawyer.

Instead, after graduating from college and moving back to his old neighborhood, González started working as a math teacher, biding his time and building his résumé until he would be considered qualified to run his own school.

The opportunity to start 223, which began with 150 students, all sixth graders, arose when he was 31. Things got off to an inauspicious start. González initially opened the school in another building with two other South Bronx middle schools, one of which was reserved exclusively for children with special needs. Special-needs students tend to be older and bigger than others at their grade level and often have behavioral issues, a mix that proved problematic for González's students. "My kids were getting their butts kicked," he says. After one such episode led to a broken nose, he decided that he had seen enough. In a freezing rainstorm on Christmas Eve, he found himself personally ferrying 30 computers out of one building and into the empty floor of another, where 223 now resides.

González still lives in East Harlem, a few blocks from where he grew up. Though his son, Laurencio, the oldest of three children, is in kindergarten at a private school on Manhattan's Upper East Side, González told me that he hoped to send him and his two other children to middle school at 223. "That's the goal, to have this school be a place where I'd want to send my own kids."

One frigid night in December, I went with González to watch him give a presentation at a community-education council meeting at an elementary school in the South Bronx. González had recently introduced a literacy initiative at 223, asking all of his parents and children to drop whatever they are doing at 6 o'clock every Thursday night and spend the next two hours reading. As part of the campaign, 223 placed free-book bins in local bodegas, health clinics and Laundromats. Now González was hoping to expand Community Reading Night into a broader, districtwide event.

González was preceded by the school's holiday concert. The moment the performance ended, parents started heading for the door. By the time González rose to speak, the auditorium, nearly full when we arrived, was mostly empty. He had prepared a PowerPoint presentation, but had to abandon it because there was a cord missing. "This community is in crisis," he said. "The literacy test scores that we have in our community are 23 percent. That is a scary number. What that means is that 23 percent of our kids are on pace to graduate from high school and go to college. *Go* to college. That doesn't mean they're going to finish college. Twenty-three percent. We cannot sustain our community on 23 percent. We have to be reading with our children. That's the only way we're going to change this scary statistic." Klein may see González as a chief executive, but González prefers to think of himself as a community activist. His vision for 223 is in some respects anachronistic in the era of school reform. Klein's animating belief, and surely what he will best be remembered for, is the notion that while low-income families may not be able to choose what neighborhood they live in, they should nonetheless be able to choose what school their children attend. It was toward that end that he brought more than 100 charter schools to New York—with at least 100 more still on the way—deliberately concentrating them in high-poverty areas like Harlem and the South Bronx to create competition for existing public schools. Without ever quite saying so, Klein was agitating against the very idea of the neighborhood school with deep roots in a community, which is precisely what González is now trying to revive and reinvent.

Broadly speaking, the modus operandi of most charter schools, or at least those in impoverished neighborhoods, is to separate children from their presumably malignant environments. González objects to this in principle. "I don't want to be part of the history of taking talented kids out of the neighborhoods and telling them to move on," he says. More practically, he doesn't think it's a realistic objective, considering 223's population. "Most of our kids are never going to leave this area just for financial reasons; they can't afford to live anywhere else, they don't have the guidance, whatever. So how do we make those places better so that their kids aren't going through the same cycle?"

Given his and Klein's conflicting agendas, it's no surprise that González is critical of many of the policies of education

reform. He has no problem with schools being held accountable for their performance, but he worries that the reform movement's infatuation with competition will undermine the broader goal of improving public education—that by grading schools against their peers you are encouraging them to hoard their successful innovations rather than to share them. He is concerned as well about the fact that the new principals being sent, disproportionately, into disadvantaged neighborhoods have little experience with or connection to the communities they're supposed to serve. And he is made uncomfortable by all of the educational experimentation, the endless stream of pilot programs, being implemented in neighborhoods like his. "I'm just afraid that our kids are being sacrificed while everyone is learning on the job," he says. "This is not some sort of urban experiment. These are kids' lives we're talking about."

González has no problem with schools being held accountable, but he is made uncomfortable by the endless stream of pilot programs. 'I'm just afraid that our kids are being sacrificed while everyone is learning on the job,' he says.

González tries to visit classrooms at least three days a week to provide informal feedback to his less experienced instructors. On a recent morning, I joined him on his rounds, sitting in on a sixth-grade science class taught by a second-year teacher named Garrett Adler.

A common assumption inside the school-reform movement, one often repeated in the wake of America's sobering performance in the recent Program for International Student Assessment exam—the U.S. ranked 17th in reading and 23rd in science—is that our nation's public-school teachers tend not to be high achievers themselves. (By contrast, in Finland teachers are drawn from the top 10 percent of their college classes.) You can't get much more high-achieving than Adler, who grew up on the Upper West Side and attended Hunter College High School, one of New York's most selective public high schools, before graduating magna cum laude from Brown University.

And yet when Adler came to 223 last year through the New York City Teaching Fellows program, which helps train and place aspiring teachers in the city's public-school system, he was at best a struggling teacher. He was incapable of controlling his classroom. Students shot rubber bands at one another, fooled around with dangerous lab equipment and ignored his repeated requests to quiet down. "I used to go into his classroom first thing in the morning scared of what I might see," González told me. "To be honest, at one point I was about ready to give him the hook." Instead, he devoted precious resources to teaching Adler how to teach, hiring a personal coach to attend his classes regularly and meet with him for 45 minutes a week.

There were 30 students in Adler's class, their desks divided into several clusters. The subject of the day was matter. Adler, a slight, anxious-looking 24-year-old with glasses and a beard, wore chinos and a button-down shirt and tie, per the unofficial dress code for male faculty members. (The U.F.T. contract prevents González from formally requiring that teachers wear ties.)

After a brief introductory movie starring an animated robot, Adler taught his students the "matter march," warning them in advance that it was "incredibly dorky" but that once they learned it, they would never forget the definition of "matter." Standing in front of his class, Adler proceeded to demonstrate the march—really more of a dance, with a spin and a clap and the words, chanted like a cheer: "Matter is anything that takes up space and has mass!"

Adler moved swiftly through the rest of the lesson, working hard not to lose his momentum. "Not right now," he said brusquely, his eyes fixed on his clipboard, to a student whose hand was raised. Over the years, González and his staff have developed a simple, rigid plan meant to help new teachers manage their classrooms and progress through lessons without getting derailed. Each 45-minute period is divided into five sections, or waves, as they're known. Adler facilitated his transitions with chants: "Work hard. Get smart. Woot! Woot!" The suggestion to do that came last year from his coach. "At first, I thought they were really cheesy; I felt like they weren't me," he told me later of the undignified sideshows he has come to deploy. "Now I feel like: You know what? They can be me."

After class, González had some criticisms. Among other things, Adler never made it to the final wave of the lesson, known as the share, when the class gathers in a circle to review and reinforce what it learned that day. ("Circle up to talk it out, to get it, get it, get it.") But González was pleased. The danger now is that like many young teachers, Adler will soon move on, and all that money González spent on his development will have been wasted. "Every time one of my teachers leaves, that's $200,000 walking out the door," he told me.

During his tenure, Klein often referred to the mission of improving our nation's public schools as "the civil rights battle of our time." Rhetoric like this helped the education-reform campaign blossom into a full-fledged movement. Young college graduates now go into blighted schools to teach in much the same way that an earlier generation went south to march. This has been a boon for González. Eight of his nine original faculty members were fresh from college via Teach for America, and today 60 percent of his teachers are in their 20s. "You really need idealists, people who are willing to do the extra work," he says.

But this dependence on young teachers brings its own challenges. "First-year teachers are pretty much useless," González says. "To me, the ideal teacher is a third-year Teach for America teacher." The problem, at least from where González sits, is that Teach for America requires only a two-year commitment. It entices the best applicants not only with the promise of changing lives in impoverished schools but also by presenting itself as a résumé-builder for elite institutions like Harvard Business School and McKinsey & Company. "I'm trying to build people who are going to stay, who want to work with our kids," González says. "This isn't where they're starting their careers; this is their life. We've had plenty of brilliant people

here from organizations like Teach for America, and they lasted two years, because their hearts weren't in it. I can't afford that. That's hurtful to our kids."

Much as he has done with his student body, González has tried to create a particular culture among his faculty, relying equally on inspiration and incentive. Last year, to discourage teachers from taking advantage of a clause in the U.F.T. contract allowing them to miss 10 days of every school year, he gave everyone with a perfect attendance record a Flip video camera. (As usual, there was an ulterior motive: González wanted them to use the cameras to record themselves in the classroom.)

A few weeks after visiting Adler's class, I stopped by his classroom at the end of the day. The place was a mess. He had just finished a lab that involved making ice cream in baggies with ice, salt, sugar, vanilla and milk. He made us a batch, spooning some into Dixie cups as we sat down to talk.

Adler said he was enjoying his job—"I like being the science teacher, being that figure in these kids' lives"—especially when he considers his friends from Brown, many of whom are still stuck in a postcollege malaise. And González, he said, is certainly an inspiring boss. "When he gets up and gives his little spiels about how we're here to change people's lives and how we do that every day, that's a powerful thing to hear as a teacher."

Still, he isn't convinced that he's well suited to teaching, particularly at this level. He's not organized enough to keep students on task and, indirectly anyway, he echoed González's concern about fundamentally not being part of the 223 community. "I have a vocabulary that comes from always having gone to really high-level schools," he said. "I feel like I'm probably talking over half the class half the time." This, he feels, diminishes his already tenuous authority in the classroom: "Who am I, this 24-year-old white kid from the Upper West Side, to tell a bunch of kids from a very different background how they're supposed to behave and act?"

M.S. 223 holds its parent-association meetings on the first Saturday morning of every month. During the preceding week, parents receive a robocall reminder from the school, either in English or Spanish. Not that such calls ever make much of a difference. Parent engagement, a given at most charter schools and middle-class public schools, is an ongoing struggle at 223. Like a door-to-door salesman, González is not ashamed to use every method at his disposal to prod participation. Each parent meeting is bookended by free raffles to encourage people to show up and to stay. Just to be safe, no one leaves empty-handed: goodie bags at the door are filled with soap, shampoo and other beauty products.

On a clear, cold Saturday in January, about a dozen parents gathered inside 223's library, an oversize classroom lined with empty metal shelves, for the first parent-association meeting of the new year. Wanda Hill, the school's parent liaison, started by raffling off a $30 gift certificate to Payless shoes. Later came a World Wrestling Entertainment clock and a set of queen-size flannel sheets from J. C. Penney. All three had been procured by Hill, who volunteers at World Vision, a Christian charity, in large part so that she can get first dibs on the corporate castoffs that the organization collects.

Sandwiched in between the raffles, in English with Spanish translation, was a presentation on gangs, as well as an update on the campaign to renovate the school's library. In closing, Hill reminded parents that anyone who made it to one of the district's monthly education meetings would be entitled to free clothes from Dress Barn, also arranged through her volunteer work at World Vision.

After the meeting, I introduced myself to the only English-speaking parent in attendance, Cheryl Thomas, the mother of a sixth grader named Terrell. Thomas told me that she moved her family to the Patterson Houses several years ago, when they had to go on public assistance after she quit her job to care for a daughter with spina bifida. Thomas said that she had decided not to enter Terrell in the lottery at a charter about 12 blocks away from 223. Because of the school's long days, he wouldn't have been heading home until close to 6, which made her nervous. She and Terrell went to an open house at 223 and liked what they saw. After he registered, Terrell returned to the school for a technology seminar run by a nonprofit; all attendees were given free computers.

On my way out of 223, I saw Hill, a cheerful, plain-spoken woman, putting away unclaimed gift bags in a supply closet. She was clearly frustrated by the school's indifferent parents. "Even knowing that they're going to get two free bags of clothing from Dress Barn, we can't get one person—not *one* person—to come to a C.E.C.—Community Education Council—meeting," she said, shaking her head. "At least we can say we're trying."

In a sense, the education-reform movement is out to demonstrate that the backgrounds of students' families don't need to be changed in order to improve schools. As reformers see it, those who cite economic circumstances as an explanation for failing schools are playing into the very "excuse-based culture" that Klein was trying to dismantle.

González has proved the reformers right, at least to an extent: his school is thriving without the benefit of consistently engaged, supportive parents. But as its English and math scores reveal, 223's success remains relative. It's also hard won. This should not come as a surprise. Studies dating to the 1960s have suggested that children's experiences inside the classroom are responsible for as little as 20 percent of their overall educational development. No less important is how they spend their evenings, their weekends, their vacations.

González sees this firsthand every September, when tests show that many of his returning students have dropped a full grade level in reading over the summer. He is trying to reverse this trend by bringing parents into their children's lives at 223 in any way he can, whether it's through sporting events (one byproduct of the school's large Dominican population is a great baseball team), plays, recitals or classroom celebrations. "We're trying to change a culture here," González says. "That's going to take time. That's going to take generations."

Eric Lincoln, M.S. 223's assistant principal, spends the first three weeks of every school year registering about 40 unplanned-for students who have just been assigned to the school by the Department of Education. This is typically a high-needs group. It includes children from failing schools who are entitled to transfer to 223 (or any other middle school in good standing) under the No Child Left Behind statute as well as children whose families recently moved to the city or the neighborhood, often under duress.

Two weeks into the 2009–10 school year, Lincoln registered a seventh grader named Saquan Townsend. Saquan's family had been living in a project in East New York, Brooklyn, when their apartment was broken into by someone who thought that one of Saquan's half-brothers had been involved in a shooting. For safety reasons, Saquan's mother felt she needed to move her family as soon as possible, but she couldn't afford another apartment. The city placed them in a one-bedroom apartment in a homeless shelter in the South Bronx. Saquan has two older half-brothers, ages 20 and 18, and a 12-year-old brother with a learning disability caused by lead poisoning that he contracted at their old apartment in Bedford-Stuyvesant, Brooklyn. For about a year, all four boys and their mother slept in the same room. Saquan's new zoned school was 223.

It didn't take Saquan long to develop a reputation as a kid who never did his homework, spoke disrespectfully to teachers and seemed unwilling to follow even the most basic instructions. He spoke in a deliberately provocative, high-pitched voice in the classroom—some of his teachers called it "the alien voice"—and raised his arms high up over his head in mock stretches to elicit laughter from classmates. Most of all, Saquan had a problem with absenteeism, missing more than 50 days over the course of the school year. "Honestly, I thought there was some sort of mental disability or something weird going on," says Emily Dodd, who had Saquan for seventh-grade science last year.

One Friday, Dodd, a 25-year-old graduate of Oberlin College, asked Saquan to stay late to catch up on some assignments he missed. Working with him one on one, she quickly discovered how wrong she had been. "I realized this kid is brilliant," she told me. "He's an intellectual. His ability to think critically, to reason critically is on a very high level."

Dodd started sending Saquan text messages every morning urging him to come to school. ("Get on the bus!!!" she would write him when she first arrived at 223 at 7.) It took him three weeks to meet her initial challenge of making it on time a total of three days in a week. They celebrated the accomplishment with cheesecake, which Saquan had never eaten. "Honestly, more than anything, I think he felt rewarded by being able to spend a half-hour with me on a Friday afternoon," Dodd says.

Having gotten the "touch" he needed from Dodd, Saquan's attendance and behavior gradually improved. He also began participating in some of 223's after-school programs. He was one of three students to join a new running club and was cast in a lead role in the school's production of "West Side Story." Directed by Dodd, it was the first play performed in 223's building in years. (The stage curtain, having sat unused for so long, collapsed at the opening of the show.) Saquan missed a lot of the rehearsals, so many, in fact, that Dodd panicked and divided his part in two. When he was there, he was often disruptive, cracking jokes and distracting other cast members. "But he was amazing in the performance," says Dodd, who recalls looking around the audience and seeing Saquan's mother in tears.

As recently as a few years ago, M.S. 223's bilingual-education program was the last place students or teachers wanted to be. Geared toward moving Spanish speakers into English-only classrooms as quickly as possible, it was known as a repository for slow learners. The perception became self-fulfilling, reinforced by the low expectations placed on students.

In an earlier era, González would have been hard pressed to change this situation, as the school would have been required to use the city's bilingual-education curriculum. But Klein's reforms gave González the freedom to try a different approach. In 2007, he asked a new teacher, Silvestre Arcos, to overhaul the program. Arcos mapped out a strategy to change virtually everything about bilingual education at 223, beginning with its primary aim. Rather than weaning children from their native tongues, the goal would be to develop and refine their Spanish skills as well as their English ones. Classes would be taught in both languages; the curriculum would include a course in which students hone their Spanish grammar and read Spanish literature.

The school's dual-language program, as it is known, is now the pride of 223, a magnet for strivers rather than a dumping ground for underperformers. This year, it was a finalist in a national bilingual-education competition run by the Spanish Embassy. Three hundred children applied for the 30 spots in next year's incoming sixth-grade class.

Evaluating teachers is an imperfect science, but by almost any measure Arcos is one of 223's finest. González basically has to rig the school's Classroom of the Month award, based on academic performance, behavior and class preparedness, to prevent Arcos from winning it every time.

A stout, goateed 33-year-old, Arcos grew up in South Texas. His father, a Mexican immigrant who worked as a gas-station mechanic, was a middle-school dropout, but Arcos excelled in school, winning a full scholarship to Cornell. He spent four years at a Kipp charter school in Los Angeles before moving to New York to get his master's at Columbia. He considered teaching at a charter in New York while pursuing his degree but decided that the schedule would be too demanding to leave him time to study, so he came to 223 instead, bringing Kipp's philosophy with him. The walls of his classroom are adorned with Kipp slogans like "All of us WILL learn" and "No short-cuts. No excuses." (Whatever ideological issues González has with charter schools, their fingerprints are everywhere at 223, beginning with its décor: the school's hallways are lined with college pennants, a design innovation popularized by the charter movement.)

Arcos's classroom has a deceptively relaxed air. He stands casually at the front of the room, his hands stuffed in the pockets of his khakis, allowing students to banter as they figure out answers to his questions. But he works relentlessly, particularly during the early part of the school year, to create and reinforce academic expectations, discipline and accountability. At the start of classes, Arcos praises students who seat themselves quietly and take out their work without being asked. When he hands back quizzes or other assignments, he singles out students who "met or exceeded expectations." Loud applause follows each name. All of his students, even the highest performers, are required to stay after school for tutoring.

I visited Arcos in his classroom one winter afternoon, the day after a huge snowstorm in New York. Even though the city's schools weren't closed, more than 50 percent of 223's students were absent. Arcos called all 12 of his 30 homeroom students who weren't there at the start of the day. Six of them came to school immediately. Arcos told me that he just received an e-mail from the United Federation of Teachers thanking its members for showing up at their jobs despite the storm. "I was like, You've got to be kidding; you're praising people for coming to work on a day when they're supposed to?" Arcos said. "I thought that was ridiculous."

As a public-school teacher, Arcos is required to be a member of the U.F.T., but he doesn't see eye to eye with the union on most issues. Among other things, he favors the public release of teacher-performance ratings, which the U.F.T. has been fighting aggressively to prevent. "What kind of message are you sending to families and communities if you're like, We don't want those evaluations to be made public?" he said. "Are you basically saying your teachers are doing a terrible job?"

Arcos told me that he has been impressed by the dedication of many of his colleagues at 223. Still, he misses the uniform standards of his Kipp school. "At Kipp, I wasn't worried that once my students left my math class and I sent them off to science or social studies or E.L.A. [English Language Arts] that they were going to fall apart, that the expectations weren't going to be there, academically, behaviorally, in terms of their intellectual habits," he said. "Two years ago, when my sixth-grade math students left for seventh-grade math, they totally fell apart. After all of the hard work we did, they went from the top of the school in their math-test scores to the bottom. I took it pretty hard." Earlier this year, Arcos was thinking about returning to a charter school, but he recently decided to stay, swayed by his commitment to the dual-language program and his faith in González's broader vision for the school.

L ast summer, Saquan's family moved out of the shelter and into a small apartment in Bedford-Stuyvesant. Saquan wanted to remain at 223 for eighth grade, even though that would mean getting up at 5:45 and making it to the subway by 6:15 for the one-and-a-half-hour commute to the South Bronx. If he stayed for after-school activities, he would not return home until after 6. Because his mother works nights, they would barely see each other. She would not yet be home when he had to leave for school and would be asleep when he returned.

I first met Saquan at a gathering of the Principal's Book Club. It was a Monday afternoon in December, and he was one of a dozen students arrayed around the conference table that dominates González's office. Manuel Santos, González's hulking executive assistant, doled out half-slices of pizza, as González and the kids discussed "Fallen," a young-adult novel about a group of fallen angels at a reform school. "Probably the biggest critique you might have of our reading program is that we don't spend much time on the classics," González says. "I can live with that. I just want our kids to read."

Toward that end, González spends close to $200,000, or 5 percent, of his annual budget at Barnes and Noble on popular new books that are more likely to interest 223's students. The strategy worked with Saquan, who joined the Principal's Book Club last April, when the book of the month was "The Hunger Games," which he had been wanting to read but couldn't find in his local library. He hadn't missed a meeting since then.

At 5-foot-3, Saquan is small for his grade, and his voice has not yet dropped, but his size 9 sneakers suggest a growth spurt in his near future. He is handsome, with smooth skin, a "faded" Afro that shoots straight up like a pencil eraser from his head, big, bright eyes and a sly smile. He poured himself a cup of orange soda and, slouching down low in his chair, said that he was annoyed by the book's main character, who obsesses endlessly over a boy without ever directly approaching him.

Several weeks later, I picked Saquan up at school and rode the subway home with him. He fiddled around with my iPhone as we talked, playing down his various activities and relationships at 223. (The play was "kind of fun." Dodd was "O.K.") When we arrived at his building, his mom didn't invite me in—she had left behind their furniture when they moved out of their place in East New York and still hadn't replaced it—but suggested we get together after school the following day at an IHOP in Brooklyn.

When we met, Saquan's mom, Tonya Henry, was operating on just a few hours of sleep. A tiny woman with dreadlocks and dark circles under her eyes, she had returned home that morning from her shift answering phones at a car-service company in Queens and gone directly to a dental clinic with Saquan to get one of his teeth pulled.

Saquan gingerly chewed his pancakes, cutting off pieces of turkey sausage to share with his mother. At one point, he told his mom with obvious pride that he'd been invited to join an after-school math program at 223 that could be applied toward his high-school credits. "You gonna do it?" his mom asked, disinterestedly. "Then do it." She went on to explain her less-than-enthusiastic response: "I try to let him make his own decisions. Sometimes he gets upset with me. He wants me to have more input than I want to. He'll ask my opinion, and he'll say, 'Mom, why can't you just give me an answer?' I'll say: 'Listen, I don't want to say this, and I don't want to say that. You've got to make up your own mind.'"

Saquan was one of 25 eighth graders at 223 who qualified for a prep course last summer for New York's specialized high-school test, used to determine admission to eight prestigious public high schools. (Run by Kaplan, the six-week course cost González $8,000.) But even after the prep course, he was at a severe disadvantage. Some of 223's students who take the test have been preparing since sixth grade, attending another twice-weekly class on Wednesday and Saturday afternoons that the city offers free to poor students.

The test was given in late October, and the results were released in mid-February. For the first time in 223's history, one of its students was accepted at Bronx Science. Another got in to Brooklyn Tech. Saquan didn't score high enough to be admitted anywhere, leaving him in the regular, citywide high-school application process.

Saquan is at grade level in reading and above grade level in math, which is nothing short of remarkable given everything he has been through. Still, his transcript is hardly impressive,

and the city's high schools place a great deal of weight on attendance records. What's more, without Dodd's full-time attention, Saquan's academic performance has faltered this year. At the end of February, he was failing social studies, having not completed any of his class projects, and was barely passing English. All of this might be mitigated by a proactive parent, the kind of mother or father who diligently researches the city's high schools until they find the right fit and a sympathetic principal. This is the sort of sophisticated shopper that Klein's consumer-driven system, with its emphasis on choice, would seem to depend on. But parents like this are in short supply at 223.

It's hard to disagree with the reform movement's insistence that poverty, like ignorant or apathetic parents, should not be accepted as an excuse for failing schools. But watching Saquan, it's just as hard to ignore the reality that poverty is an immutable obstacle in the path of improving public education, one that can't simply be swept aside by the rhetoric of raised expectations. Is it really a surprise that a child whose family had been forced to move into a homeless shelter where he was sharing a bedroom with his mother and three brothers was having trouble getting himself to school and was acting out in class? Is it realistic to think that demanding more of him and his teachers is all that is required?

In late February, after hearing about Saquan's poor grades, Dodd sought him out to encourage him to end the year strong. Even though he was no longer in any of her classes, she volunteered to personally tutor him to make sure he finished with only B's or better. "Because he has never actually known what it feels like to get A's and B's, and because I know that he is capable of A's and B's, I want him to experience this before he gets to high school," Dodd wrote me in an e-mail in early March. "He's totally into it and believes he can pull it off." By way of incentive, she was going to offer to give him and his mom tickets to a Broadway show.

Days after the meeting, though, Saquan stopped coming to school. A couple of 223's administrators called his house, as did Dodd, but they were unable to reach him or his mother. When Dodd finally managed to speak with Saquan in mid-March, he told her that he decided to transfer to his neighborhood middle school in Brooklyn.

In February, 223 received an unexpected visit from a space planner for the city. To González, it seemed to be the equivalent of getting measured for his coffin. He figured that it could mean only one thing: a charter school was coming to his building.

González was furious. "You're impacting my community, and you're not even going to have a discussion with me?" he said. It also made no sense to him. "There are three, maybe four middle schools in our district with their heads above water," he told me. "How are you not closing one of the failing schools and putting the charter there? Or better yet, you have a couple hundred more kids who need to be educated? Fine. Send them to me. I'll take them. Now I have to fight with the D.O.E., and those are the guys who are supposed to be helping me."

The prospect of a new charter for his building irks Gonzáles. 'How are you not closing one of the failing schools and putting the charter there? Or better yet, you have a couple hundred more kids who need to be educated? Fine. Send them to me.'

Battles between incoming charter schools and reluctant public-school hosts have become a recurring motif on New York's education-reform landscape. The tension often carries over into the school year in the form of bickering over access to shared facilities like cafeterias and auditoriums.

To González, though, the arrival of a charter would represent more than just an inconvenience. Not only would he lose the extra space that he deliberately carved out for teacher training and student guidance, but he also feared that a charter school could jeopardize his plans to expand 223 into a high school, perhaps even a boarding school. The idea, which he enlisted a class of students at New York University's Robert F. Wagner Graduate School of Public Service to help develop, is to create a nonprofit attached to the school and to purchase an abandoned building in the neighborhood that would be converted into a dormitory. It's a radical notion—a public inner-city boarding school—but it's also very much in keeping with González's expansive vision for 223.

When González first told me about the charter, I couldn't help sharing his outrage. It seemed a cruel joke, the most extreme example yet of him being punished for his success. From the city's perspective, however, González's building doesn't belong to him or even, really, to the city. It belongs to the students. An opportunity to use it to create another potentially successful school is not one that the city can afford to miss.

González did everything he could to have the charter placed elsewhere, arguing that, among other things, 223 had less unused space than several other middle schools in the district. (He also made it known to the D.O.E. that this article was in the works.) In late March, he received a reprieve. For at least another year, there would be no charter moving into 223's building.

The D.O.E. says that it was only considering a charter at 223 and that González's lobbying was largely irrelevant to its final decision. González says that his impression, from his interactions with the D.O.E., was that the charter had basically been a done deal. Either way, it was just another obstacle for González to overcome, along with developing and retaining young teachers, engaging parents and getting free eye tests for his students.

During one of our last conversations, González told me about a new eighth grader with a learning disability who recently turned up at 223. Already almost 16, the boy had earned the lowest possible score on both the reading and math portions of the state's standardized test. His mother had just moved to the neighborhood, and even though he was qualified to receive a host of free services connected to his disability that were not available at 223, she had heard good things about the school and waived her son's privileges so that he could attend it.

Hearing about the student and the challenges he would present, yet another hurdle in the endless row of them that make up the days at 223, made me exhausted. González, who would have a matter of weeks to somehow get the boy ready for high school, had a completely different reaction. "It's days like this that remind me why I get up in the morning," he said.

Critical Thinking

1. How do you feel about public schools, charter schools, and private schools? If money were no object, which school would you choose for yourself or your children? Why?

2. Give examples of ways in which union rules hindered the principal of M.S. 223 in the Bronx from transforming the school as he desired.

3. Describe three ways in which the principal of M.S. 233 was able to increase his students' academic performances.

Create Central

www.mhhe.com/createcentral

Internet References

Failing Public Schools: Education Reform
    www.parenting.com/article/failing-public-schools
Public Education Reform
    www.choicemedia.tv/Public_School_Reform
Recent Education Reform in the United States
    www.ascd.org/publications/books/109076

Article   Prepared by: Karen L. Freiberg, *University of Maryland*

Visiting Room 501

Middle-class Latino students in the United States negotiate life as transnational citizens, developing an identity and a culture that translate their contemporary, lived experiences and highlight within-group variances.

Margaret Sauceda Curwen

Learning Outcomes

After reading this article, you will be able to:

- Explain what is meant by "cultural capital."

- Describe how multiple cultural codes lead to a transnational identity.

- Evaluate the unidimensional portrayal of Latino students as marginalized and non-mainstream even if they are U.S.-born, with English as their home language.

I f you are in trouble, if you need money, I will help you. You are my favorite cousin," wrote Sammy as part of a "friendly letter" assignment in Room 501.

Why did Sammy, a 5th grader in an American elementary school, offer such support to his Mexican cousin? "People living in Mexico work hard and there is not very much money," he explained.

Sammy was a student in Room 501, a classroom in an upwardly mobile middle-class Latino community in Southern California where students were primarily from Mexico but differed in generational status.

I spent more than two months observing Room 501 to learn how children with Latino ancestry tap into their lived experiences, history, background knowledge, and language skills— what Paulo Freire and Donaldo Macedo (1987) describe as cultural capital—while engaged in their classroom's literacy activities.

Students in Room 501 were exploring and negotiating their lives as transnational citizens. In a globalized world of instantaneous information and communication, Latino students are shaping, morphing, and evolving into a new generation. This study highlights one group of students who were aspiring toward middle class, which is not the typical perception created when educators and policy makers identify Latino children as "at risk." The tacit and explicit addressing of students' culture through local school practices, curriculum, and pedagogy is intertwined with students' identity and contributes to their academic expectations. This research highlights the educational importance of understanding within-group differences, as well as students' contemporary experiences, to identify and access their strengths.

The vignette above illustrates two key points from my study. The first is the distinction that students, such as Sammy, make between their current middle-class neighborhood and their perceptions of life in Mexico. Now living in the United States, they consider themselves better off financially and therefore able to help relatives who remain in Mexico and whom they perceive as less fortunate.

Second, these students maintain relationships that cross geographic borders through literacy practices that incorporate cultural, social, economic, linguistic, and political domains. In this example, Sammy displays his newly constructed transnational identity, one which he seems to embrace with remarkable ease. He demonstrates not only geographical flexibility, but also an inclination to draw on multiple cultural codes that transcend his personal history and that of his parents.

A startling, and somewhat alarming, finding by sociologists triggered my initial interest in exploring the classroom interactions of young children: The education and economic gains made by first- and second-generation Latinos are not sustained in later generations. Stated another way, the prospects for economic, educational, health, and social viability for Latinos actually decreases by the third generation. This discovery compelled me to rethink my assumptions that Latino immigrants of the late 20th century would follow trajectories similar to those of 19th-century European immigrants. After all, this upward mobility was the "Great American Dream" and part of this country's cultural narrative. My research needed to move beyond pedagogy and interactions between child and teacher. Clearly, there were other issues. Although I am a former classroom teacher and currently focused on research into children's literacy development, my curiosity drew me to a much broader landscape of sociological and anthropological perspectives and readings into critical theory and public policy.

Understanding the Latino Experience

In 2003, there were 37 million Latinos in the United States, making them the "largest minority group" (Darder and Torres 2004). Much has been said about this group's educational achievement, language issues, and identity patterns. However, Latinos are not a monolithic group. As often happens with other ethnic groups, such as Asians and African Americans, a demographic umbrella descriptor subsumes the multifaceted groups within. For Latinos, these within-group variances include such distinguishing characteristics as occupation, place of residence, class, and educational attainment. For Latino immigrants, other contributing aspects include country of origin, reception in this country, availability of an existing support system, language of preference, and generational status (Orellana and Bowman 2003).

Two-thirds of the Latino population in this country have Mexican origins, and an increasing proportion is becoming middle class. However, research has shown that the academic achievement of U.S.-born, English-speaking Latinos lags behind those of their school peers. Of particular concern are U.S.-born Latinos whose home language is English. Because this group is native born and has acquired the necessary language skills, one might expect that they would logically find success in school. However, researchers point out that a disproportionate percentage of English-speaking Latino students is underachieving (Nieto 2001), as are third-generation children (Portes and Rumbaut 2001). Though the high school dropout rate for Latinos is high and might be attributed to the process, difficulties, and complications inherent in immigrating to a new country, Latino immigrants account for only one-third of this group's dropout rate.

Systemic and institutional factors have contributed to the disenfranchisement of Latinos. These include differential school resources, *de facto* school segregation, school tracking into low-level courses, disproportionate numbers in school categorical groups, lack of culturally relevant texts, and reductionist reading programs. In addition, the discourse in the education literature on children from diverse backgrounds also can unintentionally create a negative perception. Education researcher Carol Lee (2003) notes that this happens when educators and policy makers identify Latino children or other children from diverse backgrounds as "minority," "non-mainstream," "marginalized," and "at risk." A tendency is to automatically position certain populations, such as Latinos, in a low niche without considering the experiences of other socioeconomic levels, notably working class and middle-class children.

Educators are focused on the academic success of all children. For some children from diverse backgrounds, this focus is on both their English language acquisition and concerns for those living in poverty. The stark reality is that children from diverse populations disproportionately experience poverty, discrimination, and low-quality education. Without question, these needs are real and need to be part of the conversation in developing policies and programs that will advance the educational achievement of all children. Yet, to fully understand the needs of today's learners, school reform efforts must recognize the particular context and respond to the perceptions and adaptive responses of different groups.

Given this perplexing research on the academic trajectories of multigenerational, English-speaking Latinos, I began to wonder about the conversations that might occur in a well-functioning school in which a caring teacher invites children to display their cultural knowledge while engaged in reading and writing. The teacher in Room 501 was a skilled practitioner who built on students' strengths as learners. He recognized that every child had "little pieces of history." Therefore, I was surprised to discover a mismatch between these students' interests and their teacher's attempts to tap into their experiences.

Looking through New Eyes

Learning is more than a solitary "in-the-head" activity. Learning occurs in social spaces where individuals interact in purposeful activity. In doing so, they're shaped by the cultural, historical, economic, and social contexts in which they live and participate (Rogoff 2003; Vygotsky 1987). Children have fully textured lives and move through a multitude of out-of-school social groups, e.g., family, neighborhoods, friends, and clubs, in which they participate and acquire particular ways of being. This social and cultural knowledge can be a resource for their intellectual growth.

I was eager to discover how children in Room 501 might share such resources in the instructional and social setting of their classroom. I was particularly interested in how children might strategically incorporate their cultural capital, like Sammy did, when they responded to reading school texts, in writing class assignments, and during peer collaboration. Because the children's talk revealed the ever-changing nature of their lives and the instantaneous influence of technology, I was prompted to explore more current perspectives into the adaptations of immigrant groups to this country's values and beliefs.

Sociologist Yossi Shain's view of immigrant groups adopting American creed was a helpful orientation (1999). Shain provides an alternative conception of immigration processes that transcends traditional assimilation and acculturation models. In these processes, the individual subsumes aspects of their identity, culture, and language to the new dominant culture. Shain recounts recent experiences of several ethnic groups who develop transnational identities. He contends that some ethnic diasporas, such as Latinos of Mexican descent, adopt American creed, that is, this country's values of freedom, democracy, equity, justice, and human rights. This distinctive notion describes how ethnic groups simultaneously maintain an identity as a diasporic group member while espousing American values. While these aspects of immigrants' and subsequent generational differences are often explored in related fields of sociology, economics, and public policy, the literature on teaching and learning discusses these aspects less often. Thus, this broader conception of individuals as multifaceted helped provide a framework for Room 501 students' learning and negotiating in their classroom space.

Five Findings

I chose Room 501 as a case study site in part because of the teacher's progressive stance on including cultural and contemporary social issues in daily classroom life and his respect for students' diverse experiences, dual linguistic abilities, and cultural backgrounds. Constructivist literacy practices and multilingual and critical pedagogy were hallmarks of the teacher's instruction.

During the spring semester, the 5th graders in Room 501 read their language arts basal program, trade book literature, social studies, and science texts. Their writing projects were purposeful and authentic, and they included multiple genres. Students participated in the school's science fair and performed a class play. The classroom teacher honored and embraced the 5th-grade students' Latino heritage. He sought to include students' cultural heritage in the curriculum through multicultural texts, incorporation of Spanish language, and literary discussions. Often, he initiated critical class discussions surrounding societal issues of poverty and discrimination. However, a mismatch arose between his instructional overtures and his middle-class students' lived experiences. Given the students' mixed responses, I considered it important to carefully examine the nature in which children engaged, remained silent, or shied away from discussions. These instances could lead to theoretical and practical insights for students' readiness to participate in such activities.

My study led me to five key findings:

Adoption of the American creed

Room 501 students were active participants in multiple communities shaping their identity. They wove in views and beliefs from their everyday interests and concerns. They participated in Little League and tuned into popular "texts," including movies, video games, and TV shows. They were more likely to be energized by pop rock groups, teen celebrities, and Disney movies than to declare affinity for the multicultural 1970s United Farm Workers' leader Cesar Chavez or such former national baseball players as Roberto Clemente. Their response was consistent with education scholar Frederick Erickson's assertions that individuals negotiate through a variety of microcultures every day (2004). This engagement and participation shaped students' interests and formed the basis for academic connections they made to their text readings. Furthermore, Shain (1999) asserts that ethnic diasporas want to transform their outsider status and become part of the American lifestyle. Room 501 students' mainstream knowledge and community participation served social goals of peer affiliation and societal inclusion.

Homogeneity of neighborhood

These 5th graders were influenced by the homogeneity of their community and its comfortable security. Students and their families held an ethnic majority status in their neighborhood. When the teacher focused on differences, students didn't seem compelled to differentiate themselves from other racial and ethnic groups. The students' lack of engagement may have been their unwillingness to believe that being Latino could adversely affect their mainstream inclusion. Also, class discussions of contemporary discrimination and poverty, grounded in their basal program language arts and American history texts, were shadowed by a societal historical and current negative sentiment toward Mexican immigrants. Students would have had to publicly reveal exclusionary experiences that had the potential to be more personally humiliating than educationally illuminating.

Unidimensional portrayals of Latino culture

Students seemed uninspired by the teacher's well-intentioned—albeit, one-dimensional—portrayal of Latino culture. Students and their families' backgrounds and experiences defied a simplified "one-size-fits-all" categorization, as the sociologist Rubén Rumbaut notes (2004, p. 1169). They had varied generational, socioeconomic, familial, and linguistic proficiencies and varying ties to other cultures and countries. While the classroom highlighted unquestionably rich multicultural literature, such as *Esperanza Rising* (Muñoz 2000) and *Lupita Mañana* (Beatty 1981), the texts didn't automatically serve as cultural touchstones for Room 501 students.

This was a particularly perplexing finding because multicultural literature plays a key role in fostering student identity and affiliation. Upon closer inspection, however, an explanation became clearer. Cultural images were frozen in time; contemporary reflections of students' lives were absent. These texts, as well as others used in the classroom, typically portrayed Mexicans as recent immigrants or migrant laborers. They were representations of only a single facet of the ethnic diaspora's experience. Such textual depictions didn't adequately capture the full range of this ethnic diaspora's subsequent generational economic gain, social mobility, educational attainment, varied employment, and interest in participating in American society. Room 501 students' experiences as middle-class with access to a multitude of technological resources underscores the need to refine perceptions of today's students.

In discussions about a social issue such as discrimination, Room 501 students were disinclined to publicly include personal experience. On the surface, students distanced themselves from the salience of discrimination in their lives. In their view, discrimination had been erased through the efforts of Martin Luther King, Jr. and Rosa Parks; two students even said aloud that these individuals "saved our lives and stopped discrimination." Another student noted, "Discrimination doesn't happen here." But in further discussions, children repeatedly cited instances of discrimination in popular movies and TV sitcoms. For example, several students described in detail a recent episode of the teen television show, *That's So Raven*, when a black character wasn't given an opportunity to apply for a job but then overcame the issue. It was problematic that the school's sanctioned texts consisted typically of historical—not contemporary—stories. In popular movies and TV shows, racial and ethnic struggles have been resolved, which helps shape a perception among students that racism and discrimination are merely archival events.

Pursuit of upward mobility

Students and their families were not consigned to one economic class but were aspiring upwards. This was evidenced by parents' and their children's expressed interest in higher education, material attainment, parental career orientations, and English-language acquisition. Children contrasted their single-family homes in their stable suburb to other Southern California communities where recent-entry immigrants live in dense areas of apartments. The lifestyle of these 5th graders and their families symbolized middle-class standing to them.

Gravitating toward English language

English was perceived as a high-status language and was a priority for parents and their children. Families knew about political pressures and societal negative sentiment toward the Spanish language. Since the late 1990s, legislation in California and Arizona, reverberating with a strong anti-immigrant sentiment, promulgated the authority of the English language and all but eliminated bilingual education. Parents in this school were increasingly choosing English-language instruction over bilingual instruction. This finding disrupts popular beliefs that members and children of the Mexican diaspora persist in maintaining their language at the expense of national unity. When these multigenerational children were asked about their interest in speaking Spanish, their responses varied: Evita relished the chance to share a phone conversation after school in Spanish, and Conner recounted translating his school-assigned poems written in English for his Spanish-speaking grandmother. Other students expressed concern about losing their cultural language and "sounding weird" by speaking Spanish among their peers and in their home. Chloe lamented, "I don't know how to pronounce the [Spanish] words anymore," and Geraldo noted, "I can't find the words." They were adept and strategic about choosing which language to use and when. They were linguistically negotiating as transnational citizens as well as among microcultural communities of family, peers, and schools.

Of note were the generational tensions regarding the erosion of Spanish language competency. Parents expressed their desire for their children to be bilingual. This finding was consistent with the findings of anthropologist Sally Merry (2006), who described the contradictions and clashes between group members when some adopt new practices. When culture is recognized for its dynamic, fluid, and porous nature, the eruption of tensions, such as the one between parents and their offspring over language retention, can be expected.

In conclusion, these 5th-grade Latino students circulated in varied cultural worlds. This snapshot of social interaction in Room 501 captures a single point in time of one specific group. This exploration in a classroom, watching and listening closely to children talk, provides insight for educators. Similar to all ethnic diaspora groups, the students' identities were fluid and shifting. In a time of instantaneous information and communication, students were continuously shaping their identity. However, as Michael Olneck contends, "schools rarely recognize the transnational aspects of their immigrant group's identities and lives" (2004, p. 383). Modern conceptions of culture are analogous to a kaleidoscope: With each turn, culture is always shifting and changing.

The perception of culture guides institutional policy and reform efforts. Thus educators need a dynamic, fluid, and evolving conception of culture. Only then can the learning experiences of children of ethnic diasporas be understood and nurtured.

References

Beatty, Patricia. *Lupita Mañana.* New York: Morrow, 1981.

Darder, Antonia, and Rodolfo D. Torres. *After Race: Racism After Multiculturalism.* New York: New York University Press, 2004.

Erickson, Frederick. "Culture in Society and Educational Practices." In *Multicultural Education: Issues and Perspectives,* 5th ed., ed. James A. Banks and Cherry A. McGee Banks, pp. 31–60. Hoboken, N.J.: Wiley, 2004.

Freire, Paulo, and Donaldo Macedo. *Literacy: Reading the Word and the World.* Westport, Conn.: Bergin and Garvey, 1987.

Lee, Carol D. "Why We Need to Re-Think Race and Ethnicity in Educational Research." *Educational Researcher* 32 (June/July 2003): 3–5.

Merry, Sally E. "Introduction: Culture and Transnationalism." In *Human Rights and Gender Violence* (pp. 1–35). Chicago: University of Chicago Press, 2006.

Muñoz Ryan, Pam. *Esperanza Rising.* New York: Scholastic Press, 2000.

Nieto, Sonia. "Foreword." In *The Best for Our Children: Critical Perspectives on Literacy for Latino Students,* ed. Maria de la Luz Reyes and John J. Halcon, pp. ix–xi. New York: Teachers College Press, 2001.

Olneck, Michael. "Immigrants and Education in the United States." In *Handbook of Research on Multicultural Education,* 2nd ed., ed. James A. Banks and Cherry A. McGee Banks, pp. 381–403. San Francisco: Jossey-Bass, 2004.

Orellana, Marjorie Faulstich, and Phillip Bowman. "Cultural Diversity Research on Learning and Development: Conceptual, Methodological, and Strategic Considerations." *Educational Researcher* 32 (June/July 2003): 26–32.

Portes, Alejandro, and Rubén G. Rumbaut. *Legacies: The Story of the Immigrant Second Generation.* Berkeley: University of California Press, 2001.

Rogoff, Barbara. *The Cultural Nature of Human Development.* New York: Oxford University Press, 2003.

Rumbaut, Rubén. "Ages, Life Stages, and Generational Cohorts: Decomposing the Immigrant First and Second Generations in the United States." *International Migration Review* 38, no. 3 (2004): 1160–1205.

Shain, Yossi. *Marketing the American Creed Abroad: Diasporas in the U.S. and Their Homelands.* Cambridge, Mass.: Harvard University Press, 1999.

Vygotsky, Lev S. *The Collected Works of L. S. Vygotsky, Volume 1. Problems of General Psychology,* ed. Robert W. Riber and Aaron S. Carton (1934; reprint, New York: Plenum Press, 1987).

Critical Thinking

1. Why do non-Latinos view the 37+ million Latinos in the U.S. as "all alike"?

2. Support the desire of some parents to have their children be bilingual, even if they are educated in the English language.

3. What contributes to the finding that the educational and economic gains made by first- and second-generation Latinos are not sustained in later generations?

Create Central

www.mhhe.com/createcentral

Internet References

At the Intersection of Transnationalism, Latina/o Immigrants, and Education
http://muse.jhu.edu/journals/hsj/summary/v092/92.4

Latino Identity
www.huffingtonpost.com/tag/latino-identity

When Labels Don't Fit: Hispanics and Their View of Identity
www.pewhispanic.org/2012/04/04

Margaret Sauceda Curwen of Long Beach, California, is the winner of this year's PDK Outstanding Doctoral Dissertation Award.

Her dissertation was titled "The Nature of Middle-Class Latino/a Students' Cultural Capital in a 5th-Grade Classroom's Reading and Writing Activities."

Curwen received her Ph.D. from the Rossier School of Education at the University of Southern California in 2007. She is now an assistant professor of education at Chapman University in Orange, California. She is a member of the University of Southern California Chapter.

Unit 4

UNIT

Prepared by: Karen L. Freiberg, *University of Maryland*

Development during Childhood: Family and Culture

Families and cultures have substantial effects on child outcomes. How? New interpretations of behavioral genetic research suggest that genetically predetermined child behaviors may have substantial effects on how families parent, how children react, and how cultures evolve. Nature and nurture are very interactive. Is it possible that there is a genetic predisposition toward more warlike, aggressive, and violent behaviors in some children? Do some childrearing practices suppress this genetic trait? Do others aggravate it? Are some children predisposed to care for others? The answers are not yet known.

If parents and societies have a significant impact on child outcomes, is there a set of universal family values? Does one culture have more success than another culture? Laypersons often assume that children's behaviors and personalities have a direct correlation with the behaviors and personality of the person or persons who provided their socialization during infancy and childhood. Have Americans become paranoid about terrorist intentions? Do we try to justify our culture's flaws by claims that other cultures are worse? Do we teach our children this fear? Conversely, do other cultures try to hide their atrocities behind the screen that Americans are worse?

Are you a mirror image of the person or persons who raised you? How many of their beliefs, preferences, and virtuous behaviors do you reflect? Did you learn their hatreds and vices as well? Do you model your family, your peers, your culture, all of them, or none of them? If you have a sibling, are you alike because the same person or persons raised you? What accounts for all the differences between people with similar genes, similar parenting, and the same cultural background? These and similar questions are fodder for future research.

During childhood, a person's family values are compared to and tested against the values of schools, community, and culture. Peers, schoolmates, teachers, neighbors, extracurricular activity leaders, religious leaders, and even shopkeepers play increasingly important roles. Culture influences children through holidays, styles of dress, music, television, the Internet, world events, movies, slang, games, parents' jobs, transportation, exposure to sex, drugs, and violence, and many other variables. The ecological theorist Urie Bronfenbrenner called these cultural variables exosystem and macrosystem influences. The developing personality of a child has multiple interwoven influences: from genetic potentialities through family values and socialization practices to community and cultural pressures for behaviors.

Article   Prepared by: Karen L. Freiberg, *University of Maryland*

The Angry Smile

Recognizing and responding to your child's passive aggressive behaviors.

SIGNE L. WHITSON

Learning Outcomes

After reading this article, you will be able to:

- Recognize the more subtle signs of passive aggressive behavior.
- Explain why assertive expression of anger should be encouraged.

Amber had been giving her mother the silent treatment all week. She was angry about not being allowed to sleep over at a friend's house. Late Thursday night, she left a note on her mother's pillow, asking her mom to wash her uniform before Friday's soccer game. When Amber returned home from school on Friday, in a rush to pack her gear, she looked all over for her uniform. She finally found it in the washer—perfectly clean, as per her request—but still soaking wet! Amber was late for her game and forced to ride the bench.

When all was un-said and done, Amber's mother felt defeated. Having one-upped her daughter in the conflict, it was clear to her that she had lost by winning. As parents, most of us have been in situations where traveling the low road is irresistible and we become temporarily reckless in our driving. But any-time we mirror a child's poor behavior instead of modeling a healthier way to behave, our victories add up to long-term relationship damage and lasting hostilities.

So, what could Amber's mother have done differently in this hostile un-confrontation? What can any parent do to avoid the agony of victory and the defeat of healthy communication? The following guidelines offer parents strategies for maintaining their calm in a passive aggressive storm and responding in ways that lay the groundwork for less conflictual relationships with their children and adolescents.

1. Know What You Are Dealing With

Amber's silent treatment is a classic example of passive aggressive behavior, a deliberate and masked way of expressing feelings of anger. Common passive aggressive behaviors in young people include:

- Verbally denying feelings of anger (*"I'm fine. Whatever!"*)
- Verbally complying but behaviorally delaying (*"I'll clean my room after soccer."*)
- Shutting down conversations (*"Fine." and "Whatever."*)
- Intentional inefficiency (*"I did make my bed. I didn't know you meant all of the blankets had to be pulled up!"*)
- "Forgetting" or "misplacing" important items (*"I don't know where your car keys are."*)
- Avoiding responsibility for tasks (*"I didn't know you wanted me to do it. Putting away the clean dishes is his chore!"*)

Parents who are familiar with these typical patterns are able to respond directly to their children's underlying anger and to avoid misbehaving in counter-passive aggressive ways!

2. Consult the Mirror on the Wall

Passive aggressive persons master concealing their anger, and are expert at getting unsuspecting others to act it out in one of two ways. Many respond with an outburst of anger and frustration—yelling, finger wagging, threatening punishment—then feel guilty and embarrassed for having lost control. Others keep the tension low, but turn up the heat on the simmering conflict by mirroring the passive aggression. When Amber's mother purposely left the soccer uniform in the washer, she mirrored the anger that Amber had been feeling all week long. What's more, her counter-passive aggression ensured that the anger between mother and daughter would linger, fester, and grow more intense over time in its buried, unaddressed form! The second step in effectively confronting passive aggression is to refuse to act out the anger for the other person. Helping Amber learn to express her anger assertively is one of this mother's most valuable parenting opportunities!

3. Say Yes to Anger

Anger is a basic, spontaneous, neurophysiological part of the human condition. As such, it is neither good nor bad. It just is. Too often young people are held to an unrealistic social standard about what it takes to be "good." From a very early age, they begin to associate having angry feelings with being bad. Like Amber, our children perceive anger as taboo and take steps to suppress angry feelings.

When parents teach their children to say "yes" to the presence of anger and "no" to the expression of anger through aggressive or passive aggressive behaviors, they build a foundation for lifelong emotional intelligence and strong relationships.

4. Be the Change You Want to See

Each time passive aggressive behavior is answered with a mirrored counter-passive aggressive response, the hidden means of expressing anger is reinforced and an opportunity for direct emotional expression is lost. On the other hand, each time passive aggressive behavior is confronted assertively, the hidden anger is weakened.

The most effective way for our kids to learn to acknowledge and accept angry feelings is to role model this for them on a daily basis. As parents, this can be a real challenge since we, too, may have faced stringent socializing forces regarding the expression of our anger. It's never too late to learn to express anger in emotionally honest, direct ways, however, and the stakes have never been so high!

5. Allow It, Tolerate It, Encourage It, Even!

The final essential angle to confronting passive aggressive behavior in our kids is our willingness to receive their anger when they test out their new voice. If you are going to guide your child to be more open and direct with his anger, then you must also be willing to accept his anger when he expresses it. For many, this is truly difficult. But for lasting change to take hold for Amber and other young people, they must know that the assertive expression of their anger will be tolerated, respected and even honored!

Critical Thinking

1. Describe five common passive aggressive behavior patterns.
2. Give an example of counter-passive aggression to express underlying anger.
3. Describe how anger can be expressed in an emotionally honest way.

Create Central

www.mhhe.com/createcentral

Internet References

Confronting Passive Aggressive Behavior/Psychology Today
www.psychologytoday.com/blog/passive-aggressive-diaries/201305
How to Deal with Passive Aggressive People: MD Junction
www.mdjunction.com/forums/positive-thinking-discussions
Parents Division of the Life Space Crisis Intervention Institute
www.lsci.org/pros-parents

SIGNE L. WHITSON is a co-author of the book, *"The Angry Smile: The Psychology of Passive Aggressive Behavior in Families, Schools, and Workplaces, 2nd edition."* She is also the creator of the website www.PassiveAggressiveDiaries.com. Signe is a licensed social worker and therapist who has developed and delivered numerous training programs around the country in areas related to child and adolescent mental health. Copies of *The Angry Smile,* as well as information on Angry Smile seminars, can be found at www.lsci.org.

Article   Prepared by: Karen L. Freiberg, *University of Maryland*

Support Parents to Improve Student Learning

Efforts are building to translate traditionally strong family relationships among Latinos into stronger performance at school.

JOANNA CATTANACH

Learning Outcomes

After reading this article, you will be able to:

- Identify several activities that link Latino parents in partnerships with their children's schools.

- Explain how parent classes on nutrition and Zumba, for example, draw them into greater involvement in their children's educational achievement.

It is 6 P.M. on a crisp winter night, and 30 parents are seated at long folding tables covered in bright blocks of blue and yellow construction paper inside the cafeteria at Lorenzo De Zavala Elementary School in West Dallas, Texas. Soft Christmas music plays on the sound system as the group waits for the ceremony to begin. Hurried parents rush through side doors and apologize for being late. Has it started, they ask? Many carry containers of food—homemade tamales, tortillas, and rice. They place their covered dishes and crockpots on tables pressed against the back wall of the cafeteria and quickly take their seats with the other parents.

The atmosphere is eager and tense as parents—some in suits and church dresses, others in work clothes—tap their feet, look at the clock, and speak softly to each other in Spanish while a singer croons about a holly jolly Christmas in English.

Ten minutes later, the graduation ceremony begins with a train of children walking in a disjointed single-file line past their now smiling parents to the center of the cafeteria. They are excited, fighting over who gets to sit where, and waving at their parents seated nearby. The children were asked to gather in a separate room away from their parents. This night is about mom and dad, but also about the children. Soon the little ones begin cheering and clapping as their parents step forward to receive certificates of completion.

Tonight's graduation ceremony is one of dozens hosted by The Concilio, a Dallas-based nonprofit focused on helping Hispanic parents improve the education and health of their families. Tonight is about recognizing parents who completed a nine week course focused on ways they can better navigate the school system and be more actively involved in their child's education.

For parent graduate Mary Ann Martinez, the program has helped her become a better mother. "I'm here because of my daughter, Lauren," she tells the audience. Like so many Hispanic parents, she wants to see her child succeed in school, but Martinez, a Mexican-American born in the United States who speaks better English than Spanish and attended public schools in America, admits she was not involved in her daughter's education except to argue with teachers. That has changed thanks to the program. "It has really taught me and my daughter to have a better relationship," she said.

Martinez and Hispanic parents like her are a key part of efforts to close the achievement gap and this program, like so many others around the nation, is aimed and getting Hispanic parents more involved with their child's school and ultimately more invested in their child's education.

"Parent involvement is the key to improving school culture," said De Zavala principal Lisa Miramontes. When The Concilio approached her about partnering with the school, she readily agreed. Many parents at the school were not attending activities, and some would not come inside. Since the parent program began, test scores are improving, parent-teacher relationships are better, and previously uninvolved parents, including Martinez, are now volunteering and joining the PTA.

Challenges for Schools, Parents

As American schools adjust to the influx of Hispanic students, many from economically disadvantaged homes, schools and outside groups are increasingly faced with teaching not just the student but the parent as well because, as research shows, how well a child performs in school is based in large part on family and outside influence. Hispanic parents tend to feel most comfortable in small, group-based, bilingual programs.

The new engagement model has forced school administrators and leaders to become more proactive in reaching out to parents, yet school programs are often designed to address middle-class Hispanic parents, not low-income parents or those with little education. As a result, Hispanic parents, especially non-English-speaking parents, feel alienated and don't participate.

"We had a segment of our parents who were intimidated to go on to campuses because of language differences," said Sam Buchmeyer, a spokesman for the Grand Prairie Independent School District, a suburban Dallas school district with a large, predominantly poor Hispanic population.

But translating a flyer from English to Spanish is not enough. "Family engagement is more than just addressing the language issue. It goes far beyond that," Buchmeyer said. The district's parent involvement center offers classes on nutrition, computers, Zumba, and English as a second language. It also offers dual-language programs for students, has campus-based parent liaisons, and has social workers on staff to handle immigration issues.

So far, Grand Prairie's outreach efforts have paid off. Science scores for 3rd-grade Hispanic students in the district increased from 47% proficient in 2007 to 77% in 2010, and math scores went from 65% to 81% in the same period. From 2009 to 2010, Hispanic students outperformed their regional and state counterparts in every tested area including math and writing. The district said proactive, parent engagement is a major reason for the changes.

For recent immigrants, the idea of participating in their child's school can be a new concept. In Mexico, where most Hispanic parents in Texas originate, the educational success of a child is left to the school, and, because many parents are uneducated, they don't feel they can be involved with their children's education. In the U.S., that often means Hispanic parents don't enforce homework or study time at home, feel apprehensive about helping with schoolwork they don't understand, and don't know to ask about tutoring at their child's school (Schneider, Martinez, & Owens, 2006).

"We're talking about parents who don't even realize their kids need to finish their homework and turn it in," said Tara Dunn, The Concilio's education director. New immigrant parents don't know how to get involved with their child's school nor that they should be involved. They are a separate challenge from parents already familiar with the American school system. For second- and third-generation U.S.-born Hispanic parents there is often a lack of buy-in: What difference does it make if I get involved with my child's school?

Quality Engagement

By all rights, Hispanic children should be performing better than test scores show. Strong parent-child relationships at home should equal student success, yet Hispanic students remain the least educated minority group in the country (Ryan & Siebens, 2012). The Hispanic family structure epitomizes the values normally associated with high academic performance. Hispanic families typically have clear boundaries and rules, and the sort

of open communication that allows parents to inquire about school; they promote discussion about behavior and goals. Such families are engaged in activities that build emotional maturity in their children, and many parents have some contact with the school—all key factors necessary for student success (Jones & Velez, 1997). So why, then, are Hispanic students lagging?

The answer may be to focus on the quality of engagement at home and for schools to take better advantage of the sociocultural capital inherent in the Hispanic culture. Knowing your child has homework and goes to school and is passing and not in trouble often constitutes engagement in many Hispanic homes. Seeing that the homework is finished, offering to help, finding out from teachers how well their student is doing compared to others, assessing where their children can improve, and how they should be prepared for the future are not steps many Hispanic parents see as necessary for their child's educational success.

The Argument for Parent Engagement

The Concilio, which has a 30-year history in Dallas and whose volunteers, coordinators, and staff are primarily bilingual, works with schools and outside groups to involve Hispanic parents in family-based education and health programs. Other courses cover how to handle adolescents, how to navigate life after high school, and how to help parents understand what it means to be college-ready. School-based outreach efforts, they have learned, are often ignored or simply misunderstood.

"If you have parents involved, children are going to do better and your schools are going to do better," Dunn said. "You can't bypass the parents." Their own data proves it. From 2002 to 2009, 90% of the students whose parents completed The Concilio's parent education program graduated from high school, and 78% of students completed at least one year of postsecondary education, according to a survey of 2,100 parents.

"The idea that Hispanic parents don't care about education is a myth," Dunn said. "Parents do want to know how better to help their children."

Indeed, in the 2009 National Survey of Latinos, some 89% of young people said they believed a college education was important to succeed in life, yet Hispanic students continue to have the highest dropout rates among minority groups in the country, as well as the lowest high school completion rates (Dockterman, 2011).

Districts Work at It

Despite difficult challenges, some school districts are making strides. Irving Independent School District, another suburban Dallas school district, has created a new office for Student and Family Engagement to help with school-based parent outreach efforts. Over 70% of the district's students are Hispanic, over 60% are considered at-risk students, and over 80% of students live below the poverty line. Irving ISD teachers and administrators go through culture, language, and diversity training.

The district also offers dual-language classes to students, and it has partnered with community sponsors, including corporate, civic, and nonprofit groups, to send home packages of books with students, including bilingual books. Its goal is to distribute 1 million books to students.

Adam Grinage, Irving ISD's director for student and family engagement, said the district is "on fire for family engagement" and notes that the parent outreach centers in its 37 schools are among its most effective initiatives. Open to all parents, but particularly geared toward Hispanic parents, the centers offer various programs and literacy classes that are often the gateway for new parents to become involved in their child's school. The district hosts parent academies, has created a Spanish language information TV program, partners with groups such as The Concilio, and offers specific programs targeted toward at-risk Hispanic teens.

Too often, parents don't know how to access information online, what to find or where to look to check if their child attended class or completed their work, Grinage said. "Often, parents don't know the language of the system. They are intimidated by it . . . they don't know what 'curriculum' means."

The initiatives of Irving ISD and other such districts amount to a significant change in the traditional school-parent relationship. Instead of PTA fundraisers to support the schools, now schools support the parents. "It means more when school-based personnel reach out to the family," Grinage said.

In 2012, over 80% of Irving parents surveyed said they were satisfied with both the personal communication they received from their child's teacher and from school administrators—just a few points shy of the 90% approval rating the district wants.

Parents are very involved at Otis Brown Elementary School in Irving, where a group of mothers recently gathered in the parent center on campus. The brightly colored classroom is where Maria Mancillas, a parent liaison, conducts a weekly literacy class. Each week, parents are given a bilingual book with vocabulary words in English and Spanish to take home and read with their children. They read the story as a group and then discuss ways to better engage their children at home and questions to ask their children for increased comprehension.

Otis Brown Elementary strives to be a safe place, a happy place, for parents. Apple cutouts line one side of the wall next to a toddler kitchenette. When they visit school, mothers are encouraged to bring their nonschool-age children with them because childcare concerns often are an obstacle to parental involvement in school activities.

The day's lesson, Mancillas explains in Spanish, is to read from letters each mother was asked to write to her child as part of the previous week's homework assignment. Tissues are passed around the room as mothers read aloud from handwritten letters. "*Me gusta tu imaginación* (I love your imagination)," one mother said.

Part of the challenge with Hispanic parents, Mancillas explains later, is that parents do not know how to connect with their children as students or how to be involved in their life at school or at home. They also do not understand the importance of engagement and view engagement as simply asking if there is homework, visiting the school only when there is a problem

and viewing themselves primarily as a disciplinarian, not their child's first teacher.

Mancillas recruits parents at the beginning of each semester with the same message, "Give me this opportunity to show you this is important for your school and your family."

It took a while for Mancillas to recruit Laura Morales who was educated in the U.S. and is bilingual. Before entering the literacy program, the once shy and depressed mother of three was embarrassed to read to her children. Her own mother told her she was wasting her time volunteering at school. But Morales persisted and slowly came out of her shell. Now, "I can read to them without being embarrassed," she said. A volunteer at the school, she also serves as PTA vice president. When either of her two children at Otis Brown see her in the hall at school, they scream, "That's my mom!" They are proud, she said. And their behavior and test scores also have improved since she became involved at the school.

Mancillas, a former kindergarten teacher in Mexico, said the literacy class helps breakdown barriers. And while some mothers struggled with words from the week's take-home book, *Thelma La Hormiga* (Thelma the Ant), they pushed forward. They know that soon their children will surpass them in knowledge, but the objective is to create a culture of involvement, accountability, and learning in the home, said Grinage. That means following up with homework assignments, turning off the TV, making sure their child is reading, asking follow-up questions, and becoming more involved with their child's school, not just being a curbside parent at pickup time.

"We need for parents to feel connected and engaged," said Grinage.

The Road Ahead

Thirty years ago, experts said more rigorous schoolwork was the answer to improving test scores and decreasing dropout rates. In the transformational *A Nation at Risk* report, a blue-ribbon commission of experts, policy makers, educators, and administrators said educational institutions had "lost sight of the basic purposes of schooling" (Gardner et al., 1983). A lack of competent teachers, less rigorous coursework, poor completion rates in core courses such as Algebra I, and an overall acceptance of mediocre student performance were some of the main concerns the panel cited. The report, which focused primarily on teenage students, suggested that more emphasis on improving the content, expectation, time, and quality of teaching in the classroom would improve educational outcomes.

The report gave only a nod to outside factors such as parent educational achievement, community support, and the family's health and welfare, and it did not link parental involvement at school with student success.

While school districts have since embraced the engagement model, there is still an emphasis at the state and national levels on improved student test scores and student learning outcomes. Despite some successes, the dropout rate among Hispanic students remains high, students are still graduating unprepared for college, and there remains a large achievement gap between white, black, and Hispanic students.

"It's easy just to focus on the academics and not the (non-cognitive side of learning)," Grinage said, "but the affective side has a strong effect on academic success."

At Irving, the engagement process is a three-step approach. First, Irving asks parents to volunteer at school, then to join parent education classes, and finally to empower themselves by becoming leaders in their school. The district's goal is to increase participation in parent education programs by 10%.

Grinage attributes the district's success to having a proactive school board focused on parent and student engagement, which has allotted funds for outreach, placing parent outreach centers on campuses. He also said connecting with outside groups and community partners, and creating an environment of engagement in school and education at home have helped the effort. As a result, since 2003, the district has seen double-digit gains in all five testing areas across the board, and the district is ranked academically acceptable; no schools are ranked failing.

In its 2009 policy brief, the National Family, School, and Community Engagement Working Group, a leadership coalition of community stakeholders, said engagement is a shared responsibility with the parents, the school, and the community. It must be continued across a child's educational journey and carried out everywhere a child learns: at home, in the classroom, and in the community. Proactive school districts such as Grand Prairie and Irving offer access to parents and reach out to them. "Now is the time we need to make parent education programs mainstream," said Dunn from The Concilio. "Hispanic parents are a resource, not a problem."

References

Dockterman, D. (2011). *Statistical portrait of Hispanics in the United States, 2009*. Washington, DC: Pew Hispanic Center.

Gardner, D., Larsen, Y.W., Baker, W., Campbell, A., Crosby, E., Foster, C., . . . Wallace, R. (1983). *A nation at risk*. Washington, DC: U.S. Department of Education.

Jones, T.G. & Velez, W. (1997, March). *Affects of Latino parent involvement on academic achievement*. Paper presented at the annual meeting of the American Educational Research Association, Chicago, IL.

Ryan, C. & Siebens, J. (2012). *Educational attainment in the United States, 2009*. Washington DC: U.S. Census Bureau.

Schneider, B., Martinez, S., & Owens, A. (2006). Barriers to educational opportunities for Hispanics in the United States. In M. Tienda & F. Mitchell (Eds.), *Hispanics and the future of America* (pp. 179–227). Washington, DC: National Academies Press.

Critical Thinking

1. How can Latino parents be a resource to a school?

2. What steps can be taken to help non-English-speaking parents feel less alienated from their children's schools?

3. Do you support school–social work liaisons to help Latinos handle immigration issues? Why or why not?

Create Central

www.mhhe.com/createcentral

Internet References

Council of Spanish Speaking Organizations
http://elconcilio.net

Hispanic Partnerships Initiative
www.calstate.edu/externalrelationships/latino.shtml

The Concilio
www.theconcilio.org

Welcoming Latino Parents as Partners
www.principals.org/portals/0/content/54433.pdf

JOANNA CATTANACH is a freelance writer who lives in Dallas, Texas.

Cattanach, Joanna. From *Phi Delta Kappan*, March 2013, pp. 20, 22–25. Reprinted with permission of Phi Delta Kappa International. All rights reserved. www.pdkintl.org.

Article   Prepared by: Karen L. Freiberg, *University of Maryland*

Do-It-(All)-Yourself Parents

They raise chickens. They grow vegetables. They knit. Now a new generation of urban parents is even teaching their own kids.

LINDA PERLSTEIN

Learning Outcomes

After reading this article, you will be able to:

- Contrast reasons for homeschooling today with those in the past.

- Summarize what is meant by "differentiated instruction."

In the beginning, your kids need you—a lot. They're attached to your hip, all the time. It might be a month. It might be five years. Then suddenly you are expected to send them off to school for seven hours a day, where they'll have to cope with life in ways they never had to before. You no longer control what they learn, or how, or with whom.

Unless you decide, like an emerging population of parents in cities across the country, to forgo that age-old rite of passage entirely.

When Tera and Eric Schreiber's oldest child was about to start kindergarten, the couple toured the high-achieving public elementary school a block away from their home in an affluent Seattle neighborhood near the University of Washington. It was "a great neighborhood school," Tera says. They also applied to a private school, and Daisy was accepted. But in the end they chose a third path: no school at all.

Eric, 38, is a manager at Microsoft. Tera, 39, had already traded a career as a lawyer for one as a nonprofit executive, which allowed her more time with her kids. But "more" turned into "all" when she decided that instead of working, she would homeschool her daughters: Daisy, now 9; Ginger, 7; and Violet, 4.

We think of homeschoolers as evangelicals or off-the-gridders who spend a lot of time at kitchen tables in the countryside. And it's true that most homeschooling parents do so for moral or religious reasons. But education observers believe that is changing. You only have to go to a downtown Starbucks or art museum in the middle of a weekday to see that a once-unconventional choice "has become newly fashionable," says Mitchell Stevens, a Stanford professor who wrote *Kingdom of Children*, a history of homeschooling. There are an estimated 300,000 homeschooled children in America's cities, many of them children of secular, highly educated professionals who always figured they'd send their kids to school—until they came to think, *Hey, maybe we could do better.*

When Laurie Block Spigel, a homeschooling consultant, pulled her kids out of school in New York in the mid-1990s, "I had some of my closest friends and relatives telling me I was ruining my children's lives." Now, she says, "the parents that I meet aren't afraid to talk about it. They're doing this proudly."

Many of these parents feel that city schools—or any schools—don't provide the kind of education they want for their kids. Just as much, though, their choice to homeschool is a more extreme example of a larger modern parenting ethos: that children are individuals, each deserving a uniquely curated upbringing. That peer influence can be noxious. (Bullying is no longer seen as a harmless rite of passage.) That DIY—be it gardening, knitting, or raising chickens—is something educated urbanites should embrace. That we might create a sense of security in our kids by practicing "attachment parenting," an increasingly popular approach that involves round-the-clock physical contact with children and immediate responses to all their cues.

Even many attachment adherents, though, may have trouble envisioning spending almost all their time with their kids—for 18 years! For Tera Schreiber, it was a natural transition. When you have kept your kids so close, literally—she breast-fed her youngest till Violet was 4—it can be a shock to send them away.

Tera's kids didn't particularly enjoy day care or preschool. The Schreibers wanted a "gentler system" for Daisy; she was a perfectionist who they thought might worry too much about measuring up. They knew homeschooling families in their neighborhood and envied their easygoing pace and flexibility—late bedtimes, vacations when everyone else is at school or work. Above all, they wanted to preserve, for as long as possible, a certain approach to family.

Several homeschooling moms would first tell me, "I know this sounds selfish," and then say they feared that if their kids were in school, they'd just get the "exhausted leftovers" at the end of the day. Says Rebecca Wald, a Baltimore homeschooler, "Once we had a child and I realized how fun it was to see her discover stuff about the world, I thought, why would I want to let a teacher have all that fun?"

It's 12:30 P.M. on a Thursday, and Tera and her daughters have arrived home from a rehearsal of a homeschoolers' production of *Alice in Wonderland*. Their large green Craftsman is typical Seattle. There are kayaks in the garage, squash in the slow cooker, and the usual paraphernalia of girlhood: board games, dolls, craft kits. Next to the kitchen phone is a print-out of the day's responsibilities. Daisy and Ginger spend about two hours daily in formal lessons, including English and math; today they've also got history, piano, and sewing.

Laws, and home-crafted curricula, vary widely. Homeschoolers in Philadelphia, for instance, must submit a plan of study and test scores, while parents in Detroit need not even let officials know they're homeschooling. Some families seek out a more classical curriculum, others a more unconventional one, and "unschoolers" eschew formal academics altogether. There are parents who take on every bit of teaching themselves, and those who outsource subjects to other parents, tutors, or online providers. Advances in digital learning have facilitated homeschooling—you can take an AP math class from a tutor in Israel—and there's a booming market in curriculum materials, the most scripted of which enable parents to teach subjects they haven't studied before.

So far, Tera says, these books have made the teaching itself easy—insofar as anything is easy about mothering three kids nonstop. The girls have started their lessons at the kitchen table, but there are also sandwiches to be assembled, cats who want treats, and girls who want drinks or ChapStick or napkins or, in the youngest's case, attention.

"Violet, Ginger is getting a lesson, so you have to be quiet," Tera says from across the open kitchen, while heating tea and coaching Ginger on sounding out Y words. "The first word: is it two syllables? What does Y say at the beginning of a word?"

"Yuh."

"At the end?"

"Eee? Yucky."

"Yucky is correct."

Tera sits down to eat a bowl of salmon salad while helping Ginger with her reading workbook. Daisy is reading a fantasy book about wild cats. Violet is playing with a big clock.

"Sam has a c-ane and a c-ape," Ginger says. "Sam has a c-ap and a c-an."

"If you use your finger, it will work better," Tera says.

Teaching Daisy to read was a breeze. With Ginger it's been more complicated, and Tera has had to research different approaches. She gives her lots of workbook activities, because Ginger retains information better when she's writing and not just listening. Since hearing about a neurological link between crawling and reading, Tera also has Ginger circle the house on hands and knees 10 times daily.

A school, Tera says, might not have teased out precisely how Ginger learns best. This is something I heard often from urban homeschoolers: the desire to craft an education just right for each child. They worry that formal schooling might dim their children's love of learning (yet there is a flip side: a reduced likelihood of being inspired along the way by the occasional magical teacher, full of passion and skill). They want their children to explore the subjects that interest them, as deeply as they

care to go. For Daisy and Ginger, that has meant detours into herbalism, cat shows, musical theater, and deer.

Many parents are happy to sidestep environments that might be too intense, loading kids up with homework, making them feel an undue burden to perform. "The pressure from the reform movement today, from kindergarten on, has been all about 'Let's push, push, push for academic achievement,'" says Michael Petrilli, executive vice president of the Thomas B. Fordham Institute, an education think tank, and the author of a forthcoming book about urban parents' schooling decisions. Some urban homeschooled kids, particularly those with special needs, were previously enrolled in school but not served well there.

In truth, some conventional schools are making strides toward diagnosing and remedying each child's weaknesses. "Differentiated instruction"—the idea that teachers simultaneously address students' individual needs—is a catchphrase these days in public schools. And many elementary classrooms are no longer filled by rows of desks with children working in lockstep. But it is also true that you can never tailor instruction more acutely than when the student-teacher ratio is 1–1.

The Schreiber girls spend most of their time out and about, typically at activities arranged for homeschoolers. There are Girl Scouts and ceramics and book club and enrichment classes and park outings arranged by the Seattle Homeschool Group, a secular organization whose membership has grown from 30 families to 300 over the last decade. In a way, urban homeschooling can feel like an intensified version of the extracurricular madness that is the hallmark of any contemporary middle-class family, or it can feel like one big, awesome field trip.

Institutions throughout the country have discovered a reliable weekday customer in urban homeschoolers. "Everywhere you turn there's a co-op or a class or a special exhibit," says Brian Ray, founder of the National Home Education Research Institute in Oregon. Three years ago, the Museum of Science and Industry in Chicago began to court homeschoolers with free admission, their own newsletters, and courses designed specifically for them. Participation has doubled each year. "The more we offer, the more we sell out," says Andrea Ingram, vice president of education and guest services.

A mini-industry of homeschool consultants has cropped up, especially in New York City, whose homeschooling population has grown 36 percent in eight years, according to the school district. (While states usually require homeschoolers to register, many parents choose not to, so official estimates skew low.) In Seattle, even the public-school system runs a center that offers classes just to homeschoolers.

"My kids actually have to tell me to stop," says Erin McKinney Souster, a mother of three in Minneapolis, whose kids have learned to find an academic lesson in something as mundane as the construction of a roller-rink floor. "Everything is always sounding so cool and so fun."

Still, you can't help but wonder whether there's a cost to all this family togetherness. There are the moms, of course, who for two decades have their lives completely absorbed by their children's. But the mothers I got to know seem quite content with that, and clearly seem to be having fun getting together with each other during their kids' activities.

And the kids? There's concern that having parents at one's side throughout childhood can do more harm than good. Psychologist Wendy Mogel, the author of the bestselling book *The Blessing of a Skinned Knee*, admires the way homeschoolers manage to "give their children a childhood" in an ultracompetitive world. Yet she wonders how kids who spend so much time within a deliberately crafted community will learn to work with people from backgrounds nothing like theirs. She worries, too, about eventual teenage rebellion in families that are so enmeshed.

Typical urban homeschooled kids do tend to find the space they need by the time they reach those teenage years, participating independently in a wealth of activities. That's just as well for their parents, who by that time can often use a breather. And it has made them more appealing to colleges, which have grown more welcoming as they find that homeschoolers do fine academically. In some ways these students may arrive at college more prepared, as they've had practice charting their own intellectual directions, though parents say they sometimes bristle at having to suffer through courses and professors they don't like.

Tera figures that her daughters are out in the world enough to interact with all sorts of people. She feels certain they will be able to be good citizens precisely because of her and Eric's "forever style of parenting," as she calls it, not in spite of it. It's hard for Tera to get too worried when she's just spent the weekend, as the Schreibers often do, hanging out on a trip with homeschooled kids of all ages, including confident, competent teenagers who were happy playing cards with their parents all evening, with no electronics in sight.

Milo, my 3-year-old, never wants to go to preschool. So the more I hung out with homeschoolers, the more I found myself picking him up from school early, to squeeze in some of the fun these families were having. I began to think, why not homeschool? Really, there's something of the homeschooler in all of us: we stuff our kids with knowledge, we interact with them more than our parents did with us. I am resourceful enough to make pickles and playdough; why couldn't I create an interdisciplinary curriculum around Milo's obsession with London Bridge? I calculated what we'd have to give up if I cut back on work (though some homeschooling moms work full time or at least occasionally—like Tera, who writes parenting articles).

But my husband and I are loyal to what we call "detachment parenting": we figure we are doing a good job if Milo is just as confident and comfortable without us as he is with us. Family for us is more a condition—a joyous one, for sure—than a project, one of several throughlines of our lives.

For many of the homeschoolers I met, family is more: the very focus of their lives. And they wouldn't want it any other way. One comfort Tera and Eric Schreiber held on to when they started homeschooling was that if it wasn't working out, they could enroll the girls in school, literally the next day. That developed into an annual reassessment. By now their rhythms are deeply their own; they are embedded in a community they love. And at the college up the road there are plenty of calculus tutors, should they need them one day.

Critical Thinking

1. Why is homeschooling "newly fashionable"?
2. Identify some of the pros of homeschooling.
3. Identify some of the cons of homeschooling.
4. Defend the proposition that an educator should be able to address each student's individual needs.
5. Is there a happy medium between too much and not enough family togetherness? Should family togetherness increase or decrease as children age?

Create Central

www.mhhe.com/createcentral

Internet References

Homeschool Laws and Regulations
http://homeschooling.about.com/od/legal

How to Homeschool: Homeschooling Requirements and Information
www.motherearthnews.com/how-to-home-school.aspx

You Can Homeschool—Introduction
www.youcanhomeschool.org

LINDA PERLSTEIN, a freelance writer and editor based in Seattle, is the author of two books about schools and children, *Tested* and *Not Much Just Chillin'*.

Article   Prepared by: Karen L. Freiberg, *University of Maryland*

Child Welfare and Children's Mental Health Services

A Decade of Transformation

KEN OLSON

Learning Outcomes

After reading this article, you will be able to:

- Explain how mental health care for children has changed in the past 10 years.

- Identify some safety outcomes, permanency outcomes, and well-being outcomes recommended by the U.S. branch of Child and Family Services.

The line between "child welfare services" and "children's mental health services" has never been particularly clear. In general, policy makers, bureaucrats and service providers all agree that there is substantial overlap among the populations of children and families that need these services. Common sense and research both tell us that children who are victims of abuse or neglect are more likely to have mental health needs than those who are not. Similarly, children with mental health problems often live in family situations that can benefit from a range of child welfare prevention and intervention programs. It might not even be too glib to say that deeming a program to be a "mental health service" or a "child welfare service" is sometimes determined as much by the nature and requirements of the funding source as anything else.

In the most recent decade, both of these have undergone significant transformations: Underlying philosophies have been questioned, and new paradigms have emerged. Providers of these services to children and adolescents have scrambled to adapt, to differentiate "fad" from "trend" and to remain true to organizational mission, vision and values. The changes have been, at times, tumultuous, with mature agencies going out of business and new agencies and new models of care growing and disappearing rapidly. Other new models have become a new standard of excellence, with long-standing providers of one service in one location adapting and diversifying into multi-service, multi-state and multi-regional providers.

While there has been loss, there has also been a real opportunity to better serve children and families with new and more effective strategies and interventions.

Child Welfare

Approximately 500,000 children in America live in foster care—counting foster homes, residential treatment and other group care settings. Despite the best efforts of many mental health professionals, "graduates" of the foster care system have higher incidences of mental health problems, lower levels of academic achievement, higher incidences of substance abuse and legal system involvement, etc. While there are many exceptional individuals who have grown up in this system (Steve Jobs, Eddie Murphy, Alonzo Mourning, Malcolm X, John Lennon and Superman to name a few), the system itself has often failed to produce the desired outcomes for children.

Clearly, even casual observers of America's child welfare system cannot help but notice the sea of change that has occurred in this field in the last decade. Loosely called "child welfare reform" by some and "a cynical ruse to save money" by others, these changes include major reductions in the numbers of children and adolescents being served in residential treatment and group care settings, increases in the number and types of programs that provide care in community-based settings, a preeminent priority of serving children in their own community whenever possible and a near prohibition on sending youth to programs located out of state or, in some cases, out of county.

These evolving trends have altered our nation's approach to dealing with problems associated with child abuse and neglect. Long-held assumptions about the kind of help children and families need have been called into question. The goal of providing stability, for example, has been superseded by the belief that it is more important to provide permanency. From a practical standpoint, this means that a teenager who formerly might have been allowed and encouraged to "age out" to independence in a stable group home setting may now be moved to

And then he waited. And waited. "It felt like putting a note in a bottle and throwing it into the ocean," Carbonella said. "There was no way to know if anyone was out there on the other end. For me, this wasn't a situation where I knew which student was involved and could easily give it to a school guidance counselor. It was completely anonymous, so we really needed Facebook to intervene." But, to Carbonella's frustration, Let's Start Drama stayed up. He filed another report. Like the first one, it seemed to sink to the bottom of the ocean.

Facebook, of course, is the giant among social networks, with more than 1 billion users worldwide. In 2011, *Consumer Reports* published the results of a survey showing that 20 million users were American kids under the age of 18; in an update the next year, it estimated that 5.6 million were under 13, the eligible age for an account. As a 2011 report from the Pew Internet and American Life Project put it, "Facebook dominates teen social media usage." Ninety-three percent of kids who use social-networking sites have a Facebook account. (Teens and preteens are also signing up in increasing numbers for Twitter—Pew found that 16 percent of 12-to-17-year-olds say they use the site, double the rate from two years earlier.)

In the early days of the Internet, the danger to kids seemed to be from predatory adults. But it turns out that those perils are rare compared with the problems that come from other kids.

Social networking has plenty of upside for kids: it allows them to pursue quirky interests and connect with people they'd have no way of finding otherwise. An online community can be a lifeline if, say, you're a gender-bending 15-year-old in rural Idaho or, for that matter, rural New York. But as Let's Start Drama illustrates, there's lots of ugliness, too. The 2011 Pew report found that 15 percent of social-media users between the ages of 12 and 17 said they'd been harassed online in the previous year. In 2012, *Consumer Reports* estimated that 800,000 minors on Facebook had been bullied or harassed in the previous year. (Facebook questions the methodology of the magazine's survey; however, the company declined to provide specifics.) In the early days of the Internet, the primary danger to kids seemed to be from predatory adults. But it turns out that the perils adults pose, although they can be devastating, are rare. The far more common problem kids face when they go online comes from other kids: the hum of low-grade hostility, punctuated by truly damaging explosions, that is called cyberbullying.

What can be done about this online cruelty and combat? As parents try, and sometimes fail, to keep track of their kids online, and turn to schools for help, youth advocates like Robinson and Carbonella have begun asking how much responsibility falls on social-networking sites to enforce their own rules against bullying and harassment. What *does* happen when you file a report with Facebook? And rather than asking the site to delete cruel posts or pages one by one, is there a better strategy, one that stops cyberbullying before it starts? Those questions led me to the Silicon Valley headquarters of Facebook, then to a lab at MIT, and finally (and improbably, I know) to the hacker group Anonymous.

The people at facebook who decide how to wield the site's power when users complain about content belong to its User Operations teams. The summer after my trips to Woodrow Wilson, I traveled to the company's headquarters and found Dave Willner, the 27-year-old manager of content policy, waiting for me among a cluster of couches, ready to show me the Hate and Harassment Team in action. Its members, who favor sneakers and baseball caps, scroll through the never-ending stream of reports about bullying, harassment, and hate speech. (Other groups that handle reports include the Safety Team, which patrols for suicidal content, child exploitation, and underage users; and the Authenticity Team, which looks into complaints of fake accounts.) Willner was wearing flip-flops, and I liked his blunt, clipped way of speaking. "Bullying is hard," he told me. "It's slippery to define, and it's even harder when it's writing instead of speech. Tone of voice disappears." He gave me an example from a recent report complaining about a status update that said "He got her pregnant." Who was it about? What had the poster intended to communicate? Looking at the words on the screen, Willner had no way to tell.

In an attempt to impose order on a frustratingly subjective universe, User Operations has developed one rule of thumb: if you complain to Facebook that you are being harassed or bullied, the site takes your word for it. "If the content is about you, and you're not famous, we don't try to decide whether it's actually mean," Willner said. "We just take it down."

All other complaints, however, are treated as "third-party reports" that the teams have to do their best to referee. These include reports from parents saying their children are being bullied, or from advocates like Justin Carbonella.

To demonstrate how the harassment team members do their jobs, Willner introduced me to an affable young guy named Nick Sullivan, who had on his desk a sword-carrying Grim Reaper figurine. Sullivan opened the program that he uses for sorting and resolving reports, which is known as the Common Review Tool (a precursor to the tool had a better name: the Wall of Shame).

Sullivan cycled through the complaints with striking speed, deciding with very little deliberation which posts and pictures came down, which stayed up, and what other action, if any, to take. I asked him whether he would ever spend, say, 10 minutes on a particularly vexing report, and Willner raised his eyebrows. "We optimize for half a second," he said. "Your average decision time is a second or two, so 30 seconds would be a really long time." (A Facebook spokesperson said later that the User Operations teams use a process optimized for accuracy, not speed.) That reminded me of Let's Start Drama. Six months after Carbonella sent his reports, the page was still up. I asked why. It hadn't been set up with the user's real name, so wasn't it clearly in violation of Facebook's rules?

After a quick search by Sullivan, the blurry photos I'd seen many times at the top of the Let's Start Drama page appeared on the screen. Sullivan scrolled through some recent "Who's hotter?" comparisons and clicked on the behind-the-scenes history of the page, which the Common Review Tool allowed him to call up. A window opened on the right side of the screen, showing that multiple reports had been made. Sullivan checked to see whether the reports had failed to indicate that Let's Start Drama was administered by a fake user profile. But that wasn't the problem: the bubbles had been clicked correctly. Yet next to this history was a note indicating that future reports about the content would be ignored.

When I asked whether they'd rather be suspended from school or from Facebook, most middle- and high-school students picked school.

We sat and stared at the screen.

Willner broke the silence. "Someone made a mistake," he said. "This profile should have been disabled." He leaned in and peered at the screen. "Actually, two different reps made the same mistake, two different times."

There was another long pause. Sullivan clicked on Let's Start Drama to delete it.

With millions of reports a week, most processed in seconds—and with 2.5 billion pieces of content posted daily—no wonder complaints like Carbonella's fall through the cracks. A Facebook spokesperson said that the site has been working on solutions to handle the volume of reports, while hiring "thousands of people" (though the company wouldn't discuss the specific roles of these employees) and building tools to address misbehavior in other ways.

One idea is to improve the reporting process for users who spot content they don't like. During my visit, I met with the engineer Arturo Bejar, who'd designed new flows, or sets of responses users get as they file a report. The idea behind this "social reporting" tool was to lay out a path for users to find help in the real world, encouraging them to reach out to people they know and trust—people who might understand the context of a negative post. "Our goal should be to help people solve the underlying problem in the offline world," Bejar said. "Sure, we can take content down and warn the bully, but probably the most important thing is for the target to get the support they need."

After my visit, Bejar started working with social scientists at Berkeley and Yale to further refine these response flows, giving kids new ways to assess and communicate their emotions. The researchers, who include Marc Brackett and Robin Stern of Yale, talked to focus groups of 13- and 14-year-olds and created scripted responses that first push kids to identify the type and intensity of the emotion they're feeling, and then offer follow-up remedies depending on their answers. In January, during a presentation on the latest version of this tool, Stern explained that some of those follow-ups simply encourage reaching out to the person posting the objectionable material—who typically takes down the posts or photos if asked.

Dave Willner told me that Facebook did not yet, however, have an algorithm that could determine at the outset whether a post was meant to harass and disturb—and could perhaps head it off. This is hard. As Willner pointed out, context is everything when it comes to bullying, and context is maddeningly tricky and subjective.

One man looking to create such a tool—one that catches troublesome material before it gets posted—is Henry Lieberman, a computer scientist whose background is in artificial intelligence. In November, I took a trip to Boston to meet him at his office in MIT's Media Lab. Lieberman looked like an older version of the Facebook employees: he was wearing sneakers and a baseball cap over longish gray curls. A couple years ago, a rash of news stories about bullying made him think back to his own misery in middle school, when he was a "fat kid with the nickname Hank the Tank." (This is hard to imagine now, given Lieberman's lean frame, but I took his word for it.) As a computer guy, he wondered whether cyberbullying would wreck social networking for teenagers in the way spam once threatened to kill e-mail—through sheer overwhelming volume. He looked at the frustrating, sometimes fruitless process for logging complaints, and he could see why even tech-savvy adults like Carbonella would feel at a loss. He was also not impressed by the generic advice often doled out to young victims of cyberbullying. "'Tell an adult. Don't let it get you down'—it's all too abstract and detached," he told me. "How could you intervene in a way that's more personal and specific, but on a large scale?"

To answer that question, Lieberman and his graduate students started analyzing thousands of YouTube comments on videos dealing with controversial topics, and about 1 million posts provided by the social-networking site Formspring that users or moderators had flagged for bullying. The MIT team's first insight was that bullies aren't particularly creative. Scrolling through the trove of insults, Lieberman and his students found that almost all of them fell under one (or more) of six categories: they were about appearance, intelligence, race, ethnicity, sexuality, or social acceptance and rejection. "People say there are an infinite number of ways to bully, but really, 95 percent of the posts were about those six topics," Lieberman told me.

Focusing accordingly, he and his graduate students built a "commonsense knowledge base" called BullySpace— essentially a repository of words and phrases that could be paired with an algorithm to comb through text and spot bullying situations. Yes, BullySpace can be used to recognize words like *fat* and *slut* (and all their text-speak misspellings), but also to determine when the use of common words varies from the norm in a way that suggests they're meant to wound.

Lieberman gave me an example of the potential ambiguity BullySpace could pick up on: "You ate six hamburgers!" On its own, *hamburger* doesn't flash cyberbullying—the word is neutral. "But the relationship between *hamburger* and *six* isn't neutral," Lieberman argued. BullySpace can parse that relationship. To an overweight kid, the message "You ate six hamburgers!" could easily be cruel. In other situations, it could be said with an admiring tone. BullySpace might be able to tell the difference based on context (perhaps by evaluating personal information that social-media users share) and could flag the comment for a human to look at.

BullySpace also relies on stereotypes. For example, to code for anti-gay taunts, Lieberman included in his knowledge base the fact that "Put on a wig and lipstick and be who you really are" is more likely to be an insult if directed at a boy. BullySpace understands that lipstick is more often used by girls; it also recognizes more than 200 other assertions based on stereotypes about gender and sexuality. Lieberman isn't endorsing the stereotypes, of course: he's harnessing them to make BullySpace smarter. Running data sets from the YouTube and Formspring posts through his algorithm, he found that BullySpace caught most of the insults flagged by human testers—about 80 percent. It missed the most indirect taunting, but from Lieberman's point of view, that's okay. At the moment, there's nothing effective in place on the major social networks that screens for bullying before it occurs; a program that flags four out of five abusive posts would be a major advance.

The superintendent at one school felt appreciative of Anonymous for intervening. "We would have never done anything if they hadn't notified us," he said.

Lieberman is most interested in catching the egregious instances of bullying and conflict that go destructively viral. So another of the tools he has created is a kind of air-traffic-control program for social-networking sites, with a dashboard that could show administrators where in the network an episode of bullying is turning into a pileup, with many users adding to a stream of comments—à la Let's Start Drama. "Sites like Facebook and Formspring aren't interested in every little incident, but they do care about the pileups," Lieberman told me. "For example, the week before prom, every year, you can see a spike in bullying against LGBT kids. With our tool, you can analyze how that spreads—you can make an epidemiological map. And then the social-network site can target its limited resources. They can also trace the outbreak back to its source." Lieberman's dashboard could similarly track the escalation of an assault on one kid to the mounting threat of a gang war. That kind of data could be highly useful to schools and community groups as well as the sites themselves. (Lieberman is leery of seeing his program used in such a way that it would release the kids' names beyond the social networks to real-world authorities, though plenty of teenagers have social-media profiles that are public or semipublic—meaning their behavior is as well.)

I know some principals and guidance counselors who would pay for this kind of information. The question is what to do with it. Lieberman doesn't believe in being heavy-handed. "With spam, okay, you write the program to just automatically delete it," he said. "But with bullying, we're talking about free speech. We don't want to censor kids, or ban them from a site."

More effective, Lieberman thinks, are what he calls "ladders of reflection" (a term he borrowed from the philosopher Donald Schön). Think about the kid who posted "Because he's a fag! ROTFL [rolling on the floor laughing]!!!" What if, when he pushed the button to submit, a box popped up saying "Waiting 60 seconds to post," next to another box that read "I don't want to post" and offered a big X to click on? Or what if the message read "That sounds harsh! Are you sure you want to send that?" Or what if it simply reminded the poster that his comment was about to go to thousands of people?

Although Lieberman has had exploratory conversations about his idea with a few sites, none has yet deployed it. He has a separate project going with MTV, related to its Web and phone app called Over the Line?, which hosts user-submitted stories about questionable behavior, like sexting, and responses to those stories. Lieberman's lab designed an algorithm that sorts the stories and then helps posters find others like them. The idea is that the kids posting will take comfort in having company, and in reading responses to other people's similar struggles.

Lieberman would like to test how his algorithm could connect kids caught up in cyberbullying with guidance targeted to their particular situation. Instead of generic "tell an adult" advice, he'd like the victims of online pummeling to see alerts from social-networking sites designed like the keyword-specific ads Google sells on Gmail—except they would say things like "Wow! That sounds nasty! Click here for help." Clicking would take the victims to a page that's tailored to the problem they're having—the more specific, the better. For example, a girl who is being taunted for posting a suggestive photo (or for refusing to) could read a synthesis of the research on sexual harassment, so she could better understand what it is, and learn about strategies for stopping it. Or a site could direct a kid who is being harassed about his sexuality to resources for starting a Gay-Straight Alliance at his school, since research suggests those groups act as a buffer against bullying and intimidation based on gender and sexuality. With the right support, a site could even use Lieberman's program to offer kids the option of an IM chat with an adult. (Facebook already provides this kind of specific response when a suicidal post is reported. In those instances, the site sends an e-mail to the poster offering the chance to call the National Suicide Prevention Lifeline or chat online with one of its experts.)

Lieberman would like to build this content and then determine its effectiveness by asking kids for their feedback. He isn't selling his algorithms or his services. As a university professor, he applies for grants, and then hopes companies like MTV will become sponsors. He's trying to work with companies rather than criticize them. "I don't think they're trying to reflexively avoid responsibility," he told me. "They are conscious of the scale. Anything that involves individual action on their part, multiplied by the number of complaints they get, just isn't feasible for them. And it *is* a challenging problem. That's where technology could help a little bit. My position is that technology can't solve bullying. This is a people problem. But technology can make a difference, either for the negative or the positive. And we're behind in paying attention to how to make the social-network universe a better place, from a technological standpoint."

Internal findings at Facebook suggest that Lieberman's light touch could indeed do some good. During my visit to Silicon Valley, I learned that the site had moved from wholesale banishment of rule-breakers toward a calibrated combination of warnings and "temporary crippling of the user experience," as one employee put it. After all, if you're banished, you can sign up again with a newly created e-mail address under an assumed name. And you might just get angry rather than absorb the message of deterrence. Instead, Facebook is experimenting with threats and temporary punishments. For example, the Hate and Harassment Team can punish a user for setting up a group to encourage bullying, by barring that person from setting up any other group pages for a month or two. (If the account associated with the offensive group uses a made-up name, then the site's only leverage is to remove the group.) According to an in-house study, 94 percent of users whose content prompted a report had never been reported to the site before. As Dave Willner, the content-policy manager, put it when he told me about the study: "The rate of recidivism is very low."

He explained, in his appealingly blunt way, "What we have over you is that your Facebook profile is of value to you. It's a hostage situation." This didn't surprise me. In the course of my reporting, I'd been asking middle-school and high-school students whether they'd rather be suspended from school or from Facebook, and most of them picked school.

The hacker group Anonymous isn't the first place most parents would want their bullied kids to turn. Launched a decade ago, Anonymous is best known for its vigilante opposition to Internet censorship. The group has defaced or shut down the Web sites of the Syrian Ministry of Defense, the Vatican, the FBI, and the CIA. Its slogan, to the extent a loosely affiliated bunch of hackers with no official leadership can be said to have one, is "When your government shuts down the Internet, shut down your government." Anonymous has also wreaked financial havoc by attacking MasterCard, Visa, and PayPal after they froze payments to the accounts of WikiLeaks, the site started by Julian Assange to publish government secrets.

Since Anonymous is anarchic, the people who answer its call (and use its trademark Guy Fawkes mask in their online photos) speak for themselves rather than represent the group, and protest in all kinds of ways. Some, reportedly, have not been kind to kids. There was the case, for example, of a 15-year-old named McKay Hatch, who started a No Cussing Club in South Pasadena, California. When the concept took off in other cities, a group referring to itself as Anonymous launched a counter-campaign, No Cussing Sucks, and posted Hatch's name, photo, and contact information across the Web; he got 22,000 e-mails over two weeks.

But other people in Anonymous have a Robin Hood bent, and this fall, they rode to the rescue of a 12-year-old girl who'd come in for a torrent of hate on Twitter. Her error was to follow the feed of a 17-year-old boy she didn't know and then stop following him when he posted remarks she found rude. The boy took offense and, with three friends, went after her. The boys threatened to "gang bang" her, and one even told her to kill herself. "I'm gonna take today's anger and channel it into talking shit to this 12 year old girl," one wrote. "Blow up [her Twitter handle] till she deletes her twitter," another one added. The girl lived far from the boys, so she wasn't in physical danger, but she was disturbed enough to seek help online.

"I have been told to kill myself alot its scary to think people in the world want you to die :(," she wrote to another Twitter user who asked me to call her Katherine. "He has deleted some of them he was saying things like do you have a rope? and didnt the bleach work?"

Her pleas reached Katherine in the wake of the suicide of a 15-year-old Canadian girl named Amanda Todd. Before Amanda died, she posted a video of herself on YouTube, in which she silently told her story using note cards she'd written on. Amanda said that a man she'd met online had persuaded her to send him a topless photo, then stalked her and released the photo, causing her misery at school. The video is raw and disturbing, and it moved Katherine and a member of Anonymous with the screen name Ash. "It made me choke up," Ash told me. When Katherine discovered that people were still sending the compromising photo of Amanda around online, she and Ash teamed up to help organize a drive to stop them and report offending users to Twitter, which removes pornographic content appearing on its site.

As Katherine and Ash came across other examples of bullying, like rape jokes and suicide taunts, they found that "Twitter will suspend accounts even if they are not in violation of Twitter rules when simply 1000s of people mass report an account as spam," Katherine explained to me in an e-mail. A Twitter spokesperson said this was possible (though he added that if spam reports turn out to be false, most accounts soon go back online). Twitter bans direct and specific threats, and it can block IP addresses to prevent users whose accounts are deleted from easily starting new ones. But the site doesn't have an explicit rule against harassment and intimidation like Facebook does.

While monitoring Twitter for other bullying, Katherine found the 12-year-old girl. When Katherine told Ash, he uncovered the boys' real names and figured out that they were high-schoolers in Abilene, Texas. Then he pieced together Screenshots of their nasty tweets, along with their names and information about the schools they attended, and released it all in a public outing (called a "dox"). "I am sick of seeing people who think they can get away with breaking someone's confidence and planting seeds of self-hate into someone's head," he wrote to them in the dox. "What gives you the fucking right to attack someone to such a breaking point? If you are vile enough to do so and stupid enough to do so on a public forum, such as a social website, then you should know this . . . We will find you and we will highlight your despicable behaviour for all to see."

"I informed them that the damage had been done and there was no going back," he explained to me. "They understood this to be an act by Anonymous when they were then messaged in the hundreds." At first the boys railed against Ash on Twitter, and one played down his involvement, denying that he had ever threatened to rape the girl. But after a while, two of the boys began sending remorseful messages. "For two solid days, every time we logged on, we had another apology from them," Ash said. "You hear a lot of lies and fake apologies, and these guys seemed quite sincere." Katherine thought the boys hadn't understood what impact their tweets would have on the girl receiving them—they hadn't thought of her as a real person. "They were actually shocked," she said. "I'm sure they didn't mean to actually rape a little girl. But she was *scared*. When they started to understand that, we started talking to them about anti-bullying initiatives they could bring to their schools."

I tried contacting the four boys to ask what they made of their encounter with Anonymous, and I heard back from one of them. He said that at first, he thought the girl's account was fake; then he assumed she wasn't upset, because she didn't block the messages he and the other boys were sending. Then Ash stepped in. "When i found out she was hurt by it i had felt horrible," the boy wrote to me in an e-mail. "I honestly don't want to put anyone down, i just like to laugh and it was horrible to know just how hurt she was." He also wrote, "It was shocking to see how big [Anonymous was] and what they do."

Ash also e-mailed his catalog of the boys' tweets to their principals and superintendents. I called the school officials and reached Joey Light, the superintendent for one of the districts in Abilene. He said that when Anonymous contacted him, "to be truthful, I didn't know what it was. At first the whole thing seemed sketchy." Along with the e-mails from Ash, Light got an anonymous phone call from a local number urging him to take action against the boys. Light turned over the materials Ash had gathered to the police officer stationed at the district's high school, who established that one of the boys had been a student there.

The officer investigated, and determined that the boy hadn't done anything to cause problems at school. That meant Light couldn't punish him, he said. "I realize bullying takes a lot of forms, but our student couldn't have harmed this girl physically in any way," he continued. "If you can't show a disruption at school, the courts tell us, that's none of our business." Still, Light told me he that he felt appreciative of Anonymous for intervening. "I don't have the technical expertise or the time to keep track of every kid on Facebook or Twitter or whatever," the superintendent said. "It was unusual, sure, but we would have never done anything if they hadn't notified us."

I talked with Ash and Katherine over Skype about a week after their Texas operation. I wanted to know how they'd conceived of the action they'd taken. Were they dispensing rough justice to one batch of heartless kids? Or were they trying to address cyberbullying more broadly, and if so, how?

Ash and Katherine said they'd seen lots of abuse of teenagers on social-networking sites, and most of the time, no adult seemed to know about it or intervene. They didn't blame the kids' parents for being clueless, but once they spotted danger, as they thought they had in this case, they couldn't bear to just stand by. "It sounds harsh to say we're teaching people a lesson, but they need to realize there are consequences for their actions," Ash said.

He and Katherine don't have professional experience working with teenagers, and I'm sure there are educators and parents who'd see them as suspect rather than helpful. But reading through the hate-filled tweets, I couldn't help thinking that justice Anonymous-style is better than no justice at all. In their own way, Ash and Katherine were stepping into the same breach that Henry Lieberman is trying to fill. And while sites like Facebook and Twitter are still working out ways to address harassment comprehensively, I find myself agreeing with Ash that "someone needs to teach these kids to be mindful, and anyone doing that is a good thing."

For Ash and Katherine, this has been the beginning of set OpAntiBully, an operation that has a Twitter account providing resource lists and links to abuse-report forms. Depending on the case, Ash says, between 50 and 1,000 people—some of whom are part of Anonymous and some of whom are outside recruits—can come together to report an abusive user, or bombard him with angry tweets, or offer support to a target. "It's much more refined now," he told me over e-mail. "Certain people know the targets, and everyone contacts each other via DMs [direct messages]."

In a better online world, it wouldn't be up to Anonymous hackers to swoop in on behalf of vulnerable teenagers. But social networks still present tricky terrain for young people, with traps that other kids spring for them. My own view is that, as parents, we should demand more from these sites, by holding them accountable for enforcing their own rules. After all, collectively, we have consumer power here—along with our kids, we're the site's customers. And as Henry Lieberman's work at MIT demonstrates, it *is* feasible to take stronger action against cyberbullying. If Facebook and Twitter don't like his solution, surely they have the resources to come up with a few more of their own.

Critical Thinking

1. What can parents do to curb dangerous online talk?
2. What can schools do to prevent students from bullying each other online?
3. Will algorithm sites such as BullySpace solve bullying? Why or why not?

Create Central

www.mhhe.com/createcentral

Internet References

Cyberbullying Research Center
    www.cyberbullying.us/resources.php
Online Bullying: A Conversation with Emily Bazelon
    www.theatlantic.com/video/archive/2013/02/online-bullying
Online Bullying: PBS Kids
    http://pbskids.org/itsmylife/friends/bullies/article8
What Is Cyberbullying?
    www.violencepreventionworks.org/public/cyber_bullying.page

---

EMILY BAZELON, a senior editor at *Slate,* is the author of *Sticks and Stones: Defeating the Culture of Bullying and Rediscovering the Power of Character and Empathy,* from which this piece is adapted.

Article   Prepared by: Karen L. Freiberg, *University of Maryland*

Use the Science of What Works to Change the Odds for Children at Risk

The federal government should heed seven essential principles when it invests in breaking the cycle of disadvantage.

SUSAN B. NEUMAN

Learning Outcomes

After reading this article, you will be able to:

- Discuss cost-effective strategies to improve the lives of at-risk children.

- Propose tactics to recruit at-risk families into compensatory programs.

D ating back to President Lyndon Johnson's War on Poverty, Americans have relied on federal dollars to tackle our most intractable issues in education. For example, the federal government helped support school integration, recognize the needs of handicapped and challenged children, and provide for the "least restrictive environments" in classrooms. The federal push for early education led to Head Start, a program targeted to the preschool years. Federal funds also helped to defray the costs of college, allowing even the poorest student to get a high-quality college degree. In these and other cases, federal funds have provided a safety net, a kind of "emergency response system," a means of filling in the gaps when critical national priorities and needs arise that go beyond the means of individual states and local supports for education.

The federal government must once again step up to the challenge. Today, despite the great wealth for some in this nation, nearly one out of every five American children lives in poverty—one of the highest poverty rates in the developed world (Neuman 2008b). And even though our schools are in the midst of the most major and costly education reform in their history and are grappling with the federal mandates to leave no child behind, any influence a school might have is trumped by this reality. The single best determinant of a school's likely output is a single input—the characteristics of the entering children. The painful truth is that we have done almost nothing to raise or change the trajectory of achievement for our disadvantaged children.

The single best determinant of a school's likely output is a single input—the characteristics of the entering children.

The idea that schools, by themselves, can't cure educational inequity is hardly astonishing, but much of our political discourse is implicitly predicated on the notion that schools can do it alone. The national conversation has almost exclusively targeted schools as if they were the source of the problem, as well as the sole solution. The fact that 6.7% of our country's population lives in the very poorest and most vulnerable census tracts with higher proportions of very young children and higher rates of single parenting and less-educated adults, and that it is in these very same census tracts where schools supposedly are failing miserably to close the achievement gap has seemed to be lost in the ongoing conversation (Browning 2003). Expecting teachers to overcome a 30-million-word gap between high- and low-income children (Hart and Risley 2003) in kindergarten alone is beyond optimistic. It is nonsensical. Regardless of what political aisle you stand on, fixing schools has become the cure to everything but the common cold, erasing all debate about the devastating effects of entrenched poverty and what to do about it.

Good schools can go a long way toward helping poor children achieve more, but the fact remains that educational inequity is rooted in economic problems and social pathologies too deep to be overcome by school alone. Even as we work to reform schools as if there were no limits to their powers, our only hope to break the cycle of disadvantage lies outside their influence.

Ending the cycle of disadvantage requires prevention and early intervention programs that help families who are desperately struggling to do the best for their children. Childcare, family support, and community-based programs working in public settings and social service agencies are a critical part of the "closing the gap" equation. But they are not nearly

Research over the last 30 years has pointed to seven essential principles for breaking the cycle of disadvantage:

- Target interventions to children who need help the most;
- Begin early;
- Engage highly trained professionals;
- Provide intensive interventions;
- Coordinate health, education, and social services;
- Provide compensatory instructional benefits; and
- Be accountable.

enough. If we're truly serious about breaking cycles of poverty, inequality, and limited opportunity that place enormous constraints on our nation's resources, we need to recognize and appropriately support education whether it is delivered in clinics, childcare centers, community-based organizations, libraries, church basements, or storefronts. By using the science of what works, we can change the odds, helping create a more promising future for millions of children growing up in vulnerable circumstances.

How We Can Change the Odds

There is the story of 86 young children growing up in a small rural town in the Southeast in the 1960s. The families were black and poor. Isolated both geographically and socially from the larger community and the beginning stirrings of the civil rights movement, these children were about to attend segregated schools. They seemed destined to follow in their parents' footsteps—a life of poverty, discrimination, and disadvantage.

But here the predictable trajectory for what we might expect for these children took on a different, more positive twist. By age 20, these children were neither on welfare nor delinquent or indigent. Instead, most had completed high school, and a few had gone on to college. Tracking their progress, Susan Gray and her colleagues (1982) tell the story of these children's lives, their schooling, and their experiences as participants in an early intervention program, a preschool program fashioned to help children advance through school with greater success.

During the turbulent years of the late 1950s and early 1960s, a group of academics, psychologists, and social scientists began to challenge the prevailing view that ability and achievement were immutable. Recognizing the all-too-consistent correlation between poverty and achievement, these researchers realized that intellectual development couldn't possibly relate solely to the child's inherent ability. Intellectual ability had to relate to the environment. To explore this notion of "intellectual plasticity," a series of experimental early intervention programs began throughout the country, all sharing the presumption that environmental factors must play an important role in children's cognitive and social-emotional development and that early intervention could have significant, positive, long-term effects.

Susan Gray and her colleagues at Vanderbilt University took up the challenge in what became known as the Early Training

Project. Identifying characteristics of early experience that related to educability, she developed an intervention designed to offset the cumulative deficits for these three-year-olds, targeting language, concept development, and motivation. Setting up an intensive summer camp program, highly experienced expert teachers worked with children in small groups, supporting their perceptual and cognitive skills and attitudes related to achievement.

Nevertheless, soon it became clear that even 10 weeks in the highest quality program could hardly overcome the economic hardships that children had accumulated, even at three years old. So she developed a home visiting program, enlisting mature women with certified experience in early education to make weekly hour-long visits with the children and parents in an effort to bridge what had been learned from one summer to the next. These home visits weren't just about teaching, but about enlisting the mothers' emotional support for helping their children learn, explore, and communicate, with the goal of eventually meeting school requirements. Over the next 2½ years, children from ages 3 to 6 and their families participated in these summer programs and winter visits.

Yet the resolute Gray and her colleagues charted children's progress far beyond these years. In fact, at regular intervals, she continued to measure their development until they were 20 years old. And strikingly, many of the gains that Gray and her colleagues reported were enduring, some for long periods of time. Children were able to meet school requirements, fewer were placed in special education, fewer were likely to be retained or drop out of high school. Even those who became pregnant as teens were more likely to return to school. As one mother remarked, "I wasn't going to let a little old baby keep me from graduatin' from high school."

There is another story, this time in the heart of the Rust Belt—Ypsilanti, Michigan, home to automobile manufacturing—where local school administrators, despite entreaties from local families, refused to adjust the curriculum to better serve their high-risk children. With high special education referrals and high school dropout rates soaring, 123 of the poorest children in the neighborhood were about to enter these settings with all the odds against their success.

However, David Weikart and his special service staff took things into their own hands (Weikart, Bond, and McNeil 1978). Checking the local census for who might be entering from the Perry School neighborhood, Weikart and his team walked door-to-door, identifying children most likely at risk for school failure. He found them in crowded residences with over twice the number of people you might expect in a typical household, their children's intelligence bordering only on educability (79 I.Q.), the parents unskilled and too beaten down to provide much encouragement for learning. Working against all odds, Weikart was determined to change those odds by developing what was unheard of at the time, a daily preschool program starting with three-year-olds along with regular visits to their families in homes. Over a period of either one or two years, specialists in early childhood involved small groups of children—no more than five or six at a time—to actively learn, think, plan, and express their ideas in language.

Recognizing that children learn best through hands-on activities, such as sand and water play, teachers encouraged them to experiment with materials and talk about what they'd learned. They would ask "why" questions, like "Why might the cork float in water?" helping the children to discover new concepts on their own. In addition to turning around these children's lives, the enormous return on investment would be hard for an economist to ignore: 65% of these children graduated from high school, compared to only 45% of those not in the program; 61% got good jobs, compared to just 38% in the nonprogram group. The findings have remained stable some 27 years later.

Garber recognized that risk is a caution and not a condemnation, essentially proving that early intervention had the power to change children's lives.

Then there is another story that completely blows away the myth of equal opportunity for all children. In this case, the story is about 20 infants in Milwaukee, Wisconsin, born to severely low-functioning mothers. Each family's poverty conditions only exacerbated any hope for stimulation or learning. Examining surveys that yielded the likely trajectory for these children, all evidence amassed by Herb Garber (1988) suggested that by the time they entered school, these children would likely succumb to what was described as "induced retardation," declining functioning and cognitive processing skills.

Recognizing, perhaps for the first time, that disorganized multi-risk families face a level of disadvantage far different from poor but stable working families, Garber devised a two-generation program, foreshadowing others that would come later. Starting at about three months, infant caregivers helped prepare mothers and children, first visiting them for three to five hours three times a week, then transitioning them to center-based care, where the infants received seven hours of stimulating activities each day until they were four years old. At the same time, caregivers helped mothers learn basic home-management skills and got them enrolled in vocational education programs so that they could get jobs and responsibly take care of their children.

Garber's intervention effectively stopped the decline in children's cognitive development. He prevented the intergenerational transfer of risk and disadvantage. In fact, all experimental children whose mothers were mentally retarded performed at least 20 points higher than their mothers and averaged 32 points higher than did their own mothers. By providing an intensive program designed to compensate for what children were lacking in the home, Garber was able to offset the negative influences of an impoverished learning environment. By focusing on the single most important environmental influence—the intimate interaction between child and caregiver—he was able to help severely at-risk children avoid significant cognitive delays. He recognized that risk is a caution and not a condemnation, essentially proving that early intervention had the power to change children's lives.

Despite differences in location, population, and risk categories, each of these stories—backed by the solid scientific evidence that accompanies them (Consortium for Longitudinal Studies 1983; Shonkoff and Phillips 2000)—share some striking commonalities. Each recognized the extraordinary role that environment plays in children's development. Acknowledging its malleability, each modified the environment to maximize children's potential. Involving the primary caregivers in their children's education, each regarded the family as a learning unit that is a critical part of the solution.

Weaving these accounts together, however, illuminates an even more powerful story. Across these richly detailed programs is a set of principles for what is required to make a difference in the lives of highly vulnerable children. Recognizing the sense of urgency, these programs *targeted their efforts to children and families at greatest risk.* They *began early* in the child's development, engaging *highly trained professionals* to provide *intensive interventions,* operationally defining intensity as more hours, longer-term, and greater focus according to the family's needs. Together, these programs reached children and families where they were located, both psychologically and physically, through *comprehensive services,* realizing that a child who is suffering from Otis media (ear infections) and other illnesses can't possibly be successful in learning without relief from continuing pain. Furthermore, they recognized that the problem was not children's ability to learn, but the opportunities to learn, so they provided *compensatory instructional benefits* to make up for the cognitively and socially stimulating activities that many of these children lacked. Finally, all were *accountable,* using tangible, quantitative evidence and evaluations to examine whether they were achieving desired effects, adjusting when necessary in order to make that happen.

In essence, evident throughout these programs, and subsequently validated through research over the last 30 years (Bowman, Donovan, and Burns 2000; Farren 2000; Shonkoff and Phillips 2000), are seven essential principles for breaking the cycle of disadvantage:

- Target interventions to children who need help the most;
- Begin early;
- Engage highly trained professionals;
- Provide intensive interventions;
- Coordinate health, education, and social services;
- Provide compensatory instructional benefits; and
- Be accountable.

These stories, each better known by their project names and illustrative leaders—Susan Gray's Early Learning Project, David Weikart's Perry Preschool Project, and Herb Garber's Milwaukee Project—were originally conceived as research and demonstration projects and, as such, designed to examine the extent to which interventions, given adequate resources, a fully engaged and highly talented staff, and continuous and ongoing monitoring of progress, might affect the cognitive and social development of disadvantaged children. Capturing the public's attention even more than skill achievements, however, were the real life measures used in these reports, such as employment histories and declines in delinquency that, when combined with cost-benefit analysis, led to dramatic claims that early intervention was a highly sound investment, saving citizens an average of $7 for every dollar spent.

Together, they set a benchmark for what was possible, making a compelling case in public policy for early intervention and for the ways in which resources might be allocated for improving achievement for highly disadvantaged children.

The science of intervention has come a long way since these projects. Yet the principles remain the same. Programs that serve our most vulnerable children are tied to seven essentials and have a coherent and self consistent vision of pedagogy, curriculum, and structure. Interventions like the Nurse-Family Partnership, Early Head Start, and Avance provide critical parent supports early on; Reach Out and Read and Books Aloud give important access to books in community wide programs in libraries and clinics; Core Knowledge and Bright Beginnings have programs that help children develop content-rich learning in developmentally appropriate ways (Neuman 2008*a*).

These programs and others like them provide demonstrable evidence that we can remove some of the most significant risk factors through systematic intervention and support. And this new knowledge can become the foundation of a broader, bolder new effort in education to change the odds of our most at risk children, reorienting the federal role in education to become the emergency response system it was designed to be.

References

Bowman, Barbara, Suzanne Donovan, and M. Susan Burns. *Eager to Learn: Educating Our Preschoolers.* Washington D.C.: National Academy Press, 2000.

Browning, Lynnley. "U.S. Income Gap Widening." *The New York Times,* September 25, 2003, p. 10.

Consortium for Longitudinal Studies. *As the Twig Is Bent.* Hillsdale, N.J.: Lawrence Erlbaum Associates, 1983.

Farren, Dale C. "Another Decade of Intervention for Children Who Are Low Income or Disabled: What Do We Do Now?" In *Handbook of Early Childhood Intervention,* ed. Jack P. Shonkoff and Sam Meisels. New York: Cambridge University Press, 2000.

Garber, Herb. *The Milwaukee Project.* Washington, D.C.: American Association on Mental Retardation, 1988.

Gray, Susan W., Barbara K. Ramsey, and Rupert A. Klaus. *From 3 to 20: The Early Training Project.* Baltimore, Md.: University Park Press, 1982.

Hart, Betty, and Todd Risley. "The Early Catastrophe." *American Educator* 27 (Spring 2003): 4, 6–9.

Neuman, Susan B. *Changing the Odds for Children at Risk: Seven Essential Principles of Educational Programs That Break the Cycle of Poverty.* Westport, Conn.: Praeger, 2008a.

Neuman, Susan B., ed. *Educating the Other America: Top Experts Tackle Poverty, Literacy, and Achievement in Our Schools.* Baltimore, Md.: Brookes, 2008b.

Shonkoff, Jack P., and Deborah Phillips, eds. *From Neurons to Neighborhoods.* Washington, D.C.: National Academy Press, 2000.

Weikart, David, James T. Bond, and J.T. McNeil. *The Ypsilanti Perry Preschool Project.* Ypsilanti, Mich.: High/Scope, 1978.

Critical Thinking

1. Give examples of activities of daily life for children living in poverty.

2. Explain why children at-risk affect the school achievement of all students.

3. Suggest research-based solutions for high-low income inequality.

Create Central

www.mhhe.com/createcentral

Internet References

Effects of Poverty, Hunger, and Homelessness on Children and Youth
www.apa.org/pi/families/poverty.aspx

Families and Work Institute
www.familiesandwork.org/index.html

Harborview Injury Prevention and Research Center
http://depts.washington.edu/hiprc

Susan B. Neuman is a professor of educational studies at the University of Michigan, Ann Arbor, Michigan.

From *Phi Delta Kappan*, April 2009. Reprinted with permission of Phi Delta Kappa International. All rights reserved. www.pdkintl.org.

Unit 5

UNIT

Prepared by: Karen L. Freiberg, *University of Maryland*

Development during Adolescence and Young Adulthood

The term "adolescence" was coined in 1904 by G. Stanley Hall, one of the world's first psychologists. He saw adolescence as a discrete stage of life that bridges the gap between sexual maturity (puberty) and socioemotional and cognitive maturity. He believed it to be characterized by "storm and stress." At the beginning of the 20th century, it was typical for young men to begin working in middle childhood (there were no child labor laws), and for young women to work as wives and mothers as soon as they were fertile and/or spoken for. At the turn of the 21st century, the beginning of adolescence was marked by the desire to be independent of parental control. The end of adolescence, which once coincided with the age of legal maturity (usually 16 or 18, depending on local laws), has now been extended upward. Although legal maturity is now 18 (voting, enlisting in the armed services, owning property, marrying without permission), the social norm is to consider persons in their late teens as adolescents, not adults. The years between 18 and 21 are often problematic for youth tethered between adult and not-adult status. They can be married, with children, living in homes of their own, running their own businesses, yet not be able to drive their cars in certain places or at certain times. They can go to college and participate in social activities, but they cannot legally drink. Often the 21st birthday is viewed as a rite of passage into adulthood in the United States because it signals the legal right to buy and drink alcoholic beverages. "Maturity" is usually reserved for those who have achieved full economic as well as socioemotional independence as adults.

Erik Erikson, the personality theorist, marked the passage from adolescence to young adulthood by a change in the nuclear conflicts of two life stages: identity versus role confusion and intimacy versus isolation. Adolescents struggle to answer the question, "Who am I?" Young adults struggle to find a place within the existing social order where they can feel intimacy rather than isolation. In the 1960s, Erikson wrote that females resolve both their conflicts of identity and intimacy by living vicariously through their husbands, an unacceptable idea to many females today.

As adolescence has been extended, so too has young adulthood. One hundred years ago, life expectancy did not extend too far beyond menopause for women and retirement for men. Young adulthood began when adolescents finished puberty. Parents of teenagers were middle-aged, between 35 and 55. Later marriages and delayed childbearing have redefined the line between young adulthood and middle age. Many people today consider themselves young adults well into their 40s.

Jean Piaget, the cognitive theorist, marked the end of the development of mental processes with the end of adolescence. Once full physical maturity, including brain maturity, was achieved, one reached the acme of his or her abilities to assimilate, accommodate, organize, and adapt to sensations, perceptions, associations, and discriminations. Piaget did not feel cognitive processing of information ceased with adulthood. He believed, however, that cognitive judgments would not reach a stage higher than the abstract, hypothetical, logical reasoning of formal operations. Today many cognitive theorists believe postformal operations are possible.

Article   Prepared by: Karen L. Freiberg, *University of Maryland*

The Incredible Shrinking Childhood

How Early Is Too Early for Puberty?

Elizabeth Weil

Learning Outcomes

After reading this article, you will be able to:

- Appraise some of the reasons for precocious puberty.

- Suggest several ways that parents can deal with girls who experience early puberty.

One day last year when her daughter, Ainsley, was 9, Tracee Sioux pulled her out of her elementary school in Fort Collins, Colo., and drove her an hour south, to Longmont, in hopes of finding a satisfying reason that Ainsley began growing pubic hair at age 6. Ainsley was the tallest child in her third-grade class. She had a thick, enviable blond-streaked ponytail and big feet, like a puppy's. The curves of her Levi's matched her mother's.

"How was your day?" Tracee asked Ainsley as she climbed in the car.

"Pretty good."

"What did you do at a recess?"

"I played on the slide with my friends."

In the back seat, Ainsley wiggled out of her pink parka and looked in her backpack for her Harry Potter book. Over the past three years, Tracee—pretty and well-put-together, wearing a burnt orange blouse that matched her necklace and her bag—had taken Ainsley to see several doctors. They ordered blood tests and bone-age X-rays and turned up nothing unusual. "The doctors always come back with these blank looks on their faces, and then they start redefining what normal is," Tracee said as we drove down Interstate 25, a ribbon of asphalt that runs close to where the Great Plains bump up against the Rockies. "And I always just sit there thinking, What are you talking about, normal? Who gets pubic hair in first grade?"

Fed up with mainstream physicians, Tracee began pursuing less conventional options. She tried giving Ainsley diindolylmethane, or DIM, a supplement that may or may not help a body balance its hormones. She also started a blog, the Girl Revolution, with a mission to "revolutionize the way we think about, treat and raise girls," and the accompanying T.G.R. Body line of sunscreens and lotions marketed to tweens and described by

Tracee as "natural, organic, craptastic-free products" containing "no estrogens, phytoestrogens, endocrine disrupters."

None of this stopped Ainsley's body from maturing ahead of its time. That afternoon, Tracee and Ainsley visited the office of Jared Allomong, an applied kinesiologist. Applied kinesiology is a "healing art" sort of like chiropractic. Practitioners test muscle strength in order to diagnose health problems; it's a refuge for those skeptical and weary of mainstream medicine.

"So, what brings you here today?" Allomong asked mother and daughter. Tracee stroked Ainsley's arm and said, wistfully, "Precocious puberty."

Allomong nodded. "What are the symptoms?"

"Pubic hair, armpit hair, a few pimples around the nose. Some budding." Tracee gestured with her hands, implying breasts. "The emotional stuff is getting worse, too. Ainsley's been getting super upset about little things, crying, and she doesn't know why. I think she's cycling with me."

Ainsley closed her eyes, as if to shut out the embarrassment. The ongoing quest to understand why her young body was turning into a woman's was not one of Ainsley's favorite pastimes. She preferred torturing her 6-year-old brother and playing school with the neighborhood kids. (Ainsley was always the teacher, and she was very strict.)

"Have you seen Western doctors for this?" Allomong asked.

Tracee laughed. "Yes, many," she said. "None suggested any course of action. They left us hanging." She repeated for Allomong what she told me in the car: "They seem to have changed the definition of 'normal.'"

For many parents of early-developing girls, "normal" is a crazy-making word, especially when uttered by a doctor; it implies that the patient, or patient's mother, should quit being neurotic and accept that not much can be done. Allomong listened intently. He nodded and took notes, asking Tracee detailed questions about her birth-control history and validating her worst fears by mentioning the "extremely high levels" of estrogen-mimicking chemicals in the food and water supply. After about 20 minutes he asked Ainsley to lie on a table. There he performed a lengthy physical exam that involved testing the strength in Ainsley's arms and legs while she held small glass vials filled with compounds like cortisol, estrogen and sugar. (Kinesiologists believe that weak muscles indicate illness, and that a patient's muscles will test as weaker when he or she is holding a substance that contributes to health problems.)

Finally, he asked Ainsley to sit up. "It doesn't test like it's her own estrogens," Allomong reported to Tracee, meaning he didn't think Ainsley's ovaries were producing too many hormones on their own. "I think it's xeno-estrogens, from the environment," he explained. "And I think it's stress and insulin and sugar."

"You can't be more specific?" Tracee asked, pleading. "Like tell me what crap in my house I can get rid of?" Allomong shook his head.

On the ride back to Fort Collins, Tracee tried to cheer herself up thinking about the teenage suffering that Ainsley would avoid. "You know, I was one of those flat-chested girls at age 14, reading, 'Are You There God? It's Me, Margaret,' just praying to get my period. Ainsley won't have to go through that! When she gets her period, we're going to have a big old party. And then I'm going to go in the bathroom and cry."

In the late 1980s, Marcia Herman-Giddens, then a physician's associate in the pediatric department of the Duke University Medical Center, started noticing that an awful lot of 8- and 9-year-olds in her clinic had sprouted pubic hair and breasts. The medical wisdom, at that time, based on a landmark 1960 study of institutionalized British children, was that puberty began, on average, for girls at age 11. But that was not what Herman-Giddens was seeing. So she started collecting data, eventually leading a study with the American Academy of Pediatrics that sampled 17,000 girls, finding that among white girls, the average age of breast budding was 9.96. Among black girls, it was 8.87.

When Herman-Giddens published these numbers, in 1997 in Pediatrics, she set off a social and endocrinological firestorm. "I had no idea it would be so huge," Herman-Giddens told me recently. "The Lolita syndrome"—the prurient fascination with the sexuality of young girls—"created a lot of emotional interest. As a feminist, I wish it didn't." Along with medical professionals, mothers, worried about their daughters, flocked to Herman-Giddens's slide shows, gasping as she flashed images of possible culprits: obesity, processed foods, plastics.

Meanwhile, doctors wrote letters to journals criticizing the sample in Herman-Giddens's study. (She collected data from girls at physicians' offices, leaving her open to the accusation that it wasn't random.) Was the age of puberty really dropping? Parents said yes. Leading pediatric endocrinologists said no. The stalemate lasted a dozen years. Then in August 2010, the conflict seemed to resolve. Well-respected researchers at three big institutions—Cincinnati Children's Hospital, Kaiser Permanente of Northern California and Mount Sinai School of Medicine in New York—published another study in Pediatrics, finding that by age 7, 10 percent of white girls, 23 percent of black girls, 15 percent of Hispanic girls and 2 percent of Asian girls had started developing breasts.

Now most researchers seem to agree on one thing: Breast budding in girls is starting earlier. The debate has shifted to what this means. Puberty, in girls, involves three events: the growth of breasts, the growth of pubic hair and a first period.

Typically the changes unfold in that order, and the process takes about two years. But the data show a confounding pattern. While studies have shown that the average age of breast budding has fallen significantly since the 1970s, the average age of first period, or menarche, has remained fairly constant, dropping to only 12.5 from 12.8 years. Why would puberty be starting earlier yet ending more or less at the same time?

To endocrinologists, girls who go through puberty early fall into two camps: girls with diagnosable disorders like central precocious puberty, and girls who simply develop on the early side of the normal curve. But the line between the groups is blurring. "There used to be a discrete gap between normal and abnormal, and there isn't anymore," Louise Greenspan, a pediatric endocrinologist and co-author of the August 2010 Pediatrics paper, told me one morning in her office at Kaiser Permanente in San Francisco. Among the few tools available to help distinguish between so-called "normal" and "precocious" puberty are bone-age X-rays. To illustrate how they work, Greenspan pulled out a beautiful old book, Greulich and Pyle's "Radiographic Atlas of Skeletal Development of the Hand and Wrist," a standard text for pediatric endocrinologists. Each page showed an X-ray of a hand illustrating "bone age." The smallest hand was from a newborn baby, the oldest from an adult female. "When a baby is born, there's all this cartilage," Greenspan said, pointing to large black gaps surrounding an array of delicate white bones. As the body grows, the pattern of black and white changes. The white bones lengthen, and the black interstices between them, some of which is cartilage, shrink. This process stops at the end of puberty, when the growth plates fuse.

One main risk for girls with true precocious puberty is advanced bone age. Puberty includes a final growth spurt, after which girls mostly stop growing. If that growth spurt starts too early in life, it ends at an early age too, meaning a child will have fewer growing years total. A girl who has her first period at age 10 will stop growing younger and end up shorter than a genetically identical girl who gets her first period at age 13.

That morning one of Greenspan's patients was a 6 ½-year-old girl with a bone age of 9. She was the tallest girl in her class at school. She started growing pubic hair at age 4. No one thought her growth curve was normal, not even her doctors. (Eight used to be the age cutoff for normal pubic-hair growth in girls; now it's as early as 7.) For this girl, Greenspan prescribed a once-a-month shot of the hormone Leuprolide, to halt puberty's progress. The girl hated the shot. Yet nobody second-guessed the treatment plan. The mismatch between her sexual maturation and her age—and the discomfort that created, for everybody—was just too great.

By contrast, Ainsley was older, and her puberty was progressing more slowly, meaning she wasn't at much of an increased risk for short stature or breast cancer. (Early periods are associated with breast cancer, though researchers don't know if the risk stems from greater lifetime exposure to estrogen or a higher lifetime number of menstrual cycles, or perhaps something else, like the age at which a girl has her growth spurt.) In cases of girls Ainsley's age, Greenspan has been asked by parents to prescribe

Leuprolide. But Greenspan says this is a bad idea, because Leuprolide's possible side effects—including an increased risk of osteoporosis—outweigh the benefits for girls that age. "If you have a normal girl, a girl who's 8 or 9, there's a big ethical issue of giving them medicine. Giving them medicine says, 'Something is wrong with your body,' as opposed to, 'This is your body, and let's all find a way to accept it.'"

> ## "'Giving them medicine says, Something is wrong with your body, as opposed to, This is your body, and let's all find a way to accept it.'"

"I would have a long conversation with her family, show them all the data," Greenspan continues. Once she has gone through what she calls "the process of normalizing"—a process intended to replace anxiety with statistics—she has rarely had a family continue to insist on puberty-arresting drugs. Indeed, most parents learn to cope with the changes and help their daughters adjust too. One mother described for me buying a drawer full of football shirts, at her third-grade daughter's request, to hide her maturing body. Another reminded her daughter that it's O.K. to act her age. "It's like when you have a really big toddler and people expect the kid to talk in full sentences. People look at my daughter and say, 'Look at those cheekbones!' We have to remind her: 'You may look 12, but you're 9. It's O.K. to lose your cool and stomp your feet.'"

"We still have a lot to learn about how early puberty affects girls psychologically," says Paul Kaplowitz, chief of endocrinology at Children's National Medical Center. "We do know that some girls who start maturing by age 8 progress rapidly and have their first period before age 10, and many parents prefer that we use medications to slow things down. However, many girls do fine if they are simply monitored and their parents are reassured that they will get through it without major problems."

In some ways early puberty is most straightforward for families like those of the kindergartner on Leuprolide. She has a diagnosis, a treatment plan. In Greenspan's office, I asked the girl's father at what age he might choose to take his child off the drugs and let her puberty proceed. He laughed. Then he spoke for most parents when he said, "Would it be bad to say 22?"

So why are so many girls with no medical disorder growing breasts early? Doctors don't know exactly why, but they have identified several contributing factors.

Girls who are overweight are more likely to enter puberty early than thinner girls, and the ties between obesity and puberty start at a very young age. As Emily Walvoord of the Indiana University School of Medicine points out in her paper "The Timing of Puberty: Is It Changing? Does It Matter?" body-mass index and pubertal timing are associated at age 5, age 3, even age 9 months. This fact has shifted pediatric endocrinologists away from what used to be known as the critical-weight theory of puberty—the idea that once a girl's body reaches a certain mass, puberty inevitably starts—to a critical-fat theory of puberty. Researchers now believe that fat tissue, not poundage, sets off a feedback loop that can cause a body to mature. As Robert Lustig, a professor of clinical pediatrics at the University of California, San Francisco's Benioff Children's Hospital, explains, fatter girls have higher levels of the hormone leptin, which can lead to early puberty, which leads to higher estrogen levels, which leads to greater insulin resistance, causing girls to have yet more fat tissue, more leptin and more estrogen, the cycle feeding on itself, until their bodies physically mature.

In addition, animal studies show that the exposure to some environmental chemicals can cause bodies to mature early. Of particular concern are endocrine-disrupters, like "xeno-estrogens" or estrogen mimics. These compounds behave like steroid hormones and can alter puberty timing. For obvious ethical reasons, scientists cannot perform controlled studies proving the direct impact of these chemicals on children, so researchers instead look for so-called "natural experiments," one of which occurred in 1973 in Michigan, when cattle were accidentally fed grain contaminated with an estrogen-mimicking chemical, the flame retardant PBB. The daughters born to the pregnant women who ate the PBB-laced meat and drank the PBB-laced milk started menstruating significantly earlier than their peers.

One concern, among parents and researchers, is the effect of simultaneous exposures to many estrogen-mimics, including the compound BPA, which is ubiquitous. Ninety-three percent of Americans have traces of BPA in their bodies. BPA was first made in 1891 and used as a synthetic estrogen in the 1930s. In the 1950s commercial manufacturers started putting BPA in hard plastics. Since then BPA has been found in many common products, including dental sealants and cash-register receipts. More than a million pounds of the substance are released into the environment each year.

Family stress can disrupt puberty timing as well. Girls who from an early age grow up in homes without their biological fathers are twice as likely to go into puberty younger as girls who grow up with both parents. Some studies show that the presence of a stepfather in the house also correlates with early puberty. Evidence links maternal depression with developing early. Children adopted from poorer countries who have experienced significant early-childhood stress are also at greater risk for early puberty once they're ensconced in Western families.

Bruce Ellis, a professor of Family Studies and Human Development at the University of Arizona, discovered along with his colleagues a pattern of early puberty in girls whose parents divorced when those girls were between 3 and 8 years old and whose fathers were considered socially deviant (meaning they abused drugs or alcohol, were violent, attempted suicide or did prison time). In another study, published in 2011, Ellis and his colleagues showed that first graders who are most reactive to stress—kids whose pulse, respiratory rate and cortisol levels fluctuate most in response to environmental challenges—entered puberty earliest when raised in difficult homes. Evolutionary psychology offers a theory: A stressful childhood inclines a body toward early reproduction; if life is hard, best to mature young. But such theories are tough to prove.

Evolutionary psychology offers a theory: A stressful childhood inclines a body toward early reproduction; if life is hard, best to mature young.

Social problems don't just increase the risk for early puberty; early puberty increases the risk for social problems as well. We know that girls who develop ahead of their peers tend to have lower self-esteem, more depression and more eating disorders. They start drinking and lose their virginity sooner. They have more sexual partners and more sexually transmitted diseases. "You can almost predict it"—that early maturing teenagers will take part in more high-risk behaviors, says Tonya Chaffee, associate clinical professor of pediatrics at University of California, San Francisco, who oversees the Teen and Young Adult Health Center at San Francisco General Hospital. Half of the patients in her clinic are or have been in the foster system. She sees in the outlines of their early-developing bodies the stresses of their lives—single parent or no parent, little or no money, too much exposure to violence.

Some of this may stem from the same social stresses that contribute to early puberty in the first place, and some of it may stem from other factors, including the common nightmare of adolescence: being different. As Julia Graber, associate chairwoman of psychology at the University of Florida, has shown, all "off-time" developers—early as well as late—have more depression during puberty than typically-developing girls. But for the late bloomers, the negative effect wears off once puberty ends. For early bloomers, the effect persists, causing higher levels of depression and anxiety through at least age 30, perhaps all through life. "Some early-maturing girls have very serious problems," Graber told me. "More than I expected when I started looking for clinical significance. I was surprised that it was so severe."

Researchers know there's a relationship between pubertal timing and depression, but they don't know exactly how that relationship works. One theory is that going through puberty early, relative to other kinds of cognitive development, causes changes in the brain that make it more susceptible to depression. As Elizabeth Sowell, director of the Developmental Cognitive Neuroimaging Laboratory at Children's Hospital Los Angeles, points out, girls in general tend to go through puberty earlier than boys, and starting around puberty, girls, as a group, also experience more anxiety and depression than boys do. Graber offers a broader hypothesis, perhaps the best understanding of the puberty-depression connection we have for now. "It may be that early maturers do not have as much time as other girls to accomplish the developmental tasks of childhood. They face new challenges while everybody else is still dealing with the usual development of childhood. This might be causing them to make less successful transitions into adolescence and beyond."

Over the past year, I talked to mothers who tried to forestall their daughters' puberty in many different ways. Some trained with them for 5K runs (exercise is one of the few interventions known to help prevent early puberty); others trimmed milk and meat containing hormones from their daughters' diets; some purged from their homes plastics, pesticides and soy. Yet sooner rather than later, most threw up their hands. "I'm empathetic with parents in despair and wanting a sense of agency," says Sandra Steingraber, an ecologist and the author of *Raising Elijah: Protecting Our Children in an Age of Environmental Crisis*. "But this idea that we, as parents, should be scrutinizing labels and vetting birthday party goody bags—the idea that all of us in our homes should be acting as our own Environmental Protection Agencies and Departments of Interior—is just nuts. Even if we could read every label and scrutinize every product, our kids are in schools and running in and out of other people's homes where there are brominated flame retardants on the furniture and pesticides used in the backyard."

Adding to the anxiety is the fact that we know so little about how early puberty works. A few researchers, including Robert Lustig, of Benioff Children's Hospital, are beginning to wonder if many of those girls with early breast growth are in puberty at all. Lustig is a man prone to big, inflammatory ideas. (He believes that sugar is a poison, as he has argued in this magazine.) To make the case that some girls with early breast growth may not be in puberty, he starts with basic science. True puberty starts in the brain, he explains, with the production of gonadotropin-releasing hormone, or GnRH. "There is no puberty without GnRH," Lustig told me. GnRH is like the ball that rolls down the ramp that knocks over the book that flips the stereo switch. Specifically, GnRH trips the pituitary, which signals the ovaries. The ovaries then produce estrogen, and the estrogen causes the breasts to grow. But as Lustig points out, the estrogen that is causing that growth in young girls may have a different origin. It may come from the girls' fat tissue (postmenopausal women produce estrogen in their fat tissue) or from an environmental source. "And if that estrogen didn't start with GnRH, it's not puberty, end of story," Lustig says. "Breast development doesn't automatically mean early puberty. It might, but it doesn't have to." Don't even get him started on the relationship between pubic-hair growth and puberty. "Any paper linking pubic hair with early puberty is garbage. Garbage. Pubic hair just means androgens, or male hormones. The first sign of puberty in girls is estrogen. Androgen is not even on the menu."

Frank Biro, lead author of the August 2010 Pediatrics paper and director of adolescent medicine at Cincinnati Children's Hospital, began having similar suspicions last spring after he flew to Denmark to give a lecture. Following his talk, Biro looked over the published data on puberty of his colleague Anders Juul. In Juul's study, some of the girls with early breast development had unexpectedly low levels of estradiol, the predominant form of estrogen in women's bodies from the onset of puberty through menopause. Biro had seen a pattern like this in his data, suggesting to him that the early breast growth might be coming from nonovarian estrogens. That is to say, the headwaters for the pubertal changes might not be in the girls' brains. He is now running models on his own data to see if he can determine where the nonovarian estrogens are coming from.

The possibility that these early "normal" girls are reacting to estrogens that are not coming from their ovaries is compelling. Part of the comfort is that a girl who is not yet in puberty may not have developed an adolescent brain. This means she would not yet feel the acute tug of her own sexual urges. She would not seek thrills and risk. Still, the idea that there are enough toxins or fat cells in a child's body to cause breast development is hardly consoling. Besides, some of the psychosocial problems of early puberty derive from what's happening inside a girl's body; others, from how people react to her. "If a girl is 10 and she looks 15, it doesn't make any difference if her pituitary is turned on or if something else caused her breast growth," Biro says. "She looks like a middle adolescent. People are going to treat her that way. Maybe she's not interested in reciprocal sex, but she might be pressured into sex nonetheless, and her social skills will be those of a 10-year-old."

So what are families of early bloomers to do? Doctors urge parents to focus on their daughters' emotional and physical health rather than on stopping or slowing development. In this way, the concept of a new normal is not just a brushoff but an encouragement to support a girl who is vulnerable.

"I know they can't change the fact that their daughter started developing early, but they can change what happens downstream," Louise Greenspan, the pediatric endocrinologist at Kaiser Permanente, told me. Parents can keep their daughters active and at healthy body weights. They can treat them the age they are, not the age they look. They can defend against a culture that sells push-up bikinis for 7-year-olds and otherwise sexualizes young girls. "Most of the psychological issues associated with early puberty are related to risk-taking behaviors," Greenspan continued, and parents can mitigate those. "I know it sounds corny and old-fashioned, but if you're in a supportive family environment, where you are eating family meals and reading books together, you actually do have control." Early breast growth may be just that—early breast growth: disconcerting, poorly understood, but not a guarantee of our worst fears. "You don't go directly from the first signs of early puberty to anorexia, depression, drinking and early sexual debut."

In Fort Collins, Tracee, Ainsley's mother, tried to stay focused on the positive. At one point during my visit, she disappeared into her basement, the headquarters for her company, T.G.R. Body, and returned with a pink hat box filled with chemical-free samples of Peppermint Pimple Popper and Bad Hair Day Miracle Powder. "I just want to be part of the solution," Tracee said, rubbing a sample of silver hair-streaking

gel on my wrist. "I'm so tired of running away. I need to have something Ainsley is moving toward."

Mothers who have been through it urge candor. "Be honest with her, and by honest I mean brutally honest"—about what's going to happen to her body—"while still being kind," says the mother of a girl who recently turned 10 but who first showed signs of developing what she calls "a shape" at age 3. "You don't want your daughter experiencing something for which she's unprepared."

Patience and perspective may be the greatest palliatives. "The thing with puberty is that everybody is going to go through it at some point," another mother told me. Three years ago this woman was installing small trash cans in her third-grade girl's school bathroom stalls so that her daughter could discreetly throw away menstrual pads. But now that daughter is 12, in the sixth grade; her body seems less strange. "I feel so much better, and so does she. By another two or three years down the road, all the other girls will have caught up."

Critical Thinking

1. Why do some researchers insist that there is no puberty without the production of gonadotropin-releasing hormone (GnRH)?

2. Identify sources of environmental estrogens that may cause breast development in preadolescents.

3. How are cognitive development and depression correlated in females who experience early puberty? What might explain this correlation?

Create Central

www.mhhe.com/createcentral

Internet References

Link between Body Fat and the Timing of Puberty
  http://pediatrics.aapublications.org/content/121
Lolita Syndrome
  www.hindustantimes.com/Entertainment/Wellness
Onset of Puberty in Girls Has Fallen
  www.theguardian.com/society/2012/oct/21/puberty
Physical Development in Girls: What to Expect
  www.healthychildren.org/English/ages-stages/gradeschool

Article   Prepared by: Karen L. Freiberg, *University of Maryland*

Foresight Conquers Fear of the Future

Today's youth are growing up in the midst of radical social and economic transformations. Now is the time to develop the most critical skill for effectively managing their careers and personal lives: foresight.

EDWARD CORNISH

Learning Outcomes

After reading this article, you will be able to:

• Explain why many young adults are making critical decisions without parental guidance.

• Describe the problem known as "future phobia."

" **I**'m scared," the young man confessed. "I'm starting my eighteenth year in a world that makes no sense to me. All I know is that this world I'm living in is a shambles and I don't know how to put it together."

The young man bared his soul to an invisible audience during a radio call-in show. Other callers agreed with his dismal assessment of the state of the world. Nobody offered an answer for his fears.

Bill Moyers, the TV interviewer, happened to be listening that night and was profoundly affected by what he heard.

"Such lamentations," Moyers commented later, "are deep currents running throughout the liberal West today. Our secular and scientific societies are besieged by violence, moral anarchy, and purposelessness that have displaced any mobilizing vision of the future except hedonism and consumerism."

Moyers put his finger on what may be a key challenge faced by many young people today: their inability to think realistically, creatively, and hopefully about the future. Instead, these young people suffer from what can be described as "futurephobia."

Some futurephobes have an acute version of this malady, like the young man described by Moyers, but most futurephobes simply focus on their immediate circumstances and drift into the future without thinking much about it at all. Either way, they may drift into financial or other kinds of trouble.

The connection between poor foresight and serious problems is widely recognized by psychologists and sociologists. Yale sociologist Wendell Bell asserts that some authorities "go so far as to claim that all forms of deviant, criminal, and reckless behavior have the same fundamental cause: the tendency to pursue immediate benefits without concern for long-term costs, a disregard for inevitable and undesirable future consequences."

Successful self-management, says Bell, requires understanding and giving appropriate value to the likely consequences of your actions. If you have little or no foresight, you cannot think realistically and creatively about your future, so you cannot steer your career and personal life toward long-term success.

Poor foresight can threaten not just the careers of emerging adults, but even their lives. Young people lacking foresight are prone to act recklessly—drive too fast, use drugs, play with guns, commit crimes, and even kill themselves (or others).

On the other hand, when young people do manage to develop good foresight, they can think realistically, creatively, and hopefully about the future. So empowered, they can aim their careers toward achievable goals and cheerfully accept the burdens of responsibility and self-discipline required for success. Barack Obama is a recent example of foresight-empowered success.

The New Urgency of Foresight

Older people are prone to dismiss the problems of youth as just a normal part of growing up, but the fact is that today's youth are coming of age in a world undergoing an unprecedented transformation powered by multiple technological revolutions. These technological advances, all occurring simultaneously, are overturning the world's economies and undermining long-established institutions, careers, and lifestyles.

Amid such turbulence, making a good decision concerning one's career or private life can be highly problematic, and the demographic group most acutely affected are young people moving into adulthood. These emerging adults have entered a time of life when parents and teachers have diminished power to guide them, so young people must make critical decisions by themselves at a time when their experience of the world is limited and their brains are still immature. (Foresight, scientists say, is largely a function of the brain's prefrontal cortex, which does not reach maturity until about age 25.)

Adding to the challenge of making appropriate decisions in today's world is the fact that knowledgeable and trustworthy advisors are now less available to emerging adults. In bygone days, most young people lived in villages or small towns where people got to know each other well, enabling the elders to offer wise counsel for a young person trying to find a suitable job or marriage partner.

In today's highly mobile mass society, young people roam the world and can choose among thousands of potential careers and mates in countless different locations. In principle, the abundance of choice offers wonderful opportunities, but it can pose a baffling conundrum for an emerging adult with little experience of the world.

Making matters worse for many young people, technological advances have eliminated most of the jobs that could be learned quickly and paid enough for an 18-year-old to live on and maybe support a family. Now, getting a decent job is likely to require years of training at a college or university during which time the student earns little or no money and may go heavily into debt.

Improving Youth Foresight

Ironically, it was fear of the future that led to some of our most useful foresight tools.

Relatively little was done to create a science of foresight until after World War II, which had led to the development of rockets and atomic bombs. Frightened that the Soviet Union might use the new superweapons, the U.S. Air Force established the RAND Corporation in Santa Monica, California, as a "think factory." The main task of RAND's scientists and scholars was to think about future wars—how to fight and win them.

To fulfill their mission, the RAND scientists had to think seriously about the future, and in the process they developed a variety of methods for thinking more scientifically about the future than had ever been done before. Mathematician Olaf Helmer and his RAND colleague Norman Dalkey developed the Delphi technique, a way to refine and synthesize scientists' forecasts of future technological developments. In addition, Herman Kahn developed his scenario technique for exploring the implications of possible future events. The scenario method is now widely used in government and business.

Meanwhile, Arnold Brown, Edie Weiner, and others refined ways for identifying and analyzing social trends. Today trend analysis is widely recognized as one of the most useful ways for identifying significant developments in technology and society and anticipating outcomes.

Many of the methods developed since World War II can now be used in simplified forms by young people and by teachers or others trying to help young people gain a practical understanding of what is happening in the world now, where things are going, and the opportunities that young people have to make

valuable contributions to human welfare as well as succeed in their chosen careers and personal lives.

The task now is to make foresight into a recognized life skill that can empower young people to think more clearly, constructively, and hopefully about the future. The World Future Society has already initiated several projects for improving youth foresight, and more are under development.

Young people interested in participating in a Society conference now can attend at a reduced rate of $125 ($150 on site) and many members have been donating funds to cover one or more full scholarships for young people.

In addition, the Society recently sponsored a High School Essay Contest, and the first group of winners was announced in July. Other programs will be instituted as funding becomes available.

If we can equip today's young people with good foresight, we can all be much more optimistic about their future and ours.

Critical Thinking

1. Indicate forces which are transforming our social and economic worlds.

2. Identify jobs that have been eliminated by modern technology.

3. Provide a rationale for foresight and the need to practice it.

Create Central

www.mhhe.com/createcentral

Internet References

Decision-Making under Risk in Children, Adolescents, and Young Adults
    www.ncbi.nlm.nih.gov/pubmed/21687443
How to Plan Ahead with Foresight
    http://lockwoodresource.com/how-to-plan-ahead
Teaching Self-Management Skills
    www.specialconnections.ku.edu/?q=behavior_plans
World Future Society
    www.wfs.org/futuring.htm

EDWARD CORNISH, founder of the World Future Society, is editor of *The Futurist* and a member of the Society's Board. His book *Futuring: The Exploration of the Future* provides a readable description of the futures field, including many of the methods now in use. It may be ordered from the World Future Society for $19.95 (member's price $17.95). Go to www.wfs.org/futuring.htm.

Article Prepared by: Karen L. Freiberg, *University of Maryland*

Build a Curriculum That Includes Everyone

Ensuring that schools are more accepting of LGBT students and issues requires more than passing mentions of diversity in sex education classes.

ROBERT MCGARRY

Learning Outcomes

After reading this article, you will be able to:

- Evaluate the difference between states that forbid LGBT curriculum in sex education and states that include it.

- Identify ways in which educators can teach LGBT curriculum that helps all students feel safe.

In order to accommodate the education needs of lesbian, gay, bisexual, and transgender students, American schools must do more than merely add LGBT information to the curriculum in sex education class. If we believe that adolescence is the time when young people try to make sense of who they are (Erikson, 1968), and if we believe that providing positive role models for students during this period of self-discovery is an important action that schools can take to support their students, then we also must believe that lesson plans throughout the curriculum should include positive representations of LGBT people.

In his description of curriculum development in U.S. schools, Michael Sadowski (2008) suggests that the final curriculum often "reflects choices about which . . . identities are to be represented and which are not" (p. 127). Beyond supporting the identity development of LGBT adolescents, LGBT-inclusive curriculum has other equally important benefits. Findings from a recent study by the Gay, Lesbian, and Straight Education Network (GLSEN) suggest that attending a school with an LGBT-inclusive curriculum is related to both a less-hostile school experience for LGBT students and increased feelings of connectedness to the school community. The results of the lack of connection seem obvious. When students don't feel connected to their school, they're more likely to miss classes and even full days of school. Not only does this affect their learning, but it also denies them the identity development benefits that result from the activities and in-person interactions that occur in schools.

Despite the benefits, most LGBT students don't have access to LGBT-inclusive curriculum. Eight states—Alabama, Arizona, Louisiana, Mississippi, Oklahoma, South Carolina, Texas, and Utah—have laws that explicitly prohibit the development and implementation of such curriculum. Considering both legally and socially imposed limitations, it's not surprising that most of the more than 8,000 students in grades 6–12 surveyed in GLSEN's 2011 study reported never having been taught anything positive about LGBT people, history, or events. Fewer than 20 percent of LGBT students were exposed to positive representations of LGBT people in their classes, with history/social studies classes being the most likely context for LGBT-inclusive teaching and learning. Health classes were the third most likely place for students to learn about LGBT people—a slightly less likelier place than English classes. Finally, when asked about textbooks and materials, less than a fifth said textbooks or other assigned class readings included LGBT-related information (Kosciw et al., 2012).

While many forms of bias can be found in school curriculum, the most basic form is the complete or relative exclusion of individuals who represent certain groups, including LGBT people. Many school districts have policies or a set of expectations that require analyzing curriculum to identify and eliminate bias. Often, this takes the form of a checklist that asks developers to review their work. Common criteria call for curriculum plans to depict men and women of various races and ethnic groups as role models worthy of being emulated and require that curricula conform to nonsexist language guidelines. But fewer of the criteria ever call for depicting people of various sexual orientations, gender identity or gender expression, or assure that the language used is not heterosexist in nature.

Mirrors and Windows

Emily Style (1996) introduced the idea of thinking about curriculum as a way to provide students with both windows to see the world and mirrors to see themselves. Curriculum can (and does for many students) provide a mirror when it reflects individuals and their experiences. At the same time, curriculum can provide a window when it introduces and provides opportunities to understand the experiences and perspectives of those who are different from the student. By serving as a mirror for LGBT youth, curriculum that includes LGBT people validates the existence of an often-invisible population. LGBT students are able to see themselves or, at least, have the opportunity to see people with whom they share an aspect of their identity. Meanwhile, teaching about LGBT-related issues and including LGBT people in the curriculum gives other students a window into a world they might not otherwise have access to and prepares them for eventual interactions with that world. Beyond the advantage of broadening student learning, these curricular mirrors and windows help create a more positive environment for all students, regardless of sexual orientation, gender identity, or gender expression.

Differing Practices

Greytak and Kosciw (in press) analyzed various curricular approaches to sex education through the lens of LGBT inclusion and identified four different practices, each of which in its own way misses the mark for meeting the healthy learning needs of LGBT students. In fact, some of these practices may yield negative mental and physical health outcomes for these students. The practices range from complete invisibility or the "ignoring" approach as the authors refer to it, to others that "demonize," "stigmatize" or simply neglect part of the LGBT acronym.

Ignoring

This approach completely disregards the existence of LGBT people. A sex education curriculum developed within this frame would refer only to heterosexual behaviors. This approach presents heterosexuality as the absolute norm and the only conceivable option for students. The authors point out that even the very definition of sex used by some excludes LGBT people. Excluding LGBT people in a sex education curriculum is obviously problematic for LGBT students and can, among other negative health outcomes, lead to limited knowledge and a lack of skill development in terms of negotiating healthy sexual relationships.

Abstinence-only programs tend to be based on the ignoring approach and, in addition to the consequences already mentioned, may contribute to developing or maintaining a negative school climate for LGBT students. Typically, such abstinence-only programs don't mention nonheterosexual relationships or transgender people. Instead, these programs assume universal heterosexuality and emphasize that physically intimate relationships are harmful outside the context of marriage, an option that isn't widely available to same-sex couples. In fact, in GLSEN's 2011 National School Climate Survey (Kosciw et al., 2012), LGBT students who attended schools with abstinence-only programs were less likely to report that their health classes included positive representations of LGBT people than students who had access to other sexual health curricula.

By excluding LGBT people and relationships, LGBT-ignoring, abstinence-only curricular approaches can also reinforce anti-LGBT behavior by students and contribute to a hostile school climate for LGBT students. GLSEN research suggests that students in schools with abstinence-only curricula were less likely to say that their peers were "somewhat" or "very" accepting of LGBT students while LGBT students in schools with abstinence-only programs also reported feeling less connected to their school communities. It is worth noting that federal funding guidelines developed in 2010 encourage federally funded abstinence-only programs to "consider the needs of lesbian, gay, bisexual, transgender, and questioning youth and how their programs will be inclusive of and non-stigmatizing toward such participants." However, because these guidelines don't require schools to do so, they essentially give schools permission to ignore those needs.

Demonizing

This approach to sex education curriculum may have worse outcomes than that which simply ignores LGBT people. This approach may explicitly teach that homosexuality is wrong or implicitly communicate that being LGBT is undesirable and unacceptable. Defining "normal sexual attraction" or using terms such as "natural" or "unnatural" when referring to various types of sexual intercourse are just two examples of how this approach "demonizes" LGBT people.

Stigmatizing

Like the demonizing approach, stigmatizing negatively brands LGBT people by equating homosexuality with child sexual abuse or assigning responsibility for the AIDS epidemic to gay men. In doing so, sex education curriculum portrays LGBT people as dangerous risk takers or abnormal.

Transgender Excluding

With this approach, the curriculum may seem to be LGBT-inclusive, but it is actually only LGB-inclusive, leaving out transgender topics. By virtue of their definitions, the ignoring, demonizing, and stigmatizing already fit into the category. But even approaches that include LGB people and go beyond heterosexuality in an affirming, respectful manner, still most often exclude transgender people, negating their existence and value.

LGBT-inclusive Curriculum

So, what does an LGBT-inclusive sex education curriculum look like? The National Sexuality Education Standards: Core Content and Skills, K-12 (Future of Sex Education Initiative, 2012) can help answer that question or at least help curriculum developers begin to imagine what an LGBT-inclusive sex education curriculum might look like. The standards were developed to articulate the "essential minimum, core content for sexuality education that is developmentally and age-appropriate for students in grades K-12." Among the seven core topics is "identity." This standard presents lesbian, gay, bisexual, and transgender identities as possibilities as it addresses fundamental aspects of people's understanding of who they are. It also sets out what students should know and be able to do by the end of grades 2, 5, 8, and 12. (See Figure 1.)

The national standards provide an excellent starting point for the development of LGBT-inclusive sex education curriculum at the local level and can also help anchor decisions on adopting instructional materials. Another helpful resource is the *Guidelines for Comprehensive Sexuality Education: Kindergarten through 12th Grade* (2004), published by the Sexuality Information and Education Council of the United States (SIECUS). These guidelines, the authors suggest, were designed as, "a framework for comprehensive sexuality education; as such, they can be used to create new programs or evaluate existing curricula and material" (p. 81). The document includes an evaluation tool that can help educators review curriculum in terms of concepts and topics, informational accuracy, messaging, age appropriateness, responsiveness to cultural sensitivity, teaching strategies, and parental involvement.

For example, the Montgomery County (Md.) Public Schools designed its health education program around the SIECUS guidelines. How it came to be is just as important as that it came to be. After a three-year controversy that drew national attention, the school board unanimously approved a revised and LGBT-inclusive sex education curriculum for implementation in 2007. It had pulled previous versions of it from the program. Its development demonstrated how district stakeholders worked to address the kind of conflict that often thwarts efforts to do what is best for students.

IDENTITY

Core Concepts	Analyzing Influences	Accessing Information	Interpersonal Communication	Decision Making	Goal Setting	Self-Management	Advocacy
BY THE END OF THE 2ND GRADE, STUDENTS SHOULD BE ABLE TO:							
Describe differences and similarities in how boys and girls may be expected to act	Provide examples of how friends, family, media, society, and culture influence ways in which boys and girls think they should act						
BY THE END OF THE 5TH GRADE, STUDENTS SHOULD BE ABLE TO:							
Define sexual orientation as romantic attraction to an individual of the same gender or of a different gender	Analyze external influences that have an impact on one's attitudes about gender, sexual orientation, and gender identity	Identify parents or other trusted adults to whom they can ask questions about sexual orientation				Demonstrate ways to treat others with dignity and respect	Demonstrate ways students can work together to promote dignity and respect for all people
BY THE END OF THE 8TH GRADE, STUDNTS SHOULD BE ABLE TO:							
Differentiate between gender identity, gender expression, and sexual orientation	Analyze the influence of peers, media, family, society, religion, and culture on the expression of gender, sexual orientation, and identity	Access accurate information about gender identity, gender expression, and sexual orientation	Communicate respectfully with and about people of all gender identities, gender expressions, and sexual orientations				Develop a plan to promote dignity and respect for all people in the school community
Explain the range of gender roles							
BY THE END OF THE 12TH GRADE, STUDENTS SHOULD BE ABLE TO:							
Differentiate between biological sex, sexual orientation, and gender identity and expression						Explain how to promote safety, respect, awareness, and acceptance	Advocate for school policies and programs that promote dignity and respect for all
Distinguish between sexual orientation, sexual behavior, and sexual identity							

Source: Future of Sex Education, www.futureofsexeducation.org

Figure 1   National Sexuality Education Standards   The National Sexuality Education Standards present performance indicators for what students should know and be able to do by the end of grades 2, 5, 8, and 12. The standards include seven sexuality education topics: anatomy and physiology, puberty and adolescent development, identity, pregnancy and reproduction, sexually transmitted diseases and HIV, healthy relationships, and personal safety.

The curriculum includes LGBT-relevant content throughout and avoids putting forth concepts such as relationships or family in heterosexist terms. The curriculum also provides explicit lessons designed to cultivate respect for differences in human sexuality. As the guide indicates, "addressing human sexuality in an appropriate and factual fashion leads to informed teens, increasing the likelihood of students making healthy decisions" (Montgomery County Public Schools, 2006). The curriculum incorporates locally produced lessons that address the effect of stereotyping and harassment, discuss gender identity, gender expression, and sexual orientation, and examine the harmful effects of stereotyping people based on these.

Beyond the written curriculum, what educators do and say as they teach has a great deal to do with LGBT inclusion as well as safe and respectful student learning. Educators engaged in this work should:

- Make sure the analogies used when teaching don't express heterosexuality as a given instead of being one of many possibilities.
- Use inclusive language when referring to students, families, or others outside the classroom.
- Use students' preferred names and gender pronouns (although caution should be used when speaking to parents/caregivers so as not to "out" a student).
- Build knowledge of vocabulary like ally, respect, diversity, etc.
- Use gender-neutral language, such as partner when appropriate.
- Consider and control the ways stereotypes are perpetuated and intervene when students or other staff perpetuate them.

Sexuality is an integral part of each person's identity and a large body of research proves that comprehensive sex education programs can positively shape the kind of attitudes and behaviors that support healthy sexual development and overall well-being. Schools have a responsibility to promote the healthy development of every child, regardless of sexual orientation or gender identity/expression. As such, access to positive, LGBT-inclusive sex education in a manner that's free from shame and stigma, balanced with positive portrayals of LGBT people, their works and achievements, events and history in other curricular areas, is critical to enabling LGBT individuals to lead healthy and fulfilling lives. This is how schools truly succeed in meeting the healthy learning needs of all students.

References

Erikson, E.H. (1968). *Identity: Youth and crisis.* New York, NY: Norton.

Future of Sex Education Initiative. (2012). *National sexuality education standards: Core content and skills, K-12.* Bethesda, MD: Journal of School Health. www.futureofsexeducation.org/documents/josh-fose-standards-web.pdf.

Greytak, E.A. & Kosciw, J.G. (in press). Responsive classroom curriculum for LGBTQ students. In E. Fisher & K. Komosa-Hawkins (Eds.), *Creating safe and supportive learning environments: A guide for working with lesbian, gay, bisexual, transgender, and questioning youth and families.* New York, NY: Routledge.

Kosciw, J.G., Greytak, E.A., Bartkiewicz, M.J., Boesen, M.J., & Palmer, N.A. (2012). *The 2011 National School Climate Survey: The experiences of lesbian, gay, bisexual, and transgender youth in our nation's schools.* New York, NY: Gay, Lesbian, and Straight Education Network.

Montgomery County Public Schools. (2006). *Health Education Grade 10.* Rockville, MD: Author. www.teachthefacts.org/curriculumdocs/Grade10-Sec1.pdf.

Sadowski, M. (Ed.). (2008). *Adolescents at school.* Cambridge, MA: Harvard Education Press.

Sexuality Information and Education Council of the United States. (2004). Guidelines for comprehensive sexuality education: Kindergarten through 12th grade. New York, NY: Author. www.siecus.org/_data/global/images/guidelines.pdf.

Style, E. (1996). Curriculum as window and mirror. *Social Science Record, 33* (2), 21–28.

Critical Thinking

1. What happens to many students who are disengaged from their schoolmates and disconnected from their school?

2. When should sexual orientation and gender identity be introduced into sex education classes?

3. Why are demonizing and stigmatizing approaches to homosexuality worse than excluding LGBT curriculum from sex education?

Create Central

www.mhhe.com/createcentral

Internet References

Future of Sex Education Initiative
www.futureofsexeducation.org/documents/josh-fose-standards-web.pdf
Health Education Grade 10 Rockville, MD
www.teachthefacts.org/curriculumdocs/Grade10-Sec1.pdf
Sexuality Information and Education Council of the US: Guidelines
www.siecus.org/_data/global/images/guidelines.pdf

Robert McGarry (rmcgarry@glsen.org) is director of education at Gay, Lesbian, and Straight Education Network, New York, N.Y.

Article

Prepared by: Karen L. Freiberg, *University of Maryland*

Digitalk: A New Literacy for a Digital Generation

Teachers who recognize that "digitalk" is different and not deficient can find ways to harness this language en route to improving students' academic writing.

KRISTEN HAWLEY TURNER

Learning Outcomes

After reading this article, you will be able to:

- Generate a plan to help students code-switch from digital to standard, grammatically correct English.

- Defend "digitalk" as a different language rather than a deficient language/bad English.

Lily:	heyyyy (:
Michael:	waszgud B.I.G.?
Lily:	nm, chillennn; whatchu up too?
Michael:	WatchIn da gam3
Lily:	mm, y quien ta jugandoo?
Michael:	Yank33s nd naTi0naLs.
Lily:	WHAAAATT A JOKEEEEE, dime comoyankeeslosttagainstt them yesterdaii.
Michael:	i n0e, th3y suCk.
Lily:	& the nationalsss won like only 16 games . . . one of the worst teamshomieeegee.
Michael:	t3lL m3 b0uT it, i b3T y0u fIv3 d0lLaRs th3Y g00nAl0s3.
Lily:	AHA, naw gee thats easy $ for youu ! =p
Michael:	loliwaSplAyInG wI y0u. =D
Lily:	lolimma talk to you later . . . i got pizzaa awaitingggmeeeee (;
Michael:	iight pe3cE

As I copy this text conversation between two adolescents into Microsoft Word, the screen lights up with red. Every line in this exchange is marked. Microsoft Word, it seems, does not "get" the language of these speakers and attacks the black-and-white text with its red pen. For Microsoft Word, these writers are wrong.

When I first encountered "computer-mediated language" (Crystal 2001: 238), I was as confused as my word-processing program is today. An English teacher and one of our school's

"grammar gurus," I couldn't understand why students were substituting "2" for "too" or "u" for "you" in their school writing. I was completely stumped by the language they were using to talk to each other digitally. Today, when I look at the exchange between Lily and Michael, I am amazed by their ability to manipulate language and to communicate effectively across time and space. I have evolved from being a grammar guru who questioned this teen language as a degradation of Standard English to one who sees adolescent digitalk as a complex and fascinating combination of written and conversational languages in a digital setting.

The Journey of a "Grammar Guru"

I first ventured beyond e-mail into other forms of digital communication a decade ago when my brother installed an instant-messaging program on my personal computer. He taught me how to "see" him online and to exchange messages. A few years later, I used a similar instant-messaging program to "chat" with group members as we completed a class project for graduate school. Our inability to find a time for five adults to meet in person led us to use this technology, and our success in working together in a virtual space made me consider the pedagogical applications of instant messaging in my high school classroom.

When I first assigned a book discussion to be conducted by instant message (IM), my high school students looked at me quizzically. They hadn't thought about using IM as a learning tool. For them, it was a social space outside of school. They humored me, however, happy to be doing something "fun" rather than writing a literary essay about the book. As with any initial assignment, I wasn't sure what I would get when these students submitted their work. What I received were pages of writing that impressed me with truly critical thought about the text—and that shocked me with language that was far from Standard English.

Digitalk Guide

02: Your, or my, two cents worth. Also: m.02, y.02
8: Oral sex
10Q: Thank you
143: I Love you
ACORN: A Completely Obsessive Really Nutty person
AITR: Adult in the room
book: Cool
C-P: Sleepy
CICYHW: Can I copy your homework
da: There
E123: Easy as 1, 2, 3
EML: E-mail me later
EOT: End of Thread (end of discussion)
FE: Fatal error
FS: For sale
G2G: Got to go
GI: Google it
I 1-D-R: I wonder
IDK: I don't know
J/C: Just checking
K: OK
KIPPERS: Kids in parents pockets eroding retirement savings
LTTIC: Look, the teacher is coming
M4C: Meet for coffee
MOS: Mom over shoulder
N2MJCHBU: Not Too Much, Just Chillin. How Bout You?
ne1er: Anyone here?
nth: Nothing
P911: Parent alert
potato: Person over 30 acting 21
r u da: Are you there?
smt: Something
soz: Sorry
s^: What's up?
u up: Are you up?
w's^: What's up?
W8: Wait
wru: Where are you?
X-I-10: Exciting
ysdiw8: Why should I wait?
zerg: To gang up on someone

Source: NetLingo

I worked hard to decipher those first chat transcripts. I mentally capitalized letters and added punctuation marks. I translated phonetic spellings. I asked my brother or the students themselves to explain unknown acronyms. When it was time to grade the assignment, I was faced with a difficult decision. As an English teacher, I needed to hold them accountable for their use of language, and I certainly wouldn't have accepted this kind of writing had they submitted a traditional literary essay. However, the discussions of the novel were rich, and I wanted to reward their thinking despite their seemingly substandard language.

Ultimately, I let the grammar slide that time and began discussions about the nature of language and the purposes of writing. Through those discussions in my classroom, I began to realize that, to my students, writing online was separate from school writing. They used different languages in each of those contexts. By asking them to complete school-related work (the discussion of a literary text) in a social space (their IM chat rooms), I blurred the line between home and school. What they produced was a rich blend of the two discourses.

Digitalk

Since my first encounter with nonstandard IM language, the terms used to describe digital writing have changed. The shift from "netspeak" to "textspeak" followed developments in technology that affected how and where adolescents produced digital writing. However, like much in the digital age, where change occurs fast and frequently, these terms are already obsolete. Today's teens use both the Internet and their personal cell phones to communicate with peers, and patterns of language cross technological boundaries.

The manipulation of standard spellings and conventions most often occurs when teens "talk" to each other by writing in texts, IMs, and social networking tools. There are nonstandard conventions that cross these digital spaces. Writing in these venues blends elements of written discourse with those of the spoken word, and what the terms *netspeak* and *textspeak* share conceptually is an attention to the oral nature of the language used in these spaces. Whether teens are sending text messages or IMs, they invariably think of the communication as "talking." Talk, then, is the driving force behind much of the digital writing of adolescents.

For these reasons, I call the language that adolescents use in digital spaces *digitalk*. The term captures the nature of the writing, which in most cases replaces verbal communication, and it encompasses the wide variety of digital technologies (phone, Internet, computer, PDA) that allow for this exchange. Manipulating language so that it efficiently conveys an intended message and effectively represents the voice of the speaker requires both creativity and mastery of language for communicative purposes. Becoming an adept user takes practice and knowledge of the conventions of a community. For an outsider, it is difficult to decipher and even harder to produce in an authentic way. Digitalk, then, is a new literacy of the digital generation.

A recent study by the Pew Internet and American Life Project indicates that teens are writing more than ever and that much of this writing is done in digital spaces. Interestingly, 60 percent of teens do not see the writing that they do electronically as "real writing" (Lenhart et al. 2008: 4). Perhaps their view is shaped by the idea that they are talking to friends through IM, rather writing to them. However, their dismissal of digital writing also might be a product of the societal bias against the informal language they use in digital spaces.

The Pew study documents that "a considerable number of educators and children's advocates . . . are concerned that the quality of writing by young Americans is being degraded by their electronic communication, with its carefree spelling, lax punctuation and grammar, and its acronym shortcuts" (Lenhart et al. 2008: 3). I also hear these concerns from parents in my community. I'm alarmed by the prejudice that lies behind these statements.

Many adults fail to realize that today's teens are highly adept at using language and that their mastery of the digitally written word far surpasses that of many adults.

Many adults fail to realize that today's teens are highly adept at using language and that their mastery of the digitally written word far surpasses that of many adults. Teens like Lily and Michael have learned to manipulate written language for social communication. They merge multiple language systems, break rules systematically, create and manipulate language and usage, and effectively communicate ideas with an intended audience. In the process, they create their own rules and rituals that are accepted by members of their language community. Their digitalk is intricate and complex. But in school and among adults, it is seen as deficient. In school, students are expected to use academic language, a discourse that may or may not resemble the primary discourse of their out-of-school language practices.

Lily and Michael, the two writers whose conversation opened this article, are *digital natives* (Prensky 2001), high school students who have grown up in a world saturated with communication technologies. They have access to computers in their homes and even in their bedrooms, and they carry cell phones wherever they go. Though they talk to their friends on the phone, they are just as likely, perhaps more likely, to communicate by text. Lily and Michael are immersed in a world outside of school where the written discourse differs from Standard English.

In discussing the language of urban students who speak African-American Vernacular English (AAVE), Rebecca Wheeler and Rachel Swords (2006) explain that students must be taught to make choices about language, dialect, and register. They argue that teaching code-switching allows both home and academic discourse to have a place in the classroom. By valuing the language that students use outside of school, teachers can make school language more accessible. In short, out-of-school discourses are different, not deficient. Teachers should build on students' home literacy as they help them to acquire academic language.

Privileging Digitalk

Wheeler and Swords studied the patterns of error in the writing of students who speak AAVE and found that they were directly related to the grammatical structure of AAVE. They contend that these writers "are not making mistakes in Standard English. Instead, they are following the grammar patterns of their everyday language" (2006: 9). As students translate thought to writing, they unconsciously conflate the two languages.

Similarly, teens write—and perhaps even think—in digitalk. It's not surprising, then, that they require practice to switch to a more formal language in school and that many teens admit that elements of digitalk do filter into their school work. Some researchers suggest that the prevalence of these errors is not what popular opinion believes. Anecdotal evidence from teachers, however, suggests that not all students are adept at making the switch. Thus, teachers need to ask two important questions:

1. If students have trouble switching from digital language to Standard English, thus making frequent errors of standard usage in their school writing, how can teachers help them consciously switch to the appropriate language?
2. If students use digital language outside of school in creative and analytic ways to discuss real issues with their peers, how can teachers harness its power to help students learn content?

Giving digitalk a place in the classroom helps answer these questions. For example, one way to make students aware of the different contexts for language is to have them write, "Hello, how are you?" in four distinct settings: classroom with teacher, text conversation with friend, lunchroom with friend, at home with parent. As the class analyzes the language of the settings, students can begin to look critically at the way they write in different situations. (See Turner et al. 2009 for lesson ideas.)

Conversations about language begin to ignite conscious choices for student writers. Following these conversations with an analysis of the writing they do in digital spaces will help them understand the choices they make in their digitalk. Some common patterns that emerge from the digital writing of adolescents include: 1) nonstandard capitalization, 2) nonstandard end punctuation, 3) use of multiple consonants or vowels within a word, 4) nonstandard use of ellipses, 5) lack of apostrophes, 6) use of phonetic spellings, 7) abbreviations, and 8) compound constructions to form new words (Turner et al. 2009). Instances of each of these patterns can be seen in the exchange between Lily and Michael. The writers choose the convention that best expresses purpose and voice, and they rely on the recipient's understanding of the convention to properly interpret the message. As with the conventions in Standard English that a writer might use unconsciously, teens who write daily in digitalk may not recognize the conventions they use. If teachers help students identify these patterns, they can contrast digitalk choices with the conventions of Standard English. Teachers can help writers create checklists for editing that focus on these common translation errors.

Making students conscious of the conventions of digitalk can help those who struggle to make the switch from the informal language of digital writing to the formal language of academia. In addition, allowing students to write some assignments using digitalk may allow teachers to harness the power of students' out-of-school literacy. Proponents of writing-to-learn strategies have argued that writing is closely related to thinking and that writing can help students develop and retain content knowledge. In order to achieve these goals, students are often encouraged to write freely without attention to editing. Content counts more than form when writing to learn.

Rhoda Maxwell (1996) identifies three levels of writing that are useful in thinking about writing-to-learn activities. Level 1 writing allows students to develop their ideas or to reflect metacognitively on what they know about content. It does not focus on the presentation of those ideas to others. Level 2 writing, which may have a limited audience, attends somewhat more to form, but the purpose of the activity is to help students understand and develop content knowledge. Level 3 writing, on the other hand, attends to issues of grammar and mechanics. It is often published for a larger audience or to formally demonstrate a student's learning.

If language is less of an issue than content in some assignments (Level 1 and Level 2), then teachers might encourage students to use digitalk. Permitting students to take notes, write drafts, or complete other low-stakes writing assignments in whatever form of language is most comfortable places the emphasis on the content of the writing, rather than the mechanics. It also informs students that the writing they do outside of school is valuable. By giving digitalk a place in the classroom, students are able to bring their home literacy into the academic arena.

> **By giving digitalk a place in the classroom, students are able to bring their home literacy into the academic arena.**

A Shift in Thinking

My argument is bound to be attacked by adults who are concerned with standards and rigor, with state tests and federal mandates. Digitalk is, after all, an easy target. Virtually any administrator, teacher, or parent is capable of marking as deficient a text riddled with digitalk. As Microsoft Word demonstrates, red pens can attack the language easily.

We should consider a shift in thinking about digitalk. Rather than seeing it as a deficiency, a lazy representation of Standard English, we should recognize its power in the digital, adolescent community. Teens today are writing a lot, but they aren't necessarily writing in Standard English. Switching from their digital writing to the requirements of academic writing can pose problems for some students. However, by valuing the language that adolescents use outside of school and engaging students in writing about content in less formal ways, teachers can focus writing on content and critical thinking, and they can give value to the literacy that students bring to class. And by teaching code-switching practices, teachers can help young writers become conscious of the language choices they make.

There is no question that students must learn academic English. All students should be held accountable to societal standards in their learning. However, the method by which we achieve these goals can build on students' existing knowledge, using their out-of-school skills to enhance their learning.

References

Crystal, David. *Language and the Internet*. New York: Cambridge University Press, 2001.

Lenhart, Amanda, Sousan Arafeh, Aaron Smith, and Alexandra Macgill. *Writing, Technology, and Teens*. Washington, D.C.: Pew Internet and American Life Project, 2008. www.pewinternet.org/ PPF/r/247/report_display.asp.

Maxwell, Rhoda J. *Writing Across the Curriculum in Middle and High Schools*. Boston: Allyn and Bacon, 1996.

Prensky, Marc. "Digital Natives, Digital Immigrants." *On the Horizon* 9, no. 5 (October 2001): 1–6.

Turner, Kristen H., Jeta Donovan, Eytan Apter, and Elvira Katic. "Online and in Step: Community, Convention, and Self-Expression in Text Speak." Paper presented at the annual meeting of the National Council of Teachers of English, Philadelphia, Pa., 2009.

Wheeler, Rebecca S., and Rachel Swords. *Code-Switching: Teaching Standard English in Urban Classrooms*. Urbana, Ill.: National Council of Teachers of English, 2006.

Critical Thinking

1. List some instant messaging language you know.
2. What do the following digital words mean: I0Q, soz, wru, G2G, LOL?
3. Can teenagers who use digital words frequently switch easily to grammatically correct English with standard punctuation and mechanics?
4. Is digitalk bad (deficient) language or a creatively different language?
5. Should digital words have a place in a school classroom?

Create Central

www.mhhe.com/createcentral

Internet References

Digital Natives: A Defense of the Internet Community
http://opinionator.blogs.nytimes.com/2013/09/09

Digital Natives, Digital Immigrants
www.marcprensky.com/writing/Prensky%2520

How Slang Affects Students in the Classroom
www.usnews.com/education/high-schools/articles/2011/06/13

Kristen Hawley Turner is an associate professor of education at Fordham University, New York, N.Y.

Article   Prepared by: Karen L. Freiberg, *University of Maryland*

Portrait of a Hunger Artist

The anorexia began innocently enough, until eating became the point of living. Precisely because it was so special, it had to be made more perfect by hunger.

EMILY TROSCIANKO

Learning Outcomes

After reading this article, you will be able to:

- Distinguish between normal-eating thin persons and anorexic thin persons.

- Analyze the four big myths about anorexia and explain why they are incorrect.

"Y ou are welcome in our new home, but your anorexia isn't," my mother said to me one day in April 2008. How dare she imply that there was any distinction between "me" and "my anorexia"?

I couldn't imagine my life without it, nor did I want to. It dictated everything I did and was, from going to bed almost when other people were getting up, to the solitude of my existence on a boat in Oxford, studying and starving, to my absolutely nonnegotiable daily bike rides and my constantly being cold—and my incomparable pleasure in the plate of bread and low-fat margarine and boiled vegetables in bed last thing at night, followed by cereal with skimmed milk diluted with water to go further, and finally mouthfuls of creamy chocolate to send me to sleep without hunger.

That was life; that was me. How to say "I" could come to their new house, and "it" couldn't? Her words made me so angry, so upset—and so scared. I was 26, and for 10 years I and my anorexia had grown ever more inseparable.

But my mother and her partner were moving and they told me they couldn't face the idea of me and my illness coming like a black shadow over their new home. He couldn't bear my cooking for the family and never eating, sitting there and watching them eat, or my nocturnalism; she couldn't bear any of it, least of all how it threatened their relationship, too.

I wept. But a few months after that conversation, I did make the decision to start to eat more. And it felt like I was bidding good-bye to my closest, most loyal friend.

That friendship began so innocuously I'm not sure I can identify a proper beginning. I do remember the end of a family ski holiday in France. I'd had one too many vodka-and-Cokes in the hotel bar. The après-ski haze of warm fires and hilarity ended at the hotel toilets. The next morning the others got in some last skiing while I sat in the car feeling ill. Then the queasy hairpin bends all the way down the mountain, and in the evening all I could stomach were a few salty crisps.

The next day, on motorways and the ferry, I had a few more crisps, but I felt a weakness that at once demanded more food and made "more" too much effort. It was a new weakness that mutated into an almost-strength, which was no longer physical but manifested itself in ways like this: "You sure you don't want any dinner?" "Yeah, still don't feel very hungry, I'll get myself something later." And then I wouldn't.

Looking back over my diaries, though, I realize that wasn't really the beginning, but rather a stepping-stone along the way to starvation: learning how exhilarating hunger can be. The power to keep on deferring eating felt like a true triumph, even as the hunger itself became more oppressive.

Deferring food was proof of strength, so it was a victory always to be a little later than yesterday. There was always a perverse pleasure in staying hungrier longer. So the day's single meal would be at two or three or four or five in the morning.

One winter it went all the way around the clock, several times, so for a week or so I'd be going to bed at 9 or 10 in the morning, and then soon bedtime would be back around to 10 at night. This does not make for a good mood or many social opportunities. Waking up to a wintry sunset is one of the most depressing things in the world, especially when you must now have a bike ride and work eight hours or so before eating.

Starvation was the very thing that made food so sublime. I couldn't imagine any pleasure that could replace that of chocolate in bed at dawn. I knew that the sense of power, self-control, and superiority was all just my entrapment in the rigid mind-set of the starved and frail. I knew that the purity I idealized was every night belied by the feverish inspection of my stools, and by the demeaning obsessive-compulsive habits of counting and checking and memorizing and tidying that were infiltrating my brain and dragging me further into exhaustion. Yet understanding simply could not translate into action.

Starvation was the very thing that made food so sublime. And the purity I idealized was every night belied by the feverish inspection of my stools.

As to the causes of it all, there are the usual nature-nurture suspects: my parents' genes (my father stopped eating at age four in protest over his parents' arguments; my mother inherited her mother's debilitating penchant for guilt) and all the ethereal cheekboned catwalk girls. But the thread woven through the years was a line I found much earlier in my diary: "the flat stomach I've always wanted."

Through the years of my increasing starvation, I would look in the mirror and see the curves of my thighs and breasts gradually give way to sharp outcrops of hips, ribs, and sternum, and elbows become wider than the arms they held together. But I really only cared about one thing: my tummy. Right from the beginning, I'd turn this way and that, in light and shadow, pressing it in, breathing in—imagining, in the early days, being the person I was when I breathed in, and imagining staying that person when I breathed out.

I imagined being the person I was when I breathed in, and imagined staying that person when I breathed out.

Eventually, I did become the image of my imaginings. But by then I had become someone quite different. The almost-flatness of the tummy was a perpetual torment: One can always breathe in more, make it flatter still, or concave; one can never quite become the person in whom breathing out and breathing in make no difference. After a decade of losing weight so gradually that I hardly noticed, maybe I finally did reach the impossible concavity of the tummy that isn't, that doesn't contain or speak of past contents, past consumption, but simply declaims, right now, its perfection.

As my tummy withered, all sorts of things became untenable. The cold—it started at the fingertips and worked its way inwards, so that throughout the winter, and the end of the autumn and the beginning of the spring, there was an awful core of cold, which knew that warmth comes from movement but which wanted only to curl up into itself; which turned walking and sitting and lying into variations on huddling; which kept muscles taut with resistance against the outside; which saw in every activity, every location, only sources of heat or threats of cold.

It, or the fear of it, or the attempt to preempt it, was always there. A room would be reduced to its radiators, an evening outing refused for the frosty distances between bedroom and bar.

My trousers began to settle on my protruding hips instead of at my waist, and so trailed below the heels, as if my body's shrinkage had been in height as well as width. Tops began to hang shapeless, and bras became superfluous. But while all these things became too big, they were at the same time too small: They offered too little protection against the eyes of other people—who saw only bones—and against the cold.

While my clothes became too big, they were at the same time too small; they offered too little protection against the eyes of other people and against the cold.

My wardrobe now filled up with cardigans and trousers. Where once one layer was enough, now I needed two or three. Having done so much to denude the body of its padding, this body, so overly "purified," now had to be encumbered with layers of external insulation far less efficient than fat. And then even when summer came, I couldn't embrace it with open arms; I feared that all the energy hitherto expended in the attempt to keep warm might now be converted back into the fat that could warm me so much better.

Along with coldness, tiredness, and hunger came solitude. Social contact dwindled firstly because it can't be separated from food and drink, and then doubly so due to the gulf of mental separation. At first, I found it hard to talk at all about food and eating, or not eating: It was so private, so shameful, so glorifying—but simply unspeakable. An evening in a bar or a friend's family dinner—simple past pleasures—demanded excuses for not eating, which multiplied in inventive excess.

Even the seemingly unthreatening walk or shopping trip or cinema outing was precluded by a brain that counted hours not working as hours lost that had to be made up. A tangle of emotions grew between old friends. There was envy—of thinness on the one hand, and of carelessness on the other. There was resentment—of just this thinness and this carelessness. And scorn—of fatness or absence of control, which amounted to the same thing. Ultimately, I envied, scorned, and resented other people's inability to comprehend me, and made every effort to prevent their comprehending.

With my family it was even worse. On and off over the years, my father tried to persuade me to eat, with what I saw as emotional blackmail that swung between tears and rage, pity and fear. He feigned indifference—"I don't care if you eat it but it's there if you want it"—while silently screaming how he was being destroyed, and sometimes screaming it aloud: "I'm not going to let you kill yourself without a fight, it's a crisis point, you have to eat some dinner." There were moments of pure paternal tenderness—the unreserved will to help, to protect—and unreserved daughterly love and gratitude. But when the immediate danger was past these moments would fade. Gradually there was nothing but distance between us.

With my mother it was less dramatic and, for a long time, far more intimate. She never tried to force anything as he did, and I relied more and more upon her patience in letting me stay at home, not sending me away as he thought I should be. She, more than anyone, made deep and sincere attempts to

---

Four Big Myths about Anorexia

1. Anorexics don't feel hungry.

Of course they do. Hunger is the point, after a while: It's the great tormentor and the great addictive high.

2. Anorexics don't like food.

In general, anorexics love eating as much as they love being hungry. The eating, too, becomes the point: Eating can only be as perfect as it should be if you're hungry enough, if it's late enough, if you've prepared the food meticulously according to your own immutable rules.

3. Anorexics look in the mirror and see a fat person.

Of course they don't. They're not stupid. You look in the mirror and see your ribs with their thinly stretched coating of papery skin. But what you care about is some tiny, specific aspect of your body that has always to be more and more pared away: inner thighs that must be more

and more fleshless, or wrists that can be encompassed with the other hand with more and more space to spare. Anorexia isn't body dysmorphia.

4. Being thin is all that matters to an anorexic.

Being thin is in fact often only a minor matter compared to everything else that drives you. Control is probably at the center of it all. Control of food and eating might be the most obvious anorexic behavior, but the control illusion stretches its tentacles into all the rest of life—how much you work, how much you spend, how many people you spend time with—until going out for a drink on a Saturday night is as impossible as not having the next day and week and month planned into nothingness. Control equals strength, strength equals denial, denial equals simplicity, simplicity equals purity, purity equals perfection, perfection equals perfect control. It's the ultimate illusion; simplicity and perfection are equally inhuman.

---

understand. Together we would pick apart the pseudo-logic, uncover hidden paths of obsessive reasoning. And every time she would be ready to hug and hold and support me when the excavations brought tears and shameful despair at the exposed absurdities.

And so when she told me "it" wasn't welcome, I was devastated. Somehow, though, I needed to know this more and more deeply until the blackness and the narrowness became unmitigated. The thought of infertility and bones breaking with brittleness in my old age had to surface once more, hauntingly. I needed the obsessive compulsions to feel ever more like madness and the weakness to make just one more flight of stairs feel insurmountable. I needed a moment in a dressing room, seeing myself like a corpse sticking out of a silk dress I could never wear. And one more compulsive half hour in a supermarket, not being able to stop myself from checking every package I saw for nutrition information when all I'd come for was a loaf of bread. I needed my mother to tell me I could come to her new house, but not laden with all this.

Even when, at last, I decided this all must go, and my friends took matters into their own hands and found me an eating disorders clinic, I didn't believe it could. Eating was the point of living, of getting through the next interminably long day; precisely because it was so special, it had to be waited for, made more and more perfect by the hunger that would grow deeper and deeper so that nothing else mattered.

Rather than trying to visualize some unimaginable end point, I simply had to decide to eat 500 calories more every single day, without fail. I didn't really believe anything would happen. Yes, I might put on a few kilos, and although that terrified me it wouldn't change who I was. Food would still be the ultimate point and pleasure of life, made perfect by infinitely

deferring, restricting, and meticulously, secretively orchestrating the eating of it.

But then emotions came back, and I fell in love, and one night there was the first night without chocolate last thing. Funny that learning to do without food should in any sense be part of the recovery from anorexia. But it is; the most terrifying and thrilling thing I've learned in this last year since I began to eat again is that food is the means and not the end, a part rather than the whole, and that life cannot be as simple as simply longing for another day of hunger to be over.

Not long ago, I was sitting in a high-ceilinged apartment in Berlin with a cup of tea and my laptop, my boyfriend lying on the bed reading, interrupting me now and then with talk of where we might go and eat the next night, our last evening before we flew back to England. We had eaten at a restaurant the night before, too, and did so almost every night we were in Berlin. It was a holiday, after all, and we were treating ourselves.

I still get overcome with how miraculous it is: the repeated miracle of eating with other people, at a normal time of day, and of having eaten thus for days and weeks and months now. Sometimes it still feels unreal. But gradually, now, it's my old anorexic self who feels like she never really existed.

Critical Thinking

1. Support the idea that a non-living thing can be viewed as a friend.

2. Review the activities of daily life of a person with anorexia nervosa.

3. Identify the forces that helped the author recover normal eating patterns.

Create Central

www.mhhe.com/createcentral

Internet References

Anorexia Nervosa Fact Sheet

www.womenshealth.gov/publications/fact-sheet/anorexia-nervosa

Anorexia Nervosa Treatments and Drugs

www.mayoclinic.com/health/anorexia/DS00606/DSECTION

Eating Disorder Treatment and Recovery

www.helpguide.org/mental/eating_disorder_treatment.htm

Quick Facts on Anorexia Nervosa

www.childmind.org/en/quick-facts-anorexia-nervosa

EMILY TROSCIANKO is a lecturer in German at Jesus College, University of Oxford, and just completed a doctoral thesis on Franz Kafka. She writes the *PT* blog "A Hunger Artist."

Article   Prepared by: Karen L. Freiberg, *University of Maryland*

Heartbreak and Home Runs: The Power of First Experiences

From winning the science fair to losing a first boyfriend, certain youthful experiences cast a long shadow, revealing character and at times actually shaping it.

JAY DIXIT

Learning Outcomes

After reading this article, you will be able to:

- Judge how early experiences (e.g., love, loss, lies, success) affect you today.

- Explain how the primacy effect and "flashbulb memories" are linked to the neurotransmitters dopamine and norepinephrine.

Patricia was a 15-year-old high school cheerleader in her 10th year of Catholic school.

Chuck was a basketball star, a senior from the rough side of town.

One night after a high school mixer where everyone danced to jukebox music, Chuck and a friend offered Patricia a ride home. Chuck held Patricia's hand in the back seat, and when they got to her house, he walked her to the door. "Then he put both arms around me and kissed me gently on the lips," recalls Patricia. "I thought for a fleeting moment that I was floating with angels in heaven."

The next instant, their bubble was burst when Patricia's father turned on the porch light.

"It was 49 years ago and I still remember nearly all the details," says Patricia. "I was suddenly desirable," she explains. "I was kissworthy—and oh my goodness, that was enough self-esteem to propel me into a lifetime of feeling good about myself."

Beginning in our late teenage years and early 20s, we develop and internalize a broad, autobiographical narrative about our lives, spelling out who we were, are, and might be in the future, says Dan McAdams, a psychologist at Northwestern and author of *The Redemptive Self: Stories Americans Live By*. The story is peppered with key scenes—high points, low points, and turning points—and a first experience can be any of these. "These experiences give us natural ways to divide up the stories of our lives—episodic markers that help us make sense of how our life has developed over time," McAdams explains.

Part of why firsts affect us so powerfully is that they're seared into our psyches with a vividness and clarity that doesn't fade as other memories do. You may not remember the 4th real kiss you ever had, or the 20th—but you almost certainly remember your first. This is known as the primacy effect.

When people are asked to recall memories from college, 25 percent of what they come up with draws from the first two or three months of their freshman year, says David Pillamer, a psychologist at the University of New Hampshire. What people remember most vividly are events like saying goodbye to their parents, meeting their roommates for the first time, and their first college class.

In fact, when psychologists ask older people to recall the events of their lives, the ones they most often name are those that occurred in their late teens and early 20s. We're also better at recalling the world events, music, books, and movies—as well as the cultural events such as the Academy Awards or the World Series—that happened during the early parts of our lives. This "early-life memory bump" occurs because that's when we have the most first experiences, explains Jefferson Singer, a psychologist at Connecticut College who studies autobiographical memory.

Consider a first kiss or sexual encounter. These can generate sensations so new and unfamiliar that the experience feels almost unreal. "Someone can be a primitive neophyte when it comes to writing, but when you get them to talk about their first kiss, you see eloquence, poetry, metaphor, synecdoche, and hyperbole," says John Bohannon III, a psychologist at Butler University who studies first kisses. That sensation of disembodiment—pleasurable during a kiss, aversive when you first suffer the death of a loved one—is common in first experiences, as are feelings of heightened reality or unreality.

Intense emotional sensations etch first experiences deeply into memory, creating what psychologists call "flash-bulb memories." Memories like our first kiss or tryst, our first glimpse of the ocean, our first day of school, or the birth of a first child engage all our senses simultaneously.

Besides emotional engagement, these experiences also pack a heavy dose of novelty. "Novelty drives up dopamine and norepinephrine, brain systems associated with focus and paying attention and rewards," explains anthropologist Helen Fisher, author of *Why Him? Why Her?*

A first romantic relationship has one critical novel element: "It's the only time you're ever in love where you've never had your heart broken," says Laura Carpenter, a sociologist at Vanderbilt University and author of *Virginity Lost: An Intimate Portrait of First Sexual Experiences.* "You can have better relationships after that, but there's never again one where you've never been hurt."

"Powerful first relationships can stamp a template in your mind that gets activated in later interactions," says Susan Andersen, a psychologist at NYU who studies mental representations of significant others. If you meet someone who reminds you even a little of an ex—whether it's a physical resemblance or a similarity in attitudes, gestures, voice, word choice, or interests—it may engage the representation you have in your memory, says Andersen. The effect is called transference. And since your first love, by virtue of its novelty and emotional significance, is potentially your most salient, it may well be the representation that's summoned when you meet someone new, forging the lens through which you see new relationships.

It's not just a person's qualities that get transferred in your mind—your old feelings, motivations, and expectations are also reactivated. If someone new reminds you of an ex you still love, Andersen's studies show, you'll like that new person more, want to be close to them, and even start repeating the behaviors you engaged in with your ex. "The behaviors I'm engaging in will lead this new person, temporarily at least, to actually confirm my expectations," says Andersen. "By interacting in a particular way, I will draw out of this new person behaviors my ex used to engage in. That's expectation becoming reality."

In Vladimir Nabokov's *Lolita,* the tormented antihero Humbert Humbert describes Annabel, a childhood neighbor who loves him passionately for one summer, then dies of typhus. "I leaf again and again through these miserable memories," writes Humbert, "and keep asking myself, was it then, in the glitter of that remote summer, that the rift in my life began?"

First loss differs qualitatively from later losses because it submerges us in the icy reality that we're in constant danger of losing the people we love most—a concept we grasp intellectually at a certain age, but which doesn't feel real until it actually happens to us.

"We're wired for attachment in a world of impermanence," says Robert Neimeyer, a psychologist at the University of Memphis who studies how people draw meaning from loss and grief. "How we negotiate that tension shapes who we become."

Early loss can poison your ability to trust or feel safe, or give yourself fully in subsequent relationships, explains Singer. There's a strong link between early loss and depression, and early loss is also associated with diminished ability to form later attachments.

Loss: Only after the first loss of a loved one do we truly understand the finality of death. We're wired for attachment in a world of impermanence, and that tension shapes us.

Setup for a Self-Fulfilling Prophecy

Expectations about how an experience "should" feel can prime you for a lifetime of disappointment.

A negative first relationship can doom people to get trapped over and over again in self-destructive relationships. The reverse effect applies also. If your first relationship is healthy and positive, you may expect new people to be similarly friendly and safe—causing you to feel fondly, disclose your emotions, and build intimacy with that new person.

Losing one's virginity is an experience often subject to self-fulfilling expectations. People who consider their first sexual encounter to be a momentous turning point and find that it is indeed positive tend to wait for another loving relationship before they have sex again, says Laura Carpenter, a sociologist at Vanderbilt University and author of *Virginity Lost: An Intimate Portrait of First Sexual Experiences.* But if they're rejected by their partner, such people feel worthless—as if they've lost a special part of themselves. "A number of them felt they didn't have the right to say no to future sexual partners because they were already 'soiled' and 'ruined,'" says Carpenter. "They get involved in relationships they don't want and feel they have to have sex because they've already had sex. It's a spiral."

As with other first experiences, the loss of virginity can be a rite of passage—an irreversible transition from a state of ignorance to a state of knowledge. "Like a teenager learning to drive or a surgeon mastering her craft, you're knifing off the old self and building this new self," says Carpenter. "Whether it's what sex is about, a body of knowledge about religious mysteries, or medical skills, you've gained this special knowledge and you can never go back."

Love & Sex: Your first love may come to define what love means for you, and any subsequent relationships you have will be influenced by this first experience whether you realize it or not.

But many people find that after surviving a painful loss, they emerge more resilient. Optimistic people take loss better than less optimistic people, as do people who grow up with strong, secure attachment to their caregivers.

But the biggest predictor of resilience in the face of loss is "sense-making," weaving the experience into a larger narrative about who we are and what our lives are about, says Mary-Frances O'Connor, a behavioral scientist at UCLA who studies grief. Robert Neimeyer's father committed suicide when Robert was a child, for instance, and he dedicated his life to studying how people draw meaning from grief.

Getting Past the Past

You can't change the past, but you can look at it differently. Here's how.

Make a choice.

Decide to stop dwelling, suggests Susan Nolen-Hoeksema. List the pros and cons of dwelling—an exercise that will feel absurd, since cons will vastly exceed the pros. Say to yourself, "I know it's hard, but I choose to move forward."

Contain your rumination.

Schedule limited blocks of time to wallow—say, 15 minutes twice a day. You're compartmentalizing your grief—and you'll soon get bored of it and move on.

Do a reality check.

Maybe you find yourself thinking, "I'll never be happy again." Stop. True, nothing will ever be exactly the same. But there's no reason you can't find happiness in the present and future, with new people and new experiences.

Do not confuse the path with the destination.

May be you lost a youthful love and can't let go. Maybe you got fired and you feel like a failure. Clarify your values—creativity? Love? Recognize that you don't need that particular job to do creative work. You don't need that particular partner to have a loving relationship. Continue on your path.

Get present.

Join a gym, take up a hobby, find a cause, and schedule time with friends. "The best way to break free of living in the past is to get focused on the present and the future," says psychologist Jefferson Singer. "Take risks and do concrete things to create new experiences for yourself in the here and now."

People struck by loss or trauma at an early age—such as victims of crime or abuse—are at risk of drawing unwarranted conclusions about the world and their own place in it. Maybe your first boyfriend abused you. You may mistakenly infer that you're not careful enough—when the truth is that it could have happened to anybody.

That's the catch with first experiences. Because they're memorable, they come readily to mind and we overgeneralize when drawing conclusions about what kind of person we are. Positive first experiences can inspire us for a lifetime, but negative ones can be hard to get past.

So if you're overly focused on a negative event as a turning point in your life, ask yourself: Is what happened truly a reflection of who you are? Or would others have made the same choices given the same circumstances? "In repeated experiences, we understand the situational factors outside ourselves," says Singer. "But the first time, we don't have the context, so we're more likely to see it as a reflection on our own character."

Two women recounted the story of their first lie to Bella DePaulo, a psychologist at the University of California at Santa Barbara who studies deception. The first one told a story about how she wanted to go out one night as a child but was barred from doing so by her father. So she went anyway and lied to him about where she'd been. When he cluelessly swallowed the whole story, she realized she had a new talent. She lied freely from that moment on.

The other woman told a story about how, as a girl, she was very curious about her sister's boyfriend. One night she snuck into a room with a phone extension and listened in on their conversation. When her father walked in and caught her *in flagrante delicto,* she panicked, blurting, "I was just cleaning the phone!" Guilt-stricken over the lie, she immediately confessed and apologized, resolving never to lie again.

A first lie crosses a line. You recognize a capacity you didn't realize you had. For the extremely honest or the extremely dishonest, the lie may reveal character: a decision never to repeat the act, or the realization that this is a new way to behave. But for many people between these two poles, the consequences of a first lie depend on one's reaction to it, says DePaulo. If we do something we shouldn't—say, shoplifting—and get caught and punished, we're likely to internalize the lesson that stealing is wrong, incorporating it into our value system. But if no one finds out, we may decide it's no big deal.

"First experiences tell you something about yourself and what you're like in a new situation," explains DePaulo. "It's testing the social environment and seeing how other people react, but it's also testing who you are, how you think of yourself, and whether you want to be that person."

If you get a thrill out of lying, it's easier to cross that line the next time.

"It's called the abstinence violation effect," explains Singer. "If I'm willing to make that first slip, then what's the point in holding on? Now that I'm no longer a dieter, I might as well have another cookie." The principle applies not only to straying from a diet but also to major transgressions. If you're a soldier, your first kill may force you to reflect on death and morality. But killing someone may not feel like such a big deal the second time around.

Lies: Your first lie crosses a line, making it easier to go through with it the next time. And the outcome—whether you get away with it or not—can shape your patterns later in life.

With transgressions, as with other first experiences, it's important to remember that one action doesn't define you.

"When counselors treat addicts who have fallen off the wagon, they tell them, 'Look, you haven't relapsed, you've had a slip,'" explains Singer. "If you use the fallacy of saying, 'Oh, well, it's over now,' then you can easily rationalize taking the next drink and the next and the next and it will be a relapse. But a slip can be corrected."

In 1982, before Michael Jordan was Michael Jordan, he was a student at the University of North Carolina. He played good basketball, but as a 19-year-old freshman, he was constantly overshadowed by upper-classmen. When North Carolina entered the NCAA championship game against Georgetown, though, something changed in Jordan's play. In the first three quarters of the game, he scored 14 points and grabbed nine rebounds.

It wasn't enough. Georgetown, led by freshman superstar and future NBA powerhouse Patrick Ewing, was winning 62 to 61, with only 17 seconds left in the game. Then, when it looked like the game was over, Jordan made one of the most famous shots in basketball history: a 16-foot jump shot that won the game and earned North Carolina the championship.

That first game-winning shot was a turning point, Jordan recalled in later years. It gave him the confidence that he could come through in a clutch. For the rest of his career, especially when he needed to muster the intense concentration and Zen calm necessary to shoot free throws, he would summon up that moment to bring him into a winning state of mind. "He used that shot, performing in that pressure situation, as the foundation for his confidence in taking other big shots," says Richard Ginsburg, an athletic coach and author of *Whose Game Is It, Anyway?* "He'd tell himself, 'I've done this before, I can do it again.'"

Game-winning shots and home runs—as well as the times you ace an exam, nail a job interview, or win a standing ovation—provide potent fodder for your sense of identity as a successful person. "You think, 'I succeeded in this clutch situation, now I know I'm a clutch player,'" explains Singer. "It's revealing something in your character that wasn't clear before, telling you, 'This is something I can do. This is who I am.'"

"I remember the time I first won a tennis match against my father," says Tim Gallwey, author of the classic book *The Inner Game of Tennis.* Gallwey's father had promised him a new racket if he won. Gallwey was 13 at the time, and had been playing in state tournaments. During the match, he was torn between wanting to win a new racket and not wanting to beat his father. When he won, he felt regret and compassion for his dad, who'd just been defeated by his own son, but was also elated by victory, glowing with a sense that his abilities had reached a new height. "That sense of self-worth is very precious," says Gallwey.

Of course, first failures can be as memorable as first successes. If you flunk a test or miss an easy pop fly, you may start to feel like a loser. And failure is always a possibility. But what separates world-class performers from the rest of us is the ability to put negative experiences behind them (see "Getting Past the Past").

> **Success: A single victory can transform your sense of self. By telling yourself, "I've done this before, I can do it again," you realize your ability to come through when it counts.**

"Once you can see yourself doing something—once you can experience it and feel what it's like—it changes you," explains Ginsburg. "The best performers are good at forgiving themselves, dropping failure from their mental bandwidth quickly so that they can focus on the positive." If you can do that, you may strike out many times, but you'll always be the person who hit that grand slam—which in turn will breed further success.

First successes often take the form of "redemption sequences," wherein a bad event suddenly turns good, says McAdams—like when you defy the odds in a basketball game you're losing by sinking a winning buzzer-beater with seconds left on the clock. "The construction of redemption sequences in life is a very common narrative strategy," he adds, "and one that seems to bring with it a certain sense of resilience."

A single win may not be sufficient to boost your confidence permanently. True confidence comes from the gradual accumulation of self-efficacy over a long period of successes. But a dramatic first triumph can inspire and motivate you and transform your self-conception from "I'm a loser" to "I'm the kind of person who hits grand slams."

And a first success can also uncover abilities you didn't realize you had. Days before he died, I interviewed George Carlin. Toward the end of our conversation, I asked him about the first time he made his mother laugh. "I noticed the moment something had happened," Carlin immediately recalled. "This was when I was very young. My mother laughed fairly frequently. But I knew the difference between her social laugh and her really spontaneous laugh when she was caught off guard and amused—I saw that in her and it registered with me. It meant I had said something witty. It was a little mark along the way, a little badge of honor."

Critical Thinking

1. Provide two reasons why first experiences have more power than later events.

2. Give an example of transference of a mental representation.

3. Suggest ways to look at your past experiences in a new light.

Create Central

www.mhhe.com/createcentral

Internet References

Expectations and Self-Fulfilling Prophecies
  www.pon.harvard.edu/daily/negotiation-skills
Flashbulb Memories: DNA Learning Center
  www.dnal.org/view/823-Flashbulb-Memories.html
Seared in Our Memories
www.apa.org/monitor/2011/09/memories.aspx

Article   Prepared by: Karen L. Freiberg, *University of Maryland*

Will Your Marriage Last?

What social scientists have learned from putting couples under the microscope.

BROOKE LEA FOSTER

Learning Outcomes

After reading this article, you will be able to:

- Identify three things that make some couples more likely to divorce than other couples.

- Describe three things that make some couples less likely to divorce than other couples, and explain why.

- Explain the paradox of less, then more, happiness in a marriage with children.

My husband, John, and I lived together for four years before we got engaged. He's Filipino; I'm white. And we have a two-year-old. Can you guess which of these things makes us more likely to divorce than other couples?

The answer: all of the above.

People who live together before marriage are more likely to divorce than those who move in together after their engagement. Mixed-race couples don't fare as well as couples of the same race or ethnicity: According to the National Center for Health Statistics, 41 percent of couples who intermarry will divorce before the ten-year mark. And as for kids, let's just say the research doesn't paint a rosy picture of marriage post-baby.

Psychologists have been trying for decades to figure out why some marriages last while others fail. It's easy to be cynical about marriage. With the conventional wisdom saying about half of all couples will divorce, it's hard to go to a wedding without wondering if a couple will make it. At age 36, I already know several people who split up within a few years of getting married. I've got bets on others.

The secret to long-lasting relationships is particularly confounding considering that most couples start in the same place: madly in love. What happens after the wedding that alters the course of so many relationships?

It turns out that the initial years of marriage are particularly telling. Once the honeymoon is over and the fairy dust settles, the work of merging two lives begins. Talking gas bills and car payments can kill the mood. Sometimes one partner might feel disappointed in the relationship, and bad habits can form.

"The first two years are supposed to be a honeymoon," says Barry McCarthy, a professor of psychology at American University and coauthor of *Sexual Awareness: Your Guide to Healthy Couple Sexuality.* "But research says they're quite difficult. You're figuring out sexually and emotionally how to be a couple."

Most divorces happen within the first several years of marriage in part because, McCarthy says, "many couples just can't figure these things out and they end up fighting all of the time." Those who make it through aren't exactly in the clear—racking up marital years isn't the same as having a happy and fulfilling marriage.

Last December, the University of Virginia's National Marriage Project analyzed a survey of more than 1,400 couples between ages 18 and 46 about the key to a happy marriage. The project found that couples who reported higher levels of generosity toward each other also reported happier marriages. The study defined generosity as "being affectionate and forgiving of your spouse."

Is the key to marital happiness as easy as making your partner breakfast each morning—or simply saying "I love you"?

"It's not that simple," laughs the study's lead author, W. Bradford Wilcox, director of the National Marriage Project. But the study did reveal that playing nice improves your sex life, another key factor in a couple's happiness. Respondents who reported high levels of generosity, commitment, religious faith, and quality time together also said they had increased sexual satisfaction. Interestingly, women were more sexually satisfied when husbands shared the housework. Says Wilcox: "It seems that what happens outside of the bedroom has a lot to do with what happens inside the bedroom."

Pioneering marriage researcher John Gottman, a psychology professor at the University of Washington, has been trying to figure out the secret to a happy marriage for decades. He calls one of his most famous theories "the magic ratio." Gottman believes that couples who have at least five positive interactions for every negative one are more likely to make it.

In 1992, Gottman did a study of 700 newlywed couples, inviting them in for a 15-minute videotaped conversation. He counted how many positive and negative interactions they had during the interview. Based on his 5-to-1 ratio, he predicted which couples would be together ten years later and which would be divorced. In a 2002 follow-up study, his findings were astounding: He had a 94-percent accuracy rate, which means he could predict marital happiness for strangers in a quarter of an hour.

A clue to how happy your marriage is may lie in the way you talk about it. Last year, researchers at the University of California at Berkeley found that middle-aged and older couples who used words such as "we," "our," and "us" tended to treat each other better and were better at resolving conflicts. Couples who emphasized their "separateness"—using pronouns such as "I," "me," and "you"—tended to be less happy.

Do you have couple friends? If not, you should get some. Professor Geoffrey Greif and associate professor Kathleen Holtz Deal of the University of Maryland's School of Social Work recently authored a book, *Two Plus Two: Couples and Their Couple Friendships*. After interviewing 123 couples, they found that those who had a social network of couple friends reported higher levels of marital happiness. The researchers said that having couple friends promotes marital satisfaction because it increases attraction to each other and allows couples to observe how other couples interact and resolve differences.

Everyone brings some baggage to a relationship, but a parent's divorce greatly affects marital quality. If your parents split up when you were a kid, you have a 50-percent greater chance of getting divorced yourself. If you and your spouse are both children of divorce, you have a 200-percent higher risk of divorce, says Nicholas Wolfinger, an associate professor of family and consumer studies at the University of Utah and author of a book called *Understanding the Divorce Cycle: The Children of Divorce in Their Own Marriages*.

People who live together before getting engaged tend to "slide" into a lifelong commitment.

Children of divorce are also more likely to live together before marriage or to marry young—both of which increase the chance of divorce. You'd think cohabiting partners would have lower divorce rates—isn't the whole point of moving in together to test the waters, to give couples a chance to try each other on as life partners?

Apparently, it doesn't work. Researchers say that people who live together before getting engaged tend to "slide" into a lifelong commitment rather than choose it. In other words, they've already got the house, the patio furniture, and someone to split the bills with—why wouldn't they take the next step?

Experts say this inertia doesn't bode well for lasting happiness. Scott Stanley, a psychologist at the University of Denver, found that 19 percent of couples who lived together before their engagement suggested divorce at least once over the course of the five-year study, compared with only 10 percent who moved in together after the big day.

But cohabitation doesn't always spell doom: Couples who move in together after their engagement—but before marriage—appear to fare just as well as couples who moved in together after saying "I do."

As for having kids, the jury is out on whether they strain or enrich a marriage. "There's a dip in marital happiness after the birth of your first child," says the Marriage Project's W. Bradford Wilcox. A study by Texas A&M University and the University of Denver of 218 couples in their mid-twenties—roughly two-thirds of whom welcomed their first child within eight years of marrying and a third of whom had no children—showed that couples with kids were less happy than childless couples. While the study showed that overall marital happiness decreased over time for both those with kids and those without, the couples with children reported a more sudden drop in marital dissatisfaction; the childless couples' happiness levels decreased more slowly over time.

Still, Wilcox says that couples with kids often rebound and report higher levels of happiness later in life. Longitudinal data show that marital satisfaction increases as children get older and leave home. In other words, while individuals love their children and glean much happiness from them, their marriages benefit when their kids enter college and they're able to spend more quality time together.

There doesn't seem to be a magic age for getting married. Even so, couples who wed later tend to report higher levels of education, leading to greater affluence and greater marital satisfaction. If you have a college degree, you're 66 percent less likely to divorce. "It's partly because people with college degrees make more money and do better in the professional world," says Wilcox, "but it's also because many have the social skills needed to navigate married life more successfully."

Money makes a big difference in a couple's life. Research cited in a 2009 article by Jeffrey Drew of the National Marriage Project found that wives with higher incomes and assets are happier in their marriages; they're also less likely to get a divorce. Couples who reported fighting about money once a week were 30 percent more likely to split up than couples who argued about finances a few times a month. And couples with no assets at the beginning of a three-year period were 70 percent likelier to divorce than couples with at least $10,000 in assets.

But while having money can help, it's not a good sign if either spouse is too motivated by it. A Brigham Young University study of 1,734 married couples found that those who said money wasn't important scored 10 to 15 percent better on marriage stability than couples in which one or both said they highly valued "having money and lots of things."

"Couples where both spouses are materialistic were worse off on nearly every measure we looked at," says Jason Carroll, a BYU professor of family life.

A second study cited in Drew's National Marriage Project article found that perceptions of how well one's spouse handles money can also cause strain. If you feel your husband or wife doesn't handle money well, you probably have a lower level of marital happiness. "In one study, feeling that one's spouse spent money foolishly increased the likelihood of divorce by 45 percent for both men and women. Only extramarital affairs and alcohol/drug abuse were stronger predictors of divorce," Drew writes.

What do happy couples have incommon? They respect each other. They don't nitpick, criticize, or put each other down. And yes, they go out of their way to be nice. Says Wilcox: "Being an affectionate and engaging spouse is going to make both of you happier."

My husband and I may be of different ethnicities and we may have a kid, but I think we're going to make it. Here's why: When my feet are cold in winter, he'll always let me warm them up on his legs. I kiss him hello every day when he gets home. He encourages me to take time for myself when he sees I'm feeling drained. In other words, we're kind to each other—and as the studies show, that counts for a lot.

Critical Thinking

1. Why does "playing nice" improve a couple's sex life?

2. What are some of the positive interactions that contribute to the 5-to-1 ratio of positive-to-negative interactions that predict marital success?

3. How does the desire for money and lots of things decrease the chances of marital success?

Create Central

www.mhhe.com/createcentral

Internet References

Child Out of Wedlock: Huffington Post
 www.huffingtonpost.com/tag/child-out-of-wedlock

Does Living Together before Marriage Increase Chances of Divorce?
 www.eharmony.com/blog/2013/07/24/does-living-together-before-marriage-increase-chances-of-divorce

The Downside of Cohabitating before Marriage
 www.nytimes.com/2012/04/15/opinion/Sunday

U.S. Rate of Interracial Marriage Hits Record High
 http://usatoday30.usatoday.com/health/news/2012-02-16

Article   Prepared by: Karen L. Freiberg, *University of Maryland*

The Retro Wife

Feminists who say they're having it all—by choosing to stay home.

LISA MILLER

Learning Outcomes

After reading this article, you will be able to:

- Contrast traditional women's roles (stay home and nurture husband/children) with the liberated women's roles (independence, career).

- Explain why women who expect their husbands to fully share housework, child care, and money-making in careers are frequently disappointed.

When Kelly Makino was a little girl, she loved to go orienteering—to explore the wilderness near her rural Pennsylvania home, finding her way back with a compass and a map—and the future she imagined for herself was equally adventuresome. Until she was about 16, she wanted to be a CIA operative, a spy, she says, "like La Femme Nikita." She put herself through college at Georgia State working in bars and slinging burgers, planning that with her degree in social work, she would move abroad, to India or Africa, to do humanitarian work for a couple of years. Her husband would be nerdy-hip, and they'd settle down someplace like Williamsburg; when she eventually had children, she would continue working full time, like her mother did, moving up the nonprofit ladder to finally "run a United Way chapter or be the CEO." Kelly graduated from college magna cum laude and got an M.S.W. from Penn, again with honors, receiving an award for her negotiating skills.

Now Kelly is 33, and if dreams were winds, you might say that hers have shifted. She believes that every household needs one primary caretaker, that women are, broadly speaking, better at that job than men, and that no amount of professional success could possibly console her if she felt her two young children—Connor, 5, and Lillie, 4—were not being looked after the right way. The maternal instinct is a real thing, Kelly argues: Girls play with dolls from childhood, so "women are raised from the get-go to raise children successfully. When we are moms, we have a better toolbox." Women, she believes, are conditioned to be more patient with children, to be better multitaskers, to be more tolerant of the quotidian grind of playdates and temper tantrums; "women," she says, "keep it together better than guys do." So last summer, when her husband, Alvin, a management consultant, took a new position requiring more travel, she made a decision. They would live off his low-six-figure income, and she would quit her job running a program for at-risk kids in a public school to stay home full time.

Kelly is not a Martha Stewart spawn in pursuit of the perfectly engineered domestic stage set. On the day I met her, she was wearing an orange hoodie, plum-colored Converse low-tops, and a tiny silver stud in her nose. In the family's modest New Jersey home, the bedroom looked like a laundry explosion, and the morning's breakfast dishes were piled in the sink. But Kelly's priorities are nothing if not retrograde. She has given herself over entirely to the care and feeding of her family. Undistracted by office politics and unfettered by meetings or a nerve-fraying commute, she spends hours upon hours doing things that would make another kind of woman scream with boredom, chanting nursery rhymes and eating pretend cake beneath a giant *Transformers* poster. Her sacrifice of a salary tightened the Makinos' upper-middle-class budget, but the subversion of her personal drive pays them back in ways Kelly believes are priceless; she is now able to be there for her kids no matter what, cooking healthy meals, taking them hiking and to museums, helping patiently with homework, and devoting herself to teaching the life lessons—on littering, on manners, on good habits—that she believes every child should know. She introduces me as "Miss Lisa," and that's what the kids call me all day long.

Alvin benefits no less from his wife's domestic reign. Kelly keeps a list of his clothing sizes in her iPhone and, devoted to his cuteness, surprises him regularly with new items, like the dark-washed jeans he was wearing on the day I visited. She tracks down his favorite recipes online, recently discovering one for pineapple fried rice that he remembered from his childhood in Hawaii. A couple of times a month, Kelly suggests that they go to bed early and she soothes his work-stiffened muscles with a therapeutic massage. "I love him so much, I just want to spoil him," she says.

Kelly calls herself "a flaming liberal" and a feminist, too. "I want my daughter to be able to do anything she wants," she says. "But I also want to say, 'Have a career that you can walk away from at the drop of a hat.'" And she is not alone. Far from the Bible Belt's conservative territories, in blue-state cities and suburbs, young, educated, married mothers find themselves not uninterested in the metaconversation about "having it all" but untouched by it. They are too busy mining their grandmothers' old-fashioned lives for values they can appropriate like heirlooms, then wear proudly as their own.

Feminism has fizzled, its promise only half-fulfilled. This is the revelation of the moment, hashed and rehashed on blogs and talk shows, a cause of grief for some, fury for others. American women are better educated than they've ever been, better educated now than men, but they get distracted during their prime earning years by the urge to procreate. As they mature, they earn less than men and are granted fewer responsibilities at work. Fifty years after the publication of *The Feminine Mystique,* women represent only a tiny fraction of corporate and government leaders, and they still earn only 77 cents on the male dollar.

What to do? One solution is to deny the need for broader solutions or for any kind of sisterly help. It's every woman for herself, and may the best one win. "I don't, I think, have, sort of, the militant drive and, sort of, the chip on the shoulder that sometimes comes with that," said Yahoo CEO Marissa Mayer in an interview with PBS, in which she declined to label herself a "feminist." "I think it's too bad, but I do think that *feminism has become in many ways a more negative word.*" (*I went to Stanford, worked at Google, got pregnant, and still became the chief executive of a Fortune 500 company,* she seemed to say. *If you're smart enough, so can you.*) But others, as you may have read, believe it's time for women to resume the good fight. In her much-discussed *Atlantic* piece, Anne-Marie Slaughter, by profession a policy wonk (now at Princeton, formerly at the State Department), calls for better workplace programs: more parental leave, more part-time and flextime options. Facebook COO Sheryl Sandberg, in her new book, *Lean In,* acknowledges the need for better policies, but argues that the new revolution needs to start with women themselves, that what's needed to equalize U.S. workplaces is a generation of women tougher, stronger, wilier, more honest about their ambition, more strategic, and more determined to win than American women currently are.

But what if all the fighting is just too much? That is, what if a woman isn't earning Facebook money but the salary of a social worker? Or what if her husband works 80 hours a week, and her kid is acting out at school, and she's sick of the perpetual disarray in the closets and the endless battles over who's going to buy the milk and oversee the homework? Maybe most important, what if a woman doesn't have Sandberg-Slaughter-Mayer-level ambition but a more modest amount that neither drives nor defines her?

Reading *The Feminine Mystique* now, one is struck by the white-hot flame of Betty Friedan's professional hunger, which made her into a prophet and a pioneer. But it blinded her as well: She presumed that all her suburban-housewife sisters felt as imprisoned as she did and that the gratification she found in her work was attainable for all. That was never true, of course; the revolution that Friedan helped to spark both liberated women and allowed countless numbers of them to experience financial pressure and the profound dissatisfactions of the workaday grind. More women than ever earn some or all of the money their family lives on. But today, in the tumultuous 21st-century economy, depending on a career as a path to self-actualization can seem like a sucker's bet.

Meanwhile, what was once feminist blasphemy is now conventional wisdom: Generally speaking, mothers instinctively want to devote themselves to home more than fathers do. (Even Sandberg admits it. "Are there characteristics inherent in sex differences that make women more nurturing and men more assertive?" she asks. "Quite possibly.") If feminism is not only about creating an equitable society but also a means to fulfillment for individual women, and if the rewards of working are insufficient and uncertain, while the tug of motherhood is inexorable, then a new calculus can take hold: For some women, the solution to resolving the long-running tensions between work and life is not more parent-friendly offices or savvier career moves but the full embrace of domesticity. "The feminist revolution started in the workplace, and now it's happening at home," says Makino. "I feel like in today's society, women who don't work are bucking the convention we were raised with . . . Why can't we just be girls? Why do we have to be boys and girls at the same time?" She and the legions like her offer a silent rejoinder to Sandberg's manifesto, raising the possibility that the best way for some mothers (and their loved ones) to have a happy life is to make home their highest achievement.

"What these women feel is that the trade-offs now between working and not working are becoming more and more unsustainable," says Stacy Morrison, editor-in-chief of BlogHer, a network of 3,000 blogs for and by women. "The conversation we hear over and over again is this: 'The sense of calm and control that we feel over our lives is so much better than what is currently on offer in our culture.' And they're not wrong." The number of stay-at-home mothers rose incrementally between 2010 and 2011, for the first time since the downturn of 2008. While staying home with children remains largely a privilege of the affluent (the greatest number of America's SAHMs live in families with incomes of $100,000 a year or more), some of the biggest increases have been among younger mothers, ages 25 to 35, and those whose family incomes range from $75,000 to $100,000 a year.

This is not the retreat from high-pressure workplaces of a previous generation but rather a more active awakening to the virtues of the way things used to be. Patricia Ireland, who lives on the Upper West Side, left her job as a wealth adviser in 2010 after her third child was born. Now, even though her husband, also in finance, has seen his income drop since the recession, she has no plans to go back to work. She feels it's a privilege to manage her children's lives—"not just what they do, but what they believe, how they talk to other children, what kind of story we read together. That's all dictated by me. Not by my nanny or my babysitter." Her husband's part of the arrangement is to go to work and deposit his paycheck in the joint account. "I'm really grateful that my husband and I have fallen into traditional gender roles without conflict," says Ireland. "I'm not bitter that I'm the one home and he goes to work. And he's very happy that he goes to work."

A lot of the new neo-traditionalists watched their own mothers strain under the second shift, and they regard Sandberg's lower-wattage mini-mes, rushing off to Big Jobs and back home with a wad of cash for the nanny, with something like pity. They don't want a return to the confines of the fifties; they treasure their freedoms, but see a third way. When Slaughter tours the lecture circuit, she is often approached, she says, by women younger than 30 who say, "I don't see a senior person in my world whose life I want." In researching her 2010 book *The Unfinished Revolution: Coming of Age in a New Era of Gender, Work and Family,* New York University sociologist Kathleen Gerson found that, in spite of all the gains young women have made, about a quarter say they would choose a traditional domestic arrangement over the independence that comes with a career, believing not just "that only a parent can provide an acceptable level of care" but also that "they are the only parent available for the job."

The harried, stressed, multiarmed Kali goddess, with a laptop in one hand and homemade organic baby food in the other, has been replaced with a domestic Madonna, content with her choices and placid in her sphere. "I was . . . blessed," wrote one woman on the UrbanBaby message boards recently, "with the patience to truly enjoy being home with my kids and know that in the end family is what is important in life—not pushing papers at some crap job." When the UB community fired back with a fusillade of snark, the poster remained serene. "It's sacred work but not for everyone," she wrote. "I will never have regrets." In season three of *The Good Wife,* Caitlin D'arcy, the law firm's ambitious and strategically minded female associate, unexpectedly quits her job when she becomes pregnant, saying she wants to be a full-time wife and mother. Her mentor, Alicia Florrick—separated from her husband and a mother of two—tries to dissuade her. "You're smart and clever," she says. "If you give this up for someone, even someone important to you, you'll regret it."

"I'm not giving it up for my fiancé," says Caitlin. "I'm giving it up for myself. I like the law, but I love my fiancé."

"But you don't need to choose," protests Alicia. "There's no reason why you can't work, be a wife and a mother."

"But I want to choose," says Caitlin. "Maybe it's different for my generation, but I don't have to prove anything. Or if I have to, I don't want to. I'm in love."

In Friedan's day, housewives used novel technologies such as the automatic washing machine to ease the burden of their domestic work; today, technology helps them to avoid the isolation of their grandmothers and to show off the fruits of their labor. Across the Internet, on a million mommy blogs and Pinterest pages, these women—conceptual cousins of the bearded and suspendered artisanal bakers and brewers who reside in gentrified neighborhoods—are elevating homemaking to an art, crocheting baby hats, slow-roasting strawberries for after-school snacks ("taste like Twizzlers!"), and making their own laundry soap from scratch. Young mothers fill the daytime

upholstery and pattern-making courses at Third Ward, a craftspace in Williamsburg, and take knitting classes at the Brooklyn Yarn Café in Bushwick while their kids are in school.

Home, to these women, is more than a place to watch TV at the end of the day and motherhood more than a partial identity. It is a demanding, full-time endeavor, requiring all of their creativity, energy, and ingenuity. Kelly Makino set up a giant mothers' group in northern Jersey, using her M.S.W. to help other parents pool time and resources. (Such "side projects," she says, have the added benefit of "keeping us sane.") Home-schooling, once the province of Christian conservatives, is now increasingly chosen by lefty families; in New York City, the number of children being taught in their apartments rose by nearly 10 percent over the past year.

For Rebecca Woolf, maternal ambition led to the creation of her website, Girl's Gone Child, in 2005, when she was 23 and had just given birth to her son Archer. She has since had three more children (a girl, Fable, and twins named Reverie and Boheme), and every day she posts staged photos of her kids that make her family life look like one big, wholesome-but-funky romp. Here are the twins wearing adorable handmade animal hats with ears! Here is a lesson in at-home bang trimming! Woolf, who lives in Los Angeles and whose husband is a television producer, points out that as the founder of a thriving blog, she does have a job. But the image of home life she presents for popular consumption is as glossy and idealized as the mythical feminine perfection Friedan rebelled against. It is perhaps no wonder that in the world of mommy blogs, tattooed Fort Greeners and Mormons unknowingly collide, trafficking the same sites and trading recipes on the same message boards. They may vote different tickets, but on the centrality of home and family to a satisfying life, their interests are aligned.

Before they marry, college students of both genders almost universally tell social scientists that they want marriages in which housework, child care, professional ambition, and moneymaking will be respectfully negotiated and fully shared. According to a 2008 report by the Families and Work Institute, two thirds of people younger than 29 imagine for themselves partnerships not defined by traditional gender roles. Maybe she'll change the lightbulbs; maybe he'll go part time for a while after the birth of the baby. Seventy-four percent of American employees say they believe that women who work outside the home can be as good at mothering as those who don't. The institute's data also indicates that "men today view the 'ideal' man as someone who is not only successful . . . but also involved as a father, husband/partner, and son." Once married, the research shows, men are more contented over the long term, and women are happiest in an egalitarian union—so long as both parties agree about what egalitarian means.

That, of course, is where things get tricky. Despite their stated position, men still do far less housework than their spouses. In 2011, only 19 percent spent any time during the average day cleaning or doing laundry; among couples with kids younger than 6, men spent just 26 minutes a day doing what the Bureau of Labor Statistics calls "physical care," which is to say bathing, feeding, or dressing children. (Women did more than twice as much.) In her research, Gerson found that in times of stress men overwhelmingly revert to the traditional provider role, allowing them to justify punting on the dishes. "All [men]," she says, "agree that no matter what the gender revolution prescribes, it is still paramount for men to earn a living and support their families, which also implies taking a backseat as caregiver." As a romantic college student, a man may imagine he will request an extended paternity leave, but it's very likely that he won't. The average amount of time a man takes off after the birth of a child is five days. "That's exactly what happened to me!" exclaimed Kelly Makino when I relayed that stat to her. Alvin had planned on taking a two-week leave after Lillie was born but was back at the office after half that time.

All those bachelors' vows of future bathroom cleanings, it turns out, may be no more than a contemporary mating call. "People espouse equality because they conform to the current normative values of our culture," says University of Texas evolutionary psychologist David Buss. "Any man who did not do so would alienate many women—yes, espousing values is partly a mating tactic, and this is just one example." At least in one area, there's scant penalty for this bait and switch. Last year, sociologists at the University of Washington found that the less cooking, cleaning, and laundry a married man does, the more frequently he gets laid.

Feminism has never fully relieved women from feeling that the domestic domain is theirs to manage, no matter what else they're juggling. There is a story, possibly apocryphal yet also believable, of an observer looking over Secretary of State Madeleine Albright's shoulder during a Cabinet meeting in the late nineties. On the pad before her, the secretary had written not "paths to peace in the Middle East" but "buy cottage cheese." (Albright declined to comment for this story, but while promoting a book in 2009, she told an audience that all her life she made it a point always to answer phone calls from her children, no matter what else she was doing. "Every woman's middle name is guilt," she said.) Those choices have a different tenor now, one that upholds the special importance of the maternal role. "My sense," says Buss, "is that younger women are more open to the idea that there might exist evolved psychological gender differences." Among my friends, many women behave as though the evolutionary imperative extends not just to birthing and breast-feeding but to administrative household tasks as well, as if only they can properly plan birthday parties, make doctors' appointments, wrap presents, communicate with the teacher, buy the new school shoes. A number of those I spoke to for this article reminded me of a 2010 British study showing that men lack the same mental bandwidth for multitasking as women. Male and female subjects were asked how they'd find a lost key, while also being given a number of unrelated chores to do—talk on the phone, read a map, complete a math problem. The women universally approached the hunt more efficiently. Joanna Goddard, who runs the women's lifestyle blog A Cup of Jo, says she hears this refrain among her friends. "I'll just do it. It'll be easier. I'll just do it. It'll be faster. I'll do the dishes. I know where everything goes."

Psychologists suggest that perhaps American women are heirs and slaves to some atavistic need to prove their worth through domestic perfectionism: "So many women want to control their husbands' parenting," says Barbara Kass, a therapist with a private practice in Brooklyn. "'Oh, do you have the this? Did you do the that? Don't forget that she needs this. And make sure she naps.' Sexism is internalized." Perhaps this mentality explains the baffling result of a survey that the Families and Work Institute conducted last spring for *Real Simple* magazine. Women said they yearned for more free time and that they hated doing most housework. But when they got free time, they used it to do housework—convinced that no one else could do it as well.

If women and men are at odds with themselves over what they value most, if a woman says she wants a big job but also needs to be home by 5:30 to oversee homework, and her husband promises to pick up the kids from chess club but goes instead to the meeting with the boss, how can marriages with two working parents not wind up conflict-ridden? From Kelly Makino's perspective, it was a no-brainer. "Some days I just have to pinch myself," she says. "It's so easy, it's so rewarding to live this way."

Kelly and Alvin decided to change their lives one night last spring during a mini-vacation to Washington, D.C. They were there to see the cherry blossoms, and Kelly was aware, all weekend long, of the ebbing of her anxiety. "I didn't have to worry about 500 people's lives. I had to worry about four people's lives."

Connor had been in a fight at school. Lillie had been having nightmares. After the kids were in bed, the Makinos retired to the bathroom of their hotel room. "We realized that neither one of us were happy. We were sleep deprived and stressed out all the time," says Kelly. If they scaled back, they reasoned, they could live on Alvin's salary. But first Kelly had to come to terms with her unfulfilled ambition—"I knew I had it in me to be the best"—and the disapproval of her parents. Her father worried that she'd be bored out of her mind. Her mother accused her of "mooching." It took Kelly three months to quit her job.

Sitting at their kitchen table, littered with the detritus from a birthday-party goody bag, the Makinos retrace how their relationship turned out the way it has. They met at a biker bar where Kelly was waitressing, and at first, when Alvin envisioned their collective future, he thought, "*Oh, it's totally not going to be like my parents. We're going to do things equally. Both of us are working, and we'll take care of the kids together.* It just seemed so simple in my mind."

"I remember you said you wanted us to be a power couple," says Kelly.

But there was tension. Alvin earned a lot more money. Kelly felt that her job contributed more good to the world, that its emergencies were more urgent. One time, she remembers, she was just leaving work when she found herself face-to-face with an anguished child. "It's 4:30, this 12-year-old girl tells me she has been raped." Kelly attended to the girl and contacted the school authorities; after she got home, she put her own kids to bed and then was on the phone making a report to protective services until midnight. It was exhausting work but gratifying. "Honestly, before I had kids," she says, "I kind of looked down on stay-at-home moms a little. I thought, *You can't hack it. It was a prejudice that was wrong. I thought, Why can't you do it? You must've sucked at your job if you stay home.*"

Kelly's commitment to her career "put a lot more pressure on me to make sure I could pick up the kids and I could feed the kids," says Alvin. "As much as I tried to be really supportive, there were conflicts with schedule, with availability, with resource time. We would get home at 6:30 or 7:00, then we'd have to think about dinner. It's a rush to get the kids to bed. The time either of us had with the kids was short, hectic, stressful. Day to day, managing our schedules—sometimes my meeting would last two hours instead of twenty minutes—it put a lot of strain on our relationship." They got fat on takeout. At bedtime, they talked about "bills, plans, schedules, the next day, everything but spending time together," says Alvin. They never had sex, remembers Kelly. They rarely had any fun at all.

In 2006, British researchers studied work–life conflict in five European countries. They found a lot of strife in France, despite a high percentage of women in the workforce and widespread government policies aimed at helping women remain employed when their children are young: subsidized nursery schools, day-care collectives, and the like. What's more, the French expressed progressive, optimistic ideals about gender roles. Seventy-four percent of full-time employees in France disagreed with the following statement: "A man's job is to earn money, a woman's job is to look after the home and family."

The explanation for the disconnect, the researchers surmised, was that French people, like Americans, lie to themselves about what they want. French women (like their American counterparts) do the bulk of the domestic work, and the majority also work full time. Quoting from colleagues' earlier work, the sociologists showed that sexism in France is as much a part of the culture as great bread, wine, and a long lunch hour. In France, "there were numerous men who were available to look after children during the week when their partner was employed . . . but nevertheless did not take responsibility for child care even when they were free." They were saying one thing and doing another, which in marriage, says the historian Stephanie Coontz, is "a recipe for instability and unhappiness."

That same year, an American sociologist published a paper describing similar results. Predictors of marital unhappiness, found Bradford Wilcox at the University of Virginia, included wives who earned a large share of household income and wives who perceived the division of labor at home as unfair. Predictors of marital happiness were couples who shared a commitment to the institutional idea of marriage and couples who went to religious services together. "Our findings suggest," he wrote, "that increased departures from a male-breadwinning-female-homemaking model may also account for declines in marital quality, insofar as men and women continue to tacitly value gendered patterns of behavior in marriage." It's an idea that thrives especially in conservative religious circles: The things that specific men and women may selfishly want for themselves

(sex, money, status, notoriety) must for the good of the family be put aside. Feminists widely critiqued Wilcox's findings, saying it puts the onus on women to suck it up in marriage, when men should be under more pressure to change. But these days you'll find echoes of Wilcox's thesis in unlikely places. "We look at straight people," a gay friend said to me recently as we were comparing anecdotes about husbands, "and we think marriage must be so much easier for them."

When I look at Kelly and Alvin Makino, I feel the same way. I have worked full time for almost all my daughter's nine years, and only very rarely have I ever felt that nature required anything else of me. I love my job and have found work to be gratifying and even calming during periods when other parts of my life are far less so. Like 65 percent of American couples, my husband and I both work to pay our bills, but my commitment to my career extends way beyond financial necessity. My self-sufficiency sets a good example for my daughter (or so we tell ourselves), which is one reason why even if we were to win the lotto, staying at home would not likely be a course I'd choose.

And yet. I am not immune to the notion that I have powers and responsibilities as a mother that my husband does not have. I prepare our daughter's lunch box every morning with ritualistic care, as if sending her off to school with a bologna sandwich made by me can work as an amulet against all the pain of my irregular, inevitable absences. I believe that I have a special gift for arranging playdates, pediatrician appointments, and piano lessons, and I yearn sometimes for the vast swaths of time Kelly Makino has given herself to keep her family's affairs in order. In an egalitarian marriage, every aspect of home life is open to renegotiation. When two people need to leave the house at 6 A.M., who gets the children ready for school? When two people have to work late, who will meet that inflexible day-care pickup time? And who, finally, has the energy for those constant transactions?

Two of the fastest-growing religious movements in America are Mormonism and Orthodox Judaism, which clearly define gender roles along traditional lines. It's difficult not to see the appeal—if only as a fleeting fantasy. How delicious might our weeknight dinners be, how straight the part in our daughter's hair, how much more carefree my marriage, if only I spent a fraction of the time cultivating our domestic landscape that I do at work.

This veneration of motherhood is fed by popular culture. On critically praised TV shows, ambitious women are nutty and single (Claire Danes in *Homeland,* Tina Fey on *30 Rock*), while good mothers are chopping veggies with a big glass of Chardonnay at their elbow. Beyoncé and Marissa Mayer never explain how they do it all, I suspect, because they have teams of nannies and housekeepers on the payroll—and realize that outing themselves as women who rely on servants will taint them, somehow, as bad parents. (Sandberg places this feeling within "the holy trinity of fear: the fear of being a bad mother/wife/daughter.") In my Facebook feed, Michelle Obama is an object of obsession not for the causes she's pursued as First Lady but for her child-rearing tactics: two mandatory sports (one chosen by them and one chosen by her) and no screen time on weeknights. When her husband first ran for president, he delivered speeches proclaiming the heroism of the working mother: "I don't accept an America that makes women choose between their kids and their careers." Four years later, against an opponent whose home life looked like a Disney production, Obama took a sanctity-of-motherhood tack: There is "no tougher job than being a mom."

Even Anne-Marie Slaughter would say that her maternal drive ultimately superseded her professional one, which is why she was unable to achieve more in her huge State Department job. She had a troubled kid at home. Thus the policy solutions she proposes do not dispel the mind-sets that continue to haunt American couples: In a world where men still run things and women still feel drawn to the kitchen and the nursery, an army of flextime females might lock in a second-class tier of workers who will never be able to compete with men for the top jobs. "That's the criticism of my piece that I worry most about," Slaughter says. "If that turns out to be true, I'll have to live with it forever."

Even as she enjoys her new life, Kelly Makino misses certain things about her old one. She misses getting dressed for work in clothes that have buttons and hems and sexy shoes to match. She misses "eating lunch with chopsticks," a euphemism for a universe of cuisine beyond chopped fruit and yogurt cups. She acknowledges the little luxuries of an office: a desk, a quiet cup of coffee, sick days. She misses her work friends—it is vexing trying to find the same hours free—and the validation that bosses and colleagues offer for a job well done. "There is no way my wonderful, loving family can fill that need," she says. In February, a few months after I met the Makinos at their home in New Jersey, they moved to the suburbs of Washington, D.C., for Alvin's job. Out of her element and detached from her old network, she is, for the first time since quitting work, bored.

Kelly loved her old profession and does not want to be painted as betraying the goals of feminism. She prefers to see herself as reaching beyond conventional ideas about what women should do. "I feel like we are evolving into something that is not defined by those who came before us," she says. By making domesticity her career, she and the other stay-at-home mothers she knows are standing up for values, such as patience, and kindness, and respectful attention to the needs of others,

that have little currency in the world of work. Professional status is not the only sign of importance, she says, and financial independence is not the only measure of success.

I press her on this point. What if Alvin dies or leaves her? What if, as her children grow up, she finds herself resenting the fact that all the public accolades accrue to her husband? Kelly wrestles with these questions all the time, but for now she's convinced she's chosen the right path. "I know this investment in my family will be paid back when the time is right." When her kids don't need her anymore, she'll figure out what she wants to pursue next. Someday, she's sure, she'll have the chance to "play leapfrog" with Alvin; she'll wind up with a brilliant career, or be a writer, or go back to school. "You have to live in the now. I will deal with later when later comes. I'll find a way," she says. "Who knows? Maybe I will be home for ever and ever. Maybe I will have the best-kept lawn on the block for the rest of my life."

Critical Thinking

1. If a woman is benign in her confrontations, yet assertive, will her husband fully share housework and child care in a dual-career marriage? Why or why not?

2. Why are women more nurturing and men more assertive? Are these traits biological or learned?

3. What attributes foster creativity, energy, and ingenuity in child caregiving?

Create Central

www.mhhe.com/createcentral

Internet References

Genderless Child-Rearing
   www.feminagination.com/1365/genderless-childrearing

How Involved Are Fathers in Raising Children?
   www.prb.org/Publications/Articles/2000

Is Aggression Genetic?
   www.salon.com/2012/05/28/is_aggression_genetic

Is There a Genetic Contribution to Cultural Differences?
   http://scan.oxfordjournals.org/content/5/2-3/203.long

Article

Prepared by: Karen L. Freiberg, *University of Maryland*

All Joy and No Fun
Why Parents Hate Parenting

JENNIFER SENIOR

Learning Outcomes

After reading this article, you will be able to:

- Explain why children tend to reduce marital happiness.

- Summarize the reasons that money does not make parenting easier.

There was a day a few weeks ago when I found my 2½-year-old son sitting on our building doorstep, waiting for me to come home. He spotted me as I was rounding the corner, and the scene that followed was one of inexpressible loveliness, right out of the movie I'd played to myself before actually having a child, with him popping out of his babysitter's arms and barreling down the street to greet me. This happy moment, though, was about to be cut short, and in retrospect felt more like a tranquil lull in a slasher film. When I opened our apartment door, I discovered that my son had broken part of the wooden parking garage I'd spent about an hour assembling that morning. This wouldn't have been a problem per se, except that as I attempted to fix it, he grew impatient and began throwing its various parts at the walls, with one plank very narrowly missing my eye. I recited the rules of the house (no throwing, no hitting). He picked up another large wooden plank. I ducked. He reached for the screwdriver. The scene ended with a time-out in his crib.

As I shuffled back to the living room, I thought of something a friend once said about the Children's Museum of Manhattan—"a nice place, but what it *really* needs is a bar"—and rued how, at that moment, the same thing could be said of my apartment. Two hundred and 40 seconds earlier, I'd been in a state of pair-bonded bliss; now I was guided by nerves, trawling the cabinets for alcohol. My emotional life looks a lot like this these days. I suspect it does for many parents—a high-amplitude, high-frequency sine curve along which we get the privilege of doing hourly surfs. Yet it's something most of us choose. Indeed, it's something most of us would say we'd be miserable without.

From the perspective of the species, it's perfectly unmysterious why people have children. From the perspective of the individual, however, it's more of a mystery than one might think. Most people assume that having children will make them happier. Yet a wide variety of academic research shows that parents are not happier than their childless peers, and in many cases are less so. This finding is surprisingly consistent, showing up across a range of disciplines. Perhaps the most oft-cited datum comes from a 2004 study by Daniel Kahneman, a Nobel Prize–winning behavioral economist, who surveyed 909 working Texas women and found that child care ranked sixteenth in pleasurability out of nineteen activities. (Among the endeavors they preferred: preparing food, watching TV, exercising, talking on the phone, napping, shopping, *housework*.) This result also shows up regularly in relationship research, with children invariably reducing marital satisfaction. The economist Andrew Oswald, who's compared tens of thousands of Britons with children to those without, is at least inclined to view his data in a more positive light: "The broad message is not that children make you less happy; it's just that children don't make you *more* happy." That is, he tells me, unless you have more than one. "Then the studies show a more negative impact." As a rule, most studies show that mothers are less happy than fathers, that single parents are less happy still, that babies and toddlers are the hardest, and that each successive child produces diminishing returns. But some of the studies are grimmer than others. Robin Simon, a sociologist at Wake Forest University, says parents are more depressed than nonparents no matter what their circumstances—whether they're single or married, whether they have one child or four.

Mothers are less happy than fathers, single parents are less happy still.

The idea that parents are less happy than nonparents has become so commonplace in academia that it was big news last year when the *Journal of Happiness Studies* published a

Scottish paper declaring the opposite was true. "Contrary to much of the literature," said the introduction, "our results are consistent with an effect of children on life satisfaction that is positive, large and increasing in the number of children." Alas, the euphoria was short-lived. A few months later, the poor author discovered a coding error in his data, and the publication ran an erratum. "After correcting the problem," it read, "the main results of the paper no longer hold. The effect of children on the life satisfaction of married individuals is small, often negative, and never statistically significant."

Yet one can see why people were rooting for that paper. The results of almost all the others violate a parent's deepest intuition. Daniel Gilbert, the Harvard psychologist and host of *This Emotional Life* on PBS, wrote fewer than three pages about compromised parental well-being in *Stumbling on Happiness*. But whenever he goes on the lecture circuit, skeptical questions about those pages come up more frequently than anything else. "I've never met anyone who didn't argue with me about this," he says. "Even people who believe the data say they feel sorry for those for whom it's true."

So what, precisely, is going on here? Why is this finding duplicated over and over again despite the fact that most parents believe it to be wrong?

One answer could simply be that parents are deluded, in the grip of some false consciousness that's good for mankind but not for men and women in particular. Gilbert, a proud father and grandfather, would argue as much. He's made a name for himself showing that we humans are pretty sorry predictors of what will make us happy, and to his mind, the yearning for children, the literal mother of all aspirations for so many, is a very good case in point—what children *really* do, he suspects, is offer moments of transcendence, not an overall improvement in well-being.

Perhaps. But there are less fatalistic explanations, too. And high among them is the possibility that parents don't much enjoy parenting because the experience of raising children has fundamentally changed.

"I'm going to count to three."

It's a weekday evening, and the mother in this videotape, a trim brunette with her hair in a bun and glasses propped up on her head, has already worked a full day and made dinner. Now she is approaching her 8-year-old son, the oldest of two, who's seated at the computer in the den, absorbed in a movie. At issue is his homework, which he still hasn't done.

"One. Two . . ."

This clip is from a study conducted by UCLA's Center on Everyday Lives of Families, which earned a front-page story in the Sunday *Times* this May and generated plenty of discussion among parents. In it, researchers collected 1,540 hours of footage of 32 middle-class, dual-earner families with at least two children, all of them going about their regular business in their Los Angeles homes. The intention of this study was in no way to make the case that parents were unhappy. But one of the postdoctoral fellows who worked on it, himself a father of two, nevertheless described the video data to the *Times* as "the very purest form of birth control ever devised. Ever."

"I have to get it to the part and then pause it," says the boy.

"No," says his mother. "You do that *after* you do your homework."

Tamar Kremer-Sadlik, the director of research in this study, has watched this scene many times. The reason she believes it's so powerful is because it shows how painfully parents experience the pressure of making their children do their schoolwork. They seem to feel this pressure even more acutely than their children feel it themselves.

The boy starts to shout. "It's not going to take that long!"

His mother stops the movie. "I'm telling you no," she says. "You're not hearing me. I will *not* let you watch this now."

He starts up the movie again.

"No," she repeats, her voice rising. She places her hand firmly under her son's arm and starts to yank. "I *will not* have this—"

Before urbanization, children were viewed as economic assets to their parents. If you had a farm, they toiled alongside you to maintain its upkeep; if you had a family business, the kids helped mind the store. But all of this dramatically changed with the moral and technological revolutions of modernity. As we gained in prosperity, childhood came increasingly to be viewed as a protected, privileged time, and once college degrees became essential to getting ahead, children became not only a great expense but subjects to be sculpted, stimulated, instructed, groomed. (The Princeton sociologist Viviana Zelizer describes this transformation of a child's value in five ruthless words: "Economically worthless but emotionally priceless.") Kids, in short, went from being our staffs to being our bosses.

"Did you see *Babies*?" asks Lois Nachamie, a couples counselor who for years has run parenting workshops and support groups on the Upper West Side. She's referring to the recent documentary that compares the lives of four newborns—one in Japan, one in Namibia, one in Mongolia, and one in the United States (San Francisco). "I don't mean to idealize the lives of the Namibian women," she says. "But it was hard not to notice how *calm* they were. They were beading their children's ankles and decorating them with sienna, clearly enjoying just sitting and playing with them, and we're here often thinking of all of this stuff as labor."

This is especially true in middle- and upper-income families, which are far more apt than their working-class counterparts to see their children as projects to be perfected. (Children of women with bachelor degrees spend almost five hours on "organized activities" per week, as opposed to children of high-school dropouts, who spend two.) Annette Lareau, the sociologist who coined the term "concerted cultivation" to describe the aggressive nurturing of economically advantaged children, puts it this way: "Middle-class parents spend much more time talking to children, answering questions with questions, and treating each child's thought as a special contribution. And this is very tiring *work*." Yet it's work few parents feel that they can in good conscience neglect, says Lareau, "lest they put their children at risk by not giving them every advantage."

But the intensification of family time is not confined to the privileged classes alone. According to *Changing Rhythms of American Family Life*—a compendium of data about time use and family statistics, compiled by a trio of sociologists named Suzanne M. Bianchi, John P. Robinson, and Melissa A. Milkie—*all* parents spend more time today with their children than they did in 1975, including mothers, in spite of the great rush of women into the American workforce. Today's married mothers also have less leisure time (5.4 fewer hours per week); 71 percent say they crave more time for themselves (as do 57 percent of married fathers). Yet 85 percent of all parents still—still!—think they don't spend enough time with their children.

These self-contradictory statistics reminded me of a conversation I had with a woman who had been in one of Nachamie's parenting groups, a professional who had her children later in life. "I have two really great kids"—ages 9 and 11—"and I enjoy doing a lot of things with them," she told me. "It's the drudgery that's so hard: *Crap, you don't have any pants that fit?* There are just So. Many. Chores." This woman, it should be said, is divorced. But even if her responsibilities were shared with a partner, the churn of school and gymnastics and piano and sports and homework would still require an awful lot of administration. "The crazy thing," she continues, "is that by New York standards, I'm not even overscheduling them."

I ask what she does on the weekends her ex-husband has custody. "I work," she replies. "And get my nails done."

A few generations ago, people weren't stopping to contemplate whether having a child would make them happy. Having children was simply what you did. And we are lucky, today, to have choices about these matters. But the abundance of choices—whether to have kids, when, how many—may be one of the reasons parents are less happy.

That was at least partly the conclusion of psychologists W. Keith Campbell and Jean Twenge, who, in 2003, did a meta-analysis of 97 children-and-marital-satisfaction studies stretching back to the seventies. Not only did they find that couples' overall marital satisfaction went down if they had kids; they found that every successive generation was more put out by having them than the last—our current one most of all. Even more surprisingly, they found that parents' dissatisfaction only grew the more money they had, even though they had the purchasing power to buy more child care. "And my hypothesis about why this is, in both cases, is the same," says Twenge. "They become parents later in life. There's a loss of freedom, a loss of autonomy. It's totally different from going from your parents' house to immediately having a baby. Now you know what you're giving up." (Or, as a fellow psychologist told Gilbert when he finally got around to having a child: "They're a huge source of joy, but they turn every other source of joy to shit.")

Studies have found that parents' dissatisfaction only grew the more money they had, even though they could buy more child care.

It wouldn't be a particularly bold inference to say that the longer we put off having kids, the greater our expectations. "There's all this buildup—as soon as I get this done, I'm going to have a baby, and it's going to be a great reward!" says Ada Calhoun, the author of *Instinctive Parenting* and founding editor-in-chief of Babble, the online parenting site. "And then you're like, 'Wait, *this* is my reward? This nineteen-year grind?'"

When people wait to have children, they're also bringing different sensibilities to the enterprise. They've spent their adult lives as professionals, believing there's a right way and a wrong way of doing things; now they're applying the same logic to the family-expansion business, and they're surrounded by a marketplace that only affirms and reinforces this idea. "And what's confusing about that," says Alex Barzvi, a professor of child and adolescent psychiatry at NYU medical school, "is that there *are* a lot of things that parents can do to nurture social and cognitive development. There *are* right and wrong ways to discipline a child. But you can't fall into the trap of comparing yourself to others and constantly concluding you're doing the wrong thing."

Yet that's precisely what modern parents do. "It was especially bad in the beginning," said a woman who recently attended a parents' group led by Barzvi at the 92nd Street Y. "When I'd hear other moms saying, 'Oh, so-and-so sleeps for twelve hours and naps for three,' I'd think, *Oh, shit, I screwed up the sleep training.*" Her parents—immigrants from huge families—couldn't exactly relate to her distress. "They had no academic reference books for *sleeping,*" she says. (She's read three.) "To my parents, it is what it is."

So how do they explain your anguish? I ask.

"They just think that Americans are a little too complicated about everything."

One hates to invoke Scandinavia in stories about child-rearing, but it can't be an accident that the one superbly designed study that said, unambiguously, that having kids makes you happier was done with Danish subjects. The researcher, Hans-Peter Kohler, a sociology professor at the University of Pennsylvania, says he originally studied this question because he was intrigued by the declining fertility rates in Europe. One of the things he noticed is that countries with stronger welfare systems produce more children—and happier parents.

Of course, this should not be a surprise. If you are no longer fretting about spending too little time with your children after they're born (because you have a year of paid maternity leave), if you're no longer anxious about finding affordable child care once you go back to work (because the state subsidizes it), if you're no longer wondering how to pay for your children's education and health care (because they're free)—well, it stands to reason that your own mental health would improve. When Kahneman and his colleagues did another version of his survey of working women, this time comparing those in Columbus, Ohio, to those in Rennes, France, the French sample enjoyed child care a good deal more than its American counterpart. "We've put all this energy into being perfect parents," says

Judith Warner, author of *Perfect Madness: Motherhood in the Age of Anxiety,* "instead of political change that would make family life better."

MOMS: Ever feel alone in how you perceive this role? I swear I feel like I'm surrounded by women who were once smart & interesting but have become zombies who only talk about soccer and coupons.

This was an opening gambit on UrbanBaby this past April. It could have devolved into a sanctimommy pile-on. It didn't.

I totally feel this way.

I am a f/t wohm—Work Outside the Home Mom—have a career, and I don't feel smart or interesting anymore! I don't talk about soccer or coupons, but just feel too tired to talk about anything that interesting.

I freely admit that I have gained "more" than I have lost by becoming a parent, but I still miss aspects of my old life.

More generous government policies, a sounder economy, a less pressured culture that values good rather than perfect kids—all of these would certainly make parents happier. But even under the most favorable circumstances, parenting is an extraordinary activity, in both senses of the word *extra:* beyond ordinary and *especially* ordinary. While children deepen your emotional life, they shrink your outer world to the size of a teacup, at least for a while. ("All joy and no fun," as an old friend with two young kids likes to say.) Lori Leibovich, the executive editor of Babble and the anthology *Maybe Baby,* a collection of 28 essays by writers debating whether to have children, says she was particularly struck by the female contributors who'd made the deliberate choice to remain childless. It enabled them to travel or live abroad for their work; to take physical risks; to, in the case of a novelist, inhabit her fictional characters without being pulled away by the demands of a real one. "There was a richness and texture to their work lives that was so, so enviable," she says. (Leibovich has two children.)

Fathers, it turns out, feel like they've made some serious compromises too, though of a different sort. They feel like they don't see their kids *enough.* "In our studies, it's the men, by a long shot, who have more work–life conflict than women," says Ellen Galinsky, president of the Families and Work Institute. "They don't want to be stick figures in their children's lives."

And couples probably pay the dearest price of all. Healthy relationships definitely make people happier. But children adversely affect relationships. As Thomas Bradbury, a father of two and professor of psychology at UCLA, likes to say: "Being in a good relationship is a risk factor for becoming a parent." He directs me to one of the more inspired studies in the field, by psychologists Lauren Papp and E. Mark Cummings. They asked 100 long-married couples to spend two weeks meticulously documenting their disagreements. Nearly 40 percent of them were about their kids.

"And that 40 percent is merely the number that was explicitly about kids, I'm guessing, right?" This is a former patient of Nachamie's, an entrepreneur and father of two. "How many other arguments were those couples having because everyone was on a short fuse, or tired, or stressed out?" This man is very frank about the strain his children put on his marriage, especially his firstborn. "I already felt neglected," he says. "In my mind, anyway. And once we had the kid, it became so pronounced; it went from zero to negative 50. And I was like, *I can deal with zero. But not negative 50.*"

This is the brutal reality about children—they're such powerful stressors that small perforations in relationships can turn into deep fault lines. "And my wife became more demanding," he continues. "'You don't do this, you don't do that.' There was this idea we had about how things were supposed to be: *The family should be dot dot dot, the man should be dot dot dot the woman should be dot dot dot.*"

This is another brutal reality about children: They expose the gulf between our fantasies about family and its spikier realities. They also mean parting with an old way of life, one with more freewheeling rhythms and richer opportunities for romance. "There's nothing sexy or intimate between us, based on the old model," he says. "The new model, which I've certainly come to adopt, is that our energy has shifted toward the kids. One of the reasons I love being with my wife is because I love the family we have."

Most studies show that marriages improve once children enter latency, or the ages between 6 and 12, though they take another sharp dive during the war zone of adolescence. (As a friend with grown children once told me: "Teenagers can be casually brutal.") But one of the most sobering declines documented in *Changing Rhythms of American Family Life* is the amount of time married parents spend alone together each week: Nine hours today versus twelve in 1975. Bradbury, who was involved in the UCLA study of those 32 families, says the husbands and wives spent less than 10 percent of their home time alone together. "And do you think they were saying, "Gee honey, you look lovely. I just wanted to pick up on that fascinating conversation we were having earlier about the Obama administration'?" he asks. "Nope. They were exhausted and staring at the television."

"I'm not watching it," insists the boy. We're back to the videotape now, and that den in Los Angeles. Mother and son are still arguing—tensely, angrily—and she's still pulling on his arm. The boy reaches for the keyboard. "I'm putting it on pause!"

"I want you to do your homework," his mother repeats. "You are not—"

"I know," the son whines. "I'm going to pause it!"

His mother's not buying it. What she sees is him stalling. She pulls him off the chair.

"No, you're *not,*" says his mother. "You're still not listening!"

"Yes I am!"

"No, you're not!"

Children may provide unrivaled moments of joy. But they also provide unrivaled moments of frustration, tedium, anxiety, heartbreak. This scene, which isn't even all that awful or uncommon, makes it perfectly clear why parenting may be regarded as less fun than having dinner with friends or baking a cake. Loving one's children and loving the act of parenting are not the same thing.

Yet that's where things get tricky. Obviously, this clip shows how difficult and unpleasant parenting can be. What it doesn't show is the love this mother feels for her son, which we can pretty much bet has no equal. Nor does it convey that this unpleasant task she's undertaking is part of a larger project, one that pays off in subtler dividends than simply having fun. Kremer-Sadlik says that she and her fellow researchers were highly conscious of these missing pieces when they gathered each week to discuss their data collection. "We'd all remember the negative things," she says. "Whereas everything else was between the lines. So it became our moral dilemma: How can we talk about the good moments?" She pauses, and then asks the question that, to a parent (she herself has two children), is probably most relevant of all: "And why were the good moments so elusive?"

The answer to that may hinge on how we define "good." Or more to the point, "happy." Is happiness something you *experience*? Or is it something you *think*?

When Kahneman surveyed those Texas women, he was measuring moment-to-moment happiness. It was a feeling, a mood, a state. The technique he pioneered for measuring it—the Daily Reconstruction Method—was designed to make people reexperience their feelings over the course of a day. Oswald, when looking at British households, was looking at a condensed version of the General Health Questionnaire, which is best described as a basic gauge of mood: *Have you recently felt you could not overcome your difficulties? Felt constantly under strain? Lost much sleep over worry?* (What parent hasn't answered, yes, yes, and God yes to these questions?) As a matter of mood, there does seem to be little question that kids make our lives more stressful.

But when studies take into consideration how *rewarding* parenting is, the outcomes tend to be different. Last year, Mathew P. White and Paul Dolan, professors at the University of Plymouth and Imperial College, London, respectively, designed a study that tried to untangle these two different ideas. They asked participants to rate their daily activities both in terms of pleasure and in terms of reward, then plotted the results on a four-quadrant graph. What emerged was a much more commonsense map of our feelings. In the quadrant of things people found both pleasurable *and* rewarding, people chose volunteering first, prayer second, and time with children third (though time with children barely made it into the "pleasurable" category). Work was the most rewarding not-so-pleasurable activity. Everyone thought commuting was both unrewarding and unfun. And watching television was considered one of the most pleasurable unrewarding activities, as was eating, though the least rewarding of all was plain old "relaxing." (Which probably says something about the abiding power of the Protestant work ethic.)

Seven years ago, the sociologists Kei Nomaguchi and Melissa A. Milkie did a study in which they followed couples for five to seven years, some of whom had children and some of whom did not. And what they found was that, yes, those couples who became parents did more housework and felt less in control and quarreled more (actually, only the women thought they quarreled more, but anyway). On the other hand, the married women were *less depressed* after they'd had kids than their childless peers. And perhaps this is because the study sought to understand not just the moment-to-moment moods of its participants, but more existential matters, like how connected they felt, and how motivated, and how much despair they were in (as opposed to how much stress they were under): *Do you not feel like eating? Do you feel like you can't shake the blues? Do you feel lonely? Like you can't get going?* Parents, who live in a clamorous, perpetual-forward-motion machine almost all of the time, seemed to have different answers than their childless cohorts.

The authors also found that the most depressed people were single fathers, and Milkie speculates that perhaps it's because they wanted to be involved in their children's lives but weren't. Robin Simon finds something similar: The least depressed parents are those whose underage children are in the house, and the most are those whose aren't.

This finding seems significant. Technically, if parenting makes you unhappy, you should feel *better* if you're spared the task of doing it. But if happiness is measured by our own sense of agency and meaning, then noncustodial parents lose. They're robbed of something that gives purpose and reward.

When I mention this to Daniel Gilbert, he hardly disputes that meaning is important. But he does wonder how prominently it should figure into people's decisions to have kids. "When you pause to *think* what children mean to you, of course they make you feel good," he says. "The problem is, 95 percent of the time, you're not thinking about what they mean to you. You're thinking that you have to take them to piano lessons. So you have to think about which kind of happiness you'll be consuming most often. Do you want to maximize the one you experience almost all the time"—moment-to-moment happiness—"or the one you experience rarely?"

Which is fair enough. But for many of us, purpose *is* happiness—particularly those of us who find moment-to-moment happiness a bit elusive to begin with. Martin Seligman, the positive-psychology pioneer who is, famously, not a natural optimist, has always taken the view that happiness is best defined in the ancient Greek sense: leading a productive, purposeful life. And the way we take stock of that life, in the end, isn't by how much fun we had, but what we did with it. (Seligman has seven children.)

About twenty years ago, Tom Gilovich, a psychologist at Cornell, made a striking contribution to the field of psychology, showing that people are far more apt to regret things they *haven't* done than things they have. In one instance, he followed up on the men and women from the Terman study, the famous collection of high-IQ students from California who were singled out in 1921 for a life of greatness. Not one told him of regretting having children, but ten told him they regretted not having a family.

"I think this boils down to a philosophical question, rather than a psychological one," says Gilovich. "Should you value moment-to-moment happiness more than retrospective evaluations of your life?" He says he has no answer for this, but the example he offers suggests a bias. He recalls watching TV with his children at three in the morning when they were sick. "I wouldn't have said it was too fun at the time," he says. "But now I look back on it and say, 'Ah, remember the time we used to wake up and watch cartoons?'" The very things that in the moment dampen our moods can later be sources of intense gratification, nostalgia, delight.

It's a lovely magic trick of the memory, this gilding of hard times. Perhaps it's just the necessary alchemy we need to keep the species going. But for parents, this sleight of the mind and spell on the heart is the very definition of enchantment.

Critical Thinking

1. Recognize that love for children and dislike of child care can co-exist.
2. Identify several factors that make child care an emotional roller coaster.
3. Report which of the following make parenting easier: money, age of parent, age of children, being single, knowledge of child development.

Create Central

www.mhhe.com/createcentral

Internet References

Does Having Children Make You Unhappy?
http://parenting.blogs.nytimes/2009/04/01/why-does-anyone

How to Raise a Happy Child
www.babycenter.co/0_how-to-raise-a-happy-child

Marital Satisfaction When Raising Teenagers
http://technorati.com/women/article/marital-satisfaction

Parents Who Hate Parenting: The Latest Trend?
http://shine.yahoo.com/parenting

Article   Prepared by: Karen L. Freiberg, *University of Maryland*

Peek Hours

What Makes a Neighbor Nosy?

SUSHMA SUBRAMANIAN

Learning Outcomes

After reading this article, you will be able to:

- Point out two different reasons why people are snoops.

- Discuss the pros and cons of snooping.

When Danine Manette's teenage son left the house, she noticed he'd left his Myspace account open. She saw that he had told a friend that he was going to be at a party that weekend. Manette hadn't heard about a party. She waited for the weekend to roll around to see if her son would speak up about his plans. Luckily for him, he did.

Manette, a 42-year-old criminal investigator from Oakland, warns her two teenage sons that she might slowly creep downstairs to see what they're looking at online, and they might be subject to random Internet history checks. But sometimes, she also snoops behind their backs.

"I never give them my sources," Manette says. "As long as someone doesn't know how you find something out, they're more inclined to walk a straight line so they don't get caught." Once, while her son was at the gym, his friend sent him an email message asking about the girls he was talking to there. Manette deleted the message, and when he got home, she told him he shouldn't spend hours on end talking to girls when he should be doing homework. He had no clue how she knew. He still thinks she has spies at the gym.

"Some call it snooping," Manette says. "I call it monitoring and old-fashioned parenting."

Social networking sites, email, and cell phones have made it easier for all of us to spy, and most of us Google friends or maybe even Facebook-stalk. Many employers scour office emails looking for hot-button subject lines and record keystrokes and downloads. Utility company employees and government officials have been busted for looking up confidential information about friends and celebrities.

But psychologists are just now tapping into why we do it. Snoops can be separated into two main types: There are people like Manette, who search for information to protect themselves from perceived threats (a son possibly up to no good), and there are people who seek information just because they're curious.

University of Southern Florida psychologist Jordan Litman says snoops like Manette feel much more worried and distressed than the average person when they are missing information that will affect their lives, like whether they'll be laid off or whether their spouse is cheating. Because of their higher anxiety levels, people who seek out bad or threatening information are often trying to uncover problems so they can deal with them or fix them quickly. Having more information can make it seem like they have more control.

Litman says past experiences dealing with danger also contribute to how people respond to potentially threatening situations. Manette used to work with juveniles on probation, making her an extra-vigilant parent, she says. She has seen too many kids get in trouble for robbing liquor stores and buying narcotics, catching their parents off-guard.

And two years into Manette's marriage, she noticed her husband had started working longer hours and sometimes said he was hanging out with friends whose names she hadn't heard before. She knew something was up and after two months of digging, she found the evidence—a stack of love notes and cards from a mistress, and even a photo of them posing together. "I never wanted to be the fool in the corner again," she says.

Stop the Snoop

These days, it's especially important to establish realms of privacy with family members, therapist Kay Abrams says. And she suggests talking instead of snooping. "If your partner's email is open, you can ask what a certain message is about and they might tell you instead of you having to snoop."

In the case of teenagers, there's a fine line to walk between respecting their privacy and keeping a third eye in the back of your head. "It is most important to keep a relationship and maintain ways to have a dialogue with your teen," Abrams says.

She wrote about the experience in her book, *Ultimate Betrayal: Recognizing, Uncovering, and Dealing with Infidelity,* in which she urges suspecting wives to gather evidence before confronting a husband about cheating, rather than reacting to the first thing they notice. "Then, he doesn't have time to get his story straight." Manette eventually reconciled with her husband, but first he had to agree to make his life an open book. Now, years later, she trusts him enough not to snoop on him.

The other category of snoop consists of people who can be characterized as nosy, people who seek out information about others that has no consequence for them. While we're all curious about our friends and colleagues, these snoops have a higher degree of curiosity. Under ordinary conditions, most people are outgoing enough to ask questions to satisfy their curiosity, but people who are less social often revert to covert ways of gathering information, according to Britta Renner, a University of Konstanz psychologist.

The most researched form of curiosity is called interest-type curiosity, the motivation to learn about something because it's entertaining or novel. But snooping is driven more by what's called deprivation curiosity, that nagging feeling that there are gaps in your knowledge. "It's the whole reason the human brain freaks out when a picture is out of focus," Litman says. "The brain likes coherent patterns."

That tension is worse in some than in others. For a snoop, simply knowing how a friend or family member acts around them isn't enough. Eavesdropping on a personal conversation or rifling through a gym bag can help create a more complete picture.

The need to snoop is often an indication that there is poor trust or other insecurities affecting the relationship, says Kay Abrams, a Kensington, Maryland-based family therapist. In a case of infidelity, like Manette's husband's, it makes sense to offer a partner less privacy at first. But once trust is rebuilt and the threat fades, so should the snooping.

Critical Thinking

1. Are all people who snoop alike?
2. When can you trust a person not to spy on you?
3. How does cyberspace affect one's ability to snoop?
4. Do you secretly search out information about others? Why?

Create Central

www.mhhe.com/createcentral

Internet References

Rules Being Considered on Private CCTV Cameras to Stop Snooping
    http://www.dailymail.co.uk/news/article-2338703

Top Ten Ways to Deal with a Snoopy Neighbor
    http://listdose.com/top-ten-ways-to-deal-with-a-snoopy-neighbor

Types of Nosy Neighbors and How to Deal with Them
    http://voices.yahoo.com/types-nosy-neighbors

SUSHMA SUBRAMANIAN is a writer based in New York City.

Unit 6

UNIT

Prepared by: Karen L. Freiberg, *University of Maryland*

Development during Middle and Late Adulthood

Joseph Campbell, a 20th-century sage, said that the privilege of a lifetime is being who you are. This ego-confidence often arrives during middle and late adulthood, even as physical confidence declines. There is a gradual slowing of the rate of mitosis of cells of all the organ systems with age. This gradual slowing of mitosis translates into a slowed rate of repair of cells of all organs. By the 40s, signs of aging can be seen in skin, skeleton, vision, hearing, smell, taste, balance, coordination, heart, blood vessels, lungs, liver, kidneys, digestive tract, immune response, endocrine functioning, and ability to reproduce. To some extent, moderate use of any body part (as opposed to disuse or misuse) helps retain its strength, stamina, and repairability. However, by middle and late adulthood persons become increasingly aware of the effects of aging organ systems on their total physical fitness. A loss of height occurs as spinal disks and connective tissues diminish and settle. Demineralization, especially loss of calcium, causes weakening of bones. Muscles atrophy, and the slowing of cardiovascular and respiratory responses creates a loss of stamina for exercise. All of this may seem cruel, but it occurs very gradually and need not adversely affect a person's enjoyment of life.

Healthful aging, at least in part, seems to be genetically pre-programmed. The females of many species, including humans, outlive the males. The sex hormones of females may protect them from some early aging effects. Males, in particular, experience earlier declines in their cardiovascular system. Diet and exercise can ward off many of the deleterious effects of aging. A reduction in saturated fat (low-density lipid) intake coupled with regular aerobic exercise contributes to less bone demineralization, less plaque in the arteries, stronger muscles (including heart and lung muscles), and a general increase in stamina and vitality. An adequate intake of complex carbohydrates, fibrous foods, fresh fruits, fresh vegetables, unsaturated fats (high density lipids), and water also enhances good health.

Cognitive abilities do not appreciably decline with age in healthy adults. Research suggests that the speed with which the brain carries out problems involving abstract (fluid) reasoning may slow but not cease. Complex problems may simply require more time to solve with age. On the other hand, research suggests that the memory banks of older people may have more crystallized (accumulated and stored) knowledge and more insight. Creativity also frequently spurts after age 50. One's ken (range of knowledge) and practical skills (common sense) grow with age and experience. Older human beings also become expert at the cognitive tasks they frequently do. Many cultures celebrate these abilities as the "wisdom of age."

Article   Prepared by: Karen L. Freiberg, *University of Maryland*

Good Morning, Heartache

For millions, depression is a daily reality against which they must struggle to function. The many strategies now available provide what we all might envy—the knowledge that it's possible to get through the worst of times.

KATHLEEN MCGOWAN

Learning Outcomes

After reading this article, you will be able to:

- Explain why each person with depression is different from all others.
- Identify some of the types of therapies available for persons who are depressed.

Last summer, Pata Suyemoto rode her bike from Boston to Cape Cod, 125 miles in one day. An educator who has taught everything from art to English to Reiki, she's funny, she's intense, and she's passionate. Never a jock, three years ago she became a relentless road warrior, riding more than 6,000 miles the first year she took up cycling.

But she would not say that she has conquered depression. Instead, like many people who experience major depression—and there are roughly 15 million Americans who do—she has achieved a kind of delicate détente with it. She manages to live with the disorder, or in spite of it. She thinks of her depression as a recurrent illness; getting it under control demands time, creativity, and an open mind. It keeps her on her toes.

Untamed, her depression is truly ferocious. Suyemoto, 47, has been in and out of psychiatric hospitals since age 17. Ten years ago, there came a time she now refers to as the bottom of the abyss. She could hardly do her job. Mustering the energy to stand in front of a class took all her strength. After class, she'd shut the door to her office and crawl under her desk. She had a young daughter, and she was trying to write her dissertation. Then, her mother died. "I'd write a page, and cry for an hour, then write another page, and cry for another hour," she says now.

Eventually she found cracks of light in the darkness. Antidepressants didn't help much. Glimmers of hope came more from things she did. She wrote in a journal daily, even when she had to prop herself up in bed to do it. She finally found a therapist who knew how to deal with severe depression and trauma. "It was gradual, working things into my life," she says. "It was like weaving a net."

A decade later, she now cherishes a whole a list of things that help, her own personal portfolio of antidepressants. Artistic self-expression in the form of collage gives her a way to communicate the darkest feelings without getting stuck in them. Acupuncture—as often as five times a week—helps. She finally found a medication that works. She volunteers with the Massachusetts group Families for Depression Awareness, leveraging her own experience to help other people who are struggling with depression. Self-help books and tapes offer a reality check, as does a sense of spirituality that puts her troubles in context.

And then there's the bike. It's not just good exercise. It's also a way to test limits and learn when to push herself and when to play it cool.

Is she cured? No. But she has her life back.

"I still have dark times, but they don't consume me in the same way," says Suyemoto. She expects that she may have other bad times; for her as for many people, major depression comes in cycles. She is ready for it. "It's not that I'm free and clear," she says. "But in doing all these things, and weaving them into my life, I've created a much stronger net."

A lot of the news about depression these days is good: An arsenal of treatments now available allows many to lead a normal life in spite of the disorder. The best estimate is that 80 percent of people find substantial relief from their worst symptoms, which typically include persistent sadness, guilt or irritability, sleep and appetite disruption, and the absence of pleasure. "People do recover from depression," says Michael Yapko, a clinical psychologist in California who specializes in treating depression. "There are many pathways in, and there are many pathways out."

Getting there, however, is rarely easy. Few people find simple cures. Instead, they patch together many measures. "I hate it when people say, 'Just go exercise.' Or, 'Just take medication,' or 'Just' anything," says Suyemoto. "Everybody has to find their own path, Healing from depression is a not a universal thing. Everybody's going to be different."

Major depression is so common because a lot of different biological and psychological roads lead to the same place. A variety of switches get tripped—whether by genetic

Combination Therapy Still Best

Finding the best treatment for depression *today* means wading through lots of options. There are 39 antidepressant drugs on the market. And for some people, cognitive therapy works just as well, or better. Other treatments range from light therapy to the implantation of electrodes in the brain.

A major test of drugs and talk therapy, the 2006 STAR*D trial, treated 4,000 participants who are highly typical of patients with major depression: Their disorder had not responded to the first drug they took, and most also had anxiety or an eating disorder.

The study found that no one drug or therapy was clearly best. Adding either a second drug or cognitive therapy worked equally well. Only about a third of subjects saw symptoms vanish with the first drug tried. But most—67 percent—eventually found substantial relief. The bottom line: Hang in there. It may take time to find the right treatments.

"The combination with psychotherapy is very useful," says psychiatrist Dennis Charney. "It's like hand and glove." Psychotherapy can take longer to start working, but it may have the edge in preventing relapses.

What causes depression is still basically a mystery. The altered brain chemistry goes far beyond serotonin, the neurotransmitter targeted by many antidepressant drugs. Dopamine-sensitive brain circuits, which influence pleasure and reward, are off-kilter and may underlie feelings of numbness or despair. Such circuits also influence mood, which may be why people prone to depression struggle to prevent disappointments and setbacks from spiraling into full-blown depressive episodes.

Stress also plays a role, especially in early life. Prolonged childhood stress, such as neglect or abuse, may influence neurochemistry and the responsiveness of the body's alarm system, setting the stage for depression in adulthood.

No one gene causes depression, and only about one-third of the risk of depression is inherited. But genetics might one day improve upon the current trial-and-error process of choosing a drug. A gene scan may predict which antidepressant will work best for you.

For the time being, the best approach is to seek out a depression specialist. Most people rely on their family doctor. But a depression expert has more experience with the range of options—and many more tricks up his or her sleeve.

---

vulnerability, trauma in early life, chronic stress, disturbance of neurochemistry, or guilt-prone tendencies—and the end result is depression.

To successfully cope with depression, most people stumble onto their own combination of lifestyle adaptations, therapeutic techniques, medications, and mental adjustments.

Given the diversity of causes, antidepressant medications alone are rarely enough. To successfully cope with depression, most people stumble onto their own idiosyncratic combination of lifestyle adaptations, therapeutic techniques, medications, and mental adjustments. But the most successful approaches for the long term, says Yapko, all encourage you to take action in the face of a disorder that saps your resolve. "Eventually, if you're persistent, there's a high probability you'll find something."

The most successful approaches for the long term all encourage you to take action in the face of a disorder that saps your resolve.

First, It's Physical

For many people the process of gaining control over depression begins with physical changes. Researchers now know that depression is not just a mental disorder. It affects the immune system, the heart, and basic body functions such as sleep and appetite as well. So it only makes sense that a lot of people who successfully manage their depression are careful about what they eat and drink, how much they sleep, and how active they are.

Former Massachusetts state senator and attorney Bob Antonioni, for example, always makes time for hockey, bike riding, or swimming. "In the past if I was struggling I'd curl up on the couch—that's not good, because you become more isolated, and the isolation feeds the depression," he says. "Very often I find, if I go out and exercise, I'm better for it."

Now 50, he's been dealing with depression since his mid-30s. After his brother's suicide in 1999, it got worse. He was profoundly sad, and the depression also settled into his body. His chest constantly ached. Sometimes it seemed like his body was going into panic mode. At the same time, as a politician, he had a public image to maintain. "I'm supposed to be out and about, smiling," he says now. "I just wasn't able to. I'd go into withdrawal."

He now has a comprehensive strategy; Antonioni goes for regular therapy and takes an antidepressant. But other physical interventions are equally important. He doesn't drink anymore, except on rare occasions—not that he ever had a drinking problem, but the depressant effects of alcohol worsened his symptoms.

Sleep is his number one secret weapon. "Sleep makes all the difference in the world to me," he says. It's not always easy to explain to his aides and colleagues why he won't arrange early-morning meetings. So be it. "The adjustments come," he adds. "People are a lot more willing to be flexible than I might originally have given them credit for."

Mood and sleep share basic biological mechanisms, and, according to Yapko, the single most common symptom of depression is some form of sleep disturbance. Getting lots of sleep is crucial. The challenge is in admitting that you just may not be able to do as much as you want to—and then sticking to your guns, even when life throws drama or excitement your way.

Getting through Despair

"I've found that I have to be careful or I crash," says Kathryn Goetzke, a 37-year-old entrepreneur who battles major depression. "You have to be pretty disciplined about it," Goetzke has her own business, Mood-Lites, which develops decorative lighting. She also founded a nonprofit, the International Foundation for Research and Education on Depression (iFred). Then her husband ran for Congress in 2006. Of course, she got involved in the campaign. "I thought I had it all under control," she says now. "I just took on way, way, way too much."

He lost, and for maybe six months afterward she struggled to do anything at all. The marriage ended, and sometimes money was very tight—two other major sources of stress. "I learned the hard way," she says. "I have to listen to my body. I can't be ashamed. The consequences are much worse, in the long run, if I ignore it."

Goetzke reached out to her mother and brothers, who "moved mountains" to help her through the worst times. When she was closest to the brink, they pulled her back. She found a good therapist and, when she couldn't afford therapy, she turned to support groups, augmented by long walks outside.

Now, she says, she feels pretty good. "I'm happy to be around" is how she puts it. But it still takes a lot of work. She quit drinking entirely, avoids eating too much sugar, gets plenty of sleep, and hikes, plays tennis, does yoga, or bikes almost every day. She relies on her dogs, and the encouragement of a weekly women's support group. She, too, takes medication.

What might have made the biggest difference, though, was inside her own head—a major psychological shift. Before she started grappling with depression, Goetzke was an escapist. Her father, also depressed, committed suicide when she was in college, and she was eventually diagnosed with posttraumatic stress disorder. She drank, and she had an eating disorder, two ways of blunting the bleakness that only made things worse.

Finally, in her 30s, she began to confront how bad she felt and actually learned to live with her feelings of despair. "I sit through my feelings of awfulness," she says. "I let myself fully experience the bad feelings, and then move it toward something positive." Mindfulness meditation, which derails the obsessive thinking that typically intensifies negative feelings, is also useful. In these ways, she has learned to accept herself—and that includes accepting the sorrow.

Being able to withstand feeling lousy has been important to her success. As a businesswoman, she has to endure constant rejection. Once, the head of product development for a major lighting company told her that she would never get her product into a store. Her Mood-Lites are now on the shelves of hundreds of Wal-Marts, as well as in spas and chiropractors' offices across the country.

Cognitive tricks and techniques may seem insubstantial against such a formidable foe as depression, but they work. Cognitive behavioral therapy and interpersonal therapy both focus on the future, teaching mental and emotional skills that challenge negative thought patterns and counteract feelings of helplessness and self-loathing.

"Psychotherapy gives you a toolbox of approaches to handle stress, which can elicit depression," says noted mood disorder researcher Dennis Charney, dean of the Mt. Sinai School of Medicine in New York. "Part of it is getting the right treatment, the right doctor, the right psychotherapist." The important question to ask a therapist, says Charney, is whether she or he is experienced in teaching techniques that work.

"The Narcissism of Depression"

Learning how to step away from your own thoughts and see them objectively is a technique that can short-circuit the downward spiral of despair. In her 20s, Gina Barreca was drowning in sadness and emotional turmoil. Small setbacks and difficulties regularly turned into huge cataclysms that took over her life. She cried constantly, for just about any reason. "I really think of myself in those early days as somebody blindfolded, walking underneath an emotional piñata with a bat," she says now.

Now a professor of English at the University of Connecticut, Barreca, too, eventually found a medication that helped. But she got better mostly because she learned to stop torturing herself. She fills up journals with feelings of self-loathing and misery—but that is where they stay. Over time, with the help of a smart, committed therapist, she figured out how to step around emotional chaos rather than stir it up.

Barreca rejects what she calls "the narcissism of depression," the mental habit of taking wretched feelings seriously and burrowing into them. Instead, she thinks of depression and sorrow as familiar demons who arrive as unwelcome visitors. They're nasty, and they wreck the place, but eventually they move on. Enduring them is part of life. "The hardest thing in the world to learn is a sense of humility in the face of this, that these things are going to pass," says Barreca.

Now 52, she doesn't sink into sadness, but she doesn't shy away from it, either. "I'm not bubble-wrapped," she says. "I still get furious. I still get incredibly sad." But when the tormented feelings well up, she does her best to go on with her life. She shops. She talks to friends. She goes for coffee or has a nice meal. "I do those things that actually make me feel better," she says.

Barreca has written seven humor books; her latest, *It's Not That I'm Bitter*, will be out this month. She is a brilliant and witty writer. That's actually not as unlikely as it might seem.

Finding the humor in things requires seeing them from an unexpected angle, a cognitive trick that is key to dispelling depression. "Pain plus time equals humor," says Barreca. "I've had both pain and time."

Making Light of the Darkness

There are many routes out of the isolation of depression. Both Bob Antonioni and Kathryn Goetzke turn to advocacy, going public to reach out to others and to cast off the shame. Pata Suyemoto creates artworks that express her emotional tumult. But there's something especially powerful about humor. It can connect through the terrifying darkness of the disorder, not in spite of it. Humor creates sparks of instantaneous intimacy, a rare gift for anyone—but particularly for those who feel hopelessly alone.

This unique power is the fuel for Victoria Maxwell's one-woman shows, *Crazy for Life* and *Funny, You Don't Look Crazy*. In her performances, often to mental health workers, psychiatrists, and patients, she tells the epic story of her experiences with bipolar disorder. The details are hair-raising. But in her telling, they are also hilarious.

Maxwell's bouts of depression began shortly after she graduated from college, although at first neither she nor her therapist realized quite what they were dealing with. She was binge eating and oversleeping, had trouble concentrating, and was consumed with self-hatred.

At the same time, she embarked upon a spiritual quest. On a three-day meditation retreat, a lack of sleep and food, combined with the silence and stillness, pitched her into mania. During a manic episode, some people become aggressive and others feel unstoppable; her euphoria took on a powerfully spiritual tone. She felt rapturous, like a limitless being composed only of love. But when, convinced she had transcended her earthly body, she began having visions of her grave, her parents took her to the hospital.

Maxwell left with a prescription, but soon quit taking her pills. She thought she was having a spiritual struggle, not mentally ill. During the next couple of years, she went through several more manic episodes, interspersed with horrendous depressions. Finally, one night she went running through the streets of Vancouver naked, looking for God, and got picked up by the police. A wise psychiatric nurse who recognized both Maxwell's spiritual hunger and her mental illness introduced her to a sympathetic psychiatrist who finally convinced her to seek help.

Medication quickly tamed her manic upswings, but the depressions took much longer to manage. At the age of 42, Maxwell now feels pretty stable. She is careful to sleep at least eight hours a night. Intense workouts kick-start her body when she feels slow. And she practices a version of the same technique that Barreca and Goetzke use. Following Buddhist writer Pema Chodron's counsel, she treats her depressions with "compassionate witnessing": recognition and tolerance. "I'm comfortable enough to invite those demons to come in," she says. "I don't resist them."

Performing also helps. She can connect with strangers, rather than feel ashamed of her mental illness. And the sense of love and joy that she felt during her manias still resonates. "It's really liberating to tell people you ran down the street naked, and were tied to a gurney," she says. "At the time, it was terrifying. But to be able to say that to an audience is freeing. To have people laugh with you because they relate is really powerful."

Maxwell considers her bipolar disorder "in remission," but she doesn't take her health for granted. If she's overwhelmed, she takes a day off. She still sees her psychiatrist. But it's no longer a constant struggle: "My life is more about my life than my illness, which is a godsend."

Barreca, Suyemoto, and Maxwell all say they wouldn't wish what they've been through on anyone else. But they're not altogether sorry it happened. Depression required them to learn what many people, depressed or not, never find out: the knowledge that they can get through the worst of times. And after the worst times were over, they found out, it is possible to have a sense of perspective about it all—even to laugh. "Laughter is survival," says Barreca. "It's not because life is easy. It's something you wring out of life. You make joy."

Critical Thinking

1. Identify how depressed persons get through the worst of times.
2. Review the different types of therapy for depression.
3. Explain why most people differ in terms of what relieves their depression.

Create Central

www.mhhe.com/createcentral

Internet References

Acupuncture, Anxiety, and Depression
http://psychcentral.com/lib/acupuncture-anxiety-depression
Depression Symptoms and Warning Signs
www.helpguide.org/mental/depression_signs_types
Depression Traps: Social Withdrawal, Rumination, and More
www.webmd.com/ahrq/depression-traps-and-pitfalls
Depression Treatment: Therapy, Medication, and Lifestyle Changes
www.helpguide.org/mental/treatment_strategies_depression.htm
NIMH: Depression
www.nimh.nih.gov/health/publications/depression

KATHLEEN MCGOWAN is a freelance writer in New York.

Article   Prepared by: Karen L. Freiberg, *University of Maryland*

The Switched-On Brain

AMY BARTH

Learning Outcomes

After reading this article, you will be able to:

- Evaluate the research on optogenetics and defeating mental illness.

- Predict what illnesses may be abbreviated or alleviated in the near future with more knowledge about opsins and light therapy.

For all its complexity, the brain in some ways is a surprisingly simple device. Neurons switch off and on, causing signals to stop or go. Using optogenetics, Deisseroth can do that switching himself. He inserts light-sensitive proteins into brain cells. Those proteins let him turn a set of cells on or off just by shining the right kind of laser beam at the cells.

Stopped at a red light on his drive home from work, Karl Deisseroth contemplates one of his patients, a woman with depression so entrenched that she had been unresponsive to drugs and electroshock therapy for years. The red turns to green and Deisseroth accelerates, navigating roads and intersections with one part of his mind while another part considers a very different set of pathways that also can be regulated by a system of lights. In his lab at Stanford University's Clark Center, Deisseroth is developing a remarkable way to switch brain cells off and on by exposing them to targeted green, yellow, or blue flashes. With that ability, he is learning how to regulate the flow of information in the brain.

Deisseroth's technique, known broadly as optogenetics, could bring new hope to his most desperate patients. In a series of provocative experiments, he has already cured the symptoms of psychiatric disease in mice. Optogenetics also shows promise for defeating drug addiction. When Deisseroth exposed a set of test mice to cocaine and then flipped a switch, pulsing bright yellow light into their brains, the expected rush of euphoria—the prelude to addiction—was instantly blocked. Almost miraculously, they were immune to the cocaine high; the mice left the drug den as uninterested as if they had never been exposed.

Today, those breakthroughs have been demonstrated in only a small number of test animals. But as Deisseroth pulls into his driveway he is optimistic about what tomorrow's work could bring: Human applications, and the relief they could deliver, may not be far off.

That in turn makes it possible to highlight the exact neural pathways involved in the various forms of psychiatric disease. A disruption of one particular pathway, for instance, might cause anxiety. To test the possibility, Deisseroth engineers an animal with light-sensitive proteins in the brain cells lying along the suspected pathway. Then he illuminates those cells with a laser. If the animal begins cowering in a corner, he knows he is in the right place. And as Deisseroth and his colleagues illuminate more neural pathways, other researchers will be able to design increasingly targeted drugs and minimally invasive brain implants to treat psychiatric disease.

Optogenetics originally emerged from Bio-X, a multidisciplinary project spearheaded in part by Stephen Chu, then a Stanford physicist and now the U.S. Secretary of Energy. Bio-X takes some of Stanford's best engineers, computer scientists, physicists, chemists, and clinicians and throws them together in the Clark Center, where an open, glass-clad structure makes communication unavoidable. Deisseroth, whose beat-up jeans and T-shirt practically define the universal academic wardrobe, proved a natural at working across disciplines. Over the past decade, his omnivorous quest has filtered far beyond Bio-X into a thousand institutions around the world.

Although his Bio-X work involves esoteric genetics and animal experiments, Deisseroth has never forgotten the human needs that motivated him in the first place. He still divides his time between his basement lab and the psychiatry patients who desperately need his research to pay off.

Psychiatry's Core Dilemma

Karl Deisseroth was 27 when he first brushed past the curtains of the psychiatry ward at Palo Alto's VA hospital in northern California. It was 1998 and he had just completed his first two years of Stanford Medical School, where he had earned a PhD in brain cell physiology, exploring the electrical language of neuron communication. As part of his medical training, he was required to complete a rotation in psychiatry—a hazy specialty, he felt, much less compelling than the brain surgery that was his career goal.

Several patients in the ward lay in narrow beds lined up before him, awaiting a treatment called electroconvulsive therapy (ECT). After the anesthesiologist on duty put them under, the attending psychiatrist placed pads on the patients' temples and walked from bed to bed, pressing a small button on each person's control box, sending volts of electricity into their brains. Their bodies tensed and their brains rattled with seizures for a full minute. The recipients risked losing large swaths of memory, but if things went well, the current would reset their neurons, purging their depression and providing months of relief.

From that experience, Deisseroth determined that he would spend his life solving a core puzzle of psychiatric disease: A brain could appear undamaged, with no dead tissue or anatomical deformities, yet something could be so wrong it destroyed patients' lives. Perhaps because the damage was invisible, the available therapies were shockingly crude. ECT was lifesaving but usually temporary; although it was likely that just a small set of cells caused the patient's troubles, the shock jolted neurons throughout the brain. Psychoactive drugs, targeting general brain regions and cell types, were too broad as well. And scientists were so uncertain about what chemical imbalances impacted which neural circuits that one-third of people with major depression did not respond to drugs at all.

Deisseroth pondered the problem through a subsequent psychiatry residency, where he oversaw more than 200 ECT procedures over four years. Then, in 2004, he became a principal investigator at Stanford and was given his own lab. As a clinician treating patients, his arsenal was limited. But with his scientific imagination roaming free and a brand-new lab sparkling with empty chairs and beakers to fill, he began to envision elegant new strategies. One stood out: a concept first suggested by Francis Crick, the legendary genetics and consciousness researcher.

Crick's idea was that light, with its unparalleled speed and precision, could be the ideal tool for controlling neurons and mapping the brain. "The idea of an energy interface instead of a physical interface to work with the brain was what was so exciting," Deisseroth says. He thought creating a light-sensitive brain was probably impossible, but then an idea floated up: What about tapping the power of light-sensitive microbes, single-celled creatures that drift in water, turning toward or away from the sun to regulate energy intake? Such brainless creatures rely on signals from light-sensitive proteins called opsins. When sunlight hits the opsin, it instantly sends an electric signal through the microbe's cell membrane, telling the tiny critter which way to turn in relation to the sun.

Deisseroth wondered if he could insert these opsins into targeted mammalian brain cells in order to make them light-sensitive too. If so, he could learn to control their behavior using light. Shining light into the brain could then become the tool Crick imagined, providing a way to control neurons without electric shocks or slow-acting, unfocused drugs.

Lighting the Brain

The necessary tools were already out there. The first opsin—the light-sensitive protein made by microbes—had been identified in 1971, the same year Deisseroth was born. Bacteriorhodopsin, as it was called, responded to green light, and scientists have since found it in microbes living in saltwater all over the world. The next opsin, halorhodopsin, which responds to yellow light, was discovered in 1977. Like bacteriorhodopsin, it was found in bacteria living in salty lakes and seas.

Deisseroth, who read everything he could about opsins, realized that light-sensitive microbes speak the same basic language as neurons: When light hits the opsin, gates in the cell membrane open, allowing charged particles called ions to flow in and out. In microbes, ion flow tells the organism which way to turn. In neurons, ions flowing through the cell wall initiate action, setting off a string of communications that tell organisms like us how to feel and behave. This similarity suggested to Deisseroth that opsins could be manipulated to switch brain cells on and off.

Deisseroth was still mulling this over in 2003, when German biologists Georg Nagel and Peter Hegemann announced a new light-sensitive microbe, a green alga called *Chlamydomonas reinhardtii*. The 10-micrometer-wide microbe has a small eyespot, which Deisseroth describes as "kind of cute," that spins around to detect light. It makes a protein called channelrhodopsin-2 (ChR2) that acts as an antenna to receive blue light and convert it to an ion flow. When a light shines on ChR2, the cell becomes active and tells the microbe where to turn.

Deisseroth immediately wanted ChR2. The other opsins might do the trick, but because his goal—putting them into a brain and getting that brain to respond—was so tricky and success so improbable, he needed to try as many options as possible. He wrote to Nagel in the spring of 2004, requesting a copy of the gene and explaining he planned to try inserting it into neurons. "I was realistic enough to know it was worth testing but probably a long ways away from being useful," he says. "If I'd told him I was going to cure depression with it, I'm sure he would have thought I was crazy."

Deisseroth realized that even the first step of his plan—inserting the microbial opsin molecule into a mammalian neuron and getting the two to sync up—was a long shot. For one thing, there was a good chance the mammalian immune system would reject the foreign protein. Even if the opsin was tolerated, there was no way to know whether it could toggle mammalian cells in the same way it controlled algae. The opsin's electric signals would need to fire and shut down within milliseconds of the stimulus to communicate as quickly as neurons; Deisseroth doubted that the simple biology of algae required such speed.

To run the necessary tests, Deisseroth had to hire staff for his lab, and fast. Someone would have to provide expertise in handling viruses—specifically, a virus to serve as a vector, or Trojan horse, to cart algal genes into mammalian cells. The gene for the opsin would need to be inserted into the virus, which would infect the neurons, transferring the opsin gene to them. If all went as planned, mammalian neurons would then produce light-sensitive microbial opsins as if they were proteins of their own.

A Team Is Born

Luck was on Deisseroth's side that summer of 2004. As a new Stanford faculty member, he had moved into an office that had been occupied by Steven Chu, who had recently left Stanford to become director of the Lawrence Berkeley National Laboratory. Deisseroth's door still had Chu's name on it. One afternoon, a disoriented young chemistry student named Feng Zhang wandered in, looking for Chu. "I can still remember looking at him—he was a little surprised to see me," Deisseroth says. But the two started talking. Zhang wanted to understand the chemical imbalances underlying depression. He also had the skills to help Deisseroth with viruses: At age 15 he had started working with viral vectors, a project that won him the top prize at the Intel International Science and Engineering Fair. Now an aspiring Stanford PhD, he decided to join Deisseroth's team.

Next, Deisseroth required someone skilled at patch clamping, a technique that uses an electrode to record ions passing through cells. This would allow him to record when neurons fired or shut down, indicating whether they were responding to light. For this he hired Ed Boyden, a newly minted neuroscience PhD at Stanford. Boyden was brilliant and energetic, with an aggressiveness that was sometimes off-putting but was ideal for tackling nearly impossible experiments and getting them published. He also had expertise in electrophysiology, another skill required for Deisseroth's nascent optogenetics project.

That fall Deisseroth set to work with his new team. First they inserted the ChR2 opsin into a harmless retrovirus that Zhang had harvested. Then they added the engineered virus to a culture of rat neurons in a petri dish. As hoped, Zhang's virus penetrated the neurons and delivered the light-sensitive gene. The final step was observing whether the cell actually fired quickly in response to light. Boyden hooked up one neuron to a glass electrode that could also deliver light. The other end of the electrode was attached to a computer. When the cell was quiet, a steady line appeared on the computer screen; when it was active, the line jumped up in a spike.

To Deisseroth's elation, the effort was a success: As Boyden poked the electrode into the cell, Deisseroth saw pulses of bright blue light in the culture dish and spikes precisely matching those pulses on the computer screen. "For the next nine months we worked frenetically to publish it. We wanted to move quickly," Deisseroth says. The paper, published in *Nature Neuroscience* in August 2005, chronicled the first time anyone had managed to control brain cells with light.

The cell cultures still did not prove whether optogenetics would apply to brain cells inside living, freely moving mammals, however. The effort to find out required expanding the team. By 2006 Deisseroth had a tight-knit group of 15 who took frequent excursions to local Indian buffets and In-N-Out Burger when they were not working intensely side by side.

Cracking the Animal Code

In cell culture, only a small number of mild virus particles were needed to deliver the opsin gene to targeted neurons. But inserting genes into mammalian neurons inside an intact brain required a larger number of more virulent viruses. Zhang worked tirelessly on this challenge, developing a highly concentrated but still-safe retrovirus derived from HIV; in essence, he removed HIV's toxic genes and replaced them with a version of ChR2. He could brew the virus from scratch in just three days.

Deisseroth also needed a miniature flashlight that could be surgically inserted in the brain to turn cells on and off at close range. Mice weigh only about 20 grams, less than two tablespoons of sugar, so the device could not be big or heavy. And although the light needed to be 100 times as bright as room light, the system could not heat the brain as it delivered the beam. The team's solution was to implant a fiber-optic cable in the brain and connect it to a miniature laser affixed to the animal's head. The contraption was small and light enough to travel with the mouse wherever it went.

Finally, Deisseroth needed a way to tag the specific neurons he wanted to study so that only those cells would become activated in response to the light. Other brain researchers had identified certain cell types and areas of the brain associated with fear, reward, addiction, and depression. But they had no way of knowing exactly which neurons within these regions were driving a particular behavior. Deisseroth strove to find out. He used snippets of DNA called promoters to link ChR2 genes with DNA found only in the specific neurons he wanted to study. When he shined his light, it would not disturb the entire region but just the relevant cells.

Only then was Deisseroth ready to test optogenetics in a living animal. He charged Zhang with conducting a study of hypocretin neurons, sleep-related cells located deep in the brain's hypothalamus. The cells are crucial for arousal during sleep–wake cycles and are thought to play a key role in narcolepsy.

Zhang did the research at Stanford Sleep Center, where he could record brain waves of snoozing mice. He targeted ChR2 to the sleep cells and then, using optical fiber, delivered light directly to the mice's brains. In early 2007 his team placed a ChR2-altered mouse in a sleeping chamber with two implants in its skull. One was the optical fiber; the other consisted of four wires that measured the animal's brain waves.

Deisseroth vividly remembers the moment when an excited postdoc summoned him to the room. "I walked in and he whispered to me, 'Be quiet.'" A mouse was peacefully dreaming in his chamber. But when the laser was turned on, they saw a slight change on the brain-wave monitor and the animal began to twitch. It was waking up in response to a light signal inside its brain. For the first time ever, Deisseroth's team had used optogenetics to control behavior in a living animal.

Soon after, in March 2007, their results were more dramatic still. Deisseroth implanted an optical fiber in the cortex of a mouse with ChR2 in its motor neurons. When he flashed blue light through the cable, a meandering mouse began running to the left. When the laser was switched off, the mouse resumed wandering aimlessly. "You can turn it on and off and the animal isn't distressed. It's comfortable. You're just reaching in there with the fiber-optic, controlling the cells, and you're causing its behavior," Deisseroth says. "That was the moment I knew this would be amazing."

In the five years since, the Deisseroth lab, dubbed the D-lab, has expanded into an entire brain-control research center, with more than 40 scientists on the job. Molecular biologists, neuroscientists, engineers, and physicists from all over the world rush through his cavernous laboratories, tinkering with microscopes, lasers, viral soups, electrodes, and rodent brains. Located in the heart of Silicon Valley, the D-lab feels like an entrepreneurial start-up. Members enthusiastically talk among themselves, build and invent together—there is a palpable sense of enthusiasm and urgency.

One of the team's greatest accomplishments was spearheaded by Kay Tye, a former postdoc who now works at MIT. In a lab near Deisseroth's office, Tye inserted a fiber-optic cable into a mouse's little brain at just the right spot, leaving enough slack for the animal to run around. Tye was studying anxiety circuits and needed to put the cable into a specific part of the amygdala. For decades, researchers have known that the amygdala is associated with fear and anxiety but did not know exactly which neurons in what part of the amygdala played a role. Tye used data from previous studies to home in on a likely circuit, then carefully positioned the cable to deliver light right there. As the targeted neurons were stimulated, she watched to see how the mouse's behavior changed. If it suddenly became bolder, that would be a good sign that she had found a neuron set involved in anxiety.

Mice are naturally fearful of exploring open spaces, where they are vulnerable to predators. When placed in Tye's four-armed maze, they would spend most of their time in the two arms protected by high walls, occasionally poking a nose out to explore. But when Tye switched on the light and activated the circuit in her subject's brain, the mouse ventured out, exploring the open part of the maze with no visible anxiety. The results suggested that Tye had located an anxiety circuit in the brain that could someday be targeted by drugs.

Breaking the cycle of addictive behavior was another goal for the D-team. Again working with mice, they built a three-chamber cage in which one room became a designated drug den. Mice in that room received a shot of cocaine. Animals typically formed a positive association between the effects of the cocaine and the room, just as a person addicted to alcohol might form an association between feeling good and the pop of a cork. Left to their own devices, the mice hung around the room long after the cocaine wore off, even when they were free to wander elsewhere.

But when mice were injected with cocaine and also treated with halorhodopsins and light—in this case a yellow pulse sent directly to the brain's reward center—the rush of euphoria was blocked. Those mice never formed a positive association between cocaine and the room and roamed freely around the cage.

Later in 2010, Deisseroth teamed with neuroscientist Anatol Kreitzer at the University of California, San Francisco, to investigate Parkinson's disease—an important step toward using optogenetics to target a neurodegenerative disease. The ultimate cause of Parkinson's is unknown but clearly involves the loss of a set of neurons that control voluntary movement. The basal ganglia are the brain's action control center. One pathway there sends signals to "go," as in go ahead and perform this action, and one sends "stop" signals. In Parkinson's the pathways are thought to be out of balance, with interrupted motor cells causing the debilitating tremors and loss of movement control symptomatic of the disease.

Although this theory of Parkinson's had been widely considered since the 1980s, there was no way to probe the circuit directly until optogenetics came along. Working with mice, Deisseroth and Kreitzer activated the "go" and "stop" circuits with light, confirming that one in fact facilitates movement while the other inhibits it. Next they tested a more nuanced hypothesis: Might Parkinson's result from an overactive stop circuit? Deisseroth and Kreitzer tagged that circuit with ChR2 and delivered blue light directly into the brains of mice. When the light turned on, movement slowed and the mice had trouble walking, both symptoms of Parkinson's.

What the researchers really wanted, though, was insight into how to treat the disease. They thought activating the go pathway could rebalance the overactive stop network. When they targeted the go circuit, that approach worked even better than expected. The mice began walking normally again, their movement indistinguishable from the way they had moved in their healthy state. Today's leading treatment for Parkinson's—deep brain stimulation—involves inserting a large electrode deep within the patient's brain and zapping all surrounding tissue. Deisseroth hopes that his findings will bring a more targeted treatment soon.

Indeed, by combining opsins, including ChR2, which turns cells on, and halorhodopsin and bacteriorhodopsin, which turn cells off, Deisseroth can ask ever more nuanced questions about complex diseases: Epilepsy, autism, sleep disorders, and schizophrenia may all require this combination approach.

Turning cells on and off efficiently allows a whole range of new, more detailed experiments: Now Deisseroth can tell neurons to fire and shut down quickly, so they can be ready to receive the next signal telling them what to do. Using multiple opsins as well as blue, yellow, and green light, he can experiment with various combinations of activation in hopes of eliminating symptoms of disease.

Pacing the Heart with Light

Despite the fact that Deisseroth has focused on animal brains, the first optogenetic implants—which could be ready for human trials in as little as a decade—will almost surely focus on other organs, where applications are less risky. Early therapies could take the form of a heart pacemaker that uses light to activate heart cells and keep them firing on time. There has been talk of optogenetics for the blind, implanting opsins in vision cells and developing special glasses that shine light into them.

In the fall of 2011, Deisseroth cofounded a company in Menlo Park, around the corner from Stanford, dedicated to translating optogenetics research into therapies. One focus is peripheral nerve disorder, in which messages between the brain and the rest of the body are interrupted. It is often caused by spinal cord injuries, multiple sclerosis, and other nervous system disorders.

"It's not very glamorous, but there's a very large population of people who have peripheral nerve defects that keep them from having good bowel and bladder control," Deisseroth says. "And what's interesting is, if you ask the people who have paralysis if they could choose one thing, to be able to walk or to have bowel and bladder control, they essentially all pick bowel and bladder control, because it's the most limiting for them. It is a problem well suited to optogenetics." Bladder control requires both a contraction of the bladder and a relaxation of the sphincter, and optogenetics can both stimulate and inhibit those different neurons at the same time. Deisseroth hopes to introduce opsins to the crucial peripheral nerves outside the brain and then use simple LED implants to switch function back on.

Once someone has figured out how to get opsins inside the brains of primates and humans—Zhang at MIT is working on the problem now—optogenetic therapies targeting the brain can begin. The possibility also opens the door to Orwellian fears. If Deisseroth can control the brains of mice with light, what is to stop human mind control? The most cogent answer is this: Creating transgenic people by sending a retrovirus into healthy brains will never be allowed. Besides, the potential for healing is too great to ignore—starting with a better implant for those who suffer from Parkinson's, a neurodegenerative disease already treated with electrodes in the brain.

Getting into the Human Brain

Deisseroth's great insight has spawned research around the world. Every two weeks, scientists come from universities in the United States and abroad to spend a week at the D-lab learning the secrets of optogenetics, mastering everything from mouse surgery to cooking up viruses. At the end of the week they present their plans for research of their own. Deisseroth slouches in his seat, wearing coffee-stained jeans, clogs, and a short-sleeve button-down shirt that he has not tucked in. The laissez-faire demeanor is deceptive: Deisseroth is fully engaged and always on, often jumping in during a presentation to ask questions or offer suggestions. The waiting list to attend his workshop is more than a dozen labs long.

One notable alumna is Ana Domingos, who flew in from New York's Rockefeller University a few years back. She was investigating weight loss and wanted to use optogenetics to trigger dopamine, a mood-enhancing neurotransmitter, whenever mice drank water laced with an artificial sweetener, causing them to ignore their usual preference, a sugar-spiked drink. Domingos hopes to use her findings to develop weight loss therapies. "The first time I saw the mouse bingeing on water with sweetener, I got goosebumps," Domingos says. "I couldn't sleep. Karl gave me the tools to play god."

Following these presentations, Deisseroth grabs lunch before attending his weekly patient psychiatry sessions. He picks an outdoor seat at a nearby café swarming with people on a sunny, 75-degree day in mid-January. It's a rare moment of downtime for Deisseroth, who readily admits he needs to relax more.

Even with his lab in high gear, Deisseroth is constantly busy trying to help his psychiatry patients. One of them, Alicia A, has tried nearly every medication, ECT, and various electrical implants to keep her depression under control. She drives seven hours once a month to visit Deisseroth, and together they have found a successful combination of electrical nerve stimulation and antidepressant drugs that has allowed her to return to work and enjoy life. Yet she intently follows Deisseroth's optogenetics work and is adamant that if he ever starts human trials, she will be the first in line.

As much as Alicia A's life has improved from sessions with Deisseroth, the electrical stimulation is often uncomfortable, and her treatment requires constant monitoring. Deisseroth has an entirely different therapy possibility in mind for her. From his experience with ECT, he knows inducing a seizure with electricity resets individual neurons in the brain just like rebooting a computer, so those neurons fire all at once in a different order than before. But something peculiar and fascinating happens to the patient: When the therapy is over everything about the person—memories, priorities, the sense of self—comes back. Apparently these things are not generated by neurons but arise from the brain's physical structure and wiring. The wires are like superhighways, roads of activity where circuits of neurons constantly communicate, but sometimes the road might be gridlocked or icy, and the messenger can't get through.

At one level, optogenetics is nothing more than using light to control a targeted population of cells. But how these cells are wired up is a huge puzzle in itself and, to Deisseroth, one that lies at the true root of future psychiatric cures. To turn his wiring insights into therapy, he wants to use optogenetics to narrow down which circuits dictate which specific behaviors. Then, if he can determine whether the circuits are somehow impeded or blocked, he can try to physically shift them and normalize activity flow.

The Magnetic Cure

Deisseroth isn't certain which tools will allow him to study these connections—it's a capability beyond the reach of optogenetics—so he is once again on the edge of something big and unprecedented. A type of brain imaging, called diffusion tensor imaging, allows doctors to scan patients and produce vibrantly colored images of the brain's wiring. These connections vary from individual to individual. When abnormalities are detected, a machine therapy called tran-scranial magnetic stimulation (TMS) can send into the brain magnetic pulses powerful enough to shift and rewire those connections so their function is improved. TMS is already used to treat ailments like Parkinson's disease, migraines, and depression.

Years ago as a psychiatry resident, Deisseroth assisted with the clinical trial that got the therapy FDA-approved. He plans to continue using optogenetics to pin down circuits of brain cells responsible for disease and to combine that knowledge with the colorful circuit images to home in on which wires need to go where to establish normal communication. Then TMS can move the wires precisely where they need to go to cure any particular illness. If it works, scientists would have a complete understanding of an individual patient's brain.

The concept may sound extraordinary, too grand to work, but this is the type of challenge Deisseroth loves most. "I want to come up with totally new things, so I don't want to be affected by too many preconceptions," he says. Conveniently, Deisseroth's own brain is wired to generate its best ideas in moments of isolation. "I can remember a couple key insights just driving in my car. For me, that's meditative. I rarely solve a problem by thinking about it. The insights usually come from out of the blue, like a bolt."

Critical Thinking

1. Why do you think people with peripheral nerve defects would rather have good bowel and bladder control than be able to walk again?

2. Do you think the science of optogenetics will allow people to control others (e.g., mind control)? Why or why not?

3. Do you think great insights come "out of the blue" like a bolt, or from meditating on a problem? Why for either choice?

Create Central

www.mhhe.com/createcentral

Internet References

The Primary Structure of a Halorhodopsin
www.jbc.org/content/265/3/1253.abstract

Transcranial Magnetic Stimulation-Scholarpedia
www.scholarpedia.org/article/Transcranial_magnetic_stimulation

What Is Optogenetics?
http://optogenetics.weebly.com/what-is-it.html

AMY BARTH is an associate editor at *Discover*.

Article   Prepared by: Karen L. Freiberg, *University of Maryland*

The Boss Stops Here

A nonhierarchical workplace may just be a more creative and happier one. But how would you feel if the whole office voted on whether to hire you—*and* when to give you a raise?

Matthew Shaer

Learning Outcomes

After reading this article, you will be able to:

- Evaluate the pros and cons of working in a setting where every employee has equal status.

- Explain why creativity can be muffled by a hierarchy.

The headquarters of Menlo Innovations occupy the basement level of an office complex in downtown Ann Arbor, not far from the main campus of the University of Michigan. The space is airy and bright and capacious, as befits a successful software company, but unlike the standard-issue corporate hive, there are no cubicles at Menlo, and very few walls, and only a couple of doors, one of which leads to a closet full of sensitive legal documents and another that opens into a conference room—a concession to clients unaccustomed to (or unwilling to fully participate in the spirit of) what is known around here as "the Menlo Way."

At ten in the morning on a recent Wednesday, the 50-odd employees of Menlo, most of whom are young and appealingly tousled and predisposed toward navy or forest-green hoodies, rose from their desks and formed a large circle in the middle of the room. Menlo developers practice something called "pair programming"—a technique whereby two coders work simultaneously on a single machine, with one actually manning the keyboard and the other backseat driving from an adjacent chair. The groupings typically remain intact for a few days or a week, at which point they are scuttled and reassigned, the hope being that the constant mutation in team structure will help encourage creativity and prevent frustration.

Since there are no bosses at Menlo (at least not in the traditional sense) and no middle managers (ditto), all that reassigning and fluctuation falls to the team as a whole, a process that requires a lot of air-traffic control. Every morning, the entire staff circles up to discuss strategy.

On the day I attended, the meeting moved with martial efficiency. Two by two, the pairs stepped forward and, with each employee gripping one of the horns of a fat-lady-sings-style helmet, the unofficial symbol of Menlo Innovations, they laid out their plan for the eight hours ahead. The bulk of the speakers were developers and designers (or "high-tech anthropologists," a term Menlo has registered with the U.S. Patent and Trademark Office), but there were also quality-assurance and support staffers on hand, and the conversation ran from the jocular to the mundane to the technical:

"We're going to be calling this project 'Gobstopper,' because 'Jawbreaker' just sounded a little too hard-core."

"Right now, I'm doing some organizing of the storage closet."

"Every day, I'm reminded of how much human suffering in the world is related to technology. I'm talking about the new Gmail design."

"I'm Andrea, and I'm working on client invoices."

There was some clapping and some backslapping, of the kind you might observe at a particularly boisterous rec-league indoor soccer game, then all the employees were filing back to their desks, past a poster of Frank Zappa and a bust of Thomas Edison, the patron saint of Menlo and the guy whose famed laboratory, in Menlo Park, New Jersey, inspired this Michigan company's name. Later, one of the quality advocates at Menlo, Joe Rock (real name), explained that the A.M. meeting helps keep morale on the team high and, more important, encourages a feeling of camaraderie—a sense that every one of the staffers is working together toward a common goal. Hence the circle, which, in a nod to King Arthur's court, ensures that no one gets a seat at the head of the table.

As I soon discovered, basically everything at Menlo Innovations is so open and transparent and *flat* that the average office worker, upon entering the Menlo den, might be forgiven for feeling a little suspicious, intrigued, cynical, and jealous all at once.

Consider, for instance, the fact that hiring at Menlo is handled by committee, with each applicant spending a little bit of time with a group of employees, until a consensus can be reached. That same collective decision-making happens during promotions, layoffs, and flat-out firings.

Consider next the charts in the corner of the office, which display the names and titles of the Menlo employees and also their corresponding pay grades. When I first saw them, I was standing in the midst of a scrum of Menlonians, and I suggested—thus belying my own, frankly square work experience—that it might be a little unnerving to have your salary exposed to your colleagues. And the guy standing to my right actually scoffed. "No," he said. "It's the opposite. It's liberating."

It's a relatively safe assumption that most of us have, at one point in our lives, worked for a boss. There is comfort in the arrangement: Someone tells us what to do, and we do it. If we do it well—and "it" here could be anything from writing software to assembling a car—we may get a more spacious cube or more money, and if we do it poorly, we can expect to be let go. Above us, in an ever-narrowing spire, are the shift supervisors and floor managers and vice-presidents, each of whom is subject to his or her own unique hierarchical pressures, and above them is the CEO or president or otherwise-titled grand Pooh-Bah who dictates the rules that the rest of us must follow.

According to Nikil Saval, the author of *Cubed,* a forthcoming history of the modern office, the top-down management structure first proliferated in the U.S. in the rail era, as corporate barons struggled to maintain control of their sprawling new concerns. The easiest way to govern hundreds of thousands of miles of railroad, they discovered, was to erect a chain of command, which extended from the central office in New York or Chicago to the field offices on the frontier.

It was a strategy that also proved remarkably effective for the heads of large banks and telephone companies and eventually—I'm skipping a few decades here—PC manufacturers and soda-pop-makers and multinational data-processing firms. There may even be some evidence that the tiered framework is hardwired into our brains. "Hierarchy is prominent across all species and all cultures in the world," Adam Galinsky, a professor at Columbia Business School, told me recently. "It reduces conflict, helps with role differentiation, and vastly increases coordination." In other words, employees may need managers because managers define, either implicitly or explicitly, who people are as workers.

In a research paper published last year titled "The Path to Glory Is Paved With Hierarchy," Galinsky and several colleagues measured the productivity of "mixed power" work teams and found that tiered groups outperformed flat ones. The pecking order, they concluded, is the "universal default for human social organization"—a default that requires minimal social interactions to emerge. The paper cites work by poultry scientists, who have discovered that putting too many high egg producers in the same small space actually decreases overall egg production: "It turns out the best egg producers are also the most competitive birds, and in a group setting, they quickly begin fighting over food, space, and territory; these intragroup conflicts then drive egg production down and bird mortality up. Chicken farmers take note: If you want to maximize group-level productivity, you need harmony, and it seems that hierarchy provides the key."

The theory that too many bosses may be an obstacle and not a boon did not achieve widespread prominence until the early eighties. The reasons are multifarious, but business historians believe it had something to do with the economic recession, which gutted the ranks of the middle managers and

in the process helped companies realize that all those bosses had actually been slowing things down. There was also an increasing sense that creativity—an invaluable commodity at the tech firms and software companies of the new "knowledge economy"—might be muffled by hierarchy. A tiered framework had worked fine for railway bosses, but it could have a frankly inhibiting effect on a team whose sole task was to build something new, often out of thin air. For that, you needed space, you needed support, and above all, you needed freedom.

Studies, in fact, show that although *some* structure is conducive to creativity, the "time to experiment and potentially fail"—to quote Pierre Azoulay, an associate professor at the MIT Sloan School of Management—is vital to the consistent production of innovative ideas.

Among the earliest agitators for a decentralized workplace was Ricardo Semler, the chairman of Brazilian industrial-parts manufacturer Semco. Semler took over Semco from his father, in the early eighties, when he was 23; his first move was to eliminate the majority of the executives and managers. He opened up the company books, organized employees into self-sufficient work teams, and instituted profit-sharing. Semler believed that Semco would perform better as a company if the workers didn't have a platoon of "bean counters"—one of his favorite insults—constantly looking over their shoulders.

"Bureaucracies are built by and for people who busy themselves proving they are necessary, especially when they suspect they aren't," he wrote in his 1988 book *Turning the Tables* (published in the United States under the title *Maverick*). "All these bosses have to keep themselves occupied, and so they constantly complicate everything." Rules are good for prisons and armies, Semler wrote, but "for a business that wants people to think, innovate, and act as human beings whenever possible," they serve only four purposes:

1. Divert attention from the company's objectives.
2. Provide a false sense of security for the executives.
3. Create work for bean counters.
4. Teach men to stone dinosaurs and start fire with sticks.

Maverick was an international best seller, and it remains a foundational text for advocates of the flattened workplace today. Tom Preston-Werner, a co-founder of the tech firm GitHub, which allows all employees to set their own schedules and choose their own projects, told me that the book "changed my understanding of how a business could be run."

In 1980, less than 20 percent of the companies on the *Fortune* 1000 list boasted at least some sort of team management structure. By 1990, it was 50 percent. By 2000, it was 80 percent. "Companies were trying to figure out the best way to foster creativity, to effect rapid change, to deal with growing global competitiveness," says Stephen Courtright, an assistant professor at Texas A&M, who specializes in the study of self-governing workplaces. "In many cases, that involved flat, horizontal management."

But only in recent years have we really seen the ideal of the democratized workplace brought to its logical conclusion: companies that don't just have fewer managers and bosses but have hardly any bosses at all.

Last month, Fox debuted a reality show called *Does Someone Have to Go?* In each episode, a squadron of Fox producers descends on an office, puts the employees in charge of day-to-day operations, and turns on the cameras. "You will all be the boss," one of the teams is told in an early promo. Cut to a close-up of the furious, disbelieving mug of an employee who looks like he's just been asked to guillotine his golden retriever.

Much of the show works like this: It turns the concept of self-management into the stuff of nightmare. As *The New York Times* noted, the program assumes "that what's wrong with the American workplace is the workers. The problems discussed aren't about the structure of the company, or the state of its chosen industry and market, or the economy as a whole. Employees are the enemy." And bosses, by default, the heroes.

All of which would deeply surprise Simon Anderson, the CEO of the web-hosting company DreamHost. "Management is a term to me that feels very twentieth century," he says. "That 100-year chunk of time when the world was very industrialized, and a company would make something that could be stamped out 10 million times and figured out a way to ship it easily, you needed the hierarchy for that. I think this century is more about building intelligent teams."

Anderson was one of three finalists for the CEO job at DreamHost in 2011. In choosing their new chief executive, the founders of the company decided to open the floor to an online vote. To make his case, Anderson was trotted in front of a majority of its 100 employees, asked to give a little speech, and answered questions from the crowd. He won narrowly, by a margin of 53 to 47 percent. Anderson told me that he has since spoken to some of the employees who voted against him. "There were no hard feelings," he said.

DreamHost has a management structure, but workers have the freedom to select their own projects, and the offices, in downtown Los Angeles, are open 24 hours a day.

And there is an increasing number of companies around the country that function similarly. Development at Valve Corporation, a video-game company based near Seattle, is conducted by a network of self-governing teams. Employees choose which team they join and also choose when they'd like to join a new one. Jason Holtman, who until recently worked in business development at Valve, has, in the past, called the setup "an organic gravity well"—the number of people on a project helps determine which games are shipped and which are held for more work.

At W. L. Gore & Associates, the makers of Gore-Tex, there are few titles (almost everyone is referred to as an "associate"), and once a year employees gather to rank their colleagues based on their contributions to the overall success of the company. Those rankings are used by a separate committee of associates to determine pay raises or cuts.

And at IDEO—a sprawling design firm with offices in New York, Mumbai, and London, among other cities—work teams are multidisciplinary and mostly self-governing. Every team opens a project by setting a series of personal and collective goals, reviews its progress midway, and closes the project with a self-analysis session.

This structure—largely flat and very flexible—is especially appealing to those new to the workforce, twentysomethings who tend to approach work differently from their parents. "The way workers are motivated is changing," says Anderson of DreamHost. "Twenty years ago, it was about higher pay. Now it's more about finding your work meaningful and interesting." As more and more millennials enter positions of power in the business world, Anderson believes we will soon reach a point where hierarchy itself is "passé."

Then there are the employees of Morning Star, a California tomato processor that offers an interesting demographical contrast (its employees are not young creatives). Morning Star annually processes thousands of tons of ripe tomatoes, which are ground down for use in ketchup, pizza sauce, or tomato paste. A little over 2,000 people work for Morning Star at the height of the tomato season. In order to be hired, you first sign something known as a CLOU, or a Colleague Letter of Understanding. The CLOU outlines your priorities for the year ahead. If you are a tomato sorter, you pledge to sort a predetermined amount of tomatoes a day for the duration of your stay at Morning Star, and if you are the man who is responsible for helping evaporate the water out of the squishy tomato pulp, then you sign an agreement to evaporate a specific number of gallons of water every week.

Around the facilities, everywhere you turn, are whiteboards and chalkboards and big-screen TVs displaying names and cascading numbers—the tally of what is being done and what remains to be done by each worker. (Morning Star frames it as emancipative—your impetus to work is no longer tied to the whims of your boss but to your own motivation—and most employees seem to agree. But to an outsider, the whole thing seems a little oppressive. What if you have an off day?)

Morning Star was founded by Chris Rufer, a graduate of the UCLA business school. In interviews, Rufer, like Semler, has described the structure of his company as deeply humane, something that buoys the spirits of the workers. The relationships between members of a self-managed team, he has said, are more organic and thus more substantive than the traditional relationship between boss and subordinate, which he describes as both "forced" and "artificial."

To that end, yearly evaluations at Morning Star are handled not by a manager (there are none), but by a group of colleagues who administers a written evaluation of your progress. Paul Green Jr., a member of Morning Star's Self-Management Institute, a kind of internal R&D arm of the company, says the goal is to meet a series of self-defined (capital S) Steppingstones: X amount of gallons, Y number of tomatoes, and so forth.

Conflicts, meanwhile, are handled via a four-step procedure called "Direct Communication and Gaining Agreement." The first step is to attempt to "appeal directly to the colleague," Green told me. "See if you can sort out your differences." Second step is to bring in a third colleague to mediate the argument. The third is to create a panel of six to ten additional colleagues. If all that fails, Rufer can be called upon to join the panel and help render a decision, which occurs about ten times a year.

It may be worth noting that the egalitarian spirit at Morning Star only goes so far: The company is privately held, and no employee, no matter how hard-performing, is entitled to a share of the profits.

One of the first things that Rich Sheridan, the co-founder and CEO of Menlo Innovations, told me, upon my arrival, was Menlo's origin story. He tells this story a lot, at conferences and panels, and the whole spiel is practiced, and fluid, and very TED Talk–esque. It starts in the late fall of 1997, when Sheridan, at the time a V.P. at a document-translation firm called Interface Systems, invited his then-8-year-old daughter, Sarah, to join him for a day at work. Around five in the afternoon, Sheridan turned to her and asked what she had learned.

"Well, Daddy," she replied—and here, Sheridan screws up his face and crunches his body low into his chair and, for a 55-year-old man, does an admirable impression of an 8-year-old girl—"I learned that you're really important."

"What makes you say that?" Sheridan asked.

"All day long," she said, "people came in here and asked you to make a decision for them. And you made a decision, and they went on their way."

Sheridan was mortified. "I realized that the organization couldn't move any faster than me," he said. "That I was the bottleneck."

He shared his epiphany with a young consultant, James Goebel, who harbored some admittedly radical ideas about modern management. Sheridan had originally brought Goebel onboard to help teach his team some new programming techniques, but they decided instead that Goebel should help him with a redesign of Interface.

Over the next six months, cubicles were dismantled, managers were moved out of their offices and into the middle of the floor, and pair programming was introduced. No longer could any code belong to any one person—everyone would share everything. "I had one guy raise his hand," Sheridan remembers, "and say, 'Rich—blood, mayhem, murder. For God's sake, don't put us in an open room, don't make me share my computer with another human being, and please, *please* don't make me share my code.'"

Sheridan believed that by going from a "siloed" environment to a collectivized one, Interface would be more productive. And happier. And by all accounts it was, until 2001, when the dot-com bubble burst, and Sheridan and his entire team were shown the door. That same year, Sheridan and Goebel and two partners founded Menlo Innovations. There were the usual start-up obstacles (wary clients, financing challenges, anemic bank accounts), but over the past decade, Menlo vastly increased its revenue, outgrowing one office space after another.

When I first contacted Sheridan, by e-mail, he wrote that it was "quite bossless at Menlo! Team makes hiring decisions, team gives feedback, team decides promotions." This is only partially true. Overseeing strategy, the long-term vision of Menlo as a whole, still falls to Goebel (now the chief architect and COO) and Sheridan. If one worker accused another of something illegal—sexual harassment or theft—Goebel and Sheridan would be responsible for taking the appropriate measures. They also serve as representatives for Menlo at scads of management and business conferences here and abroad. (Sheridan's business card reads "Chief Storyteller and Tour Guide.")

In every other way, however, Goebel and Sheridan are not traditional bosses. Overarching strategy is their domain, but the tactical stuff—the daily squall of code-making and high-tech "anthropologizing" that drives the company—belongs entirely to the employees. On the days I spent at Menlo, I never once saw any worker pay Sheridan or Goebel any special deference. No one talked any differently in their presence. They were there as team shrinks and advisers, and yet they were also *not there*—the rest of the office thrummed on around them, regardless of what either of them did. Sheridan's troubling "bottleneck" had been removed; in its place was a largely self-sufficient software-coding machine.

I asked Sheridan if he ever missed his old office and the clout that came with it. "I liked being the person everyone came to," he admitted. "There was glory to it. I felt like the smartest guy in the room. But that doesn't matter to me anymore. It's not my goal."

Menlo's hiring process is called "Extreme Interviewing," and it bears a striking resemblance to speed-dating. Applicants, sometimes as many as five for each open position, are brought into the offices for a series of rapid-fire interviews with a range of current employees. The emphasis is on "kindergarten skills": geniality, curiosity, generosity. As the Menlo white paper on Extreme Interviewing puts it, technical proficiency is less important than a candidate's "ability to make [his or her] partner look good." (Sample interview question: "What is the most challenging bug that you helped someone else fix?")

Later the Menlonians gather to compare notes. Lobbying is common; so is argument. Eventually, the candidates are ranked partially on their technical skill and partially on what the white paper describes as the team's "value set." Offers are extended to the applicants at the top of the list.

"The collective aspect allows one of us to say, 'Okay, he did really well at this,'" one employee, Greg Haskins, told me. "And another of us to say, 'But not so well at that.' And we bounce opinions back and forth before deciding. Basically, we build our team together."

In an old-fashioned, top-down work environment, employees get rewards from three main sources. One is pay (the better we do, the more we get). The second is title (the better we do, the higher we ascend). The third is a sense of achievement (recognition for having performed a task admirably). In a bossless environment, the calculus is significantly changed. Achievement is tied to the team as a whole—you can write a particularly nice piece of code, but it won't mean squat until the whole project is up and running, and for that, you'll need the assistance of your peers. Individual achievement is obviated and replaced by shared achievement. Friendliness and congeniality start to matter more, ladder-climbing a whole lot less.

And herein an important point: Horizontally managed companies work in large part because they tend to attract people who are okay working in a bossless environment and weed out the ones who aren't. ("I can smell a corporate-ladder climber from a mile away," one Menlonian explained.)

Which is not to say that everything at Menlo is peace and love and synergistic intellectual communion. It's not. It couldn't be—no matter how lofty the theories espoused in the glossy, professionally bound 73-page Menlo guidebook (available for free to visitors), its adherents are human, who by their very nature gossip, back-talk, and bicker. "Are there fewer problems here than elsewhere?" Goebel asked me rhetorically. "I'm inclined to say no. We just deal with our problems differently. And the problems themselves are different."

Most of those problems originate in the vacuum left by the traditional management structure. Stephen Courtright told me the story of a manufacturing company that had "misunderstood," in his words, what self-management was all about—few boundaries or guidelines were set for the work teams, and the feedback loop was practically nonexistent. (Courtright, who was consulting for this company, declined to disclose its name.) "They were just kind of set loose to do their thing," Courtright said, "and they produced too much inventory, and the company ended up with a stockpile of unused stuff." An executive decision was made to go back to a top-down hierarchy.

At Menlo, employees must necessarily be self-starters and willing to work collaboratively; if they aren't, the rest of the team will show them the door. Several Menlonians recalled for me the story of a man I'll call John. At first John seemed like an ideal employee—diligent and hardworking. But the horizontal structure at Menlo clearly ate at him, and under-the-breath grumbling soon gave way to very loud bellyaching.

One afternoon at lunch, he stood up and told his colleagues that they were "insane—that they needed to be freed from this weird Nazi regime," in the recollection of someone who witnessed the explosion. Sometime after, the team fired him.

Firing, developer Kealy Opelt told me, is something the company takes very seriously. "Usually, I wouldn't think about bringing in the group unless I've had to talk to someone several times. If it keeps happening, and you both can't adjust, that's when you start talking to everybody else and see if it's just the two of you."

Over subsequent weeks, a series of meetings will be held, and as with the Extreme Interviewing process, a consensus will be reached. If it is determined by the team that a person has to go, there's very little that Sheridan or Goebel can do about it.

To illustrate, Goebel told me about his niece, Erin, who spent a couple of months at Menlo as an admin, before the other employees decided to let her go. Goebel objected, but at Menlo, nepotism has no place. "Actually, my niece lives with me," he said. "And she was really pissed. Thankfully, she didn't take it out on the relationship with my wife or my kids. Still, it was a little frosty for a while."

This kind of team decision-making can be seen as the ultimate motivational tool—always work hard, and your co-workers won't can you. It can also be the kind of thing that yields a whole lot of ad hoc office alliances.

Opelt and colleague John Martin, for instance, told me that they had both recently recommended each other for promotions. They swore it was coincidental—they both believed the other deserved it—but it's not hard to imagine the existence of a lot more deliberately constructed pacts.

And then there is that chart that's plastered prominently on the wall—the one that displays the titles of Menlo employees and their respective pay grades. This is a new innovation, introduced by Goebel over lunch a few months earlier to address curiosity from staffers about where they stood in the overall scheme of the open office. Although almost all of the employees had written their names in Magic Marker on the poster, there were a few abstainers. "I think people are still deciding how to handle that," one employee told me. "It's stirred up a little bit of controversy. Like, that it might actually be a step too far."

Goebel and Sheridan confessed that the idea was still in its infancy—"an experiment," Goebel said. Paul Green used much the same language to describe an analogous open-book policy at Morning Star. "Full transparency in terms of compensation is something we're working on," he said. "It's a process."

One afternoon, I was invited to attend the weekly "kickoff" meeting for the fifteen team members assigned to the account of a local biotech firm that manufactures flow cytometers—machines that test blood and sundry other fluids. Menlo is developing the software that organizes and analyzes data collected by the device.

The purpose of the kickoff meeting was to discuss the code that needed to be completed by the end of the week, and the fifteen Menlonians arranged themselves in a loose circle around a set of tables. Notepads and pens were produced. Goebel and Sheridan were absent—neither man typically attends these meetings because, as Jack Coy, a developer on the account, told me, "to be honest, we don't need them."

Initially the proceedings moved smoothly. A pair of programmers would walk up to one of those big easel pads and discuss the code they'd been assigned and sometimes sketch on the paper a couple of key components. The floor was then opened to the rest of the team, who might shout out questions or suggestions.

At one point, I watched Jeff Jia and Jack Coy, two programmers in their twenties, describe an issue with an important piece of code. Caveat: Software design is an extremely complex science, and people who work in software tend to talk in jargony, acronym-heavy shorthand. For that reason, I will not attempt to recount the exact parameters of the problem Jia and Coy were facing, but suffice it to say it involved a digital filter that had been built to catch certain subsets of cytometer data and arrange those subsets into colored charts.

But the filter wasn't functioning properly, and Jia and Coy were stumped. They had the look of stumped people—lips puckered, arms crossed, shoulders raised. After a little while, they were joined at the easel by Greg Haskins. Haskins is 27, with a babyish face and unruly brown hair, and although he has only been at Menlo for little over a year, he clearly maintains an outsize presence among his peers; when he talks, the other coders tend to listen.

Now Haskins gestured a few more team members to their feet and began arranging them in front of the easel pad like mannequins. What followed was a piece of anarchic and improvised street theater: Rock, the ponytailed quality-advocate dude, was assigned the role of filter, and Kristi Sitarski and Joe Ptolemy were the data that the filter was meant to be sorting. Sitarski stepped forward (she was in), and Ptolemy stepped back (he was out). Everyone laughed. This was team spirit in action. This was *collective action*.

Except it wasn't, not really. Instead it was an action that had been driven in large part by an individual—Haskins. I was reminded of the control group of chickens referenced in Galinsky & Co.'s "The Path to Glory Is Paved With Hierarchy." Some of them were prolific egg producers and some of them were low-level layers, but together, in a mixed-power group, they formed a nice symphony of egg production. Perhaps Galinsky was right that as animals, we do naturally slot ourselves into some sort of hierarchy. Certainly I was seeing something similar now: However ostensibly egalitarian this Menlo work team was, in practice, a leader had quickly emerged, and everyone else was falling in line.

A few weeks after my visit to Ann Arbor, during a conversation with Tom Preston-Werner of GitHub—itself a mostly horizontal company—I happened to use the word *flat*. He stopped me. "With people, there are *always* senses of authority and matters of seniority and so many other social factors at play," he said. "You're fooling yourself if you think a group bigger than a single person can ever really be flat." But the people at companies like Menlo or GitHub or Morning Star don't seem to care. Instead, it's possible that the triumph of the flattened office may be the creation of work environments in which leaders organically arise, and all employees feel a sense of ownership, whether real or imagined.

Jason Holtman, formerly of Valve, has said that the big negative of going bossless is the loss of the "quick mandate"—the ability to swiftly and effectively mobilize the organization. A management structure may be democratic, and thus empowering to the workers, but that does not mean it is neat, nor particularly fast.

That kickoff meeting for that biotech firm was long—it started at 11 A.M. and went until almost two in the afternoon, with a break in between—and by the midway mark, the proceedings were moving a little more slowly, with more exasperated sighs, or slight but conspicuous head shakes, and sometimes everyone seemed to be talking simultaneously, in one big, warbly squawk.

Kealy Opelt, leaning forward, attempted to wrestle the proceedings back on track.

"So where were we?" she'd say. Or: "I didn't hear that, Jeff. Could you repeat it for everyone?" Or: "One at a time, please."

Later, I asked her if she'd been frustrated.

"Look," she said, "we don't want people having their arms all crossed and not saying anything, with this brooding idea they haven't shared with anybody. That would be worse. But yeah, it can get chaotic."

Chaotic, noisy, somewhat lumbering—Menlo may be all those things, but it is also a profitable company. Revenue in 2012 was about $4 million, and employee retention rates are notably high. As the organization has grown its client list, it has expanded the number of programmers it keeps on staff, and when the company posts an advertisement for an open gig, a flood of applications typically pours in. Around Ann Arbor, Menlo Innovations is considered an extremely desirable place to work.

Not that it's an easy place to work. More than one employee told me that it took them some time to get used to the peculiar demands of the office—the lack of doors, the lack of privacy, the constant and sometimes exhausting presence of the rest of the staff.

To help relieve some of that pressure, "walkies" were introduced several years ago. A "walkie" is exactly what it sounds like—a ten-minute group walk around the block. The daily ritual is intended to allow the basement-bound Menlonians a chance to unwind and to see the sun. On one walkie, I found myself between two Menlo employees, Natalie Svaan and Jack Coy. They could not be more unalike. Svaan, a Michigan native with silver-streaked black hair, came to Menlo after a career in IT. Coy is still in college; he works at Menlo part time.

"I remember when I first got hired, I was so wiped out," Svaan was saying. "I'd just come home and collapse. But you know, it's strange; it's gotten to be energizing. The hours do actually fly right by, probably because you're always working."

"And there's the team thing," Coy added. "It's part of your task to make the team succeed and to help other people do their jobs. It's not to promote oneself at the expense of the rest of the team. I like that."

He shook his head. "I think there are actually people," he added, in a tone of deep and abiding wonder, "who want to just go to work, be told what to do, do it, and go home."

Critical Thinking

1. How can a nonhierarchical workplace deal with gossip, back-talk, and bickering?

2. Share your feelings about having no personal computer, no codes of your own, and one common workspace.

3. Predict the response of a worker whose collegial team members agreed that he or she should be fired.

Create Central

www.mhhe.com/createcentral

Internet References

A Glimpse at a Workplace of the Future
www.forbes.com/sites/stevedenning/2012/04/27

The Modern Workplace: Flat Flexible and Wired Up
www.wetfeet.com/articles/the-modern-workplace

Workplace Conflict Resolution
http://humanresources.about.com/od/managementtips/a/conflict

Article   Prepared by: Karen L. Freiberg, *University of Maryland*

When Privacy Jumped the Shark

Note to Edward Snowden and his worrywarts in the press: Spying is only spying when the subject doesn't want to be watched.

FRANK RICH

Learning Outcomes

After reading this article, you will be able to:

- Explain why a majority of Americans are not very concerned about enterprises such as email, Facebook, GPS, Skype, smartphones, etc., invading their privacy.

- Evaluate the motivations of people who use enterprises such as YouTube and Twitter.

H ere's one dirty little secret about the revelations of domestic spying at the National Security Agency: Had Edward Snowden not embarked on a madcap escape that mashed up plot elements from *Catch Me If You Can, The Fugitive,* the O.J. Bronco chase, and "Where in the World Is Matt Lauer?," the story would be over. The leaker's flight path, with the Feds and the press in farcical flat-footed pursuit, captured far more of the public's attention than the substance of his leaks. That's not his fault. The public was not much interested in the leaks in the first place. It was already moving on to Paula Deen.

At first blush, the NSA story seemed like a bigger deal. The early June scoops in *The Guardian* and the *Washington Post* were hailed universally as "bombshells" and "blockbusters" by the networks. America's right and left flanks were unified in hyperventilating about their significance: Rand Paul and *The Nation,* Glenn Beck and Michael Moore, Rush Limbaugh and the *Times* editorial page all agreed that President Obama had presided over an extraordinary abuse of executive power. But even as Daniel Ellsberg hailed the second coming of the Pentagon Papers, the public was not marching behind him or anyone else. The NSA scandal didn't even burn bright enough to earn the distinction of a "-gate" suffix. Though Americans were being told in no uncertain terms that their government was spying on them, it quickly became evident that, for all the tumult in the media-political Establishment, many just didn't give a damn.

Only 36 percent of the country felt that government snooping had "gone too far," according to CBS News. A Pew–*Washington Post* survey found that 62 percent (including 69 percent of Democrats) deemed fighting terrorism a higher priority than protecting privacy. Most telling was a *National Journal* survey conducted days *before* the NSA stories broke: Some 85 percent of Americans assumed that their "communications history, like phone calls, e-mails, and Internet use," was "available for businesses, government, individuals, and other groups to access" without their consent. No wonder the bombshell landed with a thud, rather than as a shock. What was the news except that a 29-year-old high-school dropout was making monkeys of the authorities with a bravado to rival Clyde Barrow?

An ACLU official argued that the so-what poll numbers were misleading: "If terrorism was left out, it would change the polling results dramatically." In other words, blame the public's passivity on the post-9/11 cultural signposts of *24* and *Homeland,* which have inured Americans to a bipartisan Patriot Act regimen in which a ticking terrorist time bomb always trumps the Constitution. Obama, a *Homeland* fan himself, hit the point hard to deflect criticism. "You can't have 100 percent security and also then have 100 percent privacy and zero inconvenience," he said when alluding to the terrorist plots NSA spying had disrupted. "We're going to have to make some choices as a society."

The virtue of this rationale is that it casts not just the domestic eavesdroppers in a patriotic light but also the citizenry that valiantly sacrifices its Fourth Amendment rights to the greater good of stopping the evildoers. But that's letting everyone off easy and is hardly the whole story of the choices Americans have made "as a society"—and that were made before Obama or, for that matter, George W. Bush took office. Many of those choices predate 9/11 and have nothing to do with fighting terrorism at all.

The truth is that privacy jumped the shark in America long ago. Many of us not only don't care about having our privacy invaded but surrender more and more of our personal data, family secrets, and intimate yearnings with open eyes and full hearts to anyone who asks and many who don't, from the servers of Fortune 500 corporations to the casting directors of reality-television shows to our 1.1 billion potential friends on Facebook. Indeed, there's a considerable constituency in this country—always present and now arguably larger than ever—that's begging for its privacy to be invaded and, God willing, to be exposed in every gory detail before the largest audience possible. We don't like the government to be watching as well—many Americans don't like government, period—but most of us are willing to give such surveillance a pass rather than forsake the pleasures and rewards of self-exposure, convenience, and consumerism.

R.I.P. the contemplative America of Thoreau and of Melville's Bartleby the Scrivener, who "would prefer not to"; this is the America that prefers to be out there, prizing networking, exhibitionism, and fame more than privacy, introspection, and solitude. And while it would be uplifting to believe that Americans are willing to sacrifice privacy for the sole good of foiling Al Qaeda, that's hardly the case. Other motives include such quotidian imperatives as shopping, hooking up, seeking instant entertainment and information, and finding the fastest car route—not to mention being liked (or at least "liked") and followed by as many friends (or "friends") and strangers as possible, whether online or on basic cable. In a society where economic advancement is stagnant for all but those at the top, a public profile is the one democratic currency most everyone can still afford and aspire to—an indicator of status, not something to be embarrassed about. According to the Pew-*Post* poll, a majority of Americans under 50 paid little attention to the NSA story at all, perhaps because they found the very notion of fearing a privacy breach anachronistic. After the news of the agency's PRISM program broke, National Donut Day received more American Google searches than PRISM. There has been no wholesale (or piecemeal) exodus of Americans from Google, Facebook, Microsoft, Apple, Skype, or any of the other information-vacuuming enterprises reported to have, in some murky fashion, siphoned data—meta, big, or otherwise—to the NSA. Wall Street is betting this will hold. A blogger on the investment website Motley Fool noticed that on the day PRISM was unmasked, share prices for all the implicated corporate participants went up.

I f one wanted to identify the turning point when privacy stopped being a prized commodity in America, a good place to start would be with television and just before the turn of the century. The cultural revolution in programming that was cemented by the year 2000 presaged the devaluation of privacy that would explode with the arrival of Facebook and its peers a few years later.

What we now call reality television had been around since the dawn of the medium. Allen Funt's *Candid Camera* had its television debut in 1948 (and had been on radio before that as "Candid Microphone"). But the everyday Americans spied on in Funt's wholesome Peeping Tom pranks were caught by surprise; they didn't volunteer for public exposure. The

twelve-hour 1973 PBS mini-series *An American Family* (supported by funding from the Ford Foundation, no less) was a breakthrough because the troubled Louds of Santa Barbara willingly submitted to parading their travails in close-up on-camera. By the time MTV unveiled its series *The Real World* in 1992, the advent of video, digitalization, and compact cameras had made projects emulating *An American Family* much easier to produce in quantity and at greater length.

The Real World began as a somewhat earnest docu-soap of multicultural American youth wrestling with Real Issues. But by the end of the decade, sex and alcohol were being stirred profusely into the mix. In 2000, CBS took the genre a step further by airing an American adaptation of a Dutch television hit, *Big Brother,* in which occupants of a quarantined house are captured on camera 24/7, bathroom visits included, for three months as the participants are voted out one by one. Sure enough, the coinage Big Brother would soon become unmoored from George Orwell's vision of totalitarian terror and become known as the brand of a cheesy entertainment franchise hosted by Julie Chen. As it happened, *Big Brother*'s second-season contestants were isolated in their San Fernando Valley barracks on 9/11, and one of those contestants was the cousin of a missing Aon worker on the 90th floor of World Trade Center 2. After some debate over whether the house's inmates should even be told the news in real time, which would be a violation of the show's lab-rat rules, the young woman with a familial stake in the attacks was filled in. She chose to remain on-camera with her surrogate reality-television family (and audience) rather than return to her real family in New York, which was still waiting to learn that her cousin was dead.

Big Brother began its fifteenth season last week. We now know that it was merely a harbinger of what was to come. In 2000, it and *Survivor* (also on CBS) were novelties. In 2013, more than 300 reality shows are airing on a profusion of networks, including some that have revised their identities to accommodate them. (History, formerly known as the History Channel, is home to *Ax Men* and *Swamp People.*) That count does not include YouTube, where home productions can rival the biggest TV reality hits in audience. The 2011 video of 6-year-old Lily Clem's reaction to her birthday present, a trip to Disneyland, attracted 5 million viewers in just its first three weeks.

Reality television is not a showbiz fad but a national pastime whose participants are as diverse as America in terms of class, race, creed, and ethnicity. If redneck subjects are now the rage—*Here Comes Honey Boo Boo* outdrew Fox News coverage of the GOP convention in the prime 18–49 demographic—the desperate urban middle class is at the heart of shows like the Vegas-based smash *Pawn Stars* (another History hit). Though some participants cash in—the Robertson brood of *Duck Dynasty* has transformed an already prosperous rural Louisiana business selling duck calls into a multi-platform entertainment empire—money isn't the only motive. Many reality-show performers receive nominal pay, and the workplace protections afforded to union members usually don't apply. The Kardashians notwithstanding, the payoff in fame also can be slight, not even fifteen minutes' worth on the lower-rated shows. More often, exhibitionism is its own reward. Many Americans simply want to be seen, even in financial or psychological extremis, by as many of their fellow citizens as possible. That the government may also be watching—whether in pursuit of terrorism, ordinary criminality, immigration violations, employee malfeasance, tax evasion, or whatever—seems no deterrent.

The same risk of surveillance is taken by the many more Americans who bare their lives online, trading off privacy for speedier transactions, self-expression, and self-indulgence. With the notable exception of Anthony Weiner, few are naïve about that bargain. It's no surprise that 85 percent of the country thinks it is being snooped on: Uncannily precise recommendations of products, friends, and followers stalk our every keystroke on the web. Given that Facebook's members are more than three times as numerous as the American population, all of them linked to multiple networks that often have little or nothing to do with friendship, it's a no-brainer that the infinity of data will be trolled by outsiders, whether flesh-and-blood or algorithmic, and whether the motive be investigative, prurient, mercantile, masturbatory, altruistic, or criminal. And that trolling is so easy! As Evgeny Morozov has written in *The Net Delusion,* the 2006 German film *The Lives of Others* is a potent reminder of "how costly surveillance used to be" for a totalitarian state in the Cold War era: "Recording tape had to be bought, stored, and processed; bugs had to be installed one by one; Stasi officers had to spend days and nights on end glued to their headphones, waiting for their subjects to launch into an antigovernment tirade or inadvertently disclose other members of their network." Ah, the good old days of government surveillance, when the spies had to jump through exhausting hoops to do their dirty work.

Whatever the fine points of the NSA's snooping, anyone who cared could surmise enough of the big picture to be wary long before the Snowden leaks filled in graphic details. The NSA is crying wolf when it claims that his disclosures are an enormous boon to terrorists, unless you believe terrorists are morons. There have been NSA leakers before Snowden, and they provided plenty of connectable dots. A remarkable two-year *Washington Post* investigation published in 2010 found that as of then, some 854,000 Americans had top-secret clearances—nearly one and a half times the population of the nation's capital. Nearly a third were private contractors like Snowden. The *Post* also discovered that after 2001, intelligence agencies began building 33 new facilities in the Washington area alone, with a total square footage (17 million) almost equal to three times that of the Pentagon. What could all these people possibly be up to? What was all that space needed for?

In March 2012, James Bamford, for three decades the most authoritative journalist on the NSA beat, provided answers in a *Wired* cover story prompted by a clandestine $2 billion NSA data center under construction in Utah. "Flowing through its servers and routers and stored in near-bottomless databases will be all forms of communication, including the complete contents of private e-mails, cell-phone calls, and Google searches, as well as all sorts of personal data trails—parking receipts, travel itineraries, bookstore purchases, and other digital 'pocket litter,'" Bamford reported. Why? "The NSA has turned its surveillance apparatus on the U.S. and its citizens."

In fact, the prolific public clues about the NSA's intent also predate 9/11. In the Jerry Bruckheimer–Tony Scott movie *Enemy of the State* (1998), a fictional retired NSA officer played by Gene Hackman says, "The government's been in bed with the entire telecommunications business since the forties. They have infected everything. They can get into your bank statements, computer files, e-mail, listen to your phone calls." The NSA's then-director, Michael Hayden, was so concerned about this fictional leak that he tried to mount a PR offensive to counter it. Just a few months after that film's release, Sun Microsystems CEO Scott McNealy in essence confirmed it with his own famous dictum: "You have zero privacy anyway. Get over it."

And so we did learn to stop worrying and love the promiscuous use of Big Data by business and government. Mark Zuckerberg was telling the truth, even if to serve his own interests, when in 2010 he explained his rationale for the constant, incremental loosening of Facebook's dense and ever-changing privacy policies: "People have really gotten comfortable not only sharing more information and different kinds, but more openly and with more people." The Snowden leaks show that Facebook and PRISM had aligned six months earlier, and in 2010, as the *Times* recently discovered, the keeper of Facebook's secrets, its chief security officer, Max Kelly, defected to the NSA. But even as early as 2008, an internal memo at the U.S. Citizenship and Immigration Services had recommended that the agency's fraud office start exploiting social networks as an "excellent vantage point" for observing "the daily life of beneficiaries and petitioners" suspected of wrongdoing. The memo—cited by the public-interest lawyer Lori Andrews in her book *I Know Who You Are and I Saw What You Did*—was nothing if not prescient. Facebook was a gift to surveillance that would keep on giving, it argued, because the "narcissistic tendencies in many people fuels a need to have a large group of 'friends.'"

In the aftermath of the Snowden leaks, those who want to shut down dubious NSA programs have been hard pressed to come up with ways of getting that done. The ACLU is suing, and so are Rand Paul and Larry Klayman, the right-wing activist known for his quixotic legal battles against Bill Clinton in the nineties. Commentators at *The New Yorker* and *The New Republic* are calling for a national commission. Dianne Feinstein, the chair of the Senate Intelligence Committee and a fierce NSA defender, has proposed monthly hearings, presumably to bore the country into inertia. No doubt the Obama administration will toss out a few crumbs of transparency to satisfy its liberal base, but neither the president nor his party's leaders, exemplified by Feinstein, Harry Reid, and Nancy Pelosi, want change from the status quo. Neither would Hillary Clinton. The same is true of Republican leaders, despite their professed loathing of big-government overreach in Obamacare and at the IRS. That leaves Paul on the Republican side and the two Democratic Senate apostates, Mark Udall and Ron Wyden, who have been on the NSA's case for years. They have about as much of a chance of bringing change in 2013 as the former senator Russ Feingold did in his lonely opposition to the Patriot Act in 2001. Little short of a leak stating that the NSA is tracking gun ownership is likely to kindle public outrage.

Of course, there are some steps that ordinary Americans can take to cover their daily digital tracks and limit their vulnerability to snooping of all kinds. But there aren't many. In their new book, *Big Data,* Viktor Mayer-Schönberger and Kenneth Cukier observe that "in the era of big data, the three core strategies long used to ensure privacy—individual notice and consent, opting out, and anonymization—have lost much of their effectiveness." Their proposed workarounds are laudable—why not have "new principles by which we govern ourselves"?—but not exactly an action plan. Andrews calls for a new "Social Network Constitution" but for the short term points out that citizens of Facebook, the third-biggest nation in the world as measured by population, have "little recourse other than to leave the service." This would require asceticism on a mass scale unknown to modern America.

The easiest individual solutions for trying to protect one's privacy are the obvious ones. Quit social networks. Stop using a cell phone. Pay for everything in cash (but stop using ATMs). Abandon all Google apps, Amazon, eBay, Netflix, Apple's iTunes store, E-ZPass, GPS, and Skype. Encrypt your e-mail (which will require persuading your correspondents to encrypt, too). Filter (and handcuff) your web browser with anti-tracking software like Tor. Stop posting to YouTube and stop tweeting. As *Big Data* elucidates: "Twitter messages are limited to a sparse 140 characters, but the metadata—that is, the 'information about information'—associated with each tweet is rich. It includes 33 discrete items."

So vast a cultural sea change is beyond today's politics; it would require a national personality transplant. What the future is most likely to bring instead is more of the same: an ever-larger embrace of ever-more-brilliant toys and services that invite more prying from strangers, corporations, and government. No sooner had Snowden's leaks landed than Instagram, owned by Facebook, announced a new mobile service enabling its users to post their own brief reality-television-style video nuggets much as the equivalent Twitter service, Vine, already does. Soon to ship from Microsoft is a new Xbox game console requiring a device called Kinect, which, besides monitoring bodily motions, listens to users even when the console is turned off. It's unlikely that fanboys (and girls) will shun the new Xbox any more than they will disdain the intrusiveness of the much-awaited Google Glass. If anything, they'll fight to be first in line.

Civil libertarians can protest about how the government will track us on these devices, too, but as long as the public and the political Establishment of both parties remain indifferent, the prospect of substantial change is nil. The debate would be more honest, at least, if we acknowledge our own responsibility for our "choices as a society." Those who complain about the loss of privacy have an obligation to examine their own collaboration, whether by intent or apathy, in the decline and fall of the very concept of privacy. We can blame terrorists for many things that have happened since 9/11, but too many Americans cavalierly spilling TMI on too many porous public platforms is not one of them.

Critical Thinking

1. Support or refute the saying, "Spying is only spying when the subject doesn't want to be watched."

2. How would you feel about being secretly videotaped?

3. Why do/don't you use social networks such as Facebook, YouTube, and Twitter?

Create Central

www.mhhe.com/createcentral

Internet References

Evgeny Morozov's Net Delusion: Tangled Web
www.slate.com/articles/arts/books/2011/02/tangled_web.html

Social Media Plagued by Privacy Problems: YouTube
www.youtube.com/watch%3Fv%3BD21pOkx9SVQ

Trolling Effects Privacy Policy
https://trollingeffects.org/privacy

What Is Big Data?
www.sas.com/big-data

Article   Prepared by: Karen L. Freiberg, *University of Maryland*

The New Survivors

For over 11 million Americans, cancer is no longer a definite death sentence. The dreaded disease has instead become a crucible, often remaking personality and endowing survivors with qualities not even they knew they had.

PAMELA WEINTRAUB

Learning Outcomes

After reading this article, you will be able to:

- Examine how "learning to hope" can prolong the lives of cancer patients.

- Explain what is meant by post-traumatic growth and why it is reaped long after the trauma of cancer.

Jasan Zimmerman was 6 months old when he was diagnosed with neuroblastoma of the left neck in 1976. First the cancer was surgically removed, then he was treated with radiation. Perhaps it was exposure to all that radiation that caused the thyroid cancer when he was 15. More surgery, more radiation. But this time, old enough to grasp the situation, he was terrified. "I didn't want to die" recalls Zimmerman, who grit his teeth through the grueling treatment. Almost as difficult was the aftermath: Traumatized by the experience, he spent his teen years sullen and depressed, without quite knowing why.

He tried to put it all out of his mind—until cancer appeared for a third time in 1997. He was 21 and had just graduated from college. Again Zimmerman was successfully treated. He pursued life goals, including a master's degree in microbiology, but his inner turmoil remained.

The literature on survivorship indicates that between 30 and 90 percent of patients became hardier and more upbeat after the diagnosis of cancer was made.

For 11 more years, he went for checkups, always fearing a return of the dread disease. "I'd get road rage on the way to the doctor. Even the smell of clinical antiseptic could piss me off," he reports. Despite some scares, the cancer never came back, but living with his history itself became a burden. How soon into a new relationship would he need to confess his medical past? Would he ever be free of the threat? By 2003, he was so angry that he punched a wall and broke his hand.

Today, Zimmerman is able to turn his back on the ordeal. He's done it only by embracing his role as a survivor and speaking out to many of the 1.4 million Americans diagnosed with the disease each year. His message is about the ability to *overcome,* and he openly describes his own experience. "Each time I share my story people feel hopeful," he says. And he does, too. "I was living under a thundercloud. It's taken me decades to grow from the experience, but the ability to inspire people has turned a negative into a positive and opened me up."

In the past, the very word *cancer* summoned images of hopelessness, pain, and death; little thought was given to life after cancer because it was considered brief. The cancer "victim" was seen as the passive recipient of ill fate and terrible luck. No more.

Survivorship is increasingly common; some 11.4 million Americans are alive today after treatment and are ever more vocal about their experiences. Emboldened by effective diagnosis and treatment strategies, celebrities such as Melissa Etheridge and Fran Drescher have made public disclosure of the disease increasingly routine and the fight definitely important and profound. Tour de France champion Lance Armstrong, determined to train for the world-class athletic event on the heels of treatment for advanced testicular cancer, turned his achievement into advocacy through his LiveStrong movement.

Many cancer survivors are travelers to a highly intense edge world where they battle death and return transformed. They leave as ordinary and burdened mortals and come back empowered and invigorated. In coming closer to fear, risk, and death than most of us, they wind up marshaling qualities not even they knew they had.

As more patients have lived longer, a body of research on their experiences has developed. It demonstrates that many cancer patients muster enormous grit for highly aggressive treatments and endure considerable pain to accrue small gains in the fight for survival. Despite therapies that weaken them physically, they can be especially psychologically hardy, harnessing and growing from their stress. Even the most narrow-minded or inflexible people may come to love art, beauty, and philosophical truth as a way of getting through the ordeal. Those who survive often come out of the experience with bravery, curiosity, fairness, forgiveness, gratitude, humor, kindness, and an enhanced sense of meaning.

Is there something about cancer itself that is transformative and growth-inspiring? Do we literally need to face death to go beyond the often petty limits of our workaday lives? William Breitbart, chief of the psychiatry service at Memorial Sloan-Kettering Cancer Center in New York City and an international leader in psycho-ontology, says we just might.

"It is in our nature to transcend our limitations, but too often we get distracted by everyday life. If life is always smooth, we're never challenged," he says. "Suffering is probably necessary to make us grow." The ultimate tool may be a brush with death. "The need to find meaning is a primary force," adds Breitbart, himself a cancer survivor, "but we may need to be confronted with our own mortality for that to occur." In the school of hard knocks, cancer amounts to earning a PhD.

Learning to Hope

Carol Farran, an eldercare expert from Rush University Medical Center in Chicago, sought to understand why some nursing home residents thrived despite adversity and isolation while others just withered away. The difference between the two groups, she found, was hope—not the blind or rigid optimism that usually passes for hope, but an open sense of possibility, acceptance of risk, and a willingness to work things out. Hopeful people face reality in a clear-eyed fashion, doing the best they can. One woman too sick to go outdoors, for instance, maintained an upbeat attitude by remembering the emotional riches of her past. "The hopeful person looked at reality and then arrived at solutions. If a hoped-for outcome became impossible, the hopeful person would find something else to hope for," Farran found.

The role of hope in cancer has also come under scrutiny. Psychologists at the Royal Marsden Hospital in London and Sutton studied women with early-stage breast cancer and found that risk of recurrence or death increased significantly among those who lacked hope. There was nothing mysterious or mystical about it: Hopeful patients managed their illness themselves instead of letting outsiders pull the strings. They often chose the most aggressive treatments. And envisioning the light at the end of the tunnel helped provide the strength they needed to get through each difficult day.

Yet hope was not a given for them; it was an attitude they wrested from despair. Despite being an expert on hope, Farran could not muster any when she herself was diagnosed with breast cancer. She met the news with anger, grief, and fear of death. Panic propelled her through treatment, in a total daze. Only when she went in for breast reconstruction was a wise nurse able to penetrate her panic: "A year from now you'll be where you want to be, but there is no way to get there except by going through this experience, now."

As despair loosened its hold on Farran, she tried to embrace the flexibility she had studied in others. "I told myself to get a grip," she says. Finally she thought of her love of playing piano and decided to buy a metronome, a symbol of what she called "slow time." It was a palpable reminder to calm down, confront her fear of death, and think things through. "You can start in despair but arrive at hope," says Farran, 18 years later. Hope can be learned.

True Grit

Once empowered by hope, cancer patients have been known to search out cures in the face of daunting odds. Jerome Groopman, a Harvard cancer specialist and author of *Anatomy of Hope,* tells the story of a patient, a pathologist with advanced metastatic stomach cancer that was considered fatal. Soon word spread around the hospital that the pathologist intended to do something "mad." Without any evidence that his cancer was survivable, he insisted on doses of chemotherapy and radiation so toxic they were, by themselves, probably lethal. To Groopman and other cancer doctors on staff at the time, the effort seemed "like a desperate, wrongheaded, ultimately futile effort to resist the inevitable." Surely the treatment would deprive the pathologist of a peaceful end at home. Indeed, Groopman, stopping by the man's bedside, found him bleeding as tissues were literally burned away by the strong treatment he had engineered.

Twenty-five years later, while researching his book on hope, Groopman found that the pathologist was still going strong. "If I'd been treating him, I wouldn't have authorized the therapy and he would have died."

Similar tenacity gripped Sean Patrick, a business strategist and extreme sports enthusiast from Aspen, Colorado, whose rare form of ovarian cancer was diagnosed in 1998. Instead of simply agreeing to follow her doctor's treatment advice, she hired a research firm to comb the scientific literature and come up with a list of experts studying her specific disease. She quickly learned that her doctor had recommended the wrong treatment and if she followed through she might not survive the year.

So she fired her oncologist and hired a medical team known for experimental use of drugs. The side effects of her radical treatment were devastating. "Flu symptoms magnified a thousand times," Patrick said. There was nausea, vomiting, disabling body aches, extreme weakness, chills, and diarrhea. "I would shake so hard my teeth would knock and then have a fever so high I would sweat through my clothes." She nicknamed the side effects "shake and bake." Still, she persisted, at one point even electing a surgery so risky she was not expected to wake up. "If I hadn't taken the risk, I wouldn't be here today," she said in 2006. Her grit gave her a full decade more than anyone expected; she died just before this article went to press, in 2009.

Most people don't have the financial resources to seek such customized or experimental options, but even patients dependent on treatment approvals by an insurance company can choose the most aggressive courses that might confer even a slight survival edge. That explains why so many women with stage-one breast cancer opt for removal of both breasts instead of the watch-and-wait approach. It also explains why ovarian cancer patients subject themselves to multiple rounds of chemotherapy, often rejecting studies contending the treatment will fail.

"Even if it is a long shot, someone is going to fall at the end of the bell curve," notes Groopman.

Soldiering On

Research shows that, even while dealing with the disease, large numbers of cancer patients deploy their tenacity in other realms of life, as well. Take Elizabeth Cowie, 44, a career sergeant in the Army who was headed to Iraq with her troops. There was only one problem: Months before deployment, in a routine Army physical, Cowie was diagnosed with early-stage breast cancer. Instead of going home to attend to treatment, Cowie poured her energy into finding a way to get to Iraq along with the soldiers she'd trained. She forsook the more extreme course of mastectomy for circumscribed lumpectomy, dramatically shortening surgical recovery, and decided against weeks of radiation therapy in favor of a new technique she learned of, called Mammasite, which delivers radiation directly to the tumor over the course of days. She underwent the procedures quietly, without telling the soldiers reporting to her until she was declared cancer-free, and went on with her deployment, gritting her teeth only when her vest chafed the still-healing surgical wound. Cowie endured the heat of Iraq while still recovering, all the while watching over and counseling the soldiers she'd become so close to.

"There were days I was so sore and the heat was so oppressive and it was so exhausting," Cowie recalls. "But I had a commitment to the people I was with. The soldiers counted on me being there. Just knowing that made me stronger, and I couldn't let them down. I put one foot in front of the other; that is how I saw my mission through."

Cowie's can-do attitude is a trait common among the new survivors. According to University of Utah psychologist Lisa Aspinwall, a sense of purpose and positivity is adaptive in cancer's midst. In reviewing the literature on survivorship, Aspinwall found that 30 to 90 percent of patients reported benefits, from increased optimism to better relationships, *after* diagnosis was made. At first it seemed counterintuitive. But the positive, active mind-set "is likely to help patients manage what they need to do next," she explains. "Those in treatment must make dozens of decisions. To hold things together, you need to pay attention to options. Just think about it—negative emotions orient us to threats, but they also narrow our attention. That's not the best state for navigating a complex and changing situation, just what cancer is."

Post-Traumatic Growth

The benefits seen during the trauma, however, may pale against those reaped later, after survivors have had the chance to reflect. "It's hard to grow much when you are in the middle of a war," says psychologist Lad Wenzel of the University of California at Irvine, who works with women surviving gynecologic cancer at least five years. "Instead, strength and meaning unfold for survivors as they retell their stories, again and again."

There is nothing mystical about the power of hope. Hopeful patients managed their own illness instead of letting outsiders do it. They often chose the most aggressive treatments.

University of Connecticut psychologist Keith Bellizzi says the life event is so intense that some people use it to reconstruct their lives; they don't return to the same level of functioning but to a greater level. "Post-traumatic growth is above and beyond resilience," he says. "Life after cancer means finding a new normal, but for many the new normal is better than the old normal."

Bellizzi, 39, speaks from direct experience. He was a well-paid marketing professional when, at age 25, he was diagnosed with stage-three testicular cancer so advanced it had spread to his lymph nodes and lungs. A few months later, a CAT scan revealed a golf-ball-size mass in his kidney. Almost as upsetting as the cancer was the news that he might never have biological children of his own. "It was an opportunity to reflect on my life and face my mortality," says Bellizzi.

Following several surgeries, including removal of a kidney, along with aggressive chemotherapy, he made a vow: "If I survived, I would dedicate my life to the fight against cancer." Bellizzi kept his vow. He quit his lucrative job and went back to school, earning masters degrees in public health and in psychology and a PhD in human development and family studies. In 2005, he was one of 24 cyclists chosen to ride with Lance Armstrong on the Bristol-Myers Squibb Tour of Hope to heighten awareness of cancer research. He also has three daughters—and is a leading researcher in the field of post-traumatic growth.

Bellizzi's sense of purpose is just one type of growth that survivors report. Julia Rowland, head of the Office of Cancer Survivorship at the National Cancer Institute, points to enhanced and altered relationships. "You learn who's going to be there for you and who is not—you learn who your friends are," she says. Some friends, upset by the prospect of loss, may detach temporarily or even permanently. As some friendships fade, others may be forged, especially within the community of survivors. "You also learn to empathize," says Rowland, explaining how survivors acquire new depths of feeling.

Pleasures become more meaningful, too. As a team at the University of Pennsylvania found, those suffering chronic illness end up more immersed in art, music, and books. "Appreciation is often enhanced," points out Bellizzi. Many survivors literally stop to smell the roses even if they didn't before.

Not everyone diagnosed with cancer finds a new sense of purpose. "Some people have a glimpse of the possibilities but do not change. Cancer is just wasted on them."

The sense of self is often enhanced too. "Some survivors discover an inner strength they didn't realize they had," says Bellizzi. "A situation that might have seemed daunting before cancer may, after cancer, seem like something easily handled."

In one important study, Bellizzi looked at generativity—concerns, often arising at midlife, about the legacy one is likely to leave behind. Generativity can be expressed in many ways—making the planet a better place, giving children the love they need, being creative in work or intimate with family and friends. Midlifers surveying the past may vow to do more with the time they have left. But no matter an individual's age, Bellizzi found, cancer was a catalyst for generativity.

While cancer generally sparked more generativity in women than in men, all the survivors Bellizzi studied were more likely than those without cancer to forge a new life path reflecting their core values. Those reporting the most altered perspective "expressed an increased awareness of the fragility of life and the value of loved ones," he reports. "They also said they had learned not to worry about little annoyances." A patient with colorectal cancer said her disease had convinced her to put an end to meaningless pursuits; she resigned from her management position and spent time with her friends.

A Spiritual Dimension

Cancer can also promote a sense of inner meaning and add a spiritual dimension to life. Lisa Benaron, an internist and pediatrician from Chico, California, learned she had cancer in the midst of other traumas. Her sister-in-law, a dear friend, had just died of breast cancer. And her marriage was falling apart. Six months after her sister-in-law died, Benaron, too, was diagnosed with breast cancer. Although in stage one, her cancer was a particularly aggressive kind; further, she had the gene that signals ongoing risk.

Energized by her situation, Benaron focused on researching the best treatment options and chose the most aggressive course, to gain a few points of survival advantage. The chemo was debilitating, but she still recalls fondly the days after those sessions. They were, she insists, "great times. I didn't usually get enough time off to garden, or do yoga." She did then.

She made an effort to pursue the things she loved: kayaking, walks in nature, spending time with her daughter, Molly, then 7. "I took Molly to the Galapagos Islands on Easter break in 2004," Benaron recalls. "You could sit on the beach and the seals and iguanas would be right there within arms reach. Having cancer made me aware of how fortunate I was and how much beauty was in the world."

Her own journey wasn't complete, though, until a friend she met in the local cancer community, Theresa Marcis, sought her help to travel to Abadiania, Brazil, to see a healer named John of God. "When she was first diagnosed, Theresa had a large mass and stage-three cancer; the prognosis wasn't good," says Benaron. "But she was full of hope. She wrote the word HEAL in big burgundy letters on her kitchen walls."

Under ordinary circumstances, the logical, driven doctor would have had little in common with the free-spirited Marcis, a college English teacher. But under the influence of cancer, they became a team. Benaron helped Marcis navigate the mainstream medical minefield, and Marcis exposed Benaron to acupuncture, sound therapy, and other alternative techniques. "They were enjoyable and peaceful," Benaron recalls.

In 2008, doctors found that Marcis's cancer had spread to every bone in her body. Instead of conceding defeat, she journeyed with a colleague to Brazil to see John of God. Though her condition later worsened, she spoke of going back. When she was too sick to travel, Benaron went in her stead, "to give Theresa peace."

Still very much the logical physician, Benaron doesn't believe that John's interventions can cure. But she loved taking the trip as proxy for her gentle friend, who died hoping that John's powers would stretch from central Brazil to her home in California. "I came to realize through her that every person has their own path through life; she tapped into every good feeling within herself and threw herself into being spiritual. It helped me to see the importance of love and openness to others," Benaron says.

The California physician remembers meditating in Abadiania with a huge thunderstorm whipping up around her. "It was this gorgeous experience," she reports. "But I realized I didn't have to go across the world or down a dirt road to find it. You can be in the moment wherever you are."

Tyranny vs. Transformation

The idea that cancer can be uplifting or transformative has become controversial in the cancer community itself. Posttraumatic growth, while common, does not define all survivors. Young people, whose disease may be more challenging, often grow more emotionally from the experience than older people. "It's very disruptive to have cancer while raising your family and climbing in your career," explains Bellizzi, "and it's the intensity of the experience and the realization that life is finite that forges change."

Not everyone diagnosed with cancer transcends the past, finds a new sense of purpose, or becomes more spiritual. And in the midst of a deadly disease, the pressure to remake oneself can feel harsh. "It's wrong to pressure people to be optimistic or change their lives," says Utah's Lisa Aspinwall.

"Some will not be able to take advantage of having had cancer," says Breitbart of Memorial Sloan-Kettering. "Some people with poor prognoses just want to hasten death. Some have a glimpse of the possibilities but do not change. Cancer is just wasted on some people."

Still, cancer patients have undeniably entered a new era in which long lives are very much a reality, and they are changed by having looked death in the eye and beaten it back. The experience has made them stronger and forced them to reevaluate the very foundations of their lives. "The bottom line for me is I finally realized that I want to turn the negative experiences of having cancer into a positive," says Jasan Zimmerman, "and the more I do, the more I want to do. I don't want to miss out on anything."

Critical Thinking

1. Paraphrase the following: "Suffering is necessary to make us grow."
2. Label some of the qualities "discovered" by people with cancer.
3. Relate how a battle with death can transform a person.

Create Central

www.mhhe.com/createcentral

Internet References

Connect with Spiritual Side on Cancer Journey
   www.mayoclinic.org/health/cancer-and-spirituality/MY02026

The Power of Hope: Reading between the (Head) Lines
   www.psychologytoday.com/blog/reading-between-the-headlines/201307/the-power-hope

The Transformative Effects of Illness
   www.ncbi.nlm.nih.gov/pubmed/9362651

PAMELA WEINTRAUB is a writer in New York.

Article   Prepared by: Karen L. Freiberg, *University of Maryland*

How to Fix the Obesity Crisis

Although science has revealed a lot about metabolic processes that influence our weight, the key to success may lie elsewhere.

DAVID H. FREEDMAN

Learning Outcomes

After reading this article, you will be able to:

- Generate a plan to deal with the behavioral issues of obesity.

- Explain why mass-market programs tend to fall short when it comes to maintaining weight loss.

O besity is a national health crisis—that much we know. If current trends continue, it will soon surpass smoking in the U.S. as the biggest single factor in early death, reduced quality of life and added health care costs. A third of adults in the U.S. are obese, according to the Centers for Disease Control and Prevention, and another third are overweight, with Americans getting fatter every year. Obesity is responsible for more than 160,000 "excess" deaths a year, according to a study in the *Journal of the American Medical Association*. The average obese person costs society more than $7,000 a year in lost productivity and added medical treatment, say researchers at George Washington University. Lifetime added medical costs alone for a person 70 pounds or more overweight amount to as much as $30,000, depending on race and gender.

All this lends urgency to the question: Why are extra pounds so difficult to shed and keep off? It doesn't seem as though it should be so hard. The basic formula for weight loss is simple and widely known: consume fewer calories than you expend. And yet if it really were easy, obesity would not be the nation's number-one lifestyle-related health concern. For a species that evolved to consume energy-dense foods in an environment where famine was a constant threat, losing weight and staying trimmer in a modern world of plenty fueled by marketing messages and cheap empty calories is, in fact, terrifically difficult. Almost everybody who tries to diet seems to fail in the long run—a review in 2007 by the American Psychological Association of 31 diet studies found that as many as two thirds of dieters end up two years later weighing more than they did before their diet.

Science has trained its big guns on the problem. The National Institutes of Health has been spending nearly $800 million a year on studies to understand the metabolic, genetic and neurological foundations of obesity. In its proposed plan for obesity research funding in 2011, the NIH lists promising research avenues in this order: animal models highlighting protein functions in specific tissues; complex signaling pathways in the brain and between the brain and other organs; identification of obesity-related gene variants; and epigenetic mechanisms regulating metabolism.

This research has provided important insights into the ways proteins interact in our body to extract and distribute energy from food and produce and store fat; how our brains tell us we are hungry; why some of us seem to have been born more likely to be obese than others; and whether exposure to certain foods and toxic substances might modify and mitigate some of these factors. The work has also given pharmaceutical companies numerous potential targets for drug development. What the research has not done, unfortunately, is make a dent in solving the national epidemic.

Maybe someday biology will provide us with a pill that readjusts our metabolism so we burn more calories or resets our built-in cravings so we prefer broccoli to burgers. But until then, the best approach may simply be to build on reliable behavioral-psychology methods developed over 50 years and proved to work in hundreds of studies. These tried-and-true techniques, which are being refined with new research that should make them more effective with a wider range of individuals, are gaining new attention. As the NIH puts it in its proposed strategic plan for obesity research: "Research findings are yielding new and important insights about social and behavioral factors that influence diet, physical activity, and sedentary behavior."

How We Got Here

The desperation of the obese and overweight is reflected in the steady stream of advice pouring daily from sources as disparate as peer-reviewed scientific journals, best-selling books, newspapers and blogs. Our appetite for any diet twist or gimmick that will take the pounds off quickly and for good seems to be as insatiable as our appetite for the rich food that puts the pounds on. We, the public, love to believe in neat fixes, and the media oblige by playing up new scientific findings in headline after headline as if they are solutions.

It doesn't help that the scientific findings on which these headlines are based sometimes appear to conflict. For example, a study in September's *American Journal of Clinical Nutrition* found a link between increased dairy intake and weight loss, although a meta-analysis in the May 2008 *Nutrition Reviews* discovered no such link. A paper in the *Journal of Occupational and Environmental Medicine* in January 2010 postulated a connection between job stress and obesity, but in October a report in the journal *Obesity* concluded there was no such correlation. Part of the problem, too, is that obesity researchers are in some ways akin to the metaphorical blind men groping at different parts of the elephant, their individual study findings addressing only narrow pieces of a complex puzzle.

When the research is taken together, it is clear that the obesity fix cannot be boiled down to eating this or that food type or to taking any other simple action. Many factors contribute to the problem. It is partly environment—the eating habits of your friends, what food is most available in your home and your local stores, how much opportunity you have to move around at work. It is partly biology—there are genetic predispositions for storing fat, for having higher satiety thresholds, even for having more sensitive taste buds. It is partly economics—junk food has become much cheaper than fresh produce. And it is marketing, too—food companies have become masterful at playing on human social nature and our evolutionary "programming" to steer us toward unhealthy but profitable fare. That is why the narrow "eat this" kinds of solutions, like all simple solutions, fail.

When we go on diets and exercise regimens, we rely on willpower to overcome all these pushes to overeat relative to our activity level. And we count on the reward of getting trimmer and fitter to keep us on the wagon. It *is* rewarding to lose the weight, of course. Unfortunately, time works against us. As the weight comes off, we get hungrier and develop stronger cravings and become more annoyed by the exercise. Meanwhile the weight loss inevitably slows as our metabolism tries to compensate for this deprivation by becoming more parsimonious with calories. Thus, the punishment for sticking to our regimen becomes increasingly severe and constant, and the expected reward recedes into the future. "That gap between the reinforcement of eating and the reinforcement of maybe losing weight months later is a huge challenge," says Sung-Woo Kahng, a neurobehaviorist who studies obesity at the Johns Hopkins University School of Medicine and the Kennedy Krieger Institute.

We would be more likely to stick with the regimen if it remained less punishing and more reliably rewarding. Is there a way to make that happen?

From Biology to Brain

The most successful way to date to lose at least modest amounts of weight and keep it off with diet and exercise employs programs that focus on changing behavior. The behavioral

---

Advances in the Lab

The Biology of Obesity

The National Institutes of Health has spent nearly $800 million a year on studies to understand the neurological, metabolic and genetic foundations of obesity. In the process, scientists have uncovered complex biochemical pathways and feedback loops that connect the brain and digestive system; a new appreciation for the regulatory functions of fat tissues; subtle hereditary changes that make some groups more prone to obesity than others; and the strong possibility that exposure to certain foods and toxic substances might modify and mitigate some of these factors. Given that it will likely take decades to understand the various causes of obesity, more surprises are no doubt in store.

Brain: Scientists have long known that the hypothalamus and brain stem help to regulate feelings of hunger and fullness. Over the past several years researchers have found that the pleasure-reward centers of the limbic system and the evaluating functions of the prefrontal cortex are also heavily involved. Indeed, chronic overeating bears biochemical similarities to drug addiction.

Metabolism: The ability to burn and store energy varies greatly from cell to cell. In 2009 three studies in the *New England Journal of Medicine* demonstrated that at least some women and men continue to benefit well into adulthood from small stores of brown fat, which, unlike white fat, is associated with being lean. Brown fat helps to generate heat and is apparently more closely related to muscle than to white fat, whose primary purpose is to store excess energy.

Genes: Researchers have confirmed variations in 20-odd genes that predispose people to gaining weight easily. But further investigation shows that the effects are modest at best and cannot account for the current obesity epidemic. Genes may still play a role, however, through the environment's influence on which ones get turned on or off. So far most such genetic switches for obesity have been identified in mice, although a few likely human candidates are known.

---

approach, tested over decades, involves making many small, sustainable adjustments in eating and exercise habits that are prompted and encouraged by the people and the rest of the environment around us.

The research in support of behavioral weight-loss approaches extends back more than half a century to Harvard University psychologist B. F. Skinner's development of the science of behavioral analysis. The field is founded on the notion that scientists cannot really know what is going on inside a person's brain—after all, even functional MRIs, the state of the art for peering into the mind, are crude, highly interpretable proxies for cognition and emotion that reduce the detailed firing of billions of neurons in complex circuits to a few blobs of color. But researchers can objectively and reproducibly observe and measure physical behavior and the immediate environment in which the behavior occurs, allowing them to identify links between environment and behavior. That typically includes trying to spot events or situations that may be prompting or triggering certain behaviors and noting what may be rewarding and thus reinforcing of some behaviors or punishing and thus inhibiting of others.

The effectiveness of behavioral interventions has been extensively documented for a wide variety of disorders and problem behaviors. A 2009 meta-analysis in the *Journal of Clinical Child & Adolescent Psychology* concluded that "early intensive behavioral intervention should be an intervention of choice for children with autism." A systematic review sponsored by the U.S. Preventive Services Task Force found that even brief behavioral counseling interventions reduced the number of drinks taken by problem drinkers by 13 to 34 percent for as long as four years. Review studies have found similar behavioral-intervention successes in challenges as diverse as reducing stuttering, increasing athletic performance and improving employee productivity.

To combat obesity, behavioral analysts examine related environmental influences: Which external factors prompt people to overeat or to eat junk food, and which tend to encourage healthful eating? In what situations are the behaviors and comments of others affecting unhealthful eating? What seems to effectively reward eating healthfully over the long term? What reinforces being active? Behavior-focused studies of obesity and diets as early as the 1960s recognized some basic conditions that seemed correlated with a greater chance of losing weight and keeping it off: rigorously measuring and recording calories, exercise and weight; making modest, gradual changes rather than severe ones; eating balanced diets that go easy on fats and sugar rather than dropping major food groups; setting clear, modest goals; focusing on lifelong habits rather than short-term diets; and especially attending groups where dieters could receive encouragement to stick with their efforts and praise for having done so.

If these strategies today sound like well-worn, commonsense advice, it is because they have been popularized for nearly half a century by Weight Watchers. Founded in 1963 to provide support groups for dieters, Weight Watchers added other approaches and advice in keeping with the findings of behavioral studies and used to bill itself as a "behavior-modification" program. "Whatever the details are of how you lose weight, the magic in the sauce is always going to be changing behavior," says nutrition researcher and Weight Watchers chief science officer Karen Miller-Kovach. "Doing that is a learnable skill."

Studies back the behavioral approach to weight loss. A 2003 review commissioned by the U.S. Department of Health and Human Services found that "counseling and behavioral interventions showed small to moderate degrees of weight loss sustained over at least one year"—a year being an eon in the world of weight loss. An analysis of eight popular weight-loss programs published in 2005 in the *Annals of Internal*

Medicine found Weight Watchers (at that time in its pre-2010 points-overhaul incarnation) to be the only effective program, enabling a 3 percent maintained body-weight loss for the two years of the study. Meanwhile a 2005 *JAMA* study found that Weight Watchers, along with the Zone diet (which, like Weight Watchers, recommends a balanced diet of protein, carbohydrates and fat), achieved the highest percentage (65 percent) of one-year diet adherence of several popular diets, noting that "adherence level rather than diet type was the key determinant of clinical benefits." A 2010 study in the *Journal of Pediatrics* found that after one year children receiving behavioral therapy maintained a body mass index that was 1.9 to 3.3 lower than children who did not. (BMI is a numerical height-weight relation in which 18.5 is held to be borderline underweight and 25 borderline overweight.) The *Pediatrics* report noted that "more limited evidence suggests that these improvements can be maintained over the 12 months after the end of treatments." A 2010 study in *Obesity* found that continuing members of Take Off Pounds Sensibly (TOPS), a national, nonprofit behaviorally focused weight-loss organization, maintained a weight loss of 5 to 7 percent of their body weight for the three years of the investigation. The UK's Medical Research Council last year declared that its own long-term study had shown that programs based on behavioral principles are more likely to help people take and keep the weight off than other approaches. (The study was funded by Weight Watchers, but without its participation.)

Mass-market programs tend to fall short when it comes to enlisting a full range of behavioral techniques and customizing them to meet the varied needs of individuals.

But Weight Watchers and other mass-market programs tend to fall short when it comes to enlisting a full range of behavioral techniques and customizing them to meet the varied needs of individuals. They cannot routinely provide individual counseling, adapt their advice to specific challenges, assess environmental factors in a member's home, workplace or community, provide much outreach to members who do not come to meetings, or prevent their members from shooting for fast, dramatic, short-term weight loss or from restricting food groups. As a for-profit company, Weight Watchers sometimes even mildly panders to these self-defeating notions in its marketing. "Some people join us to drop 10 pounds for a high school reunion," says Weight Watchers's Miller-Kovach. "They achieve that goal, then stop coming."

To close that gap, a number of researchers have turned their attention in recent years to improving, expanding and tailoring behavioral techniques, with encouraging results. For example, Michael Cameron, head of the graduate behavioral analysis department at Simmons College and a faculty member at Harvard Medical School, is now focusing his research on behavioral weight-loss techniques. He is one year into a four-person study—behavioral analysts generally do very small group or even single-subject studies to more closely tailor the intervention and observe individual effects—in which the subjects meet together with him via online videoconferencing for reinforcement, weigh themselves on scales that transmit results via wireless networks, and have their diets optimized to both reduce caloric density and address individual food preferences. Favorite foods are used as a reward for exercise. So far the subjects have lost between 8 and 20 percent of their body weight.

Matt Normand, a behavioral analyst at the University of the Pacific, has focused on finding ways to more precisely track subjects' calorie intake and expenditure by, for example, collecting receipts for food purchases, providing food checklists to record what is eaten, and enlisting various types of pedometers and other devices for measuring physical activity. He then provides participants with daily detailed accounts of their calorie flow and in one published study showed three of four subjects reduced calorie intake to recommended levels. Richard Fleming, a researcher at the University of Massachusetts Medical School's Shriver Center, has in *Obesity* looked at ways to encourage parents to steer their children to healthier choices. He has found, among other techniques, that showing parents in person what appropriate serving sizes of foods look like on plates is helpful. Another successful Fleming trick: letting children pick out a small treat at a food store—as long as they walk there. "Kids can really respond to that reward for being active," he says.

Our environment is one in which ubiquitous, sophisticated marketing efforts prey on our need for sensory gratification as well as our vulnerability to misinformation.

Why are behavioral interventions effective? Laurette Dubé, a lifestyle psychology and marketing researcher at McGill University's Faculty of Management, notes that our environment is currently one in which ubiquitous, sophisticated marketing efforts prey on our need for sensory gratification as well as our vulnerability to misinformation. In addition, the poor eating and exercise habits we observe in our friends, family and colleagues encourage us to follow suit. In essence, behavioral interventions seek to reconfigure this environment into one in which our needs for information, gratification and social encouragement are tapped to pull us toward healthy food and exercise choices rather than away from them. "When we are getting the right messages in enough ways, we have a better chance of resisting the urge to eat more than we need," Dubé says.

Changing Policy

There is no one-size-fits-all solution, behavioral or otherwise, to the problem of obesity. But although behavioral interventions work best when they are customized to individuals, mass-market behavioral approaches such as Weight Watchers

What Works?

Four Steps to Losing Weight

Behavior-focused studies of obesity and diets have identified some basic conditions that seem correlated with a greater chance of losing weight and keeping it off: setting clear, modest goals and focusing on lifelong habits, among others. Most of these behavior changes fall into four main categories.

Initial Assessment

Research underscores the need to determine baseline measurements. How much does an individual weigh? What rituals and routines contribute to overeating (eating under stress) or underexercising (unrealistic expectations)? A physician, a nurse practitioner or a nutrition counselor can help with the assessment.

Behavior Shifts

Many people find it is easier to make small changes at first—such as taking the stairs instead of an elevator. Studies show that surveying the entire buffet before serving themselves will help people put less food on their plate.

Self-Monitoring

Recording body weight, counting the calories eaten and logging steps taken provide objective feedback on how well individuals are changing their habits. Behavior studies have found both low-tech paper logs and wireless monitoring systems to be of benefit.

Support Groups

Studies document the benefits of encouragement by others. Being part of a group—whether an exercise group, a formal support group or even a virtual group—lets participants share triumphs, bemoan setbacks and strategize solutions.

and TOPS are at least fairly effective. Why don't more people lose weight with them? The main reason is that people simply do not sign up for them, often because would-be weight losers are chasing fad diets or supplements or have read that obesity is locked into our genes. Weight Watchers, by far the most popular behavioral weight-loss program, counts only 600,000 meeting-attending members in its ranks in North America. That means that fewer than one out of 100 obese people in the U.S. and about one out of 200 overweight people are part of a formal behavioral-modification program.

Public policy may be changing, however. The U.S. Surgeon General's office and the CDC have both publicly lined up behind behavioral approaches as the main weapon in what is becoming a war on obesity. First Lady Michelle Obama's high-profile Let's Move campaign against childhood obesity consists almost entirely of behavioral weight-loss wisdom—that is, find ways to encourage children to eat less-calorie-dense foods, to become more active, and to enjoy doing it. The recent proposed ban of toys in Happy Meals in San Francisco suggests that more officials may be getting ready to pressure the food industry into easing up on contaminating the environment with what are essentially obesity-supportive marketing tactics. To make it easier and more tempting to buy healthier food in poorer, disproportionately overweight communities, the White House has proposed subsidizing the costs of fruits and vegetables. Approaching the problem from the other direction, New York City Mayor Michael Bloomberg is among those who have advocated modifying food-assistance programs to restrict the purchase of high-sugar beverages, and last year Washington, D.C., enacted a 6 percent tax on sugary drinks. New York City has also offered vouchers for buying produce at farmers' markets to low-income families and incentives to stores to offer healthier fare.

Some experts are trying to push the government to rewrite zoning and building codes to ensure that neighborhoods and buildings become friendlier to walkers, bikers and stair climbers. A 2009 study by researchers at Louisiana State University Medical School found that a mere 2.8 percent increase in a person's stair usage alone would keep off almost a pound a year. "The correlation between activity levels and healthy weight is one of the best-established ones in all of obesity research," says William M. Hartman, a psychologist and director of the behavioral program of the highly regarded Weight Management Program of the California Pacific Medical Center in San Francisco.

Increasing access to behavior therapy would help, too. Many overweight people might only need online behavioral monitoring, support and progress-sharing tools, which have proved moderately effective in studies. Others may need much more intensive, more personal interventions of the kind Cameron is developing. Given that obesity especially plagues the economically disadvantaged, fees for these programs may have to be heavily subsidized by the government and health care insurers. A weekly session with a behavioral therapist costing $50 would amount to $2,500 a year, or a bit more than a third of the $7,000 per year societal and medical costs of obesity—and the sessions might only be needed for a year or two to establish new, permanent eating and exercise habits, whereas the savings would continue on for a lifetime.

It is too soon to say whether the public will accept government efforts to push it toward healthier choices. In San Francisco, a community known to be especially friendly to public health initiatives, the plan to ban Happy Meals has provoked angry reactions, and Mayor Gavin Newsom vetoed it. Efforts by Let's Move to bring healthier food to school cafeterias have been intensely criticized by some as overly intrusive. Even if these efforts are eventually fully implemented nationwide, there is no way of being sure they will significantly reduce obesity.

The current rate of obesity is far beyond any ever seen before on the planet, and thus a large-scale solution will necessarily be an experiment in mass behavior change. But the research suggests that such a grand experiment would be our best shot at fixing obesity and that there is reason to be hopeful it will succeed. Given that more and more scientists, public policy experts and government officials seem eager to get it off the ground, we may well have early findings within this decade.

More to Explore

About Behaviorism. B. F. Skinner. Vintage, 1974. A classic in behavior modification. You on a Diet: The Owner's Manual for Waist Management. Michael F. Roizen and Mehmet C. Oz. Free Press, 2006. Good layperson's guide to various aspects of weight management.

Determining the Effectiveness of Take Off Pounds Sensibly (TOPS), a Nationally Available Nonprofit Weight Loss Program. Nia S. Mitchell et al., in *Obesity*. Published online September 23, 2010. www.nature.com/oby/journal/vaop/ncurrent/full/oby2010202a.html.

The entry portal to the range of NIH research on obesity: obesityresearch.nih.gov.

Critical Thinking

1. What percentage of Americans are obese? What percentage are overweight? What percentage are normal weight or underweight?

2. What health risks are associated with obesity?

3. Which is a bigger reason for obesity: biology or lifestyle choices?

4. Why is behavior theory effective for many dieters?

Create Central

www.mhhe.com/createcentral

Internet References

Beyond the "i" in the Obesity Epidemic
www.mcgill.ca/desautels/channels/news/beyond-i-obesity

Boston Nutrition Obesity Research Center
http://bnorc.org

Determining the Effectiveness of Take Off Pounds Sensibly (TOPS)
www.nature.com/oby/journal/vaop/ncurrent/full/oby

Learn the Facts/Let's Move
www.letsmove.gov/learn-facts/epidemic-obesity

NIH Research on Obesity
www.obesityresearch.nih.gov

DAVID H. FREEDMAN has been covering science, business and technology for 30 years. His most recent book, *Wrong*, explores the forces that lead scientists and other top experts to mislead us.

Article   Prepared by: Karen L. Freiberg, *University of Maryland*

Brutal Truths about the Aging Brain

A graying world will have more of the experience that comes with age. It will also be slower, fuzzier, more forgetful, and just a bit hard of hearing.

ROBERT EPSTEIN

Learning Outcomes

After reading this article, you will be able to:

- Describe the four cognitive systems that tend to decline with age.

- Explain why it is easier for elders to remember things from their 20s than from a month ago.

As a graduate student at Harvard University, I worked with one of the most influential behavioral scientists of all time, B. F. Skinner. Beginning in the summer of 1977, we worked together nearly every day for more than four years, designing experiments and chatting about literature, philosophy, and the latest research. Although we were 50 years apart in age, we were also friends. We saw *Star Wars* together, had lunch frequently in Harvard Square, and swam in his backyard pool each summer. "Fred" (from Burrhus Frederic) Skinner was the happiest, most creative, most productive person I have ever known. He was also, needless to say, quite smart.

But the septuagenarian I knew was well past his intellectual peak. One day he gave me a set of tapes of a famous debate he had had with psychologist Carl Rogers in 1962. The Skinner on those tapes seemed sharper, faster, and even wittier than the man I knew. Was I imagining this?

Recently, Gina Kirkish, a student at the University of California, San Diego, and I analyzed tapes of three comparable samples of Skinner's speech: that 1962 debate, a 1977 debate, and a speech he gave from notes shortly before he died in 1990 at age 86. We found that the speech rate dropped significantly over time, from 148 words per minute in the first sample to 137 in the second to 106 in the third—an overall decrease of more than 28 percent.

Skinner's memory and analytical skills were also declining during the years when I knew him. Sometimes he had no recollection of a conversation we had had only days before. When I tried to talk with him about technical papers he had published early in his career, he often didn't seem to understand what he had written. And he had no patience for anything mathematical, even his own equations. On the other hand, Skinner was still much smarter than most of the people I knew my own age. When you fall from a high enough cliff, you remain far above ground for a very long time.

The sad truth is that even normal aging has a devastating effect on our ability to learn and remember, on the speed with which we process information, and on our ability to reason. Recent studies suggest that the total loss in brain volume due to atrophy—a wasting away of tissue caused by cell degeneration—between our teen years and old age is 15 percent or more, which means that by the time we're in our seventies, our brains have shrunk to the size they were when we were between 2 and 3 years old. Unfortunately, most of the loss is in gray matter, the critically important part of the brain composed of neurons, the cells that transmit the signals that keep us breathing and thinking.

Contrary to what scientists long believed, only about 10 percent of our neurons die during adulthood. The real loss is in the network of connections—the "dendritic trees" that allow a single neuron to be connected to a thousand others. Over the years, 25 percent or more of this network disappears. According to William Jagust, a neuroscientist at the University of California, Berkeley, adults are also losing dopamine, a critical neurotransmitter (the type of chemical involved in transmitting signals between neurons), at the rate of 5 to 8 percent per decade. "By age 80," Jagust says, "you've lost 40 percent or so of dopamine function. When you think about it, it's remarkable that old people can do so well."

Shrinkage, dopamine depletion, and lost dendritic connections are not the only problems facing the aging brain. Myelin, a substance that insulates neurons, deteriorates, and the number of nerve fibers that carry messages throughout the central nervous system also decreases. Chemical problems—such as an increase in calcium conductance, which might impair neuronal communication—also become more common in older brains, as do problems with gene expression and protein production.

With the global population of people over 80 expected to more than quadruple to nearly 400 million by 2050, the aging brain will become an increasingly big headache for humankind. Here are four cognitive systems that tend to decline as we age. Get used to these changes. You'll be seeing a lot more of them in the future.

1. Senses

Our ability to learn and remember is limited by the accuracy of our senses, our points of contact with the world. But vision, hearing, touch, smell, and taste are not just detection systems. The sense organs also comprise a primitive kind of memory, a temporary storage system or "buffer" for the brain. Much of the input to our sense organs reverberates in receptors, and that reverberation allows even weak stimuli—for example, images flashed so quickly that we have no conscious awareness of them—to impact decisions we make later on. Without the buffering ability of our sense organs, a great deal of information about the world would be lost to us. Unfortunately, as we age, our sensory systems deteriorate, and at the extreme, we become completely insensitive to a wide range of input. For example, high-pitched tones that we can detect at a mere 30 decibels when we are young have to be boosted to an earsplitting 90 decibels for the elderly to hear. (Physics buffs: That's about a million times the energy intensity.) And pupil size decreases as we age, so when it is dim, the elderly person's eyes pick up about a third as much light as people in their prime. Because the deterioration of sense organs limits our access to critical information—speech, text, music, street signs—thinking itself is impaired.

And loss of information is just part of the problem. Research by psychologist Monica Fabiani and her colleagues at the University of Illinois at Urbana-Champaign suggests that in older people the main problem might not be that the sense organ is rejecting input but rather that the brain itself is having trouble filtering out irrelevant information. In a recent study, Fabiani had people of various ages read a book while trying to ignore auditory tones piped through headphones. Overall, the older the individual, the more trouble he or she had ignoring the tones. "The background stimuli may flood your thinking with things that are irrelevant and that you cannot inhibit," Fabiani says. As a result, "you basically lose the capacity to perform tasks."

2. Memory

Most people think of human memory as a single system. But because different kinds of information are retained differently, experts speculate that distinct types of memory systems exist in the brain. Some information stays with us for only a short time—generally no more than a few seconds unless we do something with it. For example, if somebody tells you a phone number and you do not immediately repeat it, it will very likely disappear, never to return. Research suggests the existence of a short-term memory system, consisting in turn of two subsystems: immediate memory (the temporary storage system that holds on to information we don't process in some way) and working memory (a system that allows us to retain information as long as we keep using it).

As we age, our ability to process new information in working memory is severely compromised. In a typical test procedure for evaluating working memory, cognitive aging researcher Timothy Salthouse of the University of Virginia asked people to perform arithmetic computations while also trying to remember the last digit in each problem. People in their twenties were typically able to solve four or five of these problems in a row

How Some Brains Stay Razor Sharp

Facing the specter of Alzheimer's disease, the most devastating and widespread manifestation of brain deterioration in old age, worried baby boomers have inspired whole catalogs of brain-fitness books and services. That's good news for publishers, vitamin companies, and computer game designers, but probably bad news for boomers themselves. Elizabeth Zelinski, a gerontologist at the University of Southern California, told me she was appalled at the explosion of miracle cures on the market, adding bluntly, "There's no evidence that anything works." (There is some evidence that some interventions work very narrowly or for short periods of time, but generally speaking, the new industry makes outrageous claims.) And don't hold your breath waiting for neuroscience to rescue you from your upcoming decline. When I asked neuroscientist Eric Kandel, a Nobel Prize winner in medicine, how long it will be before we achieve some reasonable understanding of how memory actually works, he replied, "a hundred years."

On the bright side, some people appear to overcome the ravages of a rotting brain by recruiting new brain systems or structures to take over functions of old ones. Neuropsychologist Yaakov Stern of the Columbia University College of Physicians and Surgeons points out that upwards of 25 percent of people who function perfectly normally while alive have brains that show serious signs of Alzheimer's in autopsy. People with more education have lower rates of dementia, suggesting that brains that get more of a workout create reserves that kick in when frontline systems start to fail.

Kandel, now 82, appears to be one of those rare souls who has somehow managed to keep Father Time at bay. He remains active in research at Columbia University, and his extraordinary productivity and creativity are exemplified by his weighty 2012 book, *The Age of Insight: The Quest to Understand the Unconscious in Art, Mind, and Brain from Vienna 1900 to the Present.* Kandel's daughter, attorney Minouche Kandel, speculates that her father's clarity and energy result from an almost fanatical regimen of healthy food—mainly fish—and regular exercise. "He's lived this healthy lifestyle for as long as I can remember," she says, "and he was doing it long before it was popular."

Through some combination of luck, good genes, and a healthy lifestyle, it is possible, it seems, for a fortunate few to stay razor sharp well into old age.

R. E.

and still recall the final digits without error. With each decade, performance deteriorated; people in their seventies could typically solve no more than two such problems in a row and still get the final digits right.

One of the simplest ways to assess memory is to read test subjects a list of words and ask them, after a short time has passed, to repeat as many as they can. In a 1990 study, Hasker Davis and his colleagues at the University of Colorado found that people in their twenties could typically recall 90 percent of a list of 15 words after a short delay. With each additional decade of age, the percentage of words recalled decreased. People in their eighties could recall only about half the words.

3. Knowledge

Some information in our short-term memory system is consolidated into a long-term storage system, where it remains available to retrieve for months or years. If a memory of anything from a good meal to a coworker's name persists for 5 years, there is a good chance it will persist for another 40. But as we age, the degradation of sensory and working memory systems makes it increasingly difficult for us to transfer information into long-term storage. That's why, if you are over 50, you are more likely to remember the lyrics to a Beatles song than to any song you have heard in the past 20 years. To put this another way, our ability to learn new things is extraordinary when we are young and peaks in our teens. We can learn after that, but it becomes increasingly difficult. In an early study by psychologist Jeanne Gilbert, English speakers of different ages were asked to learn Turkish vocabulary words. People in their sixties learned 60 percent fewer words than young adults in their twenties who spent equal time and effort on the task.

One of the most frustrating experiences we have as we age is accessing a particular word from long-term memory—the so-called "word-finding" or "tip-of-the-tongue" problem. Deborah Burke, a psychology professor at Pomona College who has studied this phenomenon for more than 20 years, explains that old people suffer from a disconnect between the meaning of a word—which presumably tells you that it is the correct word to say right now—and the sound of that word. It is, she says, "the most irritating and disturbing cognitive problem" reported by older adults. We do not know what causes the disconnect.

4. Intelligence

We also get dumber as we age. IQ remains fairly stable, but that is because it is a relative measure—a quotient (the Q) that shows where we stand relative to people our own age. The problem is that raw scores on intelligence tests actually peak in our teens, remain high for a few years, and then decline throughout life; IQ remains fairly stable only because people decline at roughly the same rate. And yes, even geniuses decline. I recently asked Nobel Laureate James Watson, 84, when he reached his intellectual peak, and he replied, "Twenty, maybe 21—certainly before we found the DNA structure." That seminal work had been done when he was 25.

Intelligence, like memory, is divided into types that decline somewhat differently. Factual information is the basis of what is called crystallized intelligence, and much of the crystallized knowledge we acquire stays fairly strong at least into our sixties. However, fluid intelligence—our ability to reason—declines dramatically in most people, in large part because we get *slow*. Generally speaking, on tasks involving reasoning, what a 20-year-old can do in about half a second takes a healthy 80-year-old more than two seconds—if, that is, he or she can do it at all. As Douglas Powell of the Harvard Medical School puts it in his recent book, *The Aging Intellect,* "No other single mental ability declines as rapidly during the adult years as processing speed."

Neuroscientists tackle the decline in reasoning and working memory under an umbrella concept called executive function. Somewhere in the brain there seems to be a coach: a system or structure that schedules and prioritizes, garnering resources, redirecting attention, or switching tasks as needed. Adam Gazzaley, a neurology professor at the University of California, San Francisco, has conducted research documenting how that coaching ability declines as we age. For example, older people are bad at multitasking, Gazzaley says, because they have trouble redirecting attention back to a task after it has been interrupted. On average, people in their seventies generally require twice as much time to do two things at once as do young adults, and they also make more errors on the tasks. That inability to focus takes its toll. "I would not be capable of doing groundbreaking work today," renowned physicist Freeman Dyson, 88, told me recently. When he was young, Dyson said, he could focus on a single problem nonstop for a week. "Today," he said, "I'm limited to two hours a day of serious work—which wouldn't be enough."

The deterioration of these four systems appears to be an inevitable part of normal, healthy aging, although the rate of decline varies among individuals. When you add disease to the picture, things truly look bleak. Half of Americans over 85 are suffering from Alzheimer's disease, which eventually robs people of their memories, identities, and the ability to function even minimally. Alzheimer's becomes increasingly common with age—so common that neurologist Gary Small of UCLA suggests that if we all lived to 110, we all would have it. These are the brutal truths we must face as we and our loved ones age.

Critical Thinking

1. What two processes are involved in the decline of the accuracy of the senses with age?
2. Why is crystallized intelligence much stronger than fluid intelligence in elders?

Create Central

www.mhhe.com/createcentral

Internet References

Changes in Cognitive Functioning in Human Aging
www.ncbi.nlm.nih.gov/books/NBK3885
Lifestyle Factors Affecting Late Adulthood
www.school-for-champions.com/health/lifestyle_elderly.htm
The Long Beach Longitudinal Study: USC Davis
http://gero.usc.edu/lbls/publications.shtml
What Happens to the Aging Brain?
www.psychologytoday.com/blog/memory-medic/201211

Epstein, Robert. From *Discover*, October 2012, pp. 48–50, 76. Copyright © 2012 by Robert Epstein. All rights reserved. Reprinted by permission of Robert Epstein.

Article   Prepared by: Karen L. Freiberg, *University of Maryland*

More Good Years

Want to live longer—and healthier? These secrets from a sleepy Greek island could show you the way.

DAN BUETTNER

Learning Outcomes

After reading this article, you will be able to:

• Break down the secrets of longevity of the people of Ikaria.

• Describe the staples of a Mediterranean diet.

In 1970 Yiannis Karimalis got a death sentence. Doctors in Pennsylvania diagnosed the Greek immigrant with abdominal cancer and told him he'd be dead within a year. He was not yet 40 years old.

Devastated, Karimalis left his job as a bridge painter and returned to his native island of Ikaria. At least there he could be buried among his relatives, he thought—and for a lot less money than in the United States. Thirty-nine years later, Karimalis is still alive and telling his amazing story to anyone who will listen. And when he returned to the States on a recent visit, he discovered he had outlived all the doctors who had predicted his death.

On Ikaria, a mountainous, 99-square-mile island, residents tell this story to illustrate something they've known all their lives: on average, Ikarians outlive just about everyone else in the world.

Ikaria's heart disease rate is about half the American rate, and its diabetes rate is one-ninth of ours.

For three weeks in April, I led a scientific expedition to Ikaria to investigate the reasons for the islanders' remarkable longevity. It was part of my research into the earth's few Blue Zones: places where an extraordinarily high proportion of natives live past 90. Our team of demographic and medical researchers—funded by AARP and *National Geographic*—found that an amazing one in three Ikarians reaches 90. (According to the U.S. Census Bureau, only one in nine baby boomers will.) What's more, Ikarians suffer 20 percent fewer cases of cancer than do

Americans and have about half our rate of heart disease and one-ninth our rate of diabetes. Most astonishing of all: among the islanders over 90 whom the team studied—about one-third of Ikaria's population who are 90 and older—there was virtually no Alzheimer's disease or other dementia. In the United States more than 40 percent of people over 90 suffer some form of this devastating ailment.

How do we explain these numbers? History tells part of the story.

In antiquity Ikaria was known as a health destination, largely for its radioactive hot springs, which were believed to relieve pain and to cure joint problems and skin ailments. But for much of the ensuing two millennia, civilization passed over this wind-beaten, harborless island. To elude marauding pirates, Ikarians moved their villages inland, high up on the rocky slopes. Their isolation led to a unique lifestyle.

Over centuries with no outside influences, island natives developed a distinctive outlook on life, including relentless optimism and a propensity for partying, both of which reduce stress. Ikarians go to bed well after midnight, sleep late, and take daily naps. Based on our interviews, we have reason to believe that most Ikarians over 90 are sexually active.

But what about the Ikarians' culture best explains their long lives? To find out, we let visitors to AARP.org/bluezones direct our team's quest. Our online collaborators voted on what we should research next. One day, for example, we interviewed hundred-year-old Ikarians to discover what they'd eaten for most of their lives. The next day we investigated the chemical composition of herbal teas.

In all, we found 13 likely contributors to Ikarian longevity. The formula below may be the closest you'll get to the fountain of youth:

Graze on greens. More than 150 varieties of wild greens grow on Ikaria. Some have more than ten times the level of antioxidants in red wine.

Sip herbal teas. Steeping wild mint, chamomile, or other herbs in hot water is a lifelong, daily ritual. Many teas lower blood pressure, which decreases the risk of heart disease and dementia.

Throw out your watch. Ikarians don't worry about time. Work gets done when it gets done. This attitude lowers stress, which reduces the risk of everything from arthritis to wrinkles.

Nap daily. Ikarian villages are ghost towns during the afternoon siesta, and science shows that a regular 30-minute nap decreases the risk of heart attack.

Walk where you're going. Mountainous terrain and a practice of walking for transport mean that every trip out of the house is a mini workout.

Phone a friend. With the island's rugged terrain, family and village support have been key to survival. Strong social connections are proven to lower depression, mortality, and even weight.

Drink goat's milk. Most Ikarians over 90 have drunk goat's milk their whole lives. It is rich in a blood-pressure-lowering hormone called tryptophan as well as antibacterial compounds.

Maintain a mediterranean diet. Around the world, people who most faithfully stick to this region's diet—a regimen high in whole grains, fruits, vegetables, olive oil, and fish—outlive people who don't by about six years. The Ikarian version features more potatoes than grains (because they grew better in the mountains) and more meat than fish (because the sea was a day's journey away).

Enjoy some Greek honey. The local honey contains antibacterial, anticancer, and anti-inflammatory properties. (Unfortunately, the health benefits of Ikarian honey do not extend to American honey, as far as we know.)

Open the olive oil. Ikaria's consumption of olive oil is among the world's highest. Residents drizzle antioxidant-rich extra-virgin oil over food after cooking, which preserves healthful properties in the oil that heat destroys.

Grow your own garden (or find farmers' markets). Fruits and vegetables eaten soon after picking are higher in compounds that decrease the risk of cancer and heart disease.

Get religion. Ikarians observe Greek Orthodox rituals, and regular attendance at religious services (of any kind) has been linked to longer life spans.

Bake bread. The island's sourdough bread is high in complex carbohydrates and may improve glucose metabolism and stave off diabetes.

Do Ikarians possess the true secret to longevity? Well, some combination of their habits is helping them live significantly longer than Americans, who live on average to age 78. We can't guarantee that Ikarian wisdom will help you live to 100. But if Yiannis Karimalis's example is any indicator, it may help you outlive your doctor.

Critical Thinking

1. Explain why people in Ikaria, a very small island, outlive most other people.

2. Name the components of Ikarians' diet that contribute to their longevity.

3. Recall other information you have heard about extending lifespan.

Create Central

www.mhhe.com/createcentral

Internet References

Exercising Your Brain into Old Age May Keep Memory Sharp
www.livescience.com/37958-brain-activities
Ikaria, Greece: The Oldest People on Earth Reveal the Secrets
www.businessinsider.com/ikaria-greece-longevity-2012-7
Mediterranean Diet May Keep Aging Mind Sharp
www.webmd.com/healthy-aging/news/20110107
New Data: Some Brain Functions Improve with Age
www.rense.com/general75/NEWDAT.HTM

DAN BUETTNER is the author of *The Blue Zones: Lessons for Living Longer from the People Who've Lived the Longest* (National Geographic, 2008).

Reprinted from *AARP The Magazine*, September/October 2009, pp. 22, 24. Copyright © 2009 by Dan Buettner. Reprinted by permission of the author via Quest Network, Inc.

Article   Prepared by: Karen L. Freiberg, *University of Maryland*

Age-Proof Your Brain
10 Easy Ways to Stay Sharp Forever

Beth Howard

Learning Outcomes

After reading this article, you will be able to:

- Tell an elder how to delay memory loss and/or dementia.
- Predict which chronic health impairments lead to an early dementia and explain why.

Alzheimer's isn't inevitable. Many experts now believe you can prevent or at least delay dementia—even if you have a genetic predisposition. Reducing Alzheimer's risk factors like obesity, diabetes, smoking and low physical activity by just 25 percent could prevent up to half a million cases of the disease in the United States, according to a recent analysis from the University of California in San Francisco.

"The goal is to stave it off long enough so that you can live life without ever suffering from symptoms," says Gary Small, M.D., director of the UCLA Longevity Center and coauthor of *The Alzheimer's Prevention Program: Keep Your Brain Healthy for the Resf of Your Life*. Read on for new ways to boost your brain.

Get Moving

"If you do only one thing to keep your brain young, exercise," says Art Kramer, professor of psychology and neuroscience at the University of Illinois. Higher exercise levels can reduce dementia risk by 30 to 40 percent compared with low activity levels, and physically active people tend to maintain better cognition and memory than inactive people. "They also have substantially lower rates of different forms of dementia, including Alzheimer's disease," Kramer says.

Working out helps your hippocampus, the region of the brain involved in memory formation. As you age, your hippocampus shrinks, leading to memory loss. Exercise can reverse this process, research suggests. Physical activity can also trigger the growth of new nerve cells and promote nerve growth.

How you work up a sweat is up to you, but most experts recommend 150 minutes a week of moderate activity. Even a little bit can help: "In our research as little as 15 minutes of regular exercise three times per week helped maintain the brain,"

says Eric B. Larson, M.D., executive director of Group Health Research Institute in Seattle.

Pump Some Iron

Older women who participated in a yearlong weight-training program at the University of British Columbia at Vancouver did 13 percent better on tests of cognitive function than a group of women who did balance and toning exercises. "Resistance training may increase the levels of growth factors in the brain such as IGF1, which nourish and protect nerve cells," says Teresa Liu-Ambrose, head of the university's Aging, Mobility, and Cognitive Neuroscience Laboratory.

Seek Out New Skills

Learning spurs the growth of new brain cells. "When you challenge the brain, you increase the number of brain cells and the number of connections between those cells," says Keith L. Black, M.D., chair of neurosurgery at Cedars-Sinai Medical Center in Los Angeles. "But it's not enough to do the things you routinely do—like the daily crossword. You have to learn new things, like sudoku or a new form of bridge."

UCLA researchers using MRI scans found that middle-aged and older adults with little Internet experience could trigger brain centers that control decision-making and complex reasoning after a week of surfing the net. "Engaging the mind can help older brains maintain healthy functioning," says Cynthia R. Green, Ph.D., author of *30 Days to Total Brain Health*.

Say "Omm"

Chronic stress floods your brain with cortisol, which leads to impaired memory. To better understand if easing tension changes your brain, Harvard researchers studied men and women trained in a technique called mindfulness-based stress reduction (MBSR). This form of meditation—which involves focusing one's attention on sensations, feelings and state of mind—has been shown to reduce harmful stress hormones. After eight weeks, researchers took MRI scans of participants' brains that showed the density of gray matter in the hippocampus increased significantly in the MBSR group, compared with a control group.

Eat Like a Greek

A heart-friendly Mediterranean diet—fish, vegetables, fruit, nuts and beans—reduced Alzheimer's risk by 34 to 48 percent in studies conducted by Columbia University.

"We know that omega-3 fatty acids in fish are very important for maintaining heart health," says Keith Black of Cedars-Sinai. "We suspect these fats may be equally important for maintaining a healthy brain." Data from several large studies suggest that older people who eat the most fruits and vegetables, especially the leafy-green variety, may experience a slower rate of cognitive decline and a lower risk for dementia than meat lovers.

And it may not matter if you get your produce from a bottle instead of a bin. A study from Vanderbilt University found that people who downed three or more servings of fruit or vegetable juice a week had a 76 percent lower risk for developing Alzheimer's disease than those who drank less than a serving weekly.

Spice It Up

Your brain enjoys spices as much as your taste buds do. Herbs and spices such as black pepper, cinnamon, oregano, basil, parsley, ginger and vanilla are high in antioxidants, which may help build brainpower. Scientists are particularly intrigued by curcumin, the active ingredient in turmeric, common in Indian curries. "Indians have lower incidence of Alzheimer's, and one theory is it's the curcumin," says Black. "It bonds to amyloid plaques that accumulate in the brains of people with the disease." Animal research shows curcumin reduces amyloid plaques and lowers inflammation levels. A study in humans also found those who ate curried foods frequently had higher scores on standard cognition tests.

Find Your Purpose

Discovering your mission in life can help you stay sharp, according to a Rush University Medical Center study of more than 950 older adults. Participants who approached life with clear intentions and goals at the start of the study were less likely to develop Alzheimer's disease over the following seven years, researchers found.

Get a (Social) Life

Who needs friends? You do! Having multiple social networks helps lower dementia risk, a 15-year study of older people from Sweden's Karolinska Institute shows. A rich social life may protect against dementia by providing emotional and mental stimulation, says Laura Fratiglioni, M.D., director of the institute's Aging Research Center. Other studies yield similar conclusions: Subjects in a University of Michigan study did better

on tests of short-term memory after just 10 minutes of conversation with another person.

Reduce Your Risks

Chronic health conditions like diabetes, obesity and hypertension are often associated with dementia. Diabetes, for example, roughly doubles the risk for Alzheimer's and other forms of dementia. Controlling these risk factors can slow the tide.

"We've estimated that in people with mild cognitive impairment—an intermediate state between normal cognitive aging and dementia—good control of diabetes can delay the onset of dementia by several years," says Fratiglioni. That means following doctor's orders regarding diet and exercise and taking prescribed medications on schedule.

Check Vitamin Deficiencies

Older adults don't always get all the nutrients they need from foods, because of declines in digestive acids or because their medications interfere with absorption. That vitamin deficit—particularly vitamin B_{12}—can also affect brain vitality, research from Rush University Medical Center shows. Older adults at risk of vitamin B_{12} deficiencies had smaller brains and scored lowest on tests measuring thinking, reasoning and memory, researchers found.

Critical Thinking

1. Name three categories of foods that are heart-friendly.
2. Identify five herbs or spices that are antioxidants.
3. Why are friends important to brain health?
4. Which exercise stimulates brain circuits more: a daily crossword puzzle or learning something new?

Create Central

www.mhhe.com/createcentral

Internet References

Aging in Different Ways
www.brainfacts.org/across-the-lifespan/agingarticles/2012
Alzheimer's Disease Research Center
http://alzheimer.wustl.edu
AARP
www.aarp.org
Stockholm Gerontology Research Center
www.aldrecentrum.se/Havudmeny/English
Vitamin B12 Deficiency in the Elderly
www.ncbi.nlm.nih.gov/pubmed/10448529

BETH HOWARD last wrote for *AARP The Magazine* about medical breakthroughs, in the September/October 2011 issue.

Article

Prepared by: Karen L. Freiberg, *University of Maryland*

The Old World

Populations everywhere are getting older faster. This leads to more globalization—and more globalization means even older countries.

TED C. FISHMAN

Learning Outcomes

After reading this article, you will be able to:

- Explain how the economic climate is pitting young against old.

- Evaluate the evidence that more globalization leads to more older countries.

You may know that the world's population is aging—that the number of older people is expanding faster than the number of young—but you probably don't realize how fast this is happening. Right now, the world is evenly divided between those under 28 and those over 28. By midcentury, the median age will have risen to 40. Demographers also use another measure, in addition to median age, to determine whether populations are aging: "elder share." If the share, or proportion, of people over 60 (or sometimes 65) is growing, the population is aging. By that yardstick too, the world is quickly becoming older. Pick any age cohort above the median age of 28 and you'll find its share of the global population rising faster than that of any segment below the median. By 2018, 65-year-olds, for example, will outnumber those under 5—a historic first. In 2050, developed countries are on track to have half as many people under 15 as they do over 60. In short, the age mix of the world is turning upside down and at unprecedented rates.

This means profound change in nearly every important relationship we have—as family members, neighbors, citizens of nations and the world. Aging populations also alter how business is done everywhere. The globalization of the economy is accelerating because the world is rapidly aging, and at the same time the pace of global aging is quickened by the speed and scope of globalization. These intertwined dynamics also bear on the international competition for wealth and power. The high costs of keeping our aging population healthy and out of poverty has caused the United States and other rich democracies to lose their economic and political footing. Countries on the rise amass wealth and geopolitical clout by refusing to bear those costs. Older countries lose work to younger countries.

To see this process at work, look at China. In its march to prosperity, the country has encouraged hundreds of millions of its young people to move into cities. Chinese metropolises—some, like Beijing, ancient but newly sprawling, others, like Shenzen, built from scratch—are where the factories are. Foxconn Technology Group, for example, the giant electronics manufacturer that builds components for Dell, Hewlett-Packard and Apple in gigantic plants in Shenzen and elsewhere in urban China, will soon employ enough people to fill 60 percent of the jobs in Manhattan. Foxconn has close to 920,000 workers, nearly all of whom are under 25; in August, the company announced plans to add 400,000 more workers in the next year. But China's is a kind of Dorian Gray economy, its young and footloose global identity hiding a grayer reality. By and large, older workers have been excluded from its remade, globalized economy. They are left behind in their rural villages, or they are pushed from their urban homes into the ghettos of dour apartment blocks on the urban edge to make room for the new apartments and offices occupied by younger urbanites and the companies eager to hire them. Discrimination—"age apartheid" might be a better term—is one way to describe what's going on here: no country sorts its population more ruthlessly by age.

The problem for China is that it is rapidly approaching the point after which it will no longer be the relatively young country we see today. In 2015, China's working population below the age of 65 will begin to shrink. Meanwhile, the number of people over 65 will be rising to 300 million by 2050, a threefold increase. Richard Jackson, the director of the Global Aging Initiative at the Center for Strategic and International Studies, notes that China will be older than the United States within a generation, making it the first big national population to age before it joins the ranks of developed countries. One of China's biggest fears, expressed repeatedly in public pronouncements, is that it will grow old before it grows rich.

To avoid this fate, China is doing all it can to lure the world's production and capital while its work force is young. In large part, it does this by denying meaningful pensions and health care to its people today. Not only do the vast majority of elderly Chinese have little more than their meager savings, but today's workers have pensions so measly as to be irrelevant. To keep the cost of manufacturing in China low for the rest of the world, the young Chinese work force is, for now, rarely provided more than token pensions, health care or disability insurance. In aging, developed countries, older workers with long tenure are usually at their peak in terms of pay and the cost of their benefits. Here in the United States, for example, health care costs for workers who are between 50 and 65 are, on average, almost two times what they are for their peers in their 30s and 40s. When the median age of workers climbs in the United States, so does the cost of insurance their employers must buy for them. China's leadership clearly believes its young workers would lose their allure if the future costs of old age were added to their costs today. When state-owned companies trimmed their ranks of tens of millions of workers following the country's transition to a market economy, older workers—many only in middle age—were often let go with small pensions and replaced by younger workers. So what China offers now is workers with short tenure and negligible benefits (as well as something of a free social safety net in the form of all the relatively young, physically fit grandparents who move in with their children to care for their grandchildren).

Companies that move production to China or buy goods from Chinese suppliers gain the leverage they need to rewrite the terms of employment with their older workers at home or the ability to push those workers off the payrolls altogether. In a 2006 analysis of how aging work forces influence global flows of capital, the economists Ronald Davies and Robert R. Reed noted that because "older" economies have smaller work forces and higher wages, they push investment to younger economies, which offer higher rates of return. And high costs in older economies reach beyond wages—into taxes, which are used to pay for age-related public spending like social security. China's youthful labor force thus helps the country maintain its low-cost economic ecosystem and attract foreign investment that seeks the higher returns a "younger" economy offers, whether or not any particular pot of foreign money goes to employ young people.

China is not the only country in which a young labor force attracts global businesses and investors. Much of the developing world, particularly in Asia and Latin America, operates the same way. An outspoken champion of outsourcing, Nandan Nilekani, a former head of Infosys, the Indian technology giant, is well known for promoting India as a place to corral young workers in an otherwise aging world. Call it "global age-arbitrage."

The other part of the feedback loop, the role globalization plays in speeding up how fast a country ages, is tied to the two big reasons that populations grow older. First and most obviously, more and more individuals are living longer than ever before. Average life expectancy is increasing nearly everywhere. Longer life is itself a kind of byproduct of globalization, the result of the worldwide exchange of public-health technology, medical breakthroughs and, perhaps the most life-giving development of all, the spread of literacy. Every person who can read has access to the world of health information, including Internet sites and government pamphlets on diseases. Countries educate their people in order to make it possible for them to enter the mainstream of global commerce and that extends their life spans—making the countries older.

Above all, however, for communities or countries to age, people must have far fewer children. Today, almost no place in the developed world has a total fertility rate of 2.1 children, the replacement rate needed to keep a population from declining. The population of nearly every developed country is expected to shrink before midcentury. When emerging nations gear up for the global economy, they tend to take two steps that encourage smaller families: they extend educational and employment opportunities to young women, and they urbanize. Urban women postpone having children until they are prepared for and established in their jobs. Rearing children in the city is also more expensive. Cities serve the global economy, and the global economy drives people to cities. (According to the U.N. Population Fund, about half the world's population was urban in 2007, but by 2030 nearly 80 percent of it will live in the cities of the developing world.) The world gets older.

Such urbanization and globalization can take hold with remarkable swiftness. Japan was one of the youngest countries in the world until around 1950, and now its population is arguably the world's oldest. (Its median age will exceed 56 by midcentury, up from 43 today.) The median age in Western Europe today is just over 40; it will rise to near 50 by 2050. Population aging did not always happen so quickly. France was the first country in the world to see its share of 65-year-olds double, from 7 percent to 14 percent; this took about 115 years, starting in 1865. But China will experience the same doubling in 25 years.

One exception is the United States. The country is subject to the same two big trends—longer lives, smaller families—that are aging much of the world's populations, but we are not growing old as fast as countries in East Asia and Western Europe. Our median age will climb only 3 years, to 40, by 2050, a rate slowed by the arrival of young immigrants, including millions from Latin America.

Of course, immigration for one country means emigration from another—and an older population left behind. Spain, which rivals Japan as the world's oldest country, was for much of the 20th century one of the youngest nations in the West. Before 2000, it had virtually no foreign-born residents. Today, nearly 12 percent of Spain's population is foreign born. Among the arrivals are hundreds of thousands of Ecuadoreans (many of them female caregivers for elderly Spanish) whose absence at home increases the median age of Ecuador's population. More than one in 10 Ecuadoreans has left in search of work, and the loss of so many of the country's youngest and most enterprising workers means Ecuador has little chance of developing. Recently, its president initiated the Welcome Home Program to lure emigrants back with tax breaks and money to start businesses.

How do globalization and an aging population affect the American workplace? According to the Economic Policy Institute, 2.3 million American jobs were lost to China alone between 2001 and 2007. Susan Houseman, an economist at the Upjohn Institute for Employment Research in Kalamazoo, Mich., notes that older employees in manufacturing jobs who are low-skilled have been among the most vulnerable workers of all. And when older workers lose their jobs, they search longer for new ones than people do in other age groups. They find it hard to remake themselves with new skills and grow less employable over time and more desperate to accept low pay. This, along with the prospect of additional outsourcing abroad, drives down the earnings of those older workers who manage to stay employed. Looking at data ending in 2002, a team of researchers including economists from the World Bank and the National Bureau of Economic Research found that older workers suffered greater income losses because of foreign outsourcing than women and union workers.

Keep in mind that these results predate the recent recession and the even more difficult times that have resulted for older workers. The ranks of the unemployed who are 55 and older grew 331 percent over the decade that ended last December. U.S. unemployment levels for workers over 50 are now at their all-time highs, nearly double what they were three years ago. AARP's Public Policy Institute reports that from December 2007 to February 2010 the number of workers 55 and older who gave up looking for work rose more than fivefold, to 287,000 from 53,000. Far more people have retired early than anyone predicted. In 2009, there were 465,000 more applications for Social Security and disability benefits than there were the year before, as employers made it clear to older workers that they were not wanted. This increase was nearly 50 percent greater than what the Social Security Administration expected.

One conundrum for aging societies is how to keep older people employed at a time when economic conditions favor the young, whether nearby or far away. The workplace left to itself comes up with some solutions, but they require older workers to accept more "flexible" conditions, which often means joining the so-called contingent work force of part-timers, self-employed contract workers and temps hired through agencies. According to the AARP Public Policy Institute, 21 percent of workers over 65 are part time, compared with 16 percent for the overall work force. Self-employment is also climbing among older workers, and Americans over 50 are the most active group of entrepreneurs, often out of necessity. This partly explains an apparent contradiction: at the same time that unemployment among older workers is at a peak, the percentage of older people with jobs is also near a high, because more people must work to make ends meet.

In the United States, the transformation of older workers into a giant contingent work force is just getting started. This year, as baby boomers begin to hit 65, the "elder share" of the U.S. population begins a sharp climb. From 2010 to 2030, the number of Americans between 25 and 64 will climb by 16 million, but two-thirds of the increase will consist of people 55 and 64. Countries that are older than the U.S., that are further along in reshaping their workplaces, give a glimpse of the future. In Japan, retirees from the biggest companies are well provided for, but for many of the rest—workers at smaller companies, the self-employed—the fear of outliving their money is real. One in five elderly Japanese lives in poverty. So the Japanese stay on the job when they can. Since 2006, the number of Japanese still working after the customary retirement age of 60 has risen by more than 11 million. Most are officially retired but are back at their companies, under contract. They typically earn about half their former wages.

Will the world ever grow young again? Perhaps, but not anytime soon. Today, many of the places that are growing old the fastest are in the developing world, largely because that's where urbanization is most rapid. It is hard to conjure a situation in which people move back to the countryside and again have larger families. Instead, if past is prelude, today's young countries like China will be the countries that in the not-distant future go shopping for younger workers in younger places. Those places will be transformed by satisfying an older China's needs, and the cycle will repeat itself: when the world finds its next young place, that country may well age even more quickly than the formerly young countries that preceded it.

The rough adjustments that global aging imposes on populations can sound bleak. Nonetheless, the challenges do not trump what we gain by living longer. Remember, too, that smaller families enable parents to make greater investments in themselves and the children they do have. Still, as the world gets older, we need to anticipate how this extraordinary change might undermine our communities, weaken nations and push able older people to the side. There are also sobering geopolitical consequences to consider. It now looks as if global power rests on how willing a country is to neglect its older citizens. Faults in the welfare states of the West are highlighted by the world debt crisis. Fiscal woes driven by age-related expenses plague every level of government in the United States. Europeans take to the streets, strike and close down governments struggling to cover unsupportable pensions. The most advanced countries owe trillions in age-related public expenses. The most straightforward solutions, like higher payroll taxes to pay for benefits, raise the cost of doing business and chase off investors and producers to lower-cost economies. Mark Haas of Duquesne University has argued that aging forces all high-income democracies into triage mode. They can pay for income support and services for their elderly and drastically reduce financing for schools, defense, infrastructure and everything else, or they can decide older people will have to make do with far less.

China has gained new financial clout in relation to advanced industrial nations because it has grown rich enough as the youthful factory of the world to act as the developed countries' banker. Yet the Chinese government says the country is still too poor to put a more comprehensive social safety net in place. Perhaps, but it is the financial sacrifices of its people that give China the means to lend trillions of dollars to the United States and other industrialized nations. That's a bargain China may be happy to accept, but it, too, is caught in the irreversible dynamic of aging, and its demographic denouement is coming. By then, the United States will be older than it is now, but younger than most of the rest of the developed world, younger than much of the developing world and far younger than China. If we understand how aging populations and economic forces interact, perhaps we can make the most of our age and our youth.

Critical Thinking

1. Describe reasons why the United States' jobs are outsourced to China and India.
2. Predict what will happen to services for elders if more tax dollars are spent on crumbling infrastructure and schools.
3. Recognize the economic effects of increased longevity.

Create Central

www.mhhe.com/createcentral

Internet References

AARP Public Policy Institute
www.aarp.org/research/ppi

Aging and Globalization
http://sincronia.cucsh.udg.mx/powellfal/2011b.htm

Aging, Globalization, and Inequality: Book Introduction
http://baywood.com/books/previewbook.asp?id=AGA

Globalisation and Support in Old Age/London: LSE Research
http://eprints.lse.ac.uk/archive/00001032

TED C. FISHMAN is the author of *Shock of Gray: The Aging of the World's Population and How It Pits Young Against Old, Child Against Parent, Worker Against Boss, Company Against Rival and Nation Against Nation,* from which this article is adapted.

Fishman, Ted C. From *The New York Times Magazine,* October 17, 2010, pp. 50, 52–53; adapted from *Shock of Gray: The Aging of the World's Population and How It Pits Young Against Old, Child Against Parent, Worker Against Boss, Company Against Rival, and Nation Against Nation* (Simon & Schuster, 2010). Copyright © 2010 by Ted C. Fishman. Reprinted by permission of the author.

Article   Prepared by: Karen L. Freiberg, *University of Maryland*

The Real Social Network

It's not only a neighborhood—it's a *village*. And it might just give you a chance to stay in your own home.

MARTHA THOMAS

Learning Outcomes

After reading this article, you will be able to:

- Distinguish between life in one's own neighborhood when old or moving to a retirement community.

- Describe the "village movement" among American elders.

On a bitterly cold morning a few years ago, Eleanor McQueen awoke to what sounded like artillery fire: the ice-covered branches of trees cracking in the wind. A winter storm had knocked out the power in the rural New Hampshire home that Eleanor shared with her husband, Jim. "No heat, no water. Nada," Eleanor recalls.

The outage lasted for nine days; the couple, both 82 at the time, weathered the ordeal in isolation with the help of a camp stove. Their three grown kids were spread out in three different states, and the McQueens weren't very close to their immediate neighbors. "We needed someone to see if we were dead or alive," Eleanor says.

But the McQueens were alone, and it scared them. Maybe, they admitted, it was time to think about leaving their home of 40 years.

Luckily, last year the McQueens found a way to stay. They joined Monadnock at Home, a membership organization for older residents of several small towns near Mount Monadnock, New Hampshire. The group is part of the so-called village movement, which links neighbors together to help one another remain in the homes they love as they grow older.

The concept began in Boston's Beacon Hill neighborhood in 2001, when a group of residents founded a nonprofit called Beacon Hill Village to ease access to the services that often force older Americans to give up their homes and move to a retirement community. More than 56 villages now exist in the United States, with another 120 or so in development, according to the Village to Village (VtV) Network, a group launched in 2010 that provides assistance to new villages and tracks their growth nationwide.

It works like this: Members pay an annual fee (the average is about $600) in return for services such as transportation, yard work, and bookkeeping. The village itself usually has only one or two paid employees, and most do not provide services directly. Instead, the village serves as a liaison—some even use the word concierge. The help comes from other able-bodied village members, younger neighbors, or youth groups doing community service. Villages also provide lists of approved home-maintenance contractors, many of whom offer discounts to members. By relying on this mix of paid and volunteer help, members hope to cobble together a menu of assistance similar to what they would receive at a retirement community, but without uprooting their household.

The earliest villages, like Beacon Hill, were founded in relatively affluent urban areas, though new villages are now sprouting in suburbs and smaller rural communities, and organizers are adapting Beacon Hill's model to fit economically and ethnically diverse communities. Each is united by a common goal: a determination to age in place. A recent AARP survey found 86 percent of respondents 45 and older plan to stay in their current residence as long as possible. "And as people get older, that percentage increases," says Elinor Ginzler, AARP expert on livable communities.

In its own quiet way, the village movement represents a radical rejection of the postwar American ideal of aging, in which retirees discard homes and careers for lives of leisure amid people their own age. That's the life Eleanor and Jim McQueen turned their backs on when they joined Monadnock at Home.

"To dump 40 years of building a home to move into a condominium doesn't appeal to me at all," Jim says. "The idea of Monadnock at Home is, I won't have to."

You could call it the lightbulb moment—literally: A bulb burns out in that hard-to-reach spot at the top of the stairs, and that's when you realize you're dependent on others for the simplest of household chores. "It's horrible," says Candace Baldwin, codirector of the VtV Network. "I've heard so many stories from people who say they can't get on a ladder and change a lightbulb, so they have to move to a nursing home. A lightbulb can be a disaster."

Especially when the homeowner won't ask for help. Joining a village can ease the resistance, says Christabel Cheung, director of the San Francisco Village. Many members are drawn by the opportunity to give aid as well as receive it. "A lot of people initially get involved because they're active and want to do something," she says. "Then they feel better about asking for help when they need it."

Last winter Blanche and Rudy Hirsch needed that help. The couple, 80 and 82, live in a three-story brick town house in Washington, D.C.; they pay $800 per year in dues to Capitol Hill Village (CHV). During the blizzard-filled February of 2010, Rudy was in the hospital for hip surgery and Blanche stayed with nearby friends as the snow piled up. On the day Rudy came home, Blanche recalls, the driver warned that if their walkways weren't clear "he'd turn around and go back to the hospital." She called CHV executive director Gail Kohn, who summoned the village's volunteer snow brigade. A pair of young architects who lived nearby were quickly dispatched with shovels.

The Hirsches have discussed moving; they've postponed the decision by installing lifts so Rudy can get up and down the stairs. Remembering her visits to a family member who lived in a retirement home, Blanche shudders: "Everyone was so old. It's depressing."

Avoiding "old-age ghettos," says Kohn, is a major draw for villagers. She touts the intergenerational quality of Capitol Hill, full of "people in their 20s and people in their 80s," and CHV organizes a handful of events geared toward people of different ages. One program brings high school freshmen and village members together in the neighborhood's public library, where the kids offer informal computer tutoring to the older folks.

Such social-network building is a natural outgrowth of village life. Indeed, Beacon Hill Village was founded on the idea of forging stronger bonds among members. "There was a program

What a Village Takes

Want to organize a village of your own? The Village to Village (VtV) Network offers information on helping villages get started. Membership benefits include tools and resources developed by other villages, a peer-to-peer mentoring program, and monthly webinars and discussion forums. Call 617-299-9638 or e-mail via the VtV website (vtvnetwork.org) for more info.

- To find out if a village exists in your region, the VtV website has a searchable online map of all U.S. villages now open or in development.
- The creators of Boston's Beacon Hill Village have written a book on starting a village: *The Village Concept: A Founders' Manual* is a how-to guide that provides tips on fundraising, marketing, and organizational strategies.
- Existing resources can make your neighborhood more "villagelike," says Candace Baldwin, codirector of the VtV Network. The best place to start is your local agency on aging. The U.S. Department of Health and Human Services offers a searchable index of these services (800-677-1116; www.eldercare.gov). —*M.T.*

committee in existence before the village even opened its doors," says Stephen Roop, president of the Beacon Hill Village board. "Most of my friends on Beacon Hill I know through the village."

One fall evening in Chicago, Lincoln Park Village members gathered at a neighborhood church for a potluck supper. A group of about 80—village members and college students who volunteer as community service—nibbled sushi and sipped Malbec wine as they chatted with Robert Falls, artistic director of Chicago's Goodman Theatre.

Lincoln Park Village's executive director, Dianne Campbell, 61, doesn't have a background in social work or gerontology; her experience is in fundraising for charter schools and museums, and she lives in Lincoln Park. To village member Warner Saunders, 76, that's a big plus. "She doesn't see us as elderly clients who need her help," says Saunders, a longtime news anchor for Chicago's NBC affiliate, WMAQ-TV. "I see Dianne as a friend. If she were a social worker, and I viewed my relationship with her as that of a patient, I would probably resent that."

For Saunders, Lincoln Park Village makes his quality of life a lot better. He recently had knee and hip surgeries, and his family—he lives with his wife and sister-in-law—relies on the village for transportation and help in finding contractors. "I'd call the village the best bargain in town," he says.

Others, however, might balk at annual dues that can approach $1,000 for services that might not be needed yet. To expand membership, many villages offer discounts for low-income households.

At 93, Elvina Moen is Lincoln Park Village's oldest, as well as its first "member-plus," or subsidized, resident. She lives in a one-room apartment in an 11-story Chicago Housing Authority building within Lincoln Park. The handful of member-plus residents pay annual dues of $100 and in return receive $200 in credit each year for discounted services from the village's list of vetted providers. Since joining, Moen has enlisted the village to help paint her apartment and install ceiling fans.

But beyond home improvements, Moen doesn't ask a lot from the village yet—she's already created her own village, of a sort. When she cracked her pelvis three years ago, members of her church brought her meals until she got back on her feet; she pays a neighbor to help clean her apartment. Her community-aided self-reliance proves that intergenerational ties and strong social networks help everyone, not just the privileged, age with dignity.

Social scientists call this social capital, and many argue that we don't have enough of it. What the village movement offers is a new way to engineer an old-fashioned kind of connection. "As recently as 100 years ago most everyone lived in a village setting," says Jay Walljasper, author of *All That We Share: A Field Guide to the Commons,* a book about how cooperative movements foster a more livable society. "If you take a few steps back and ask what a village is, you'll realize it's a place where you have face-to-face encounters." He compares the village movement to the local-food movement, which also started with affluent urbanites. Think of a village as a kind of "artisanal retirement," a modern reinterpretation of an older, more enlightened way of life. And just as there's nothing quite like homegrown tomatoes, "there's no replacement for the direct connection with people who live near you," Walljasper says.

Strong, intergenerational communities—just like healthy meals—are good for everyone.

Bernice Hutchinson is director of Dupont Circle Village in Washington, D.C., which serves a diverse neighborhood. Many members are well-off; some are getting by on Medicaid. "But at the end of the day," says Hutchinson, "what everyone wants is connectedness."

Connectedness alone, of course, can't ensure healthy aging. What happens next—when villagers' needs grow beyond help with grocery shopping or the name of a reliable plumber?

To meet the growing health demands of members, villages boast a range of wellness services, and many have affiliations with health care institutions. Capitol Hill Village, for example, has a partnership with Washington Hospital Center's Medical House Call Program, which provides at-home primary care visits for elderly patients.

A new village—Pennsylvania's Crozer-Keystone Village— flips the grassroots Beacon Hill model: It's the first village to originate in a health care institution. Barbara Alexis Looby, who oversees the village, works for Keystone, which has five hospitals in the southeastern part of the state. A monthly fee gives members access to a "village navigator," who schedules medical appointments and day-to-day logistics like errands. Members also get discounts on Keystone's health services. Because the village and the hospital system are aligned, says Looby, "the boundaries are flexible. You care for people when they come to the hospital, and you are in a position to coordinate their care when they leave." Keystone hopes this integration will lead to fewer ER visits and hospital readmissions.

How long can a village keep you safe at home? It depends. But Candace Baldwin, of VtV, says that the trust factor between members and the village can help family members and caregivers make choices and find services.

Michal Brown lives about 30 miles outside Chicago, where her 89-year-old mother, Mary Haughey, has lived in a Lincoln Park apartment for more than 20 years. She worries about her mom, who has symptoms of dementia. Brown saw a flyer about Lincoln Park Village in a pharmacy and immediately signed her mother up. Through the village, Brown enrolled her mom in tai chi classes and asked a village member to accompany her as a buddy.

Just before Christmas, Haughey became dizzy at her tai chi class. With her buddy's help, she made it to the hospital, where doctors discovered a blood clot in her lung. Without the village, Brown is convinced, her mother might not have survived.

Through the village, Brown has also learned about counseling services at a local hospital to help plan her mother's next steps. "We can add services bit by bit, whether it's medication management or home health care. The village knows how to get those services."

Nobody knows what Mary Haughey's future holds, but the village has given her options. And it has given her daughter hope that she can delay moving her mother to a nursing home. For now, it helps knowing that her mother is safe, and still in her own apartment, in her own neighborhood.

Critical Thinking

1. Name several ways in which the village movement connects younger and older adults.

2. What is "social capital" and why is it advantageous to elders?

3. Which is more expensive: moving to a retirement community or paying an annual fee for elder services while staying in your current residence?

Create Central

www.mhhe.com/createcentral

Internet References

Beacon Hill Village: Home
www.beaconhillvillage.org

Liveable Communities: AARP Public Policy Institute
www.aarp.org/research/ppi/liv-com

U.S. Department of Health and Human Services
www.eldercare.gov

Village to Village Network
www.vtvnetwork.org

MARTHA THOMAS is a Baltimore-based freelance writer.

Article   Prepared by: Karen L. Freiberg, *University of Maryland*

Elder Abuse Identification: A Public Health Issue

HELEN M. SORENSON

Learning Outcomes

After reading this article, you will be able to:

- Identify six ways in which elders can be abused.
- Describe some of the warning signs of elder abuse.

Elder abuse wears many hats. As defined by the World Health Organization, elder abuse is a single or repeated act or lack of appropriate action occurring within any relationship where there is an expectation of trust that causes harm or distress to an older person.[1] It can be manifested as physical, mental, financial, emotional, sexual, or verbal abuse. Abuse can also be in the form of passive or active neglect. Elder abuse is not confined to any country, any culture, or any age group (young-old to old-old). However, the very old seem to be most vulnerable. Determining the extent of elder abuse in any specific population is difficult, as much of it is unreported. There is a stigma associated with being abused that affects both the victim and the perpetrator, especially when it occurs within the family. Fear, loyalty, and/or shame may prevent the abused from taking any action to stop it. Suffering in silence for some seems to be a badge of honor. For those brave enough to report the abuse, it may not be considered a legitimate complaint coming from someone who has been diagnosed with delirium or dementia or from someone who is judged to "just be senile."

In all likelihood, respiratory therapists unknowingly care for patients who are or who have been abused. Unless questioned, the victim will usually not share information about the mistreatment. Brief encounters may not elicit information. Established relationships can develop between therapists/patients in smaller community hospitals, in home care, or in rehabilitation settings. These may be instances in which abusive situations can be addressed and stopped. Awareness of the possibility is the key.

Scenario

Doris and Frank live in a small house in the rural Midwest. Doris is 72, Frank is 84, and both are retired. Two years ago their daughter, who lives nearby, decided that Mom didn't really need all the "stuff" she had collected over the years. When Doris and Frank were away, she disposed of many items. After repeatedly asking her not to do this to no avail, they changed the locks on the house. Not deterred by this action, the daughter broke the window, got inside the house, and threatened to "burn the house down" if they ever locked her out again. When they disagreed, she struck Frank.

Will they report this? No, because she is their daughter, and it wouldn't be right. Are her actions justified? Is she legitimately concerned about their safety, or is this elder abuse? This is a difficult situation. Elderly individuals can be institutionalized (for their safety) after reporting abuse. Since most older adults prefer to remain in their homes, they do not report abuse. Another option is to take out a restraining order against their child, which may also have adverse consequences. What is needed is counseling for both the victims and the offender, which is a complex process and involves the local Department of Social Services. There are no easy answers.

Incidence of Abuse

Elder abuse is a public health issue that affects a significant percentage of the population and in the future is likely to get worse. A systematic review of studies by Cooper et al measuring the prevalence of elder abuse or neglect was published in 2008.[2] This summary of the best evidence determined the following: 25% of dependent older adults reported significant levels of psychological abuse, and 1% reported physical abuse. Twenty percent of the older adults who presented to the emergency department were experiencing neglect, and the incidence of financial abuse has been estimated to be about 6%–18%.[2] Another prevalence survey published in 2010 included data from 5,777 (60.2% female) respondents.[3] Abuse during a one-year period was as follows: 4.6% emotional abuse, 1.6% physical abuse, 0.6% sexual abuse, 5.1% potential neglect, and 5.2% financial abuse. Overall, 10% of those interviewed reported abuse of some kind. Factoring in demographic information, women and frail elders were more likely to experience verbal abuse. African-Americans were more likely to experience financial abuse, and Latinos were less likely than respondents from any other ethnic group to report any form of abuse. Overall, low social support increased the risk for suffering any form of mistreatment, and relatively little of this abuse was reported to the authorities.[3]

Understanding that abuse and mistreatment of older adults happens is the easy part of the dilemma. Determining the form of abuse, who is at risk, who is doing the abusing, and how it can be stopped is more difficult. The National Center on Elder Abuse (NCEA), in conjunction with the Administration on Aging, has provided a list of warning signs (see Table 1).[4] While one sign does not necessarily indicate abuse, it may raise a red flag that other signs may be present but not yet assessed. There may be many other logical reasons for the presence of the warning signs, but awareness of potential abuse is key to prevention.

Identification of Abuse

Warning signs of abuse may not be readily apparent to the RT providing routine therapy on a newly admitted patient. Respiratory therapists who work in intensive care may be more likely to notice bruises and burns, but their focus is generally on ventilation and respiration. RTs who work in home care or rehabilitation may be the most likely to pick up on the fact that "something is just not quite right" with their elderly patient. If during the course of a visit or an examination, any of the warning signs of abuse are noticed, it is time to ask questions. Any licensed health care provider is qualified to ask questions. Respiratory therapists routinely ask about shortness of breath, quality of sleep, and frequency of cough. If bruises are noted, asking "has someone hurt you" or "did someone do this to you" are not unusual questions.

To increase the odds of getting an honest response, it may be necessary to interview the older adult without others present. If family members or caregivers seem reluctant to leave you alone with the individual in question, this may also be a potential "red flag." If the patient seems afraid to answer two simple questions or seems elusive with a response, contact your hospital social worker or case worker for a follow-up. Respiratory therapy education does not always cover assessing for abuse; but despite lack of training, awareness is vital. Educators could add a unit on elder abuse to a disease management course or give reading assignments to students to increase their awareness of the problem. Classroom discussions can and often do result in attitudinal changes not measurable by examinations.

Questions for the RT to Ask

Questions that may elicit a response to warning signs or bruises include:[5]

- ? Has someone hurt you?
- ? Did someone do this to you?
- ? Has anyone ever touched you without your consent?
- ? Does anyone yell at you or threaten you?
- ? Who cares for you at home?
- ? Are you afraid of your caregiver?
- ? Do you feel safe where you live?
- ? Who manages your finances?
- ? What happens when you and your caregiver disagree?

Keep in mind that skin tears and bruises in older adults are not always the result of abuse, but assuming that they are "just signs of old age" may be doing a disservice to the patient.

Elder Abuse Screening Instruments

In an effort to facilitate early identification of elder abuse, a number of screening instruments have been created to help nurses detect mistreatment.[6–9] One of the more current instruments, the Geriatric Mistreatment Scale, is available in both Spanish and English versions and screens for five different types of elder mistreatment.[9] While useful, it is also important to realize that even when assessed, many older adults will not report and will not admit that they are the victims of abuse. Another screening instrument published by the American Medical Association and available at www.centeronelderabuse.org/docs/AMA_Screening_Questions.pdf suggests questions that physicians should incorporate into their daily practice. While presenting all aspects of elder abuse is beyond the scope of this article, a chapter authored by Tom Miller in "Elder Abuse: A Public Health Perspective" contains a very useful algorithm for elder abuse intervention designed for health professionals.[10] Unfortunately, sometimes it is the caregiver who is abusive.

Table 1 Warnings of Potential Elder Abuse

Warning Signs	Potential Causes
Bruises, pressure marks, broken bones, abrasions and burns	Physical abuse, neglect, or mistreatment
Unexplained withdrawal from normal activities, new onset of depression, change in alertness	Emotional abuse
Bruises around breasts, genitalia	Sexual abuse
Sudden change in financial status	Financial exploitation
Bed sores, unattended medical needs, poor hygiene, unusual weight loss	Neglect
Controlling spouses/caregivers, threats, belittling comments	Verbal/Emotional abuse
Frequent arguments between caregiver/older adult, tense relationships	Emotional abuse

Source: National Center on Elder Abuse, U.S. Administration on Aging, www.ncea.aoa.gov

Abuse at the Hands of Caregivers

In response to an increased awareness of elder abuse, in 1987 the Omnibus Budget Reconciliation Act (OBRA) enacted major reforms that ultimately led to improved training of caregivers working with elderly clients.[11] Additional initiatives across the country have attempted to address the problem in a variety of ways. An earlier publication estimated that at least 4% of elderly people are maltreated by their caregivers.[12] Reasons cited have been stress, dependency of the caregiver on the abused older adult for finances and living arrangements, and social isolation.[13] Marshall et al have offered that caregiver stress, rather than malicious intent, is often the cause of abuse.[14] Considering that neglect is also considered a form of abuse, how many patients develop bedsores for lack of being turned or have their call-lights ignored because they are "needy patients who whine a lot"?

Recognizing and Reporting Abuse

Health care professionals need to be able to recognize the "at-risk" factors for elder mistreatment. It is imperative to abide by all reporting laws and equally important is to maintain a therapeutic relationship with the potential victim. Communication and trust issues can make a big difference in the cooperation and willingness of older adults to share incidences of abuse. Legislatures in all 50 states have passed some form of elder abuse prevention laws. In March of 2011 Congress passed a comprehensive federal elder abuse prevention law.[15] Help for our older adults is out there; but first, abuse must be recognized. While not a comfortable situation to address, there are ways to let authorities know of a potential problem without violating the Health Insurance Portability and Accountability Act (HIPAA) rules and regulations. Anyone can report a case of elder abuse in good faith. The Elder Abuse and Neglect Act provides that people—who in good faith report suspected abuse or cooperate with an investigation—are immune from criminal or civil liability or professional disciplinary action. It further provides that the identity of the reporter shall not be disclosed except with the written permission of the reporter or by order of a court. Anonymous reports are accepted. While not easy to do, these actions may be as important as starting an IV, delivering a medication, or viewing an x-ray to get at the root of what is causing the older adult to suffer.

The following are resources that one can refer to for help if abuse is suspected or confirmed:

- Eldercare Locator: (800) 677-1116. Monday–Friday, 9 A.M. to 8 P.M. EST. Trained operators will refer you to a local agency that will help.
- The National Domestic Violence Hotline: (800) 799-SAFE (800-799-7233).
- National Committee for the Prevention of Elder Abuse: www.preventelderabuse.org.
- National Center on Elder Abuse/Administration on Aging: www.ncea.aoa.gov.
- Center of Excellence on Elder Abuse & Neglect: www.centeronelderabuse.org.

References

1. McAlpine CH. Elder abuse and neglect. Age Ageing 2008; 37(2):132–133.
2. Cooper C, Selwood A, Livingston G. The prevalence of elder abuse and neglect: a systematic review. Age Ageing 2008; 37(2):151–160.
3. Acierno R, Hernandez MA, Amstadter AB, et al. Prevalence and correlates of emotional, physical, sexual, and financial abuse and potential neglect in the United States: the National Elder Mistreatment Study. Am J Public Health 2010; 100(2):292–297.
4. National Center on Elder Abuse (NCEA), Administration on Aging website. www.ncea.aoa.gov.
5. Gray-Vickrey P. Combating elder abuse. Nursing 2004; 34(10): 47–51.
6. Yaffe MJ, Wolfson C, Lithwick M, Weiss D. Development and validation of a tool to improve physician identification of elder abuse: the Elder Abuse Suspicion Index (EASI). J Elder Abuse Negl 2008; 20(3):276–300.
7. Neale AV, Hwalek M, Scott R, Stahl C. Validation of the Hwalek-Sengstock elder abuse screening test. J Appl Gerontol 1991; 10(4):406–418.
8. Schofield MJ, Mishra GD. Validity of self-report screening scale for elder abuse: Women's Health Australia Study. Gerontologist 2003; 43(1):110–120.
9. Giraldo-Rodriguez L, Rosas-Carrasco O. Development and psychometric properties of the Geriatric Mistreatment Scale. Geriatr Gerontol Int 2012; June 14 [Epub ahead of print].
10. Summers RW, Hoffman AM, editors. Elder abuse: a public health perspective. Washington DC: American Public Health Association; 2006.
11. Hawes C, Mor V, Phillips CD, et al. The OBRA-87 nursing home regulations and implementation of the Resident Assessment Instrument: effects on process quality. J Am Geriatr Soc 1997; 45(8):977–985.
12. Pillemer K, Finkelhor D. The prevalence of elder abuse: a random sample survey. Gerontologist 1988; 28(1):51–57.
13. Penhale B. Responding and intervening in elder abuse and neglect. Ageing Int 2010; 35:235–252.
14. Marshall CE, Benton D, Brazier JM. Elder abuse. Using clinical tools to identify clues of mistreatment. Geriatrics 2000; 55(2):45–53.
15. The Elder Justice Coalition EJA Update, May 20, 2012. Available at: www.elderjusticecoalition.com *Accessed Sept. 11, 2012.*

Critical Thinking

1. How can a health-care worker maintain a therapeutic relationship with an elder who is being abused but does not want the abuse reported?

2. Why are people who report elder abuse immune from criminal or civil liability, even if they have betrayed their elder person's confidentiality and trust?

3. Under what conditions would you report suspected elder abuse?

Create Central

www.mhhe.com/createcentral

Internet References

Center of Excellence on Elder Abuse and Neglect
www.centeronelderabuse.org

Eldercare Locator
www.eldercare.gov

Eldercare Locator Resource Center
www.n4a.org/programs/eldercare-locator

National Center on Elder Abuse/Administration on Aging
www.ncea.aoa.gov

National Committee for the Prevention of Elder Abuse
www.preventelderabuse.org

HELEN M. SORENSON, MA, RRT, FAARC, is adjunct faculty and an associate professor (retired) with the department of respiratory care at the University of Texas Health Science Center at San Antonio, TX.